Frommer's®

Munich & the Bavarian Alps

7th Edition

by Darwin Porter & Danforth Prince

Here's what the critics say about Frommer's:

"Amazingly easy to use. Very portable, very complete."
BOOKLIST

"Detailed, accurate, and easy-to-read information
for all price ranges."
—GLAMOUR MAGAZINE

"Hotel information is close to encyclopedic."
—DES MOINES SUNDAY REGISTER

"Frommer's Guides have a way of giving you a real feel
for a place."
—KNIGHT RIDDER NEWSPAPERS

WILEY

Wiley Publishing, Inc.

Published by:

WILEY PUBLISHING, INC.

111 River St.
Hoboken, NJ 07030-5774

ISBN 978-0-470-39896-8

Editor: Michael Kelly, with Naomi Kraus
Production Editor: Jonathan Scott
Cartographer: Elizabeth Puhl
Photo Editor: Richard Fox
Production by Wiley Indianapolis Composition Services

Front cover photo: Munich Town Hall clock with mechanical figures.
Back cover photo: Hiking the path to the Nebelhorn in the Bavarian Alps.

For information on our other products and services or to obtain technical support, please contact our Customer Care Department within the U.S. at 800/762-2974, outside the U.S. at 317/572-3993 or fax 317/572-4002.

Wiley also publishes its books in a variety of electronic formats. Some content that appears in print may not be available in electronic formats.

Manufactured in the United States of America

5 4 3 2 1

CONTENTS

4 SUGGESTED ITINERARIES — 69

5 WHERE TO STAY IN MUNICH — 83

6 WHERE TO DINE IN MUNICH — 104

7 EXPLORING MUNICH — 126

MUNICH & THE BAVARIAN ALPS

CONTENTS

LIST OF MAPS

AN INVITATION TO THE READER

In researching this book, we discovered many wonderful places—hotels, restaurants, shops, and more. We're sure you'll find others. Please tell us about them, so we can share the information with your fellow travelers in upcoming editions. If you were disappointed with a recommendation, we'd love to know that, too. Please write to:

Frommer's Munich & the Bavarian Alps, 7th Edition
Wiley Publishing, Inc. • 111 River St. • Hoboken, NJ 07030-5774

AN ADDITIONAL NOTE

Please be advised that travel information is subject to change at any time—and this is especially true of prices. We therefore suggest that you write or call ahead for confirmation when making your travel plans. The authors, editors, and publisher cannot be held responsible for the experiences of readers while traveling. Your safety is important to us, however, so we encourage you to stay alert and be aware of your surroundings. Keep a close eye on cameras, purses, and wallets, all favorite targets of thieves and pickpockets.

ABOUT THE AUTHORS

As a team of veteran travel writers, Darwin Porter and Danforth Prince have produced dozens of previous titles for Frommer's, including guides to Europe, the Caribbean, Bermuda, the Bahamas, and parts of America's Deep South. A film critic, columnist, and radio broadcaster, Porter is also a noted biographer of Hollywood celebrities, garnering critical acclaim for overviews of the life and times of, among others, Marlon Brando, Katharine Hepburn, Howard Hughes, and Michael Jackson. Prince was formerly employed by the Paris bureau of the New York Times and is today the president of Blood Moon Productions and other media-related firms. In 2008, Porter and Prince collaborated on the release of their newest book about Hollywood, sexuality, and sin as filtered through 85 years of celebrity excess, *Hollywood Babylon—It's Back!*

FROMMER'S STAR RATINGS, ICONS & ABBREVIATIONS

Every hotel, restaurant, and attraction listing in this guide has been ranked for quality, value, service, amenities, and special features using a star-rating system. In country, state, and regional guides, we also rate towns and regions to help you narrow down your choices and budget your time accordingly. Hotels and restaurants are rated on a scale of zero (recommended) to three stars (exceptional). Attractions, shopping, nightlife, towns, and regions are rated according to the following scale: zero stars (recommended), one star (highly recommended), two stars (very highly recommended), and three stars (must-see).

In addition to the star-rating system, we also use seven feature icons that point you to the great deals, in-the-know advice, and unique experiences that separate travelers from tourists. Throughout the book, look for:

(Finds)	Special finds—those places only insiders know about
(Fun Facts)	Fun facts—details that make travelers more informed and their trips more fun
(Kids)	Best bets for kids and advice for the whole family
(Moments)	Special moments—those experiences that memories are made of
(Overrated)	Places or experiences not worth your time or money
(Tips)	Insider tips—great ways to save time and money
(Value)	Great values—where to get the best deals

The following **abbreviations** are used for credit cards:

| AE | American Express | DISC | Discover | V | Visa |
| DC | Diners Club | MC | MasterCard | | |

FROMMERS.COM

Now that you have this guidebook to help you plan a great trip, visit our website at www.frommers.com for additional travel information on more than 4,000 destinations. We update features regularly to give you instant access to the most current trip-planning information available. At Frommers.com, you'll find scoops on the best airfares, lodging rates, and car rental bargains. You can even book your travel online through our reliable travel booking partners. Other popular features include:

- Online updates of our most popular guidebooks
- Vacation sweepstakes and contest giveaways
- Newsletters highlighting the hottest travel trends
- Podcasts, interactive maps, and up-to-the-minute events listings
- Opinionated blog entries by Arthur Frommer himself
- Online travel message boards with featured travel discussions

What's New in Munich & the Bavarian Alps

MUNICH ACCOMMODATIONS In hotel news, Munich witnessed the opening of the **Charles Hotel** ((℃ 089/544-555-0; www.charleshotel.de), a luxurious hotel that's linked to the famous Rocco Forte chain of European first-class and deluxe establishments, and is rated five stars by the government. Guests may enjoy the Charles's own gardens. Its spacious and beautifully furnished bedrooms open onto the Alps in the distance. Near the Hauptbahnhof (the city's main railway station), **Sofitel Munich Bayerpost** (℃ 089/599480; www.sofitel.com) now graces the Munich skyline. It combines a state-of-the-art modernity with a lot of architectural overtures to yesterday, including Wilhelminian architecture. Its beautifully furnished bedrooms use natural materials and tasteful fabrics.

Media exposure has led to the discovery of a gem of a hotel in the suburb of Nymphenburg, near the famous palace. It's the **TOP Hotel Erzgiesserei Europe** (℃ 089/12-68-20; www.topinternational.com), a 5-minute U-Bahn ride from the center of Munich. It's a first-class hotel with sleekly modern and comfortable bedrooms, plus a restaurant where tables overflow into a garden courtyard in summer. Also in Nymphenburg, **Laimer Hof** (℃ 089/17-80-38-0; www.laimerhof.de), is a restored Renaissance villa in a parklike setting. It was turned into a hotel in 1937, but had grown shabby until an energetic young couple took it over and completely modernized it while keeping its traditional overlay.

To the north of the center in the Schwabing district, **Renner Hotel Carlton** (℃ 089/28-20-61; www.carlton-garni.de) is the showcase of an emerging little hotel chain that maintains comfortable and well furnished bedrooms. If this one is full, there are two other members of the chain, the Savoy and Antare, both of which lie nearby and are comparably priced.

For more information on Munich's accommodations, see chapter 5.

MUNICH RESTAURANTS The Bavarian capital still competes with Berlin for the title of culinary capital of Germany. For more information on Munich restaurants, see chapter 6.

Seven Fish (℃ 089/23-00-02-19) has emerged as one of the best seafood restaurants of Munich, lying near the open-air market, Viktualienmarkt. Its menu is based on the freshest and best catches of the day. The menu, overseen by two Greek brothers, even includes sushi.

Bier- und Oktoberfest Museum (℃ 089/2423-1607) has opened as an offbeat choice for dining. You're given a tour, a Bavarian snack, and a glass of beer for only 4€ ($6.40). Or else you can stick around and enjoy one of the most authentic Bavarian dinners in town. In genuine Bavarian style, the staff even serves *Schmaltz* (chicken fat) to spread over your rye bread.

One of the most innovative restaurants in town is **G-Munich** (℡ 089/7474-7999), where some of the most original dishes are served. Feast on such delights as glazed quail with a purée of green olives and caper-flavored butter or a divine gooseliver crème brûlée.

The main restaurant at the Hotel Vier Jahreszeiten Kempinski München has been transformed into the **Restaurant Vue Maximilian** (℡ 089/2125-0), serving some of the most refined French and international cuisine in Munich. Most of the haute cuisine follows classic French tradition, but the chefs show their range by adding Asian inspirations, including recipes from Thailand.

In 1898, the building housing **Lutter & Wegner** (℡ 089/54-59-49-0) was the headquarters of an association of artists. Today a new restaurant has been installed, a branch of a chain well known in Germany and Austria for its savory international and Mediterranean cuisine. Take your choice of the romantically decorated dining rooms and enjoy such dishes as rack of veal stuffed with pesto and served with a fresh tomato ragout.

The leading vegan restaurant of Munich is **Saf im Zerwirk** (℡ 089/2323-9191), which has been installed in a building that is more than 700 years old. Organic produce—but, of course—is used at this establishment where food is cooked at a very low temperature to preserve flavor and nutrition. The location is around the corner from the famed Hofbräuhaus.

MUNICH ATTRACTIONS Munich is a new city built over the old (after World War II), and it's filled with both ancient and modern treasures.

The **Jüdisches Museum München** has moved to a new location at St. Jakobsplatz (℡ 089/233-96096). The venue has better lighting on its three exhibition floors and a more sophisticated arrangement of its cherished artifacts.

ZAM, the name of a single museum that housed a series of galleries, ranging from a chamber pot museum to an Easter bunny museum, has regrettably closed. Too bad, as it was one of the most unusual museums in Germany.

For more details about Munich attractions, see chapter 7.

MUNICH SHOPPING Let's face it: Berlin is still the shopping mecca of Germany. But the city of Munich gives it close competition. For complete shopping information, see chapter 9.

The best place to shop for Bavarian arts and crafts is now the aptly named **Bavarian Association of Arts and Crafts** (℡ 089/29-01-47-0), where objects ranging from pewter to handicrafts are selected from top-rated artisans throughout the province. Some Bavarians go here just to shop for charming Christmas decorations.

Now that the milkmaid-style dress, the dirndl, is making a comeback, naturally a retail chain has opened with six outlets around Munich. **Wies'n Tracht & mehr** (no phone) sells both new and vintage forms of this dress.

MUNICH AFTER DARK Munich nightlife continues to bloom as faded flowers of yesterday disappear. See chapter 10 for complete information.

"Anything can happen," management promises, and it does at **Café am Hochhaus** (℡ 089/890-581-52), featuring boogie and soulful reggae, retro, disco, even gay T-dances. Another cafe, **Café Puck** (℡ 089/280-22-80), has become a rendezvous for students and artists, and it's also a restaurant. Many patrons come in at any time of the day or night for a "big American breakfast."

The Cuban craze sweeping Europe has hit Munich with the opening of the spicy **Havana Club** (℡ 089/291884), a lively singles bar fueled by rum-based drinks. Designers and artists have discovered **Holy Home** (℡ 089/2014546), a little hideaway bar attracting a crowd in their 20s and 30s who listen to DJs spin their best.

Homesick ex-pat Aussies and Irish head for **Killians Irish Pub/Ned Kelly's Australian Bar** (© **089/24219899**) for a taste of home brew, live music, broadcasts of sports events, and food like dear ol' mum cooked it.

SIDE TRIPS FROM MUNICH Within an hour's drive of Munich, you can visit everything from the former concentration camp at Dachau to mountains, lakes, spas, and medieval towns. For complete information on these side trips, refer to chapter 11.

Before Dachau became one of the most notorious concentration camps in world history, it was a beloved artists' town. Many visitors are not only visiting the Nazi concentration camp but also sticking around to enjoy some of the charms of the historic Old Town. You can visit Schloss Dachau, a hilltop Renaissance castle, and any number of art galleries that are opening up.

THE BAVARIAN ALPS Stretching from Munich to the Austrian border, the fir-clad Bavarian Alps is a land of summer flowers, shimmering Alpine lakes, and half-timbered houses. For complete information on the Bavarian Alps, see chapter 12.

The most romantic place to stay in Garmisch-Partenkirch, the chief resort, is a faux English manor house that has opened in the outskirts. **Das Kranzbach** (© **08823/92-800-0;** www.daskranzbach. de) is a swanky retreat reached by an old private toll road built by King Ludwig II. Today the elegant property boasts one of the finest spas in the area, along with beautifully decorated bedrooms opening onto scenic views.

The Best of Munich & the Bavarian Alps

Sprawling Munich (München), home to some 1.5 million people, is the capital of Bavaria and one of Germany's major cultural centers. (Only Berlin outranks it in terms of museums and theaters.) It's also one of Germany's most festive cities, and its location, at the foot of the Bavarian Alps, is idyllic. We've scoured the region in search of the best places and experiences, and we've shared our favorites below.

1 FROMMER'S FAVORITE MUNICH EXPERIENCES

- **Socializing at the *Biergarten*:** If you're in Munich between the first sunny spring day and the last fading light of a Bavarian-style autumn, head for one of the city's celebrated beer gardens *(Biergarten)*. Our favorite is Biergarten Chinesischer Turm (p. 124) in the Englischer Garten. Traditionally, beer gardens were tables placed under chestnut trees planted above storage cellars that kept beer cool in summer. Naturally, people started to drink close to the source of their pleasure, and the tradition has remained. It's estimated that, today, Munich has at least 400 beer gardens and cellars. Food, drink, and atmosphere are much the same in all of them. See the "Beer Gardens" section of chapter 6 for more recommendations.

- **Enjoying Munich's World-Class Music:** The city is home to outstanding classical music; notable are the Bavarian State Opera (p. 168) and the Munich Philharmonic (p. 168). Prices are affordable and the selection is diverse. The season of summer concerts at Nymphenburg Palace (p. 130) alone is worth the trip to Munich.

- **Nude Sunbathing in the Englischer Garten:** On any summery sunny day, it seems that half of Munich can be seen letting it all hang out. The sentimental romantic founders of this park surely had no idea they were creating a public nudist colony. Even if you don't want to take it all off, you can still come here to enjoy the park's natural beauty. See p. 142.

- **Snacking on *Weisswurst*:** Munich's classic street food, *Weisswurst* ("white sausage") is made of calf's head, veal, and seasoning, and is about the size of a hot dog. Smooth and light in flavor, you eat it with pretzels and beer—nothing else. *Weisswurst* etiquette calls for you to remove the sausage from a bowl of hot water, cut it crosswise in half, dip the cut end in sweet mustard, then suck the sausage out of the casing in a single gesture. When you learn to do this properly, you will be a true Münchner. See "Eating & Drinking in Munich," in chapter 2, for more about *Weisswurst*.

- **Getting Away from It All at the Hirschgarten:** For a glimpse of what Munich used to be, flee from the tourist hordes and traffic to the Hirschgarten,

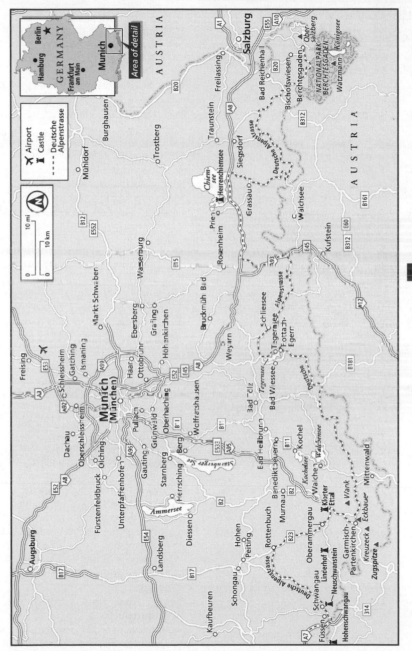

or "Deer Meadow." A "green lung" between Donnersberg Bridge and Nymphenburg Park, the area has been a deer park since 1791. In 1890, the largest beer garden in the world was built here, seating 8,000 drinkers. The Hirschgarten remains Munich's most tranquil retreat, a land of towering oaks, chestnuts, and beeches, attracting lovers of the great outdoors—and those who like to pack a picnic lunch or enjoy an open-air game of chess. See p. 142.

- **Exploring Trendy Haidhausen:** For decades, this district on the right bank of the Isar River was known as a blue-collar and low-rent sector of Munich. In the 1970s, however, hippies and artists created a cross-cultural scene that made Haidhausen, not Schwabing, the hip place to hang out. Today, it is the place to see and be seen—especially if you're a *Schicki-Micki* (a club-going Bavarian yuppie), a person who dresses only in black, or one of the Müeslis (European granolas). The place to go is one of the bars or cafes around Pariser Platz or Weissenburger Platz. Take the S-Bahn to Ostbahnhof or Rosenheimerstrasse and get with it! See p. 72.

- **Attending Oktoberfest:** It's called the biggest keg party in the world. Münchners had so much fun in 1810 celebrating the wedding of Prince Ludwig to Princess Therese von Sachsen-Hildburghausen that they've been rowdying it up ever since for 16 full days from September 21 to October 6. The festival's tent city is at the Theresienwiese fairgrounds, and the Middle Ages lives on as oxen are roasted on open spits, brass bands oompah you into oblivion, and some 750,000 kegs of the brew are tapped. There are even tents where *Bierleichen* (beer corpses) can recover from drunkenness, listening to soothing zither music.

- **Seeking R&R at Olympiapark:** Site of the 1972 Olympic Games, this 296-hectare (731-acre) park and stadium is a premier venue for various sporting events and concerts. You can swim in one of the pools, and you'll find jogging tracks, gyms, and even an artificial lake. To cap off your visit, take the elevator to the top of the Olympiaturm for a panoramic view of Munich and a look at the Bavarian Alps. In summer, free rock concerts blast from the amphitheater, Theatron, by Olympic Lake. See p. 143.

- **Going from Vie de Bohème to *Schicki-Micki* in Schwabing:** In *fin de siècle* (end of the 19th c., or Belle Epoque) Munich, Schwabing was the home of the avant-garde. Artists, writers, poets, and musicians of the era, including Thomas Mann, called it home. Jugendstil (Art Nouveau), the Blue Rider painters, and Richard Wagner made this area the cultural capital of Europe before 1914. A revival came in 1945, as new cultural icons such as Rainer Werner Fassbinder arose. Schwabing lives on, although today it's gentrified and populated by fashion editors and models, along with what have been called swinging aristocrats. Although you might come here to walk in the footsteps of Wassily Kandinsky or to see where Paul Klee or Rainer Maria Rilke lived and worked, you'll also get exposure to *Schicki-Mickies*. Walking, strolling, shopping, and people-watching are the chief activities today. See p. 73.

- **Soaking Up the Wittelsbach Lifestyle:** Northwest of Munich lies Nymphenburg Palace, an exquisite baroque extravaganza surrounded by a 200-hectare (494-acre) park dotted with lakes, pavilions, and hunting lodges. It was the summer home of Bavarian rulers. We prefer to visit in summer, when outdoor concerts are on, or spring, when the rhododendrons are in bloom. Go inside the palace for a look at the painted ceiling in the Great Hall. In such works as *Nymphs Paying Homage to the Goddess Flora,* Bavarian rococo reached its apogee. See p. 136.

- **Spending an Afternoon in the Botanischer Garten:** If you're not a plant lover, you'll be converted here. Laid out between 1909 and 1914 on the north side of Nymphenburg Park, it's one of the most richly stocked botanical wonders in Europe. You can wander among the 22 hectares (54 acres) and some 15,000 varieties of plants; a highlight is the Alpine garden with rare specimens. In late summer, the heather garden is a delight. See p. 142.

- **Checking Out Market Day at Viktualienmarkt:** The most characteristic scene in Munich is a Saturday morning at this food market at the south end of the Altstadt. Since 1807, Viktualienmarkt has been the center of Munich life, dispensing fresh vegetables and fruit from the Bavarian countryside, just-caught fish, dairy produce, poultry, rich grainy breads, moist cakes, and farm-fresh eggs. Naturally, there's also a beer garden. There's even a maypole and a statue honoring Karl Valentin (1882–1948), the legendary comic actor and filmmaker. Even more interesting than the market produce are the stallholders themselves. See p. 165.

- **Rafting along the Isar:** Admittedly, it doesn't rival the Seine in Paris, but the Isar is the river of life in Munich. If you can't take in a country walk in the Bavarian Alps, a walk along the left bank of the Isar is an alternative. Begin at Höllriegelskreuth and follow the scenic path along the Isar's high bank. Your trail will carry you through the Römerschanze into what Münchners call the Valley of the Mills (Mühltal). After passing the Bridge Inn (Brückenwirt), you will eventually reach Kloster Schäftlarn, where you'll find—what else?—a beer garden. After a mug, you'll be fortified to continue along signposted paths through the Isar River valley until you reach Wolfrathausen. Instead of walking back, you can board a raft made of logs and "drift" back to the city, enjoying beer and often the oompah sound of a brass band as you head toward Munich. See p. 186.

- **Taking a Dip at Müller's Public Baths:** Müllersches Volksbad, at Rosenheimer Strasse I (S-Bahn to Isartor), is one of the most magnificent public baths in all of Germany. This is no dull swimming pool but a celebration of grandeur, *fin de siècle* style. Karl Hocheder designed this Moorish/Roman spectacle between 1897 and 1901, an era of opulence. When the baths opened, they were hailed as the most modern in Europe, surpassing all but those in Budapest. Completely renovated, the baths today have a "gentlemen's pool" with barrel vaulting and a "ladies' pool" with domed vaulting. There are also sweat baths and individual baths for those who like to let it all hang out—but in private. Alas, the *Zamperlbad,* or doggie bath, is no more.

- **Spending a Night at the Hofbräuhaus:** Established in 1589 by Duke Wilhelm V to satisfy the thirst of his court, the Hofbräuhaus is not only the city's major tourist attraction but also the world's most famous beer hall, seating more than 4,000 drinkers. In 1828, the citizens of Munich were allowed to drink "the court's brew" for the first time, and it turned out to be habit forming. A popular song, "In München Steht ein Hofbräuhaus," spread the fame of the brewery. To be really authentic, you drink in the ground-floor Schwemme, the historic beer hall considered the heart of the Hofbräuhaus. Here, some 1,000 beer buffs down their brew at wooden tables while listening to the sounds of an oompah band. More rooms, including the Trinkstube, a restaurant for 350, are found upstairs, and in summer, beer is served in a colonnaded courtyard patio with a lion fountain. The waitstaff, in Bavarian peasant dress, appears carrying 10 steins

at once. Pretzels are sold on long sticks, and white *Radis* (radishes) are cut into fancy spirals. See p. 174.

2 FROMMER'S FAVORITE BAVARIAN ALPS EXPERIENCES

- **Boating on the Königssee:** A romantic poet would praise this lake, near Berchtesgaden in Bavaria, for the forest-covered mountains that surround its cold, deep, dark waters. The baroque chapels and fairy-tale hamlets on its shores supplement its natural grandeur. The boat you ride will be powered by very quiet electric motors, so you can hear the extraordinary echoes that bounce off the rock faces. See p. 197.
- **Hiking in the Bavarian Alps:** In summer, Alpine hiking is a major attraction in Germany. Hikers can observe a variety of wildlife, often including endangered species. Two of the best areas are the 1,240m (4,070-ft.) **Eckbauer** peak, on the southern fringe of Partenkirchen, and the **Berchtesgaden National Park,** bordering the Austrian province of Salzburg. See chapter 12.
- **Ascending the Zugspitze:** If the gentle inclines of the Harz Mountains or the

Thuringian forests aren't dramatic enough for you, ride the cable car from Garmisch-Partenkirchen to the top of Germany's tallest mountain, 2,960m (9,700 ft.) above sea level. The view from the top is suitably panoramic, and you'll find an appealing aura of German-ness that comes from the climbers and trekkers who fan out across the hiking trails. See p. 216.

- **Experiencing a Bavarian Spa:** In Germany, the question isn't whether to visit a spa, but rather which spa to visit. Each resort has its own virtues and historical associations and can supply a list of the health benefits associated with its awful-tasting waters. Whatever your choice, you'll emerge more relaxed and with a greater appreciation of German efficiency and sensuality. The most famous spa in the Bavarian Alps is **Bad Reichenhall** (p. 200), 135km (84 miles) southeast of Munich.

3 THE BEST MUSEUMS

Financial prosperity, artistic flair, and academic curiosity have helped the people of Munich develop some of the finest museums anywhere.

- **Deutsches Museum,** Munich: Since 1925, this museum has been one of the most important showcases of science and technology in the world. Occupying an island in the Isar River, it features many hands-on and historical exhibits. See p. 131.

- **Alte Pinakothek,** Munich: This massive and symmetrical building is one of the most visible in Munich, with a wraparound garden where urbanites like to walk during lunch hour. Inside is a staggering assortment of important paintings from every era. See p. 127.
- **Dachau Concentration Camp Memorial Site,** Dachau, near Munich: Heinrich Himmler first organized Dachau as a concentration camp for enemies of

the Reich in 1933. An escaped inmate, Joseph Rovan, described it as "implacable, perverted, an organization that was totally murderous, a marvelous machine for the debasement and dehumanizing of man." Today, it's one of the most poignant museums in the world. See p. 176.

- **Lenbachhaus,** Munich: Housed in the former villa of portrait painter Franz von Lenbach, this museum has a stunning and internationally renowned collection of modern art, including the Blaue Reiter (Blue Rider) period, best represented by Kandinsky. It also has a rich collection of Gothic artwork. See p. 141.

- **Bayerisches Nationalmuseum** (Bavarian National Museum), Munich: One of the largest and most impressive of the history museums of Germany, the exhibits range from classical antiquity until the 1800s. The nucleus of the collection dates from the reign of the Wittelsbachs, and was donated to Bavaria in 1855 by Maximilian II. See p. 131.

- **Pinakothek der Moderne,** Munich: This is Munich's version of Tate Britain in London or the Pompidou Center in Paris. It is one of the world's largest museums devoted to the visual arts of the 19th and 20th centuries. Artists from Picasso to Warhol are exhibited, as are 400,000 drawings ranging from Leonardo da Vinci to Cézanne. See p. 132.

4 THE BEST CASTLES & PALACES

During the Middle Ages, Germany, including Munich and Bavaria, was divided into intensely competitive feudal states and principalities. This unstable atmosphere encouraged the construction of fortified castles. As hostilities died down, architects began to design for comfort, style, and prestige, adding large windows, gilded stucco and plaster, frescoes, and formal gardens. As a result, Bavaria is full of all kinds and styles of *Burgen* (castles) and *Schlösser* (palaces).

- **Neuschwanstein,** near Füssen: When the creators of California's Disneyland needed an inspiration for their fairy-tale castle, this was their model. Neuschwanstein is the most lavishly romantic (and impractical) castle in the German-speaking world. A 19th-century theatrical set designer drew it up in a neofeudal style. The man who ordered its construction was (who else?) "Mad" King Ludwig II of Bavaria. See p. 228.

- **Hohenschwangau Castle,** near Füssen: It was completed in 1836 and built on the ruins of a 12th-century fortress. Its

patron was the youthful prince regent, Maximilian II of Bavaria, who used it to indulge his taste for "troubadour Romanticism" and the life of the English country manor. See p. 229.

- **Schloss Nymphenburg,** Munich: It was originally conceived and constructed between 1664 and 1674 as an Italian-inspired summer home for Bavarian monarchs. Subsequent Bavarian kings added to its structure, and by around 1780, the building and lavish park bore a close resemblance to the French palace at Versailles. A highlight of the interior is the green, gold, and white banqueting hall, with frescoes and ornate stucco that are among the most memorable in Bavaria. See p. 136.

- **Schloss Linderhof,** near Oberammergau: This palace, built in the 1870s, was a teenage indulgence of Ludwig II. Its architects created a whimsically eclectic fantasy, inspired by Italian baroque architecture. In the surrounding park, Moorish pavilions and Mediterranean cascades appear against Alpine vistas in combinations that are both startling and charming. See p. 221.

- **Residenz,** Munich: The official residence of the Wittelsbach dynasty from 1385 to 1918, the Residenz is a grand royal palace. Of particular fascination is the Antiquarium built in 1569, the largest Renaissance ceremonial hall north of the Alps and the oldest surviving part of the palace. The Cuvilliés Theater is one of the finest rococo theaters in the world, and the treasure trove that forms the Schatzkammer is one of the grandest in Germany. See p. 134.

- **Neues Schloss,** Chiemsee: Called "a monument to uncreative megalomania," this castle, begun in 1878 by Ludwig II, stands on the island of Herrenchiemsee, in the midst of Chiemsee, one of the most beautiful lakes in the Bavarian Alps. The chief attraction is its splendid Great Hall of Mirrors, the most authentic replica of the more famous hall at Versailles outside Paris. Ludwig was able to spend only 9 days in the palace. At his death, only 20 of the 70 rooms he envisioned had been completed. See p. 204.

5 THE BEST WALKS

- **The Royal Castle Walk:** For one of the grandest panoramas in all of the Alps (in any country), hike up to the Marienbrücke, the bridge that spans the Pöllat Gorge behind Neuschwanstein Castle. From here, if you're up to it, you can continue uphill for about an hour for an amazing view of "Mad" King Ludwig's fantasy castle. See "Neuschwanstein & Hohenschwangau" in chapter 12.

- **Partnachklamm:** One of the most dramatic walks in all of the Bavarian Alps starts from the great winter sports resort of Garmisch-Partenkirchen. A signposted trail leads to the dramatic Partnachklamm Gorge. Carved from solid rock, the route passes two panoramic bottlenecks amid the thunder of falling water and clouds of spray. See "Hiking in the Bavarian Alps" in chapter 12.

6 THE BEST SPAS

- **Bad Reichenhall:** Many spa lovers head for this remote corner of Bavaria to "take the waters." Europe's largest saline source was first tapped in pre-Christian times, though the place now has a 19th-century aura. Some of the hotels in the town are better than others, but all have equal access to the spa and lie about a 5-minute walk away. See "Bad Reichenhall" in chapter 12.

- **Bad Tölz:** On the Isar River, this resort town became a spa in 1946 when its iodine-rich springs were discovered. Its water park, Alpamare, is one of the largest in Germany, and it's filled with saunas and solariums. Even if you don't take the spa waters, the well-preserved Old Town

is worth a stopover, with many houses dating from the 17th and 19th centuries. See "Bad Tölz" in chapter 11.

- **Bad Wiessee:** Within easy reach of Munich, only 53km (33 miles) to the north, this spa town opens onto the beautiful lake, the Tegernsee. It is known for its mineral springs rich in iodine and sulfur. Bad Wiessee, with its advanced medical facilities, is a year-round resort, with swimming and boating in summer, and skiing on the nearby Bavarian Alps in winter. While having a holiday at this spa, you can also take day trips to Salzburg and Innsbruck in Austria. See "Bad Wiessee" in chapter 12.

7 THE MOST CHARMING LAKE RESORTS & VILLAGES

- **Sternbergersee:** This beautiful lake is where many a Münchner go for a holiday. It's only 27km (17 miles) to the southwest of Munich. Centering around the town of Berg, the unofficial capital of the lake region, Sternbergersee enjoys a 6.4km (4-mile) scenic coastline studded with historic castles, including one where Ludwig II was imprisoned after he was certified as insane. See "Sternbergersee" in chapter 11.

- **Tegernsee:** A lake and a resort town on the eastern shore of its water share the same name. Long known as one of the most beautiful lakes of Bavaria, Tegernsee lies just 48km (30 miles) southeast of Munich. It is surrounded by mountain peaks, one reaching a height of 1,890m (6,200 ft.). The ritziest resort town along the lake is Rottach-Egern where you find the best hotels and cuisine. See "Tegernsee" in chapter 11.

- **Ammersee:** Many Münchners have summer homes at this lake region 39km (24 miles) southwest of Munich. One of the best places for food and lodging along the lake is the large village of Herrsching, a venue for summer concerts and known as

a retreat for artists. A short ferry ride takes you to Diessen, the lake's most idyllic fishing village. Summer steamship cruises traverse the lake, and you can also rent various boats. See "Ammersee" in chapter 11.

- **Berchtesgaden:** Although its reputation is somewhat tainted by its association as a retreat for Hitler, Berchtesgaden is one of the most idyllic Alpine towns in the Bavarian Alps. It is celebrated for its beautiful scenery on the Ache River at the foot of the Watzmann, the second highest peak in Germany. It's a center for exploring the splendid lake of Königssee with its crystal clear waters in a fjordlike setting. See "Berchtesgaden" in chapter 12.

- **Mittenwald:** A town on a former trade route at the foot of the Karwendel mountain range, this town, one of the most colorful and beautiful in Bavaria, is especially popular for its winter sports. The town is also known for its violin making trade, a tradition dating back to 1684. See "Mittenwald" in chapter 12.

8 BEST HOTEL BETS

- **Best Historic Hotel: Hotel Vier Jahreszeiten Kempinski München** (*C* **089/2125-0;** www.kempinski-vierjahreszeiten.de) is one of the most famous hotels in the world—the lineage of this hostelry stretches back to 1858. Maximilian II himself took a personal interest in the hotel's establishment, even going so far as to aid its founder financially. The Walterspiel family brought it to worldwide prominence,

and over the years it has entertained the greats and near-greats. See p. 86.

- **Best for Business Travelers:** The **Hilton Munich Park** (*C* **800/445-8667** in the U.S. and Canada, or 089/3-84-50; www.hilton.com) is a modern 15-story structure geared to business travelers, with the necessary business amenities. It is close to many corporate headquarters and has the best conference facilities of any hotel in the city. Actually, the hotel was an office block until pressed into service as a hotel for the 1972 Olympics. After business is concluded, you can unwind at the hotel's health club. See p. 88.

- **Best for a Romantic Getaway: Romantik Hotel Insel Mühle** (© 089/8-10-10; www.insel-muehle.com), built around a 16th-century mill, has a romantic, antique decor and rooms with sloping, garretlike ceilings. It is known for its old-world restaurant with massive beams and a wine cellar. Though far removed from the hustle and bustle, it's only 9.5km (6 miles) west of Munich's Marienplatz. See p. 100.

- **Best Trendy Hotel: The Mandarin Oriental** (© 089/290-980; www.mandarinoriental.com/munich) is the choice of visiting celebrities, including fashion models, dress designers, and the media elite. Its discreet style and formal elegance appeal to those who don't want to be "too obvious" by staying at one of the lavish, bigger hotels. See p. 86.

- **Best Lobby for Pretending You're Rich: Bayerischer Hof & Palais Montgelas** (© 089/21-20-0; www.bayerischerhof.de) is an old-fashioned European formal hotel with a deluxe lobby filled with English and French furniture and oriental rugs. It's been called the "living room" of Munich. "Meet you in the lounge of the Bayerischer Hof" is often heard. As hotels go, there's no more impressive place to meet for a drink. See p. 83.

- **Best for Families: Four Points Hotel by Sheraton München Olympiapark** (© 800/368-7764 in the U.S. and Canada, or 089/357510; www.starwoodhotels.com) is right at Europe's biggest sports and recreation center and rents many triple rooms that are ideal for families. It's among the most modern and best-kept places in the city, and your child may meet some of the sports heroes who often stay here. At Olympiapark,

the entire family can use the sports facilities, including a large Olympic-size swimming pool. See p. 66.

- **Best B&B: Gästehaus Englischer Garten** (© 089/3-83-94-10; www.hotel englischergarten.de), close to the Englischer Garten and its summer nudes, is an oasis of charm and tranquillity in fashionable Schwabing. It offers attractively furnished rooms; those in the annex are really small apartments with tiny kitchenettes. When the weather's right, breakfast is served in the rear garden. See p. 98.

- **Best Service: Eden Hotel Wolff** (© 089/55-11-5-0; www.ehw.de) employs some of the most thoughtful staff in Munich. The attentive, efficient, unhurried, yet down-to-earth English-speaking staff here gets the job done, anticipating all your needs. See p. 88.

- **Best Location: An der Oper** (© 089/290-02-70; www.hotelanderoper.com) is in the heart of Munich, steps away from the central Marienplatz. Stay here and in moments, you're shopping along the Maximilianstrasse or exploring the traffic-free malls near the Bavarian Nationaltheater. See p. 90.

- **Best Health Club: München Marriott Hotel** (© 800/228-9290 in the U.S. and Canada, or 089/36-00-20; www.marriott.com) has a well-equipped fitness center that includes a swimming pool almost 14m (44 ft.) long, whirlpools, hydrojets, a solarium, and state-of-the-art exercise equipment. There's also a *Kosmetik-Kabine* for beauty treatments and massages, plus separate saunas for men and women. See p. 97.

- **Best Hotel Pool:** The state-of-the-art indoor pool at the **Arabella Sheraton Grand Hotel München** (© 800/325-3535 in the U.S. and Canada, or 089/9-26-40; www.starwoodhotels.com) is on the 22nd floor, offering its own waterfall to go with the city views. Although many hotels in Munich have pools, none competes with this choice. And that's not all—the hotel also has five whirlpools, two mixed saunas (open to both men and women), and a trio of steam rooms inspired by ancient Rome, each ideal for *après*-swim (after your swim). See p. 99.

- **Best Spa Hotel:** The curative spa of Bad Reichenhall is the finest and best equipped in the Bavarian Alps. The best hotel here is **Steigenberger Axelmannstein** (℃ 08651/77-70), which is set in lovely gardens of 3 hectares (7¹/₂ acres). Its spa equipment is always kept in the finest condition, and its bedrooms, cuisine, and on-site entertainment make it one of the great discoveries of Bavaria. See p. 201.

9 BEST RESTAURANT BETS

- **Best All-time Favorite:** In business since 1901, albeit not in the same location, **Boettner's** (℃ 089/22-12-10) offers a cuisine that is better than ever and still uses only top-quality ingredients like lobster and fresh white truffles. Housed in a Renaissance structure in the center of Munich, the restaurant has a cuisine lighter than in the past but still featuring those rich old Bavarian favorites for those who want to indulge. See p. 104.

- **Best Fusion Cuisine:** A luxe restaurant ranking at the top of all those in Bavaria, **Schuhbecks in den Südtiroler Stuben** (℃ 089/21-66-900) evokes California freestyle. A culinary celebrity, chef Alfons Schuhbeck blends Eastern and Western cuisine in his sublime offerings, depending a lot on California for his inspiration. The menu changes based on the best produce in any season. See p. 108.

- **Best Spot for a Romantic Dinner:** At this great Italian restaurant, **Acquarello** (℃ 089/470-4848), he or she will definitely say yes to your proposition. Classical music sets the stage for a romantic evening, and the host promises that the perfumelike fragrance of the restaurant will linger for a lifetime. From figs to almonds, the food is from the gods—at least that. See p. 120.

- **Best Spot for a Business Lunch:** Restaurant Mark's (℃ 089/29098-875),

in the prestigious Mandarin Oriental, is the chic business luncheon spot of Munich. The movers and shakers of the Bavarian capital gather in the informal lobby-level setting of Mark's Corner to make the big deal. Menu items change according to the season and the inspiration of the chef, and, as you dine, you can practically feel euros changing hands. See p. 109.

- **Best Spot for a Celebration:** A coveted address known to savvy local foodies, **Gasthof Weichandhof** (℃ 089/891-1600) is set in an old farmhouse where diners always seem to be celebrating something—a marriage, a divorce, or whatever. The Bavarian food is good and affordable and you can hang out until midnight, feasting on everything from roast suckling pig to endless servings of apple strudel. See p. 122.

- **Best Wine List:** Geisel's Vinothek (℃ 089/55-13-71-40), in the Hotel Excelsior, is the best spot in Munich for a taste of the grape. Dedicated to Bacchus, this deliberately unpretentious choice has one of the city's finest collections of Italian, French, Austrian, and German wines—all sold by the glass. You can also order Italian cuisine. See p. 110.

- **Best Value:** Palais Keller (℃ 089/2-12-09-90) is housed in the cellar of one of the most elegant hotels in Munich (the Bayerischer Hof), but it still offers the most bang for your euro. Its well-prepared cuisine of Bavarian and German dishes is priced about the same as that found in far less desirable beer halls and *Weinstuben* (wine taverns) nearby. Let a smiling waitress in a frilly apron introduce you to Tafelspitz here, the fabled boiled-beef dish. See p. 116.

- **Best Continental Cuisine: Tantris** (© 089/36-19-59-0), in Schwabing, serves the city's most refined cuisine, a treat to the eye as well as the palate. Hans Haas is one of the top chefs of Germany and is forever sharpening his culinary skills as he wines and dines the celebrated people of Europe. Nothing in Munich equals the service, flavors, and delight found here. See p. 118.

- **Best French Cuisine: Bistro Terrine** (© 089/28-17-80) has food that tastes so authentically French that you'll think you're in Lyon. Menu items are often more inventive than the Belle Epoque atmosphere of this Art Nouveau bistro in Schwabing implies. The menu changes with the seasons—for example, in autumn, nuggets of venison might appear with hazelnut-flavored gnocchi and port-wine sauce. See p. 119.

- **Best Seafood: Austernkeller** (© 089/298-787) prepares not only the freshest oysters in town but also an array of delectable seafood selections that range from mussels to clams and sea snails to the wonderful lobster Thermidor. The kitsch collection of plastic lobsters shouldn't put you off: The food is far more worthy than the decor. See p. 108.

- **Best Bavarian Cuisine: Nürnberger Bratwurst Glöckl am Dom** (© 089/291945-0) is Munich's coziest restaurant. Here you can enjoy Bavarian cuisine so authentic that it's hardly changed since the restaurant opened in 1893. Bavarians, often looking as stern as one of the Dürer prints on the wall, come here for all their favorite dishes—just like great-grandmothers made 100 years ago. See p. 116.

- **Best for Celebrity-Watching:** One of the most iconoclastic restaurants in Munich, **Lenbach** (© 089/549130-0) serves first-rate Continental and Asian cuisine. Its diners often make the next day's gossip columns. That might be Catherine Zeta-Jones devouring a plate of foie gras and sweet roasted peppers, Richard Gere digging into the grilled scampi with fresh herbs, or Robert Redford ordering the Thai curry with tiger prawns. See p. 111.

- **Best Beer Garden:** In the Englischer Garten center of Munich, **Biergarten Chinesischer Turm** (© 089/3-83-87-30) is our favorite place for soaking up the local suds—some of the best in the world—and lingering over long, filling Bavarian meals such as homemade dumplings, a specialty. To the sound of an oompah band, you can drink the night away while devouring huge baskets of pretzels with your beer. See p. 124.

- **Best for People-Watching:** Right on the Marienplatz (what Times Square is to New York), the virtual heart of Munich, you can enjoy coffee and snacks at **Café Glockenspiel** (© 089/26-42-56). This is the most frequented cafe in Munich, and it gets especially busy around 10:30am daily when hordes show up to watch a miniature tournament staged by the clock on the city hall facade. Sit back and enjoy your coffee and pastry as an international parade of humanity marches before you. See p. 123.

- **Best Picnic Fare: Alois Dallmayr** (© 089/213-51-00) offers not only Munich's best picnic fare but also Germany's. With the food you can gather up here, you could even invite the queen of England for lunch in the Englischer Garten. One of the world's most renowned delis, this supermarket of goodies has elegant selections like foie gras, but it also offers more democratically priced (and mundane) fare. See p. 104.

- **Hofbräuhaus am Platz,** Munich (① **089/22-16-76**): The Hofbräuhaus is the world's most famous beer hall and can accommodate some 4,500 beer drinkers on any given night. Music from live bands and huge mugs of beer served at wooden tables combine to produce the best of Bavarian nighttime fun. See p. 174.

- **Biergarten Chinesischer Turm,** Munich (① **089/3-83-87-30**): In the Englischer Garten between the Isar River and Schwabing, this is the best *Biergarten* in the largest city-owned park in Europe. Beer and plenty of Bavarian food, hail and hearty, are served until the cold winds of autumn blow. It's riotous fun. See p. 124.

- **Hirschgarten,** Munich (① **089/1799-9199**): In Nymphenburg Park, west of the center, this beer garden lies in a 200-hectare (494-acre) park. It can handle an astonishing 8,000 beer drinkers at once and is, in fact, the largest open-air restaurant in Munich.

Munich in Depth

Thomas Mann, a longtime resident of Munich, wrote something about the city that might have been coined by an advertising agency: "Munich sparkles." Although the city he described was swept away by two world wars, the quote is still apt. Munich continues to sparkle, drawing temporary visitors and new residents like a magnet from virtually everywhere.

Some of the sparkle comes from its vitality. With its busy factories, media outlets, and service and electronics industries, it's one of Europe's liveliest cities. More subtle is Munich's amazing ability to combine Hollywood-type glamour and stylish international allure with its folkloric connections. Few other large cities have been as successful as Munich in marketing folklore, rusticity, and nostalgia for the golden days of yesteryear. This rustic ambience coexists with the hip and avant-garde, the high-tech industries, and a sharp political sense, which is what lends the city such a distinctive flair.

As Americans head to New York or San Francisco to seek opportunity and experience, so Germans migrate to Munich. The city is full of non-Bavarians. More than two-thirds of the German citizens living in Munich have come from other parts of the country, and tens of thousands are expatriates or immigrants from every conceivable foreign land. Sometimes these diverse elements seem unified only by a shared search for the good life.

Outsiders are found in every aspect of Munich's life. The wildly applauded soccer team, FC Bayern München, is composed almost entirely of outsiders—Danes, Belgians, Swedes, Prussians. The city's most frequently quoted newspaper mogul (Dieter Schröder) and many of the artistic movers and shakers are expatriates, usually from northern Germany. What's remarkable is the unspoken collusion of the whole population in promoting Bavarian charm, despite the fact that real dyed-in-the-wool Bavarians risk becoming a distinct minority in their own capital.

Munich's self-imposed image is that of a fun-loving and festival-addicted city—typified by its Oktoberfest. This celebration, which began as a minor sideshow to a royal wedding, has become a symbol of the city itself. Redolent with nostalgia for old-time Bavaria, it draws more than 7 million visitors each year. For these 16 days every fall, raucous hordes cram themselves into the city to have a good time.

Oktoberfest is so evocative, and so gleefully and unashamedly pagan, that dozens of places throughout the world capitalize on its success by throwing Oktoberfest ceremonies of their own. These occur even in such unlikely places as Helen, Georgia, in the U.S., where citizens and merchants reap tidy profits by wearing dirndls and lederhosen, playing recordings of the requisite oompah music, and serving ample provisions of beer in oversize beer steins. No one has ever marketed such stuff better than Munich, but then, few other regions of Europe have had such alluring raw material from which to draw.

A somewhat reluctant contender for the role of international megalopolis, Munich has pursued commerce, industry, and the good life without fanfare. You get the idea that in spite of its economic muscle, Munich wants to see itself as a large agrarian village, peopled by jolly beer drinkers who cling to their folkloric roots despite the presence of symbols of the high-tech age.

Underneath this expansive, fun-loving Munich is an unyielding, ongoing conservatism and resistance to change, both religious and political. But as a symbol of a bold, reunited Germany forging a new identity for the 21st century, Munich simply has no parallel.

While you will find reminders of the past all around you in the Altstadt, or Old Town, of Munich, the city is by no means standing still or living off its past. The city has embarked on a building program that will transform its 20th-century skyline into a 21st-century look with lots of new office and commercial buildings. However, the historic core, which has zoning rules that forbid any building to rise higher than the spires of the city's symbol, the Frauenkirche cathedral, will remain relatively unchanged.

1 MUNICH TODAY

Today, Munich's position as the centerpiece of southern Germany conveys at least the illusion that life here is more easygoing, sunnier, and emotionally richer than life in the foggy and windswept Teutonic cities along, for example, the Baltic. As such, Munich continues to captivate the imagination of Germans as a place less reactionary, and less conservative, than German-speaking counterparts farther north.

That notion is only partially true. Despite new influences from virtually everywhere, and a proud role as high tech capital of Germany, Munich continues to be permeated with the spirit of the bourgeoisie that helped mold it during the 18th and 19th centuries. Consequently, although some aspects of Munich are boldly innovative and experimental, the city is at the same time defiantly reactionary and proudly opposed to new ideas. Munich's avant-garde and its reactionary elements coexist, not always comfortably, and with very little of the indulgent laissez-faire and resigned world-weariness that's more obviously prevalent in such places as Berlin.

At least some of Munich's modern-day smugness derives from the comforts, prestige, and economic power it has enjoyed since the end of World War II. This tends to be bitterly resented by residents of cities farther east, which enjoy almost no hope of ever, in their lifetimes, achieving the prosperity that bourgeois and sometimes complacent Munich attracted partly as an accident of its geography. In Munich, what you see is what you're likely to get. This flies in direct opposition to the more frenetic, more cerebral, more innovative, and more (dare we say it?) hysterical Berlin, where the rigors of reuniting the two Germanies occasionally borders on the surreal.

There's lots of room for economic creativity and trading profits in the dynamic tension that surrounds modern Munich, a fact that's been rapidly developed since the end of the Cold War. Although traditional trade patterns throughout the Cold War positioned Munich as the gateway between northern and southern Europe, the collapse of the Soviet regime in 1989 opened fertile markets in the east as well. Unfortunately, although the collapse of the Soviet regime did indeed reinforce the role of Munich as a center of postindustrial technology and trade, it initiated stiff competition in the touristic sphere as well.

In the bad old days of the Cold War, Munich was the end of the line, about as far east as most mainstream tourists cared to go during their explorations of the Continent. Rather disturbingly in the eyes of tourist officials, Munich today seems relegated to the status of stopover on the way to more exotic cities such Berlin, Budapest, and Prague.

Today, Munich boasts many laurels and superlatives. Its academic infrastructure, with more than 100,000 students, is the second largest in Germany, with a distinctly urbanized and cosmopolitan flavor. Greater Munich (third-largest city in Germany) has more heavy industry than any other city in Germany and, at least in theory, the possibility of more jobs. It has produced more Nobel Prize winners than any other city in Germany, and civic boosters claim, not without justification, that Munich is the most beautiful city in the country. Its museum of science and industry (Deutsches Museum) is the largest of its type in the world, and the Gasteig Center, completed in 1985, is a model for other symphonic halls throughout Germany.

The city recognizes 14 official holidays, more than any other city in Germany, and this is a remnant of medieval traditions when almost a third of any calendar year was devoted to religious holidays.

Cynics, many of them envious residents of Berlin, Hamburg, or the aristocratic Rhineland, claim that the only thing that really motivates a native Münchner is an aggressive pursuit of leisure time. Although that's probably not true, Munich offers more options for leisure than anywhere else in Germany, including a setting that is the most conducive in the world to beer drinking. It has some of the finest theaters (more than 60 that are legitimate, many others that are less so) and German-language repertory companies, with performances that are usually packed. By some standards, it's also the most expensive city in a reunited Germany. But despite its schizophrenic ambivalence—part class, part kitsch—and the encroachment of urban sprawl, Munich manages to retain many aspects of an Alpine village. Fortunately for urban claustrophobics, there are many verdant parks, and the open spaces of the Bavarian and Austrian Alps lie within about an hour's drive.

Modern Munich contains a lot of elements designed to amuse and divert. A visitor can while away the time pursuing sports and cultural activities, or simply sit for hours in beer halls and taverns that are, on the average, more authentically folkloric than those within any other metropolis in Europe. Even if you don't happen to be Bavarian, or even German, you can still enjoy some of the most deeply entrenched traditions about beer drinking, and its attendant social rituals, of anywhere in the world. Six major breweries are based in Munich, as well as entire industries devoted to supplying the pastime's accessories. Not least of these are rehearsal halls and recording studios for the oompah bands that help make beer-drinking rituals so delightful.

Drawbacks in Munich include the same kinds of things residents of New York or Paris complain about: impossibly high rents, urban stress, and urban anonymity. And despite the jovial facade, there's a rising incidence of urban crime and—something Munich has always seen a lot of—civil unrest.

Fortunately, Munich today offers a wider range of personal choices and different types of lifestyle options than ever before. As you'll learn, modern Munich is more than folkloric kitsch, although two or three steins of beer go a long way toward helping its citizens ease any pain that's involved while forging the city's new identity.

2 LOOKING BACK AT MUNICH

THE BRIDGE OVER THE ISAR Munich is a young city compared with some of its neighbors. It had its origins in 1156 in an unpleasant struggle between two feudal rulers over the right to impose tolls on the traffic moving along the salt road that stretched between the cities of Salzburg, Hallein, Reichenhall, and Augsburg. Up to that time, Bishop Otto von Freising had controlled a very lucrative toll bridge across the Isar River, directly on the salt route.

The ruler of the Bavarian territory, Guelph Heinrich der Löwe (Duke Henry the Lion), was in need of cash. So, with the customary ferocity that had earned him his nickname, he simply burned down the bishop's bridge and built his own bridge a few miles upstream, co-opting the profitable tolls. Emperor Frederick Barbarossa was called upon to settle this dispute between his cousin Heinrich and his uncle, Bishop Otto. However, the bishop's fully justified rage did little to influence the faraway emperor, who was too busy to worry about a minor clash between church and state. This particular squabble, however, was to have far-reaching consequences.

Henry's new bridge was adjacent to a tiny settlement of Benedictine monks, a small community on the banks of the Isar River that was referred to as *zu den Münichen*—"at the site of the little monks." The name stuck—though it was later shortened to *München*, and the little monk, or *Münichen*, remains the symbol of the city of Munich.

Henry the Lion had already had successful experiences in founding trading centers. With this knowledge, he granted Munich the right to mint its own coins and to hold markets, basic tools that any city needed for survival. Tolls from his new bridge, which now funneled the lucrative salt trade across the Isar, went directly into Henry's coffers.

Within a few months, Barbarossa validated the crude but effective actions of his duke, legitimizing the establishment of Munich on June 14, 1158, the date that is commemorated as the official debut of the city. Henry, however, had to accept a price: Barbarossa ordered that a third of all tolls generated by the new bridge be paid to the bishop of Freising, whose bridge Henry had destroyed.

MEDIEVAL PROSPERITY The first of the city's fortifications, a stone wall studded with watchtowers and five gates, was built in 1173 and enclosed 2,500 people. One of the most important survivals from this period (most of the wall was long ago demolished) is the Marienplatz—then and now the centerpiece of the city and the crossing point of the Salzstrasse (Salt Route), a crossroads that is still marked on the city map. During its early days, the Marienplatz was known as the "Marketplace" or the "Grain Market."

In 1180, Duke Henry quarreled with Emperor Barbarossa and was banished forever from Munich and the rest of Bavaria. Gleefully, Henry's nemesis, the bishop of Freising, attempted to eradicate the upstart young city and reroute the salt trade back through his stronghold of Oberföhring. By this time, however, Munich was simply too well established to succumb to his efforts.

ENTER THE WITTELSBACHS By 1240, a new force had arisen in Munich, the Wittelsbach family. They were part of a new generation of merchant princes, and through a shrewd imposition of military and economic power, their family patriarch, Otto von Wittelsbach, succeeded in having himself designated as the ruler of Bavaria shortly after the banishment of Henry the Lion. Thus began the longest and most conservative reign of any dynasty in Germany. The Wittelsbachs ruled in Munich and the rest of Bavaria until the forces of socialism swept them away during the final days of World War I. Today, they are still viewed by the Bavarians with a kind of nostalgic affection.

Between 1250 and 1300, the population of Munich increased fivefold, the result of migration from the countryside and a period that was relatively free from plagues. Members of at least three religious orders established monasteries, convents, and hospitals within the city walls.

SOCIAL UNREST As the population grew, the city's encircling fortifications were enlarged to protect new suburbs. Although predominantly Catholic, the city fostered a small population of much-persecuted Jews as well. The worst pogrom against them occurred in 1285, when 150 of Munich's Jews, accused of the murder of a small Catholic child, were burned alive inside their synagogue, which was, at the time, just behind the present-day location of the Neues Rathaus (New Town Hall). Two years later, other groups of Jews came to Munich, but ironically, the handicaps the city imposed upon them (exclusion from all trades except moneylending) led to a modest if precarious degree of prosperity. Pogroms were repeated throughout the rest of the Middle Ages, and in 1442, the Jews were banished from Munich altogether.

Just before the dawn of the 14th century, the artisans and merchants of Munich staged a revolt against the Wittelsbach family because of debased coins that were being issued by the dukes' mint. A mob destroyed the mint and killed its overseer, and they were fined for it by the dukes, as punishment and for reimbursement for the loss.

IMPERIAL MUNICH During the 1300s, Munich was the richest of the several cities ruled by the Wittelsbachs. Grains, meats, fish, and wine were traded within specifically designated neighborhoods (a medieval form of zoning thought to lead to greater efficiency). The collection of tolls from the roads leading in and out of the city continued to help make their controllers (in this case, the Wittelsbachs) very rich.

In 1314 a Wittelsbach, Duke Ludwig IV, later to be known as Ludwig the Bavarian, was elected (by a tribunal of secular and ecclesiastical authorities called the Electors) as the German kaiser, thanks to his status as the least threatening choice among a roster of more powerful contenders. The election suddenly threw Munich into the center of German politics. Ludwig traveled to Rome for his coronation and brought back from his visit one of the treasured religious icons of medieval Munich—the severed arm of St. Anthony, which still can be seen in the church of St. Anna in Lehel.

In 1319, one of the Wittelsbachs' most vindictive enemies, the Habsburg family in the person of Frederick the Handsome, attacked Munich and laid siege to its walls. Against expectations, the Wittelsbachs prevailed, eventually capturing the Habsburg leader and holding him prisoner. However, the pope sided with the Habsburgs and excommunicated Ludwig. Despite this serious handicap, Ludwig retained his throne. Consequences of the excommunication were enormous and were widely viewed as an example of a pope overplaying his cards. (Two hundred years later, when various German princes were forced to choose between allegiance to Rome and allegiance to the new Protestant order, the meddling of the popes in the secular affairs of Germany was widely remembered, often with disdain, a fact that played into the hands of the Protestants.) To reward Munich for its loyalty (and also to line his own pockets), Ludwig created a lucrative monopoly for the city in 1322 by ordering that all the salt mined within Hallein or Reichenhall must pass directly through Munich.

Although Bavaria remained Catholic, and continued to be Catholic even after the Protestant Reformation, Munich had positioned itself as a centerpiece of resistance to papal authority. Along these lines, Ludwig offered shelter to William of Occam, a brilliant scholar trained in the monasteries of both England and France and persecuted as a heretic by the pope. Occam spent his last years in Munich, striving for reform of the Catholic Church. His presence helped to define Munich as a hardheaded Catholic city that catered only reluctantly to the whims of the faraway religious potentate.

While hunting bear in the Bavarian forest in 1346, Ludwig the Bavarian was accidentally killed. His enemies joked that he was killed "just at the right time" to escape trouble from those who wanted to overthrow or assassinate him. His unbridled ambition and his successful defiance of the pope in Rome had earned Ludwig enemies, notably some of the most powerful German princes, who were poised to overthrow him. Although he escaped battle with his powerful enemies, Ludwig's death signaled the end of Munich's role as the headquarters of the German-speaking empire.

During Ludwig's tenure, the city had experienced explosive growth, and a new wall was built in 1327, so spacious that it encompassed the city throughout the next 400 years. Despite a strong temptation to alter Munich's central core, the Marienplatz was never changed from its original form—which it more or less retains today.

BEER, PIGS & PROSPERITY Throughout the 1400s, Munich became a boomtown. More than 28,000 four-wheeled carts bearing marketable goods passed through the city gates every year in addition to the vast number of two-wheeled carts and people on foot. In response to this traffic, some of the town's main avenues, narrow though they were, were paved. Between 1392 and 1492, the city's increasingly prosperous merchant class built or altered into their present form many of the city's centerpieces, including the Ratsturm, the Altes Rathaus (Old City Hall), the Frauenkirche, and St. Peter's Church. Munich had graduated from a dependence on the salt trade, and was now reaping most of its profits from trade with Italy, especially Venice. In the same year Columbus stumbled upon his landfall in the New World, the Münchners opened a mountain pass over Mt. Kesselberg to speed up trade routes to the "Queen of the Adriatic."

By 1500, Munich had a population of almost 14,000 persons, 400 of whom were beggars, and 750 of whom were priests,

nuns, or monks. It also included about three dozen brewers whose products were quickly becoming associated with the town. Pigs were engaged to eat the garbage strewn in the streets, and about two dozen innkeepers supplied food, drink, and lodgings to the medieval equivalent of the business traveler. The city's core (but not the surrounding fields that kept it fed) was protected from invasion by an ever-expanding ring of fortifications and towers. The most serious dangers were plagues and fires, both of which devastated the city at periodic intervals.

In 1516, the city adopted legislation that later helped confirm its role as beer capital of the world. Known as the Bavarian Beer Purity Law, it was the first law in Europe to regulate the production of any food or beverage by setting minimum standards for quality and cleanliness in production.

RENAISSANCE EXPANSION The showy and sometimes pompous building boom associated with the Counter-Reformation marked the debut of the Renaissance in Munich. The lavish building programs as well as the entertainments of the Wittelsbach rulers became legendary, both for their grandeur and extravagance (some feasts lasted for 3 weeks) and for the burdens they imposed on the citizenry who had to pay for them.

Munich blossomed with the appearance of Michaelskirche (St. Michael's Church), begun in 1583. The largest Renaissance-style church north of the Alps, it was conceived as a German-speaking response to St. Peter's Basilica in Rome. It took 14 frenetic years to build, and its construction costs almost bankrupted the Bavarian treasury. Despite the grumbling of the taxpayers, other buildings of equivalent splendor soon followed, including the Wittelsbach family stronghold, the Residenz.

Munich was also becoming a cultural center. By the late 16th century, the city was regarded as an artistic beacon. Credit must go to the reigning Wittelsbachs, founders of the art collection that eventually became the Alte Pinakothek, and the book collections that eventually became the Bayerischen Staatsbibliothek (Bavarian State Library).

Despite the prestige all these endeavors conveyed, virtually every tradesman and merchant in town complained of the burden such acquisitions and improvements placed upon the treasury, evidence of a fundamental conservatism that has demarcated Munich ever since.

THE THIRTY YEARS' WAR Beneath the city's newly acquired glitter were other, darker tendencies. In the early years of the 17th century, witches were hunted down and burned, flagellants paraded through the town, and foreboding sermons predicted an apocalypse. At least the spirit of those predictions was fulfilled during the Thirty Years' War (1618–48). This struggle, between the Protestant princes and the Catholic League, swept across Europe, bringing devastation in its wake.

Munich wasn't directly affected until 1632. At that time, the Protestant king of Sweden, Karl Gustav Adolf, laid siege to "the German Rome." Munich surrendered almost immediately, since the city's rulers and citizens were worried about being hopelessly outnumbered and having their city destroyed. The terms of surrender included payment of a huge ransom; in exchange, the city was spared being sacked and burned. The war, however, wasn't the only problem faced by the Münchners—at about this time, the Black Plague killed 7,000 people, more than a third of the population. After the disease had run its course, Maximilian I ordered the construction of the Mariensäule (Virgin's Column—a statue dedicated to the Virgin) on the Marienplatz as a votive offering to God for having spared the city from total destruction.

In 1643, the authority of the town's merchants was greatly undermined by the removal of their right to elect the mayor of Munich. The Wittelsbachs were now able to place in power anyone who would cater to their interests.

BAROQUE CASTLES & BAROQUE DREAMS The legacy of the Thirty Years' War left Munich demoralized and shattered. Although Bavaria was not to play a vital role in European politics during the next century, this period saw a building boom and the development of baroque architecture.

The flamboyant, richly gilded, free-flowing but symmetrical baroque style was used not only by the city's architects to the glory of God but also in secular construction. Notable are Nymphenburg Palace, Munich's answer to the palace at Versailles; the Green Gallery within the Residenz; ornate theaters; and countless villas, pavilions, and garden structures. Funds for this construction were derived, as in the past, from sometimes crippling taxes imposed on the citizenry and the forced sale of farming land to wealthy aristocrats who wanted to build ever-larger palaces for their own use.

Deep resentment was felt by the townspeople. In 1674, when the seat of the Wittelsbach family, the Residenz, accidentally caught fire, the town sullenly and deliberately postponed a response to calls for help for at least an hour, a vital delay that contributed to more enormous rebuilding costs and an increased mistrust among the various levels of society.

Part of the public resentment against Munich's leaders lay in the aristocracy's often disastrous meddling in international affairs. Among these were Bavaria's murky role in the War of the Spanish Succession, which resulted in the occupation of Bavaria by Austrian soldiers between 1705 and 1715. The first year of this occupation witnessed one of the cruelest massacres in 18th-century history: Led by a local blacksmith, an army of peasants, craftsmen, and burghers, armed only with farm implements and scythes, marched upon Munich to protest against the Austrian regime. A short march from Munich's city walls, near the hamlet of Sendling, the entire army was betrayed (one of its members sold information to the enemy), then obliterated. The *Sendlinger Mordweihnacht* ("Sendling's Night of Murder") has ever since been the source for sculptures, plays, and popular legend.

In 1715, Max Emanuel was able—with the help of the French—to evict the Austrians. Aftereffects of these fruitless conflicts included countless deaths, a profound national disillusionment, and a national debt that historians assess at around 32 million guilders, a burden imposed upon an already impoverished population.

REFORM & REFORMERS The tides of liberalization slowly spread to Bavaria. Newspapers were founded in 1702 and 1750, and in 1751, some vaguely liberal reforms (involving issues dealing with land use, penal codes, taxation, indentured labor, military service, and more) were made in the Bavarian legislature. An Academy of Sciences, whose discoveries sometimes opposed traditional Catholic teachings, was established in 1759.

To recover from the disasters initiated prior to his reign, Prince Elector Max III Joseph, one of the most enlightened Bavarian rulers, attempted to introduce economic reforms. He inaugurated new industries, including workshops for tapestry making and cloth making. Few of them worked out; the noteworthy exception was the outfit that manufactured Nymphenburg porcelain, founded in 1758, which consistently made a profit, and still does today.

In 1771, he revised the school system, making some aspects of public education a legal requirement. During his regime, the city opened its doors to playwrights, composers, and conductors from all over Europe. Munich was the site of the inaugural performance of one of Mozart's early operas *(Idomeneo)* in 1781; it wasn't

particularly well received, and Mozart's request for an ongoing creative stipend from the Wittelsbach family was rejected.

THE REBIRTH OF CONSERVATISM When Max III Joseph died in 1777, his branch of the Wittelsbach dynasty died with him. The new Wittelsbach, from an obscure family branch in the Palatinate, was Karl Theodor, one of the least popular of all the Wittelsbachs. Caring little about Bavarian national destiny, he rather amazingly negotiated to cede Munich and all of Bavaria to Austria in exchange for the Habsburg-dominated Netherlands. Relief from this plan came in the form of the French Revolution.

Ironically, although he was despised as a ruler, Karl Theodor, as a builder, did many things well and skillfully, adding the Karlsplatz and the Englischer Garten to the roster of Munich's attractions. Politically, however, he continued to play his hand badly, outlawing most personal liberties and placing repressive measures on freethinkers. His death in 1799 prompted several days of drunken celebration throughout Munich.

THE AGE OF NAPOLEON Except for distant rumblings on the western horizon and the hope it gave to Bavaria's liberals, the effects of the French Revolution weren't immediately felt in reactionary Munich. All of that changed, however, with the rise of Napoleon. In 1799, French troops laid siege to the capital. The Bavarian court had already fled to the safety of their villas at Amberg, where they realized that they had to capitulate to Napoleon's overwhelming forces and side with the French dictator against their brethren in other parts of Germany. On the first night of occupation, in June 1799, French officers enjoyed a performance of Mozart's *Don Giovanni* in the Residenz's royal theater.

To reward his Bavarian vassal, Napoleon more than doubled the territory controlled by Bavaria (at the expense of Franconia and Swabia), thereby tripling the size of its population overnight. Bavaria was eventually made a kingdom, and in 1806, Napoleon personally conducted the coronation of Max IV Joseph as King Maximilian I.

A final irony was when the territory formerly controlled by the bishop of Freising was swallowed up by the new Bavarian nation created by Napoleon, and the bishop's administrative headquarters—now no more than a ceremonial shadow of its former power—moved into the heart of its old "enemy territory" (the destruction of Freising's bridge over the Isar had led to the original founding of Munich)—downtown Munich.

TOWARD A MODERN STATE The new king's son, Crown Prince Ludwig (later, Ludwig I), gets the credit for establishing what is now the most famous autumn festival in the world, *Oktoberfest.* Originally designated as a *Volksfest,* it was scheduled, along with some horse races, as a sideshow of the crown prince's wedding in 1810.

Beginning around 1820, with the gears of the Industrial Revolution already starting to turn, the first foundations of a modern state were established. A Bavarian constitution was drawn up, and Munich became the seat of a newly founded Bavarian Parliament, designed to afford the citizenry more clearly defined legal rights. Not all Münchners were happy, however—they were attached to their roster of religious holidays, complete with complicated processions and relief from workaday cares, which the new constitution swept away.

"THE ATHENS OF THE NORTH" Crown Prince Ludwig, inspired by an idealized version of ancient Athens, made enormous changes to Munich. The old city walls were demolished, with the exception of a small stretch that still runs parallel to the Jungfernturmstrasse. The city moat was filled in and redesignated as the Sonnenstrasse, and new neighborhoods were designed with formal parks and gardens. The prince

wanted the Munich equivalent of a triumphal promenade, and commissioned the street that has been known ever since as the Ludwigstrasse.

In 1821, the Frauenkirche became the official cathedral *(Dom)* of the archbishops of Munich and Freising. In 1826, the university was transferred from the town of Landshut to Munich, bestowing on the Bavarian capital the status of intellectual centerpiece.

BOURGEOIS MUNICH By 1840, with a reported population of around 90,000 residents, Munich had been made into a neoclassical gem with a distinct identity. Munich's first railway line was laid in 1846—the foundation of a network of railways that soon converged on the city from all parts of southern Germany.

Initially a supporter of liberal reforms, Ludwig I gradually grew more and more conservative as his reign went on. In 1832, he began a campaign of censoring the press, repressing student activism, and stressing his role as an absolute monarch, casting himself in a romantic and heroic mold. Münchners considered his affair with actress and dancer Lola Montez even more odious than his rigid politics. All of this came to a head in the revolt of 1848. In a series of lurid events, Ludwig flaunted his affair with Lola so publicly that the fabric of the Wittelsbach dynasty itself was threatened. As the scandal raged, Ludwig was forced to abdicate in favor of his son, Maximilian II.

Maximilian II continued the building programs of his father, established the Bavarian National Museum (1855), and played a role in encouraging writers to settle in Munich. One of these, Paul Heyse, was the first German to win the Nobel Prize in Literature. Maximilian built an avenue (the Maximilianstrasse) in his own honor and held a series of competitions among architects for the design of such public buildings as the Regierung

(Administrative Building) and the Maximilianeum (Bavarian Parliament Building).

Maximilian's role in the promotion of science, industry, and education made him one of the most enlightened despots of the 19th century. When he died in 1864, the administration of many of his programs was continued by what had developed into a massive governmental bureaucracy. The new king, Ludwig II, unfortunately, was not so beneficial to Bavaria.

ROMANTIC BAVARIA & THE DREAM
KING Rarely has the king of a nation so despised the citizens of his capital city as Ludwig II did the Münchners. Trouble began shortly after the new king ascended the Bavarian throne in 1864 at the age of 18. The king had become the patron of Richard Wagner, and four of Wagner's operas—*Tristan und Isolde* (1865), *Die Meistersinger von Nürnberg* (1867), *Das Rheingold* (1869), and *Die Walküre* (1870)—made their debuts in Munich. One of the many visions of the composer and his royal patron was the construction of a glittering opera house. However, this project, and its estimated cost of 6 million guilders, found little support and led to the collapse not only of plans for the hoped-for opera house, but also of the friendship between the king and the composer. A spate of arrogant public outbursts by Wagner (newspapers published his statements that the citizens of Munich had no artistic imagination) led to the composer and his lofty romantic ideals leaving Munich forever.

Curiously, although viewed as hopelessly eccentric, a bizarre member of a family riddled with other mental aberrations, Ludwig seemed to captivate an age obsessed with Romanticism. Although his mania for the building of neo-Romantic castles and palaces far from the urban bustle of Munich helped bankrupt the treasury, he rarely meddled in the day-to-day affairs of his subjects and was consequently considered an expensive-to-maintain but relatively unthreatening monarch.

Actually, the lack of interest in politics on the part of Ludwig II is one of the factors that helped Bismarck, from his base in Prussia, arrange the unification of Germany in 1871. The unification transformed Berlin into the capital of a united Germany and stripped Bavaria of its status as an independent nation, a designation it had enjoyed since Napoleon's time. Some historians maintain that Bismarck induced the unstable king to give up his independent status by secretly subsidizing the building costs of his fairy-tale castles. Because the castles, especially Neuschwanstein, have brought billions of tourist dollars to the German nation ever since, he probably made a wise investment.

In 1886, the Bavarian cabinet in Munich stripped the 40-year-old Ludwig of his powers. A few days later, Ludwig's death by drowning in Starnberg Lake led to endless debate as to whether his death was prearranged because he planned an attempt at a royal comeback. His heir to the tattered remnants of the Bavarian throne was a mentally inept brother, Otto, whose day-to-day duties were assumed by a royal relative, Crown Prince Luitpold, who wore the much-diminished crown until 1912.

The only vestige of Bavaria's imperial past that remained was the designation of the local postal network and railways as "Royal Bavarian" (*Koeniglich-Bayerisch*). The Bavarian monarch was allowed to retain his position as figurehead during a transition period when real power slowly flowed toward Berlin.

Munich forged ahead in its role as an economic magnet within a unified Germany. In 1882, Munich began electrifying its street lamps. Three years later, public transport was aided by a network of streetcars. And scientist Max von Pettenkofer, who discovered the source of cholera in

(Fun Facts The Notorious Lola Montez

The sensational career of Lola Montez (1820–61) was hot copy in the newspapers all over the world during her lifetime. A woman who behaved as she pleased in the Victorian age, her liaison with Bavaria's king, Ludwig I, led to his forced abdication.

She was born in Limerick, Ireland, as Eliza Gilbert and grew up in India. An outstanding beauty with jet-black hair and alabaster skin, one admirer wrote of her, "Mrs. James looked like a star among the others." Her marriage to Lieut. Thomas James had broken up in scandal (both she and her husband frequently cheated on each other, but she could never divorce him, because she couldn't find him to serve papers to), and she was forced to leave India. She went to Spain and then to London, where she reinvented herself as the dancer Lola Montez. Though she was a mediocre performer, her erotic "spider dance" catapulted her to notoriety. Subsequently, she went through dozens of lovers, including pianist Franz Liszt and novelist Alexandre Dumas.

When Lola arrived in Munich in 1846, she was refused an engagement at the Hof Theatre. Fighting her way past security guards, she stormed the palace of Ludwig I and demanded an audience with the king. Barging into his chambers, she slit the front of her dress open. Upon looking at her body, Ludwig asked his security guards and his chief aide to leave his chambers. Thus began one of the most romantic and scandalous royal adventures of all time.

Although married to Princess Therese of Saxonia since 1810, the old, deaf, yet romantic Ludwig came under Lola's spell. Ludwig indulged her every whim, bestowing the treasures of his kingdom upon her. In return, she catered to his sexual needs, including a foot fetish he had, as widely reported by his biographers. Lola was called "the Bavarian Pompadour," but Richard Wagner dubbed her a "demonic beast."

Ludwig gave her the titles of Baroness of Rosenthal and Countess of Lansfeld. Her enemies (Lola was deeply resented in Munich) suspected that she meddled in politics; it was rumored that she virtually ran the Bavarian government. Public sentiment against Lola and her outlandish behavior was so powerful that it contributed to the Revolution of 1848 and ultimately to the king's abdication.

Fleeing to London in the wake of the king's abdication, Lola settled into her next adventures. By July 19, 1849, she'd married George Trafford Heald, scion of a wealthy, aristocratic family. There was a problem, however: She'd never been granted a divorce from Lieut. James. Learning that the state planned to arrest her on a bigamy charge on August 6, she fled first to Mexico, then to California, where she ended her days as a cigar-smoking, stage-strutting artiste who entertained miners during the California gold rush. An amazing life came to an end when she retired, found religion, and devoted the rest of her life to helping wayward women. She died in poverty in Brooklyn.

contaminated water, was instrumental in the installation of a city water supply that was hailed as one of the best in Germany.

ARTISTIC FERMENT Toward the end of the century, Munich became a center of creativity and artistic ferment. In 1892, the Secession movement was founded as a protest against traditional aesthetics. In 1896, the magazine *Jugend* helped define Munich (along with its closest rival, Vienna) as a centerpiece of the German Art Nouveau movement, Jugendstil. In 1902, a Russian expatriate, Lenin, spent a brief stint in Munich, publishing a revolutionary magazine called *Iskra*. Schwabing, once a farm village, then a summer retreat for the stylishly wealthy, became an icon for the avant-garde, the home base of satirical magazines whose contributors included Thomas Mann (who spent many years of his life in Munich), Rainer Maria Rilke, Hermann Hesse, and Heinrich Mann. In 1911, Franz Marc and Wassily Kandinsky, later joined by Paul Klee, founded the *Der Blaue Reiter* (the Blue Rider) group to promote and define the role of abstract art.

WORLD WAR I & REVOLUTION World War I (1914–18) led to more bloodshed and greater disillusionment than Europe had ever known. Hunger was rampant in Munich even in the war's early years, and by 1918, social unrest was so widespread that a rash of demonstrations, burnings, mob executions, and brawls between advocates of the left and right became increasingly frequent. On November 7, 1918, more than 10,000 workers mobilized for a mass demonstration, ending at the gates of the Wittelsbachs' hereditary stronghold, the Residenz. To the rulers' horror, their guards were persuaded to join the revolutionaries, causing the dynasty's final scion to flee Munich under cover of darkness. The event marked the end of a dynasty that had ruled longer than any other in Europe.

The next day, Munich was declared capital of the Free State of Bavaria *(Freistaat Bayern)*, an independent revolutionary people's republic, led by the Revolutionary Workers Council. The conservative, so-called legitimate Bavarian government went into immediate exile, and Kurt Eisner, an articulate political leader who was much less radical than many of those who elected him, ruled briefly and tempestuously. Within a few months, he was assassinated on Munich's Promenadeplatz. Power shifted in a rapid series of events between centrists and leftists and ended in a horrendous blood bath when troops, sent by Berlin in 1919, laid siege to the city as a means of restoring the status quo.

THE RISE OF HITLER Conservative reaction to the near takeover of Munich by revolutionaries was swift and powerful, with long-ranging effects. After the events of 1919, and the humiliating terms of surrender imposed upon Germany at Versailles, Munich became one of the most conservative cities in Germany. Combine that with staggering inflation and a deep distrust of any Prussian interference from the despised city of Berlin, and Munich, unfortunately, became a kind of incubator for reactionary, anti-Semitic, and sometimes rabidly conservative political movements.

One of these was the NSDAP (National Socialist Workers Party of Germany), of which Adolf Hitler was a member. Hitler's early speeches, as well as the formulation of his ideas as written in *Mein Kampf (My Struggle)*, were articulated in Munich's beer halls, including the famous Hofbräuhaus, where meetings were often held. Many members of Hitler's inner circle (including Heinrich Himmler and Hermann Göring) were from the region around Munich, and thousands of the dictator's rank and file originated from the city's long-suffering, endlessly deprived slums.

Under its reactionary civic government, Munich's cultural scene degenerated—anything racy or politically provocative was banned, and many creative persons (including Bruno Walter and Berthold Brecht) left Munich for the more sophisticated milieu of Berlin.

After Hitler came to power as chancellor in Berlin, there was little opposition in Bavaria to the National Socialists, whose candidates swept the city's elections of March 5, 1933, and whose swastika flew above city hall by the end of the day. By July 1933, it was painfully obvious that anyone who opposed the all-Nazi city council was deported to Germany's first concentration camp, Dachau, on Munich's outskirts.

The headquarters of the Nazi Party was established on the corner of Brienner and Arcis streets, later to be the site of the 1938 signing by Neville Chamberlain, Daladier, Mussolini, and Hitler of the Munich Agreement. Around the same time, a torture chamber was set up in the cellar of what had always been the city's symbol of power: the Wittelsbach Palace. Hitler himself even referred to Munich as "the capital of our movement," a statement heard then, as now, with great ambivalence.

Beginning in 1935, vast sums of money were spent on grandiose building projects that followed the Nazi aesthetic. In 1937, a Nazi-sponsored exhibition, permeated with anti-Semitic, xenophobic references, *Entartete Kunst (Denatured Art),* mocked the tenets of modern art.

Jews then began to be persecuted in earnest. The city's largest synagogue was closed in 1938, the same year that *Kristallnacht* ("Night of Broken Glass"; Nov 9, 1938) resulted in the vandalism of Jewish-owned homes and businesses across Germany. Despite the persecution, some 200 Jews managed to evade the Nazi net and were still alive at the end of World War II (though the city's prewar Jewish population had been more than 10,000). After the war, Jews returned in very slow numbers to Munich because many had long-rooted family ties with the Bavarian capital.

In 1939, a Marxist attempt to assassinate Hitler as he drank with cronies in a Munich beer hall (the Bürgerbräukeller) failed, and Germany (and Munich) continued the succession of aggressions that eventually led to World War II and the destruction of much of historic Munich.

WORLD WAR II & ITS AFTERMATH Resistance to Hitler was fatal. Nonetheless, a handful of clergymen opposed the Nazi regime. One notable opponent was Father Rupert Mayer, who was imprisoned for many years at Dachau, Germany's first concentration camp. Built in 1933 in Bavaria, Dachau became a model for other death camps, as thousands upon thousands of "undesirables" were murdered, often in the most brutal fashion there. When Allied troops, in May 1945, liberated the Oranienburg-Sachsenhausen concentration camp, they found that the priest from Munich had been transferred there and was still alive at the end of the war. Mayer has since been beatified by the Catholic hierarchy. Other heroic resistance came from the Weisse Rose (White Rose) coalition of university students and professors. At the risk of their lives, they published secret leaflets calling for the downfall of the Nazi regime. The White Rose leaders, Hans and Sophie Scholl, Willi Graf, and Hans Huber, were later arrested and beheaded.

By the war's end, almost half of the city's buildings lay in rubble, many having been blown to pieces as early as 1942. Most of Munich's Renaissance and neoclassical grandeur had been literally bombed off the map, a fact that's easy to overlook by modern visitors who admire the city's many restored monuments.

Munich paid a high price in the blood of its citizens: About 22,000 of its sons died in military campaigns, and the civilian population of the city was reduced by almost a quarter million before the end of the war.

THE POSTWAR YEARS & A FOLK HERO

The tone was set after the war by the city's mayor, Thomas Wimmer. He was much beloved by Münchners, and his weekly meet-the-people sessions, when anyone could talk to him personally, made the people in the street feel he was really their representative. His call to clean up Munich met with overwhelming response—the rubble was assembled into decorative hillocks in the city's parks.

Unlike other German cities, Munich was able to unearth the original plans for many of the demolished buildings, which were tastefully restored, even if at astronomical expense, to their original appearance. Today, the city's historic core is surrounded by the same church steeples and towers as in the past.

As capital of the Federal *Land* (state) of Bavaria within the Federal Republic of Germany, Munich took up its new role as focal point for trade between northern and southern Europe. Manufacturers of computers, weapons manufacturers, publishing ventures, fashion houses, movie studios, and companies such as Siemens made Munich their base. The city boomed, with a population that numbered over a million before the end of 1957. As home to BMW (Bayerisches Motoren Werke), Munich is at least partly responsible for Germany's image as home to Europe's fastest drivers.

As the city's population exploded in the 1960s, sprawling masses of concrete suburbs were thrown up hastily, designed for ease of access by cars. Older buildings were demolished to make room for yet another Munich building boom.

The obsession with rebuilding and modernizing at any price was halted when the then-mayor of Munich paid an official visit to Los Angeles. Munich's press gleefully reported that the automobile-dominated society of L.A. so horrified him that he introduced a new emphasis on historical preservation. Since then, active partici-

pation by historic-minded groups has encouraged careful renovations of older buildings.

The 1972 Summer Olympic Games were meant to show the entire world the bold new face of a radically rebuilt Munich from the premises of the innovative Olympic City. However, the terrorist attack on the Israeli athletes, and the collective murder of 11 of them, revived recollections of the past and left behind ambivalent memories.

In a surprise development in 2005, Angela Merkel became the first woman to govern modern Germany and the country's first leader to grow up under communism in the Soviet-occupied East. In a close election influenced heavily by voters in Bavaria, Merkel's conservative Christian Democratic Union party finished just one percentage point ahead of Chancellor Gerhard Schroeder's center-left Social Democrats, with neither party getting a majority.

As Germany, with Munich as a major player, went into the uncertainties of 2008, it still boasted the third-largest economy in the world and continued to be a European Union power player.

MODERN MUNICH

The traditional stereotypes still exist in Munich. Men on occasion wear lederhosen, at least at Oktoberfest, when the ladies put on their dirndls. They drink as much beer as ever in the beer halls and gardens, and the oompah bands are heard through the night.

Munich is also the country's headquarters for high-tech industry. It competes with Berlin, and some local industry leaders are concerned that Berlin as the capital of a reunified Germany could also shift trade and power to the north and east of Germany.

That's not likely to happen soon, if ever. Munich is rather firmly entrenched in the industrial market and is a base for such worldwide industries as the electronics company Siemens and the car manufacturer BMW. Munich is actually more

2

prosperous than Berlin. As the home of three universities, the city has both a vibrant cultural scene and a bustling nightlife.

Munich believes in keeping up to date with changing travel patterns. In decades gone by, Bavarians were traditional and many of them homophobic. Although pockets of that still exist, Munich has blossomed into one of Europe's most gay-friendly destinations. Gays and lesbians by the thousands are moving from the countryside into Munich, and gays and lesbians from abroad make up about 10% of the tourist revenue.

3 MUNICH ART & ARCHITECTURE

ROMANESQUE Bavarian art, as we know it today, had its beginning during the 10th and early 11th centuries, an era identified as the Ottonian period in honor of Emperor Otto I. Builders and stonemasons, virtually all anonymous, built churches whose principles of engineering were based on adaptations of the basilica developed centuries earlier by the ancient Romans. Noteworthy features included barrel vaults, rounded arches, very thick walls, and (usually) symmetrical, rather squat towers.

Today, the few Romanesque buildings that remain intact are among the most cherished in Germany. They are the first architectural flowering of a nation that centuries later developed architecture and engineering into art forms in their own right.

Decorative ivories, crucifixes, and book illuminations were also characteristic of the Romanesque Age. Monasteries established painting schools, but most of that period's paintings have deteriorated or disappeared.

The typically Romanesque Cathedral of Speyer was the 12th-century prototype for the imperial cathedrals in Mainz and Worms. Door carvings, bronze figures of Christ, and stained glass from this period show striking force despite their crudity. Ironically, Munich is not the best place in Germany for insights into this early style of architecture. Although during the city's earliest days, Romanesque architecture dominated the town's low skyline, a series of disastrous fires, the most severe of which occurred in 1327, and the destructive power of medieval rot caused most of them to be modified and rebuilt during later eras into whatever was fashionable at the time.

Munich's oldest parish church, St. Peters, is a good example of this. Built on the site of four small churches in the dim prehistory of Munich, when the town was little more than a riverside enclave of Benedictine monks, it was reconstructed in the late 1100s, then rebuilt again after the city's disastrous fire of 1327. Its foundations date from the dim early medieval days of Munich, although its superstructure, including a bell tower, is from around 1386. Compounding the relative newness of that church is the fact that most of its interior decor, statues, sarcophagi, and frescoes date from the 1400s and 1500s. In other words, admire this church for its Gothic splendor and venerable age, but not as a pure example of Romanesque.

GOTHIC ARCHITECTURE Gothic architecture allowed bigger and more impressive buildings, higher and thinner walls, taller belfries, and—thanks to "broken" (that is, pointed) arches and flying buttresses—larger windows than the small and rather dark openings that illuminated Romanesque buildings. This architectural style flowered in Europe (especially in northern France) between the 13th and 16th centuries, and because of the many communal activities that were needed for its successful execution, it encouraged the growth of trade, commerce, and such satellite industries as woodcarving and the making of stained glass. The Romanesque influence remained pervasive, however, and Gothic design never established as strong a foothold in Germany as it did in France and England. The greatest of the German Gothic cathedrals, the Dom at Cologne, was begun in 1284 but was not completed, as astonishing as it may sound, until 1880.

Perhaps most representative of the German Gothic period is the hall-type church *(Hallenkirche),* which originated in Westphalia. It was characterized by aisles constructed at the same height as the nave, separated from the nave by tall columns. Many of these churches were built during the late Gothic period, the 14th and 15th centuries, a period of great artistic growth in Germany. In Munich, the Gothic style peaked during a period of great prosperity and civic growth. Excellent examples within the city limits include the somber brick profile of the Frauenkirche. Its cornerstone was laid by Duke Sigismund in 1468 on the site of a decrepit Romanesque basilica, whose raw materials, along with the headstones from a nearby graveyard, were incorporated into the new structure. The towers were completed in 1525, as part of a rapid construction that reflected the civic muscle of Munich at the time.

THE RENAISSANCE The art and architecture of the Renaissance, which began in Italy around 1520 and lasted a century, never became widespread within northern Germany, where motifs from Flanders (southern Belgium) and Holland were much more popular. As the prosperity of the rich trading centers of the Hanseatic League grew, they adopted a distinctive design (the Weser Renaissance) almost never seen in the south. Historians attribute the lack of Renaissance motifs to the fact that the emerging Protestant principalities of northern Germany tended to reject Italian and most baroque influences as being too closely tied to the Catholic sensibility.

That was the exact opposite of the situation with Munich and most of the rest of southern Germany, where baroque motifs inspired directly by Italy ran rampant in a city that defined itself as the capital of the Counter-Reformation. The movement's most spectacular example of Counter-Reformation zeal appears in the form of the massive St. Michael's Church. The largest baroque building north of the Alps, and loaded with references to Catholic iconography that defied the growing power of the Protestants farther to the north, it was begun in 1583, and erected and embellished within a record-breaking 14 years. It was built during a pompous and superstitious era. One of its towers collapsed during the seventh year of its construction. Its royal patron, Duke Wilhelm V, interpreted the accident as a sign of displeasure from God that the building wasn't impressive enough. Consequently, it was enlarged and modified into an airy and soaring interior you'll see today. A victim of intense aerial bombardment, it was laboriously rebuilt as a symbol of civic pride after World War II.

Other examples of Renaissance Art in southern Germany include the funerary chapel of Fugger the Rich, in Augsburg, and the entire inner core of the towns of Rothenburg on the Romantic Road.

BAROQUE, NEOCLASSICISM, AND ROMANTIC Baroque style, an Italian import whose influence in Germany began around 1660 and continued into the 18th century, brought a different kind of renaissance to Germany. The baroque swept southern Germany, especially Munich and Bavaria, permeating hundreds of Alpine villages with the reassuring form of onion-shaped domes thrusting skyward between snow-capped peaks. Architectural forms no longer followed regular patterns, as individual artists and craftsmen were granted increased freedom and more variety in design. The German and Danubian baroque artists, such as those of the Vorarlberg School, sought to give an impression of movement to their florid building designs. The splendor of the period is exemplified in the work of such architects as Lukas von Hildebrandt and J. B. Fischer von Erlach. Munich, as the economic and cultural focal point of south Germany, moved into prominence as a seat of art and architecture.

The baroque movement eventually dipped its brushes into the flippant paint of the rococo, and that movement brought even greater freedom and gaiety. Examples of architecture from this period are scattered throughout Bavaria, although within Munich, many were damaged, then rebuilt after wartime destruction. Examples of rococo include the Asamkirche (Asam Church), completed in 1746, the Mariensaule (column of the Virgin) which dominates the Marienplatz, and—inside the Residenz—the Cuvilliés Theater. Another excellent example is the Theatinerkirche, built by Prince Elector Ferdinand Maria in 1662 in gratitude for the birth of his heir, Max Emanuel. Its construction was among the most complicated in Munich because of its completion date more than a century after its inauguration.

Many of these monuments were filled with frescoes commemorating heroic, sacrificial, or transcendental deeds of martyrs, saints, and angels descending on clouds to manifest themselves to the faithful in the church below.

By the 19th century, many members of the rising and prosperous middle class in Germany preferred to decorate their homes in the Biedermeier style, with its lighter designs and carefully balanced symmetry. By now the baroque and rococo styles were dead (the French Revolution, with its de-emphasis on the decorative themes of the ancient regime, had seen to that).

Neoclassicism, with its references to the grandeur of ancient Greece and imperial Rome, became the venue of choice. Once again, the south of Germany brought a lighter touch to this style than did the north. Munich was particularly receptive to this mode. Between 1825 and 1848, Munich and its transformation into a suitably royal capital became the arena for bitter conflicts between the royal patrons and their royal architects, who usually defended every nuance of their designs with something approaching obsessive mania. At least part of Munich's neoclassical grandeur derived from the autocratic Crown Prince Ludwig's (later Ludwig I) devotion to the style. Many of the buildings erected during this era exist thanks to his direct intervention between 1825 and 1848. Examples include the Alte Pinakothek (begun in 1826, and at the time the largest art gallery in the world), the Königsplatz, the Glyptothek, and, within the Residenz complex, the Königsbau (King's Building).

An emphasis on painting, however, did not follow in as fertile a mode as that associated with architecture. Although the city had wonderful art collections—in 1698, Max Emanuel had spent vast amounts of money on the core of what eventually became the Alte Pinakothek collection—most were imported from outside of Munich. Later, the autocratic Ludwig I focused on acquiring early German masters, including Dürer, and such early Italian paintings such as Giotto, Botticelli, and da Vinci.

The Romantic movement followed the neoclassical period. For inspiration in this neo-Gothic arena, which was loaded with political implications for Germany's sense of national identity, architects looked back to a rose-colored interpretation of Germany's medieval history, myth, and folklore. Permeating much of it was an almost obsessive rebirth of interest in Teutonic lore, myth, legend, as expounded by such writers as the Brothers Grimm and Goethe, or such composers as Richard Wagner.

Neo-medieval, or Neo-Romantic buildings from the era include the Staatsbibliothek (State Library), the University complex, and such focal points along the Ludwigstrasse as the Feldherrnhalle, the Siegestor, the Mariahilf-Kirche, the Church of St. Boniface, and the New Pinakothek.

The era that characterized German architecture in the latter 1800s is often termed Historicism. No one represented this flamboyant and eclectic movement better than Ludwig II of Bavaria at his palace Neuschwanstein. Outrageously ornate, with all the fairy-tale ornamentation you'd expect from a Teutonic version of Disneyland, it's one of the major tourist attractions of modern Germany. The most prominent painter of the era was Franz von Lenbach, a socially prominent portraitist who painted virtually every important person of his era from the premises of a lavish villa that today functions as a museum, the Lenbachhaus. His contemporary, Franz von Stuck, greeted his disciples in the costume of a Roman emperor, and painted works that later modernists considered unbearably pompous.

FROM JUGENDSTIL TO MODERNISM
By the end of the 19th century, the Art Nouveau movement—called *Jugendstil* in German after the magazine *Jugend* (Youth) was established in Munich in 1896, swept the country and marked the distant beginnings of contemporary architecture. It was characterized by mass production and solid, semi-industrialized construction, as architects used such materials as glass, steel, and concrete, usually crafted into curved lines inspired by the sinuous forms of nature.

In the aftermath of World War I, Walter Gropius (1883–1969) gained prominence as leader of the Bauhaus movement. Art and technique were wed at this architectural school whose primary aim was to unify Arts and Crafts within the context of

architecture. Its appeal derived from the changing sensibilities of the Industrial Age, as well as from the need for cost-effective construction techniques during an era of rising costs and exploding demand for housing. He stressed the idea of functional designs that reflected the tastes of the postindustrial revolution. Founded at Weimar and directed there by Gropius from 1919, it moved to Dessau in 1925. (Gropius eventually settled in the United States.) For a variety of personal and political reasons, the movement was formally dissolved in 1933, but not before its influence had been felt in Munich and around the rest of Europe as well.

By around 1935, the so-called National Socialist, or Third Reich, style of architecture was the law of the land, with Munich (site of most of Hitler's earliest successes) providing the experimental background for many of its ideas. Under Hitler and such designers as Albert Speer, art and architecture became propaganda tools; pompous, monumental, innately frightening, and devoid of any real humanity.

Postwar Munich did its best to conceal the Nazi roots of some of its buildings, skillfully transforming them into more humanitarian venues. An example is the *Zentralministerium* (Central Ministry), a predictably pompous but anonymous building on the Von-der-Tann-Strasse, cutting through the otherwise orderly progression of the Ludwigstrasse. An even better example, recycled after the war into an art gallery, is the *Staatsgalerie Moderner Kunst* (State Gallery of Modern Art). Originally erected between 1933 and 1937, its angular Fascist architecture seems curiously appropriate for the starkly modern paintings it showcases today. Ironically, virtually everything inside would have been outlawed as "degenerate" by the Nazis who built it originally. Fortunately, the *Führer's* dream of rebuilding a war-torn Munich in his preferred architectural style eventually collapsed.

One sad legacy of World War II was the virtual leveling of many of Germany's greatest architectural treasures by Allied bombing raids. Notable among these tragedies was the destruction of Dresden, until 1945 one of the most beautiful cities of Europe. More than 50 years after its firebombing by British and American planes, its loss is felt more poignantly than that of any other city. Munich fared better, not because it wasn't blasted apart (45% of its buildings were destroyed, all the others damaged in some way), but because it had the economic muscle to rebuild itself. Today, this is just one of the ongoing sources of jealousy and envy that sparks controversy between such prosperous enclaves as Munich and Frankfurt and newly emerging economies in what used to be Germany's Soviet bloc. On-site witnesses claim that the first two years after the end of the war were devoted almost exclusively to clearing away the rubble. In some cases, the architectural rubble of the Munich's past was swept away, never to be restored. However, many cathedrals, churches, houses, town halls, and other buildings were laboriously (at enormous expense) reconstructed in the original style.

Unlike more ancient German cities as Cologne, which has reconstructed a dozen Romanesque churches, Munich's emphasis on postwar building focused on the baroque, the neoclassical, and the neomedieval, of which it had been particularly rich before the conflicts. Regrettably (but understandably), many of Munich's postwar buildings, both domestic and commercial, were hastily erected more for convenience than for architectural grandeur. However, in the prosperous Germany of today, there has been an intense interest and concern for elegance and style in modern architecture.

In painting and sculpture, the often dreary, imitative art of the 19th century in Munich, with its emphasis on historical subjects, gave way to 20th-century vitality. Often deliberately "revolutionary" and shocking, the works of many of these artists were labeled as decadent and many were destroyed during the Third Reich, when painting was supposed to express the ideals of National Socialism. The new century began with the Expressionist school, whose haunted, tormented view of the world was inspired by Van Gogh as well as Scandinavia's greatest painter, Edvard Munch. Expressionism grew out of the work of *Die Brücke (The Bridge)*, a group of artists founded in 1905. Artists in Munich, as well as those throughout Germany, reacted strongly (favorably or unfavorably) to the input from this iconoclastic, Berlin-based group of painters and theoreticists.

Another major artistic movement, *Der Blaue Reiter* (the Blue Rider), was developed in Munich in 1911 by Franz Marc and Wassily Kandinsky, an expatriate Russian. Later, August Macke and Paul Klee reinforced the movement. Absorbed by the Romantic and the lyrical, their dreamy works influenced abstract painting in the decades to come. Disillusioned by the ravages of World War I, the group disbanded after the political crises of 1918.

If the Blue Riders wanted to free art from rigid constraints, the Dadaists carried such a desire to the ultimate. However, at the same time, such eminent artists as George Grosz (1893–1959) practiced a brutal realism. This painter and graphic artist, who immigrated to the United States in 1932, was noted for his satirical pictures of German society and of war and capitalism.

Art developed during the postwar era with what critics described as a frenzy of energy, and architecture zoomed into bursts of creative energy, sparked by the urgent need of Munich to expand into the computer age. This outburst of creativity produced dozens of young artists, so many, in fact, that a widely accepted way for

Münchners to meet and greet one another is at any of the hundreds of art openings sponsored within the city every year.

What, you might ask, is a *kir royale?* Other than a bubbly drink composed of currant juice and champagne, it refers to the scornful adage applied (usually by artists from the more cerebral and highstrung milieu of Berlin) to *Munchner* artlovers who appreciate the parties and *vernissages* of the art world more than the paintings themselves. As in New York, Düsseldorf, or Paris, dozens of artists continue to produce canvases in Munich, struggling as best they can to ride the fine line between their inner artistic vision and the demands of the marketplace.

4 THE LAY OF THE LAND

The National Park Berchtesgaden ★★★ occupies the southeast corner of Germany, comprising a large portion of the state of Bavaria and bordering Austria's province of Salzburg. The park was established in 1978 by a decree from the Bavarian government. It is a lush expanse of 218 sq km (84 sq. miles), with altitudes ranging from 540m (1,772 ft.) at lowland Königssee to the towering Watzmann Mountain.

The 2,670m (8,760-ft.) Watzmann, the Königssee, and parts of the Jenner—the pride of Berchtesgaden's four ski areas—are within the boundaries of the national park, which has well-mapped trails cut through protected areas. Conservation goals and preservation of the natural ecosystems take precedence in the park. An effort is made to keep visitor impact low and to make visitors aware of the ecosystem's fragility.

Limestone dominates most of the rock bed, suggesting that this was once a highly aquatic region. Formed by sediment deposited on the ocean floor 200 million years ago, the rock folded and lifted. Although most of the accompanying sandstone has eroded away, the limestone remains. The steep mountain valleys and moraines suggest recent glacial recession was responsible for many of the grand landscapes found in the park. Of the several Alpine lakes that dot the landscape, the most significant is the Königssee, Germany's cleanest, clearest lake.

Atlantic and continental influences characterize the climate. A substantial annual rainfall fosters the heavy forestation of the region. The valleys receive approximately 152cm (60 in.) of rainfall a year, while the mountains are doused by approximately 279cm (110 in.) annually.

Vegetation varies according to the altitude. Nearly half of the vegetation is deciduous forest, interspersed with spruce and pines, and a third of the vegetation sprouts on rock debris and in crevices. The mixed mountain forest thrives below 1,350m (4,429 ft.); the coniferous forest above it reaches up to 1,650m (5,413 ft.); and above that, wind-dwarfed bushes and Alpine meadows predominate. Once the forest was exploited for salt mines; it's now overpopulated and overgrazed by game.

In spring, summer, and autumn, many different rare species of plants flower. (They are protected, and don't live long once picked, so they should be left for the next person to enjoy.) Alpine animals such as the chamois, ibex (reintroduced in 1930), marmot, snow hare, Alpine salamander, golden eagle, ptarmigan, black grouse, capercaillie, Alpine chough, black woodpecker, and three-toed woodpecker still inhabit the area, but other animals—the wolf, lynx, bear, and golden vulture—once thriving inhabitants, have not survived.

Information about hiking in the park is provided by the **Nationalparkhaus,** Franziskanerplatz 7, 83471 Berchtesgaden (✆ **08652/64343**).

THE NATURAL WORLD OF THE ALPS

Many Alpine animals such as the lynx, otter, and Alpine ibex have all but disappeared from the Bavarian Alps. Other endangered animals include wildcats, susliks, certain nesting birds, toads, and fish.

An effort undertaken to reintroduce species eradicated from their habitats by hunters and farmers has been an unqualified success. Brown bears have been sighted in increased numbers over recent years, along with migrating elk. Wolves have not reemerged since their ultimate annihilation in the 1950s (attempts in the U.S. to reintroduce wolves in the American Rocky Mountains has been mired in controversy). Without any check on their numbers by their natural enemies, the deer and stag population has enjoyed such exponential growth that hunting in some regions has become necessary to keep the population in check and preserve the natural balance.

Other species continue to thrive in the Alpine environment. Unobtrusive hikers will find the Alps teeming with creatures— the chamois gracefully bounding up Alpine heights, golden eagles in circling flight, the griffon vulture floating with its intimidating 9-ft. wingspread. A hiker might even be befriended by a marmot or an Alpine chaugh basking in a sunny meadow. Never threaten the gentle marmot or you might learn why it's nicknamed the whistle pig. The hill country and low mountain ranges are often home to badgers, martens, and hares. Hedgehogs are rare, one of the endangered species of rodents.

Ornithologists literally have a field day in the Bavarian Alps. The range of birds is immense. Great white herons guide you on a teasing trail—they pause for respite along the Danube's banks long enough for you to catch up to them, only to depart in flight to another sanctuary 20 meters downstream. Storks, marsh warblers, gray geese, spoonbills, and terns can also be sighted. The streak of blue you see may be a blue kingfisher, diving for insects in the rippling of streams and rivers. The distinctive red and black wings of the gray Alpine wall creeper distinguish it from the gray cliff faces it ascends. The spotted woodpecker, goldfinch, redstart, thrush, and bluelit barter sing all winter, but the finch, lark, and song thrush save their voices for spring. Keen eyes only will spot falcons, buzzards, and other birds of prey. Don't forget to watch for nocturnal birds like the tawny owl if you're hiking at night.

Of course, if you spend the entire time with your head in the clouds, you'll miss what's underfoot. Edelweiss are the harbingers of spring. They blossom ahead of most wildflowers, often cropping up amid a blanket of snow, enjoying a short and fragile life. The season for mountain wildflowers varies depending on spring temperatures and snowpack. Most wildflowers blossom by the end of July or early August. Many are protected; it is against the law to pick them or take the plants. More than 40,000 plant species are threatened by extinction worldwide, and the Alps are no exception. In any case, the snowdrop, the pink meadow saffron, and the gorgeous colors of the mountain rose and gentian are finest in their natural setting in flowering Alpine meadows. You can, however, pick the bluebills, pinks, cornflowers, buttercups, daisies, and primroses that blossom in such abundance.

You might even find a snack along your trail—wild raspberries, strawberries, bilberries, blackberries, cranberries, flap mushrooms, chanterelles, and parasol mushrooms are often found. However, edible varieties can be easily confused with inedible or poisonous varieties—know what you're picking and be careful. Autumn in the mountains brings an array of colors and splendor with the turning of the leaves. Those interested in finding out more about the flora of Bavaria can visit an

Alpine garden or an instructional guided path.

An ongoing effort is being made to conserve the area's valuable biotopes—high-altitude forest, water marshes, and the specialized plant life of steep cliffs and mountain banks. Nature reserves buffer the detrimental impact of agriculture and forestry, and outside their domains, farmland has been reallocated to include low-yield cultivation and extended pastures. But it's also important that hikers be sensitive to their ecological impact as they enjoy nature in the Alps.

37

5 MUNICH IN POPULAR CULTURE: BOOKS, FILMS & MUSIC

BOOKS If you're a hiker and plan extensive touring in the Bavarian Alps, a useful guide is *Walking in the Bavarian Alps* by Grant Bourne (published by Sabine Kroner-Bourne). All the most intriguing trails are highlighted, and the walks or hikes range from easy to difficult. The book describes 57 walks, covering such places as the Tegernsee and Berchtesgaden, along with varying recommendations for Alpine huts.

For background and understanding of the German experience, any of the works by Thomas Mann (1875–1955) are recommended. As one of Germany's most celebrated writers (*Buddenbrooks*, 1901; *Death in Venice*, 1925; *The Magic Mountain*, 1927), he won the Nobel Prize in Literature in 1929. If you're politically minded, *Munich and Memory: Architecture, Monuments, and the Legacy of the Third Reich*, by Gabriel David Rosenfeld (University of California Press), explores the fascinating saga of Munich's postwar architectural reconstruction and social de-Nazification. Especially intriguing is the behind-the-scenes look at the clearing of both "rubble and rabble" from the German landscape.

A fun read is *The Beer Drinker's Guide to Munich*, by Larry Hawthorne and Eliska Jezkova (Freizeit Publishers). This is an entertaining guide to the best watering holes in the beer-drinking capital of the world. You're taken on a tour of 70 of the city's finest *Biergarten* (beer gardens) and *Bierhalle* (beer halls), along with a selection of pubs and late-night spots, and you'll also learn the history behind them.

Making its appearance in 2002, the latest work on "mad king" Ludwig is *Ludwig II of Bavaria: A King's Passion for Castles*, by Rolf Toman (published by Konemann).

Bavaria's most fascinating courtesan was Lola Montez, mistress of King Ludwig I. See the box "The Notorious Lola Montez," earlier in this chapter. Her fascinating tale lives on in *Lola Montez: A Life*, by Bruce Seymour (Yale University Press).

The intriguing story of the history behind the Eagle's Nest, once the vacation retreat of Hitler, is explored in the book *Battle for Hitler's Eagles Nest*, by Leo Kessler (Severn House Publishers)

FILMS Of late, the only film with a Munich setting to gain millions of viewers has been Steven Spielberg's 2005 film, *Munich*, with a screenplay co-authored by the award-winning Tony Kushner. It dramatically depicted the story of the "Black September" aftermath, about the five men chosen to eliminate the murderers of that fateful day when the world was watching in 1972 as 11 Israeli athletes were killed at the Munich Olympics. Daniel Craig (later James Bond) was one of the stars of this thriller known for its graphic violence. With worldwide audiences, *Munich* raised a provocative question: "What distinguishes justice from vengeance?"

Released the same year as *Munich* was director Marc Rothemund's *Sophie Scholl—die letzten Tage*. The film is a dramatization of the final days of Sophie Scholl, nicknamed the White Rose. In 1943 this brave

MUNICH IN DEPTH

7

MUNICH IN POPULAR CULTURE: BOOKS, FILMS & MUSIC

young woman stood up to members of the Nazi army as part of a resistance movement. Her courage made her a legend in Germany. Actress Julia Jentsch plays Sophie. Some scenes were filmed at the University of Munich, the original location where Scholl was arrested, followed by her interrogation and ultimate sentence of death.

Munich was also the setting for *Beerfest* (2006), director Jay Chandrasekhar's tale of two brothers who travel to Germany for Oktoberfest. Here they stumble upon a secret, centuries-old competition described as a "Fight Club." Watching all the beer drunk in this movie is guaranteed to give you a hangover the next morning.

MUSIC Contrary to its reputation, Munich is not all oompah. The city enjoys renown as a distinguished home of classical music, much of which is available on recordings. Munich was the domain of many prominent composers, including (on and off) Orlando di Lasso, W.A. Mozart, Carl Maria von Webr, and Gustav Mahler. The Nationaltheater premiered several of Richard Wagner's operas when he was under the patronage of Ludwig II. Munich is also the home of the Bavarian State Opera and the Bavarian State Orchestra.

One of the most celebrated of all Munich-born composers is Richard Strauss (1865–1949), whose works are widely recorded and performed today around the world. He was the leader of the New Romantic school. From 1886 to 1898, he was *Kappelmeister* (musical director) of the city, and later with Franz Schalk, headed the State Opera in Vienna, where he worked with all the major European orchestras. He composed both operas and symphonic works. Of his 15 operas, his most famous are *Salome* (1905), *Elektra* (1908), and *Der Rosenkavalier* (1911).

Founded in 1893, the Munich Philharmonic is one of the greatest orchestras of Europe, having performed premieres of such composers as Anton Bruckner or Gustav Mahler, among others.

Born here in 1952, Harold Faltermeyer is a musician, keyboardist, composer, and record producer. He best captured the Zeitgeist of 1980s synth-pop in film scores, including the much-imitated electronic theme, "Axel F," from *Beverly Hills Cop* and "Top Gun Anthem" from the soundtrack of Tom Cruise's *Top Gun*. For this work, he won two Grammy Awards, first in 1986 and again in 1987.

The German conductor and pianist, Wolfgang Sawallisch, was born in Munich in 1923, but became known in America when he was the music director of the Philadelphia Orchestra from 1993 to 2003.

Born in Munich as the child of a U.S. Army chaplain, Brent Mydland (1952–90) was the fourth keyboardist to play for the Grateful Dead. Two of Mydland's most popular songs with the band were "Far From Me" and "Easy to Love You."

One of the most unusual musical sons to come out of Munich is Lou Bega, born here in 1975, the son of a Ugandan father who had come to Germany in 1972 to study biology. Bega is the Latin pop musician famous for his first single, "Mambo No. 5," which became an instant worldwide hit and is still widely played. A lot of fans who hail the singer-rapper as the King of Mambo don't know of his German background and that he's fluent in the language.

6 EATING & DRINKING IN MUNICH

THE TRADITIONAL CUISINE

Bavarians like to eat, justifying their appetites with the very reasonable assertion that any type of human interaction operates more smoothly when it's lubricated with ample amounts of food and wine, or, even better, food and beer.

Calorie- and cholesterol-conscious North Americans might recoil at the sight of meals made up of dumplings, potatoes, any of a dozen different types of *Wurst* (sausages), roasted meats flavored with bacon drippings, breads, and pastries. Munich, of course, has many restaurants that specialize in cuisine moderne, as well as nouvelle counterparts of the traditional cuisine. But the standard old-fashioned *Kuchen* (cake) is still widely served and enjoyed.

The Bavarian affair with sausage is of ancient lineage, wurst having been a major part of the national diet almost since there were people and livestock in the area. Bavarians tend to view their wurst with some superstition, nostalgically adhering to such adages as "Never let the sunshine of noon shine on a *Weisswurst*," and the reservation of *Ratwurst* for consumption in the evening.

Every Bavarian professes a love for his or her favorite kind of wurst (a choice that's often based on childhood associations). Many visitors' favorite is *Bratwurst*, which came originally from nearby Nürnberg and is concocted from seasoned and spiced pork. *Weisswurst*, Munich's traditional accompaniment to a foaming mug of beer, wasn't "invented" until 1857, a date remembered by Münchners as an important watershed. The ingredients that go into it are less appetizing than the final result—usually including veal, calves' brains, and spleen. Modern versions contain less offal and better quantities of veal, as well as spices and lemon juice to enhance the flavor. Two are usually considered a snack. Five or six are a respectable main course. Most aficionados try not to eat the skin, but some die-hards wouldn't think of removing it.

Bauernwurst (farmer's sausage) and *Knockwurst* are variations of the Frankfurter, which, although it originated in the more westerly city of Frankfurt, achieved its greatest fame in the New World. While *Leberwurst* is a specialty of Hesse, and *Riderwurst* (beef sausage) and *Blutwurst* (blood

sausage) are specialties of Westphalia, all of them are widely served and enjoyed in Munich. Regardless of which you choose, the perfect accompaniment for wurst consists of mustard, a roll (preferably studded with pumpernickel seeds), and beer.

As savory as the wursts of Munich might be, they're considered too simple to grace the table at any truly elaborate Bavarian meal, unless accompanied by other dishes. From the long-ago repertoire of agrarian Bavarian cuisine comes *Züngerl* (pig's tongue) or *Wammerl* (pig's stomach), most often served with braised or boiled cabbage. Potato dumplings (*Klösse*, or *Kartoffelknödel*) and *Leber* (liver) dumplings are mandatory features. *Semmelknödel* (bread dumplings) generally accompany the most famous meat dish of Bavaria, *Schweinebraten* (roast pork). Also popular with many devotees are *Kalbshaxen* (veal shank) and *Schweinshaxen* (roasted knuckle of pork). Carp is prized by Munich's gastronomes, as is a succulent variety of trout, or *Forelle*.

Feeling hungry during your sightseeing promenades around Munich? Step into the nearest *Metzgerei* (butcher shop) and order such items as a *Warmer Leberkäs*, which has nothing to do with either liver or cheese, but instead with ground beef and bacon, baked like a meatloaf and sold in slices of about 100 grams each. It's best consumed with mild mustard and a roll. Another worthy choice is *Wurtzsemmel*, sliced sausage meat on a roll, or *Schinkensemmel*, sliced ham served on a roll. You can carry it away for consumption at a spot where there's a view or take it into a *Bierkeller* or *Biergarten* (it's been legal for centuries to bring in your own food and order a small beer to go with it).

AND WHAT BEER SHOULD YOU DRINK?

No self-respecting Münchner will refuse a sparkling glass of wine, and will even praise highly the light, slightly acidic wines from the Rhineland. But the real

The Bavarian Brew

Few cities in the world cling to a beverage the way Munich clings to beer. Münchners—with a little help from their visitors—consume a world's record of the stuff: 280 liters a year, per capita (as opposed to a wimpy 150 liters in other parts of Germany). This kind of "heroism" usually prompts a cynical comment from the wine drinkers of Berlin and the Rhineland—they say that Bavarians never open their mouths except to pour in more beer! The Münchner response is that settling questions of politics, art, music, commerce, and finance, as well as the affairs of the human heart, requires plenty of beer and lots of good, unfussy food.

Some of Munich's most notable events have floated on the suds. There was Hitler's Beer Hall Putsch (Hofbräuhaus, 1923); a bungled attempt to assassinate Hitler (in the Bürgerbräukeller in 1939); and, most recently, the Beer Garden Revolution, a 1995 event, when the proposed closing of a neighborhood beer garden at 9:30pm was seen as a threat to the civil liberties of all the city's beer drinkers and prompted mass rallies by infuriated Münchners. These, along with dozens of smaller but still sudsy tempests, have trained Munich's politicians to view the effects of the brew on their constituents with considerable respect.

The perfect accompaniment for beer (especially if it happens to be consumed before noon), as everyone knows, is *Weisswurst,* those little white sausages. And every year, the anniversary of their invention, in 1857, is celebrated as something of a national holiday. *Prost!* (Toast!)

glint enters a Münchner's eye when the relative merits of beer are discussed. You won't lack for variety within the beer halls of Munich—there are even beers available according to season.

Both because it's the law and as a matter of pride, breweries make their beer with yeast, barley, hops, and water. Preservatives aren't usually added—in a city where a 200-liter cask of beer can be drained by a thirsty crowd in fewer than 12 minutes, the beer never lasts long enough to really need them. Legally required adherence to certain standards dates back to 1516—before the establishment of standards anywhere else in Europe.

Here's a rundown on what you're likely to need in your dialogue with a Münchner bartender.

"Normal" Bavarian beer, also referred to as light beer (ask for *ein Helles*), is slightly less potent than the brew consumed in North Germany, France, or England. Its relative weakness is the main reason why many visitors can consume several liters before beginning to feel the least bit giddy.

Don't think, however, that "normal" beer is the same as *Weiss* or (in Münchner dialect) *Weizenbier,* which is brewed with a high concentration of fermented wheat. In springtime, along with spring lamb and fresh fruits and vegetables, Munich offers *Bock* and *Doppelbock* (Double Bock), *Märzenbier,* and *Pils.*

Beck's Dark is an example of dark beer *(ein Dunkles)* known to many North Americans. There's even a dark *Weiss* beer, which happens to be wheat beer brewed in such a way as to make it smoky-looking rather than pale. And in case you've forgotten a particularly unpleasant episode in Munich's civic history, there's even a beer named after the doomed socialists (the Red Guards) who forcibly took over the city's government for a few months in 1918—a *Russe,* which consists of *Weiss* (wheat) beer and lemonade.

What is the polite thing to ask for if you think you're too drunk to handle another liter of "normal" beer? Ask for a *Radlermass* (literally, "a mug for the bike"), composed of half "normal" beer, half lemonade.

The ideal place to go for consuming this amazing variety of fermented grains is any of the city's dozens of beer cellars and beer gardens, which serve simple, snack-like food items—sausages, white radishes, cheese, and the kind of salted pretzels that are guaranteed to make you thirstier. Munich's most historic drinking sites include the Hofbräuhaus and the Bürgerbräukeller, both of which carry local associations of everyone from Adolf Hitler to the boy or girl next door.

Planning Your Trip to Munich & the Bavarian Alps

This chapter covers everything you need to know to make trip planning a snap, from when to go to how to shop for the best airfare. Browse through it to get started and make sure you've touched all the bases.

1 VISITOR INFORMATION

TOURIST OFFICES

For info before you go, you can find a **German National Tourist Office** in **New York** at 122 E. 42nd St., 52nd Floor, New York, NY 10168 (© **800/651-7010** or 212/661-7174); in **Toronto** at 480 University Ave., Ste. 1410, Toronto, ON M5G 1V2 (© **877/315-6237** or 416/968-1685); and in **London,** P.O. Box 2695, London W1A 3TN (© **020/7317-0908**).

The **German National Tourist Board** is at Beethovenstrasse 69, 60325 Frankfurt am Main (© **069/975-1903**).

In Munich, tourist information is available at the Munich International Airport in the central area (© **089/97-50-00**) as you step off the plane. The desk is open Monday to Saturday from 8:30am to 10pm and Sunday from 1 to 9pm. The main branch of the Munich Tourist Office, **Fremdenverkehrsamt,** at the Hauptbahnhof, Bahnhofplatz 2 (© **089/233-96-500;** www.muenchen.de), is found at the south exit opening onto Bayerstrasse. It's open Monday to Friday 9am to 8pm and Saturday 10am to 4pm. You can pick up a free map of Munich, and you can also reserve rooms there. You will find another branch of the Munich Tourist Office at Marienplatz inside the Neues Rathaus, open Monday to Friday 10am to 8pm and Saturday 10am to 4pm.

OUR FAVORITE GERMAN WEBSITES

If you open a site that's in German, look for the little British or American flag, or for the word *English* on some, but not all, to see the pages in English.

- The **German National Tourist Board** site (www.germany-tourism.de or www.cometogermany.com) has an online tour of several cities and highlights attractions. You can access facts on weather, transportation, events, and so forth. A new, related site (www.visits-to-germany.com) designed especially for U.S. travelers lets you design and price specific itineraries and vacation packages.

- The **Hotelguide Germany Hotel Association** (IHA; www.hotels-germany.com) lets you book a room at any of more than 750 German hotels through its site. Conduct a search according to location and amenity preferences, or check out the special offers for accommodations conducive to family travel, cultural activities, sports, biking, special events, or last-minute travel.

- Get started on the appealing, if daunting, task of eating in Germany with the help of **Gastroscout.com**. Search for a schnitzel-filled *Gasthaus* or eateries by city, price, ethnicity, child friendliness, wheelchair accessibility, or any of a slew of other criteria. Recommendations are also given on this site.

- The **Munich Tourist Office** site (www.muenchen.de) offers information about the city's history, economy, places of interest (museums, parks, churches, and so on), accommodations, and an entire section devoted to Oktoberfest.

2 ENTRY REQUIREMENTS

PASSPORTS

Every U.S., Canadian, British, and Australian traveler entering Germany must hold a valid passport. You won't need a visa unless you're staying longer than 3 months. Once you've entered Germany, you won't need to show your passport again at the borders of Belgium, France, Italy, Luxembourg, the Netherlands, Portugal, or Spain. Safeguard your passport in an inconspicuous, inaccessible place like a money belt. If you lose your passport, visit the nearest consulate of your home country as soon as possible for a replacement. You should always carry a photocopy of your passport (stored separately) to expedite replacement.

For information on how to get a passport, go to "Passports" in the "Fast Facts" section of appendix A—the websites listed provide downloadable passport applications and the current fees for processing passport applications. For an up-to-date, country-by-country listing of passport requirements around the world, go to the International Travel Web page of the U.S. State Department at http://travel.state.gov (click on "International Travel for U.S. Citizens").

It's always wise to have plenty of documentation when traveling in today's world with children. For changing details on entry requirements for children traveling abroad, go to the U.S. State Department website at http://travel.state.gov, and click on "Children & Family."

To prevent international child abduction, European Union governments have initiated procedures at entry and exit points. These often (but not always) include requiring documentary evidence of relationship and permission for the child's travel from the parent or legal guardian not present. Having such documentation on hand, even if not required, facilitates entries and exits. All children must have their own passport. To obtain a passport, the child *must* be present—that is, in person—at the center issuing the passport. Both parents must be present as well. If not, then a notarized statement from the parents is required. Any questions parents or guardians might have can be answered by calling the National Passport Center at (C) **877/487-6868** Monday to Friday 8am to 8pm Eastern time.

CUSTOMS
What You Can Bring into Germany

In general, items required for personal and professional use or consumption may be brought into Germany duty-free and without hassle. No duty is levied for a private car, provided that it is reported. You can also bring in gifts duty-free up to a total value of 175€ ($280).

The following items are permitted into Germany duty-free from non-E.U. (European Union) countries: 200 cigarettes; 1 liter of liquor above 44 proof, or 2 liters of liquor less than 44 proof, or 2 liters of wine; 50 grams of perfume and .25 liters of eau de cologne; 500 grams of coffee; and 100 grams of tea. Travelers bringing in tobacco or alcohol products must be 17 years or older, and those bringing coffee or tea must be 15 years or older. From E.U. countries the duty-free limits are higher. Duty-free allowances are authorized only when the items are carried in the traveler's personal baggage.

What You Can Take Home from Germany
U.S. Residents

Returning U.S. residents who have been away for at least 48 hours are allowed to bring back, once every 30 days, $800 worth of merchandise duty-free. You'll be charged a flat rate of 4% duty on the next $1,000 worth of purchases. Any dollar amount beyond that is dutiable at whatever rates apply. On mailed gifts, the duty-free limit is $200. Be sure to have your receipts or purchases handy to expedite the declaration process. *Note:* If you owe duty, you are required to pay on your arrival in the United States, by cash, personal check, government or traveler's check, or money order, and in some locations a Visa or MasterCard.

To avoid having to pay duty on foreign-made personal items you owned before you left on your trip, bring along a bill of sale, insurance policy, jeweler's appraisal, or receipts of purchase. Or you can register items that can be readily identified by a permanently affixed serial number or marking—think laptop computers, cameras, and CD players—with Customs before you leave. Take the items to the nearest Customs office or register them with Customs at the airport from which you're departing. You'll receive, at no cost, a Certificate of Registration, which allows duty-free entry for the life of the item.

With some exceptions, you cannot bring fresh fruits and vegetables into the United States. For specifics on what you can bring back and the corresponding fees, download the invaluable free pamphlet *Know Before*

You Go online at **www.cbp.gov**. Or contact the **U.S. Customs & Border Protection (CBP)**, 1300 Pennsylvania Ave., NW, Washington, DC 20229 (© **877/287-8867**), and request the pamphlet.

Canadian Residents

For a clear summary of Canadian rules, write for the booklet *Be Aware and Declare*, issued by the **Canada Border Services** (© **800/461-9999** in Canada, or 204/983-3500; www.cbsa-asfc.gc.ca). Canada allows its residents a C$750 exemption, and adults are allowed to bring back duty-free one carton of cigarettes, one can of tobacco, 40 imperial ounces of liquor, and 50 cigars. In addition, you're allowed to mail gifts to Canada valued at less than C$60 a day, provided they're unsolicited and don't contain alcohol or tobacco (write on the package "Unsolicited gift, under C$60 value"). Declare all valuables on the Y-38 form before departure from Canada, including serial numbers of valuables you already own, such as expensive foreign cameras. *Note:* The C$750 exemption can be used only once a year and only after an absence of 7 days.

U.K. Residents

U.K. residents who are **returning from a European Union country** go through a separate Customs Exit (the "Blue Exit") especially for E.U. travelers. In essence, there is no limit on what you can bring back from an E.U. country, as long as the items are for personal use (this includes gifts) and you have already paid the necessary duty and tax. However, Customs law sets out guidance levels. If you bring in more than these levels, you may be asked to prove that the goods are for your own use. Guidance levels on goods bought in the E.U. for your own use are 3,200 cigarettes, 200 cigars, 400 cigarillos, 3 kilograms of smoking tobacco, 10 liters of spirits, 90 liters of wine, 20 liters of fortified wine (such as port or sherry), and 110 liters of beer.

For information, contact **HM revenue Customs** at (✆) **0845/010-9000** (from outside the U.K., 02920/501-261), or visit www.hmrc.gov.uk.

Australian Residents

The duty-free allowance in Australia is A$900. Residents can bring in 250 cigarettes or 250 grams of loose tobacco, and 2.25 liters of alcohol. If you're taking valuables you already own, such as foreign-made cameras, you should file form B263. A helpful brochure available from Australian consulates or Customs offices is *Know Before You Go*. For more information, call the **Australian Customs Service** at (✆) **1300/363-63**, or go to www.customs.gov.au.

New Zealand Residents

The duty-free allowance for New Zealand is NZ$700. Residents 18 and over can bring in 200 cigarettes, 50 cigars, or 250 grams of tobacco (or a mixture of all three if their combined weight doesn't exceed 250g); plus 4.5 liters of wine and beer, or 1.125 liters of liquor. New Zealand currency does not carry import or export restrictions. Fill out a certificate of export, listing the valuables you are taking out of the country; that way, you can bring them back without paying duty. Most questions are answered in a free pamphlet available at New Zealand consulates and Customs offices: *New Zealand Customs Guide for Travellers, Notice No. 4*. For more information, contact **New Zealand Customs Service**, the Customhouse, 17–21 Whitmore St., Box 2218, Wellington ((✆) **04/473-6099** or 0800/428-786; www.customs.govt.nz).

---

3 WHEN TO GO

CLIMATE

In Bavaria and in the Alps, it can sometimes be very cold in winter, especially in January, and very warm in summer, but with cool, rainy days even in July and August. Spring and fall are often stretched out. In fact, we've enjoyed many a Bavarian-style Indian summer into October. The most popular tourist months are May to October, although winter travel to the Alpine ski areas is becoming increasingly popular.

Munich's Average Daytime Temperature & Days of Rain

	Jan	Feb	Mar	Apr	May	June	July	Aug	Sept	Oct	Nov	Dec
Temp. (°F)	33	35	40	50	60	65	70	73	65	50	39	33
Temp. (°C)	1	2	4	10	16	18	21	23	18	10	4	1
Days of Rain	19	16	19	19	21	24	18	17	18	15	17	18

MUNICH CALENDAR OF EVENTS

All dates and events are subject to change. Contact the Munich Tourist Office at Sendlinger Strasse 1 at the Hauptbahnhof ((✆) **089/233-96-500**) for more information. The board publishes a free calendar of forthcoming events three times a year: in April, October, and January; the first two are biannual calendars and the last is a yearly preview. The calendars list the dates of trade fairs and exhibitions, theatrical and musical performances, local folk festivals, sporting events, conferences, and congresses throughout Germany.

For events beyond those listed here, check http://events.frommers.com, where you'll find a searchable, up-to-the-minute roster of what's happening in cities all over the world.

FEBRUARY

Fasching (Carnival). Pre-Lenten revelry characterizes this weeks-long bash, with a whirl of colorful parades and masked balls. Special events are staged at the Viktualienmarkt. The celebration, which culminates on Fasching Sunday and Shrove Tuesday, lasts 4 to 6 weeks, depending on the dates of the Lenten season. For specifics, call the Munich Tourist Office (✆ **089/233-96-500**).

Munich Fashion Week. The latest and often most elegant parades of fashion are staged at various venues across the city. Mid-February.

MARCH

Starkbierzeit. The "strong beer season" provides serious beer drinkers with a fresh crop to tide them over until Oktoberfest. Just a pint of one of the dense brews churned out specifically for the season (beginning the third Fri of Lent and lasting 2 weeks) ought to satiate most buzz seekers. Beers with the suffix "-ator" (Salvator, for example) were created to be consumed at Lent. This dalliance from the strict fasting rules of Lent was approved by the pope long ago: When he tasted what Münchners had been imbibing, he found it unpleasant enough to think that anyone who drank it would not be violating the fast. (What he didn't realize was that the beer had traveled a considerable distance to get to him, which is why it was bad!) The tradition continues.

APRIL & MAY

Auer Dult. A Munich tradition, Auer Dult is a colorful 8-day flea market that occurs three times a year. Prize antiques and vintage junk await the most disciplined bargain hunters. Merchants set up shop on the Mariahilfplatz on the last Saturday in April (Maidult), the end of July (Jakobidult), and the end of October (Herbst Dult).

Corpus Christi Street Processions. Street parades with dressed-up horses, a carried statue symbolizing Christ, girls dressed in white, a canopy, priests, and other functionaries are seen all around the region on the Thursday following the eighth Sunday after Easter.

JUNE

Munich Film Festival. This festival isn't as popular as the February International Film Festival in Berlin, but it draws a serious audience. Late June.

Tollwood. This summer music festival, originated by environmentalists, honors the free spirit of jazz, blues, and rock from the third week in June through the first week of July in Olympiapark. Ask at the Munich Tourist Office.

JULY

Opera Festival and Munich Summer of Music. The Munich Philharmonic Orchestra's Summer of Music and the Bavarian State Opera Festival highlight the work of Munich's prodigal son, Wagner, and other masters including Mozart, Orff, Mahler, and Strauss. Contact the Munich Tourist Office (✆ **089/233-96-500**) for details. All month.

Christopher Street Day. The big day for the estimated 100,000 gay men and lesbians who live in the city attracts people from across Bavaria. This fun-filled parade, with its outrageous costumes, is one of the largest such events in Europe. It is named after the street in New York's Greenwich Village that was the site of the 1960s Stonewall Riots, said to have launched the gay liberation movement. Mid-July.

AUGUST

Olympiapark Sommerfest. This well-attended summer festival near Coubertin Platz is an outdoor musical scene that ranges from classical music to rock and jazz, along with productions staged in the park's open-air theater. Admission is free. For details, call ✆ **089/30-67-0,** or visit www.olympiapark muenchen.de.

Oktoberfest. Germany's most famous beer festival takes place mostly in September, despite the name. Hotels are packed, and beer and revelry flow on the Theresienwiese, where gigantic tents hold as many as 6,000 beer drinkers. It lasts from mid-September to the first Sunday in October.

Christkindlmarkt. Every evening at 5:30pm, classic Christmas music bellows throughout the Christmas market on seasonally lit Marienplatz. You may even catch a glimpse of the *real* St. Nick. Traditionally runs from late November to Christmas Eve.

4 GETTING THERE & GETTING AROUND

GETTING THERE BY PLANE

Most airlines price fares seasonally. During peak season, the summer months, flights to Munich are at their most expensive. Excluding the Christmas holidays, winter months offer the lowest fares. This fits in fine with those who wish to ski in the Bavarian Alps. Shoulder season is in between.

Most direct flights to Munich from North America are offered on Lufthansa. On most airlines flying to Germany from North America, connections to Munich must be made through Frankfurt, Düsseldorf, or another gateway city. **Lufthansa** (℃ **800/645-3880** or 01/805-838-426 within Germany; www.lufthansa-usa.com), the German national carrier, has an alliance with **United Airlines** and **Air Canada** to provide seamless air service to Germany and other parts of the globe from North America. "Star Alliance" allows cross-airline benefits, including travel on one or all of these airlines on one ticket and frequent-flier credit to the participating airline of your choice.

Air Canada (℃ 888/247-2262; www.aircanada.com), **American Airlines** (℃ 800/443-7300; www.aa.com), **Continental Airlines** (℃ 800/525-0280; www.continental.com), **Delta Airlines** (℃ 800/241-4141; www.delta.com),

United Airlines (℃ 800/538-2929; www.ual.com), and **US Airways** (℃ 800/428-4322; www.usairways.com) all fly daily to Germany.

From the U.K., **British Airways** (℃ **0870/850-9850**; www.britishairways.com), **Lufthansa** (℃ **0871/945-9124**; www.lufthansa.com), and **British Midland** in London (℃ **0870/607-0555**; www.flybmi.com) fly regularly to major German cities.

ARRIVING AT THE AIRPORT About 27km (17 miles) northeast of central Munich at Erdinger Moos, **Munich International Airport (MUC; ℃ 089/97500;** www.munich-airport.de) is among the most modern, best-equipped, and most efficient airports in the world. The airport handles more than 400 flights a day, serving at least 65 cities worldwide. Passengers can fly nonstop from New York, Miami, Chicago, and Toronto, among other places.

GETTING INTO TOWN FROM THE AIRPORT S-Bahn (℃ 089/210-33-0) trains connect the airport with the Hauptbahnhof (main railroad station) in downtown Munich. Departures are every 20 minutes for the 40-minute trip. The fare is 10€ ($16); Eurailpass holders ride free. A taxi into the center costs 50€ to 60€ ($80–$96). Airport buses, such as those operated by Lufthansa, also run between the airport and the center.

(Tips) Getting Through the Airport

- Arrive at the airport at least 2 hours before an international flight to Germany. You can check the average wait times at your airport by going to the TSA **Security Checkpoint Wait Times** site (http://waittime.tsa.dhs. gov).
- Know what you can carry on and what you can't. For the latest updates on items you are prohibited to bring in carry-on luggage, go to **www.tsa. gov/travelers/airtravel**.
- Beat the ticket-counter lines by using the self-service electronic ticket kiosks at the airport or even printing out your boarding pass at home from the airline website. Using curbside check-in is also a smart way to avoid lines.
- Help speed up security before you're screened. Remove jackets, shoes, belt buckles, heavy jewelry, and watches, and place them either in your carry-on luggage or the security bins provided. Place keys, coins, cellphones, and pagers in a security bin. If you have metallic body parts, carry a note from your doctor. When possible, keep packing liquids in checked baggage.
- Use a TSA-approved lock for your checked luggage. Look for Travel Sentry certified locks at luggage or travel shops and Brookstone stores (or online at www.brookstone.com).

If you're going to rent or pick up a car at the airport, see "Car Rentals," below, for more information.

Flying for Less: Tips for Getting the Best Airfare

- Passengers who can book their ticket either **long in advance or at the last minute,** or who **fly midweek** or **at less-trafficked hours** may pay a fraction of the full fare. If your schedule is flexible, say so, and ask if you can secure a cheaper fare by changing your flight plans.
- Search the **Internet** for cheap fares. The most popular online travel agencies are **Travelocity.com** (www.travelocity.co. uk); **Expedia.com** (www.expedia.co. uk and www.expedia.ca); and **Orbitz. com.** In the U.K., **Travelsupermarket** (© 0845/345-5708; www.travelsuper market.com) is a flight search engine

that offers flight comparisons for the budget airlines whose seats often end up in bucket-shop sales. Other websites for booking airline tickets online include **Cheapflights.com,** **SmarterTravel. com, Priceline.com,** and **Opodo** (www. opodo.co.uk). Meta search sites (which find and then direct you to airline and hotel websites for booking) include **Sidestep.com** and **Kayak.com**—the latter includes fares for budget carriers such as jetBlue and Spirit as well as the major airlines. **Site59.com** is a great source for last-minute flights and getaways. In addition, most **airlines** offer online-only fares that even their phone agents know nothing about. British travelers should check **Flights International** (© 0800/0187050; www.flights-international.com) for deals on flights all over the world.

- Keep an eye on local newspapers for **promotional specials** or **fare wars,** when airlines lower prices on their most popular routes.
- **Consolidators,** also known as bucket shops, are wholesale brokers in the airline-ticket game. Consolidators buy deeply discounted tickets ("distressed" inventories of unsold seats) from airlines and sell them to online ticket agencies, travel agents, tour operators, corporations, and, to a lesser degree, the general public. Consolidators advertise in Sunday newspaper travel sections (often in small ads with tiny type), both in the U.S. and the UK. They can be great sources for cheap international tickets. On the downside, bucket shop tickets are often rigged with restrictions, such as stiff cancellation penalties (as high as 50%–75% of the ticket price). And keep in mind that most of what you see advertised is of limited availability. Several reliable consolidators are worldwide and available online. **STA Travel** (www.statravel.com) has been the world's leading consolidator for students since purchasing Council Travel, but their fares are competitive for travelers of all ages. **Flights.com** (© 201/541-3826; www.flights.com) has excellent fares worldwide, particularly to Europe. They also have "local" websites in 12 countries. **FlyCheap** (© 800/FLY-CHEAP; www.1800fly cheap.com) has especially good fares to sunny destinations. **Air Tickets Direct** (© 888/858-8884; www.airtickets direct.com) is based in Montreal and leverages the occasionally weaker Canadian dollar for lower fares; they also book trips to places that U.S. travel agents won't touch, such as Cuba.
- Join **frequent-flier clubs.** Frequent-flier membership doesn't cost a cent, but it does entitle you to free tickets or upgrades when you amass the airline's required number of frequent-flier points. You don't even have to fly to earn points; **frequent-flier credit cards** can earn you thousands of miles for doing your everyday shopping. But keep in mind that award seats are limited, seats on popular routes are hard to snag, and more and more major airlines are cutting their expiration periods for mileage points—so check your airline's frequent-flier program so you don't lose your miles before you use them. *Inside tip:* Award seats are offered almost a year in advance, but seats also open up at the last minute, so if your travel plans are flexible, you may strike gold. To play the frequent flier game to your best advantage, consult the community bulletin boards on **FlyerTalk** (www.flyer talk.com) or go to Randy Petersen's **Inside Flyer** (www.insideflyer.com). Petersen and friends review all the programs in detail and post regular updates on changes in policies and trends.

GETTING THERE BY CAR

Most motorists in Europe travel to Munich by autobahn (express hwy.). When getting off any autobahn, take the signs that read STADTMITTE into the center of Munich. Autobahns from Salzburg and points east, Garmisch-Partenkirchen, and destinations to the south, link up with the Millerer Ring (Munich's beltway). From Stuttgart and points west, the autobahn comes to an end at Obermenzing, the most westerly suburb of Munich. If you're coming from the north, perhaps Frankfurt, get off the autobahn at the exit marked Schwabing.

In theory, there is no speed limit on the autobahns (in the left, fast lane), but many drivers going too fast report that they have been stopped by the police and fined on the spot. So reasonable caution is recommended here, for safety if not other reasons. A German driver on the autobahn can be a ferocious creature, and you may prefer the slow lane. The government recommends an autobahn speed limit of

130kmph (80 mph). In congested areas, the speed limit is about 50kmph (around 30 mph). On all other roads except the autobahns, the speed limit is 100kmph (about 60 mph).

In Germany, you drive on the right side of the road. Both front-seat and back-seat passengers are required to wear safety belts. Children can't ride in the front seat.

Easy-to-understand international road signs are posted, but U.S. travelers should remember that road signs are in kilometers, not miles.

Note: Drinking and driving is a very serious offense in Germany. Therefore, be sure to keep any alcoholic beverages in the trunk or some other storage area. Avoid even the appearance of drinking alcohol while driving.

Car Rentals

It's usually cheaper to rent a car before leaving for Germany though you can also rent one here, keeping in mind that competition in the Munich car-rental industry is fierce.

Major car-rental companies have easy-to-spot offices at the airport. You can make reservations and do comparison shopping by calling their toll-free numbers in the United States: **Avis** (© **800/331-1084;** www.avis.com), **Budget** (© **800/472-3325;** www.budget.com), and **Hertz** (© **800/654-3001;** www.hertz.com). You can also try **Kemwel Drive Europe** (© **877/820-0668;** www.kemwel.com) and **Auto Europe** (© **888/223-5555;** www.autoeurope.com). All the major car-rental companies offer competitive rates that tend to be more attractive if you reserve your car from North America between 1 day and 2 weeks in advance of your departure. Promotional rates offered by car-rental corporations should be researched for the best value.

American and Canadian drivers, and those from E.U. countries, need only a domestic license to drive, but it's recommended that you carry an international driver's permit in case of an accident or other problems. Both in Germany and throughout the rest of Europe, you must also have an international insurance certificate, known as a green card *(carte verte).* Any car-rental agency will automatically provide one of these as a standard part of the rental contract, but it's a good idea to double-check all documents at the time of rental, just to be sure you can identify the card for the border patrol or police.

Breakdowns & Assistance

The major automobile club in Germany is **Automobilclub von Deutschland (AvD),** Lyoner Strasse 16, 60329 Frankfurt (© **069/6606-600;** www.avd.de). If you don't belong to it and have a breakdown on the autobahn, call from an emergency phone. These are spaced about a mile apart. On secondary roads, go to the nearest phone and call © **01802/22-22-22** (**Deutscher Automobil Club,** or **ADAC;** www.adac.de). In English, ask for road service assistance. Emergency assistance is free, but you pay for parts or materials.

The best maps, available at all major bookstores throughout Germany, are published by **Michelin,** which offers various regional maps. Other good maps for those who plan to do extensive touring are published by **Hallweg.**

Service stations appear frequently along the autobahns. The cheapest gasoline is at stations marked SB-TANKEN (self-service), but remember that gas will always be much more expensive than in the U.S. Of course, gasoline prices throughout the world are currently changing almost weekly. Gasoline pumps labeled BLEIFREI offer unleaded gas.

GETTING THERE BY TRAIN

British Rail runs four trains a day to Germany from Victoria Station in **London,** going by way of the Ramsgate-Ostend ferry or jetfoil. Two trains depart from London's Liverpool Street Station, via

Harwich–Hook of Holland. Most trains change at Cologne for destinations elsewhere in Germany. Tickets can be purchased through British Rail travel centers in London (© **866/BRIT-RAIL** in the U.K. or 0845/748-4950; www.britrail. com). Train journeys can be lengthy. Travel from London to Munich, depending on the connection, can take from 18 to 22 hours; it's often cheaper to fly than to take the train.

From **Paris** several trains depart throughout the day for points east, fanning out across eastern France to virtually every part of Germany.

Most trains arrive at Munich's main rail station, the **Hauptbahnhof,** on Bahnhofplatz, one of Europe's largest stations. Located near the city center and the trade fairgrounds, it contains a hotel, restaurants, shopping, car parking, and banking facilities. All major German cities are connected to this station. Some 20 daily trains connect Munich to Frankfurt (trip time 3³/₄ hr.), and 23 to Berlin (trip time 6³/₄ hr.). The rail station is connected with the **S-Bahn** rapid-transit system, a 418km (260-mile) network of tracks, providing service to various city districts and outlying suburbs. The **U-Bahn** (subway) system serving Munich is also centered at the rail station. In addition, buses fan out in all directions from here.

If you're planning travel by train outside Munich, you can get complete details about the **German Federal Railroad** and the many plans it offers, as well as information about Eurailpasses, at Rail Europe (© **877/272-RAIL;** www.raileurope.com).

GETTING THERE BY BUS (COACH)

You can travel by bus to Germany's major cities from London, Paris, and many other cities in Europe. The continent's largest bus operator is **Eurolines,** the Collonades, London SW1 (© **08717/818181;** www.euro lines.com), which operates out of Victoria Coach Station in Central London. In Paris, Eurolines is at 28 avenue du Général de Gaulle, 93177 Bagnolet (© **08/92-89-90-91**). For information about Eurolines in Germany, contact **Deutsche Touring** (Eurolines Stadtbüro), Am Römerhof 17, 60486 Frankfurt am Main (© **069/79-03-51**). Eurolines does not maintain a U.S.-based sales agent, but many travel agents can arrange for a ticket on the bus lines linking Europe's major cities.

Buses arrive at and depart from the section of the Hauptbahnhof called the West-Wing Starnberger Bahnhof, or the Deutsche Touring Terminal on Arnulfstrasse 3, about a block away. For information about connections, fares, and schedules, call **Deutsche Touring GmbH** at © **089/88989513**. Regional service to towns and villages within Bavaria can be arranged through **Oberbayern Autobus,** Heidemannstrasse 220 (© **089/323040**).

GETTING AROUND MUNICH

The best way to explore Munich is by walking. In fact, because of the vast pedestrian zone in the center, many of the major attractions can be reached only on foot. Pick up a good map and set out.

Public Transportation

The city's underground rapid-transit system, the **U-Bahn** or Untergrundbahn network, is modern and relatively noise-free. The aboveground **S-Bahn,** or Stadtbahn, services suburban locations. At the transport hub, Marienplatz, U-Bahn and S-Bahn rails cross each other. (See the inside back cover of this book for a full-color map of the U-Bahn and S-Bahn systems.)

The same ticket entitles you to ride both the U-Bahn and the S-Bahn, as well as **trams** (streetcars) and **buses.** The U-Bahn is the system you'll probably use most frequently. You're allowed to use your Eurailpass on S-Bahn journeys, as it's a state-owned railway. Otherwise, you must purchase a single-trip ticket or a strip ticket for several journeys at one of the blue vending machines positioned at the entryways to the stations.

If you're making only one trip, a **single ticket** will average 2.20€ ($3.50), although it can reach as high as 8.80€ ($14) to an outlying area. A more economical option is the **strip ticket,** called *Streifenkarte* in German. It's good for several rides and sells for 11€ ($18). A trip within the metropolitan area costs you two strips, which are valid for 2 hours. In that time, you may interrupt your trip and transfer as you like to any public transportation, as long as you travel in one continuous direction. When you reverse your direction, you must cancel two strips again. Children 6 to 14 use the red *Kinderstreifenkarte,* costing 5.20€ ($8.30) for five strips; for a trip within the metropolitan area, they cancel only one strip. Children 15 and over pay adult fares. A **day ticket** for 5€ ($8), called a *Tageskarte,* is also a good investment if you plan to stay within the city limits. It's good from the moment of purchase until 4am of the following morning. If you'd like to branch out to Greater Munich—that is, within an 80km (50-mile) radius—you can purchase a day card for 12€ ($19). For public transit information, call *C* **089/210-33-0,** or visit www.mvv-muenchen.de/en.

Taxi

The meter on cabs you hail on the street or find waiting at a taxi stand begins at 2.70€ ($4.30). If you phone for a taxi, 1€ ($1.60) is added to the fare. Within the city of Munich, you'll be charged 1.60€ ($2.55) per kilometer, unless your ride is

longer than 10km (6^1/₄ miles), in which event, the per-kilometer rate goes down to between 1.25€ to 1.40€ ($2–$2.25), depending on the distance you travel. Drivers who wait for passengers within their cabs receive a prorated waiting fee of 23€ ($37) per hour. For more information, call *C* **089/21610** or 089/19410.

Car

Because of heavy traffic, don't attempt to see Munich itself by car. And beware if your hotel doesn't have parking. Parking garages tend to be expensive, often 18€ to 25€ ($29–$40) per night.

If you're in Munich and plan to make excursions into the Bavarian countryside, it's often more convenient to rent a car in the city center instead of trekking out to the airport. Car-rental companies are listed under *Autovermietung* in the Yellow Pages of the Munich phone book. Contact **Sixt Autovermietung,** Einsteinstrasse 106 (*C* **1805/4180050**), to rent a car locally. (See "Car Rentals," above, for more details.)

Bicycle

The tourist office sells a pamphlet for 0.50€ (80¢) called *Rad-Touren für unsere Gäste;* it outlines itineraries for touring Munich by bicycle. One of the most convenient places to rent a bike is **Radius Bikes** (*C* **089/59-61-13**), at the far end of the Hauptbahnhof, near lockers opposite track 32 (open May to early Oct daily 9:30am–6pm). The charge is 3€ to 4€ ($4.80–$6.40) per hour, or 15€ to 18€ ($24–$29) all day; mountain bikes are about 25% more. A 50€ ($80) deposit is assessed; students and Eurailpass holders get 10% off.

---

5 MONEY & COSTS

Munich is an expensive city. Although prices in Germany are high, you generally get good value for your money. Hotels are usually clean and comfortable, and restaurants

generally offer good cuisine and ample portions made with quality ingredients. Trains are fast and on time, and most service personnel treat you with respect.

Many people come to Germany just for winter sports. The most expensive resorts are places like Garmisch-Partenkirchen (see chapter 12). However, if you avoid the chic places, you can enjoy winter fun at a moderate cost. Some of the winter spots in the Bavarian Alps that haven't been overrun by the beautiful people offer great value. And prices in a village next to a resort are often 30% lower than at the resort itself.

In Germany, many prices for children (generally ages 6–17) are considerably lower than for adults. Fees for children under 6 are often waived entirely.

CURRENCY

The **euro (€)**, is the single currency of Germany and other participating countries. Exchange rates of participating countries are locked into a common currency fluctuating against the dollar.

Foreign Currencies vs. the U.S. Dollar

Conversion ratios between the U.S. dollar and other currencies fluctuate, and their differences could affect the relative costs of your trip. The figures reflected in the currency chart below were valid at the time of this writing, but they might not be valid by the time of your departure. This chart would be useful for conversions of relatively small amounts of money, but if you're planning on any major transactions, check for updated rates prior to making any serious commitments.

The U.S. Dollar and the Euro: At the time of this writing, US$1 was worth approximately .625 Eurocents. Inversely stated, 1€ was worth approximately US$1.60.

The U.S. Dollar, the British Pound, and the Euro: At press time, US$1 equaled approximately 50p (or £1 equaled approximately US$2). Against the euro, £1 equaled approximately 1.25€ (or 1€ equaled about 80p).

The chart below reflects the conversions above, but because international currency ratios can and almost certainly will change prior to your arrival in Europe, you should confirm up-to-date currency rates shortly before you go.

Euro	US$	UK£	Euro	US$	UK£
1.00	1.60	0.80	75.00	120.00	60.00
2.00	3.20	1.60	100.00	160.00	80.00
3.00	4.80	2.40	125.00	200.00	100.00
4.00	6.40	3.20	150.00	240.00	120.00
5.00	8.00	4.00	175.00	280.00	140.00
6.00	9.60	4.80	200.00	320.00	160.00
7.00	11.20	5.60	225.00	360.00	180.00
8.00	12.80	6.40	250.00	400.00	200.00
9.00	14.40	7.20	275.00	440.00	220.00
10.00	16.00	8.00	300.00	480.00	240.00
15.00	24.00	12.00	350.00	560.00	280.00
20.00	32.00	16.00	400.00	640.00	320.00
25.00	40.00	20.00	500.00	800.00	400.00
50.00	80.00	40.00	1000.00	1,600.00	800.00

You can exchange money at your local **American Express** (☎ 800/528-4800; www.americanexpress.com) or **Thomas Cook** (☎ 800/223-7373; www.thomas-cook.com) office or your bank. If you're far away from a bank with currency-exchange services, American Express offers traveler's checks and foreign currency, though with a $15 order fee and additional shipping costs.

ATMS

The easiest way to get cash is from an ATM, sometimes referred to as a *Geldautomat*. The **Cirrus** (☎ 800/424-7787; www.mastercard.com) and **PLUS** (☎ 800/843-7587; www.visa.com) networks span the globe; look at the back of your bank card to find out which network you're on, and then call or check online for ATM locations at your destination. Be sure you know your personal identification number (PIN) and daily withdrawal limit before you depart. *Note:* Remember that many banks impose a fee every time you use a card at another bank's ATM, and that fee can be higher for international transactions (up to $5 or more) than for domestic ones (where they're rarely more than $2). In addition, the bank from which you withdraw cash may charge its own fee. For international withdrawal fees, ask your bank.

Note: Banks that are members of the **Global ATM Alliance** charge no transaction fees for cash withdrawals at other Alliance member ATMs; these include Bank of America, Scotiabank (Canada, the Caribbean, and Mexico), Barclays (U.K. and parts of Africa), Deutsche Bank (Germany, Poland, Spain, and Italy), and BNP Paribas (France).

CREDIT CARDS

Credit cards are another safe way to carry money. They also provide a convenient record of all your expenses, and they generally offer relatively good exchange rates. You can withdraw cash advances from your credit cards at banks or ATMs but high fees make credit-card cash advances a pricey way to get cash. Keep in mind that you'll pay interest from the moment of your withdrawal, even if you pay your monthly bills on time. Also, note that many banks now assess a 1% to 3% "transaction fee" on **all** charges you incur abroad (whether you're using the local currency or your native currency).

In Germany, American Express, Diners Club, MasterCard, and Visa are commonly accepted, with the latter two cards predominating.

For tips and telephone numbers to call if your wallet is stolen or lost, go to "Lost & Found" in the "Fast Facts" section of appendix A.

TRAVELER'S CHECKS

You can buy traveler's checks at most banks. They are offered in denominations of $20, $50, $100, $500, and sometimes $1,000. Generally, you'll pay a service charge ranging from 1% to 4%.

The most popular traveler's checks are offered by **American Express** (☎ 800/528-4800 or 800/221-7282 for cardholders—this latter number accepts collect calls, offers service in several foreign languages, and exempts Amex gold and platinum cardholders from the 1% fee); **Visa** (☎ 800/732-1322—AAA members can obtain **Visa** checks for a $9.95 fee for checks up to $1,500 at most AAA offices or by calling ☎ 866/339-3378); and **MasterCard** (☎ 800/223-9920).

American Express, Thomas Cook, Visa, and **MasterCard** offer **foreign currency traveler's checks,** which are useful if you're traveling to one country, or within the euro zone; they're accepted at locations where U.S.-dollar traveler's checks may not be.

If you carry traveler's checks, keep a record of the serial numbers separate from your checks, in the event that they are stolen or lost. You'll get a refund faster if you know the numbers.

What Things Cost in Munich	US$	UK£
Taxi from airport to center of town	96.00	48.00
Average ride on the underground (U-Bahn)	3.50	1.75
Double room at the Bayerischer Hof (very expensive)	430.00	215.00
Double room at the King's Hotel First Class (expensive)	256.00	128.00
Double room at the Hotel Brack (moderate)	158.00	79.00
Double room at the Hotel-Pension Am Siegestor (inexpensive)	96.00	48.00
Lunch for one at Lenbach (moderate)	32.00	16.00
Lunch for one at Bier- und Oktoberfest Museum (inexpensive)	13.00	6.50
Dinner for one (no wine) at Restaurant Königshof (expensive)	131.00	66.00
Dinner for one (no wine) at Pfistermühle (moderate)	42.00	21.00
Dinner for one (no wine) at Andechser am Dom (inexpensive)	21.00	11.00
Half a liter of beer	5.95	3.00
Coca-Cola in a restaurant	4.00	2.00
Cup of coffee	4.00	2.00
Glass of wine	5.60	2.80
Admission to Alte Pinakothek	8.80	4.40
Movie ticket	14.00	7.00
Ticket to Bavarian State Opera	24.00	12.00

6 HEALTH

STAYING HEALTHY

German medical facilities are among the best in the world. If a medical emergency arises, your hotel staff can usually put you in touch with a reliable doctor. If not, contact your embassy or consulate; each one maintains a list of English-speaking doctors. Medical and hospital services aren't free, so be sure that you have appropriate insurance coverage before you travel. The water is safe to drink throughout Germany; however, do not drink the water in mountain streams, regardless of how clear and pure it looks.

If you suffer from a chronic illness, consult your doctor before departing. Pack **prescription medications** in your carry-on luggage and carry them in their original containers, with pharmacy labels—otherwise they won't make it through airport security. Carry the generic name of prescription medicines, in case a local pharmacist is unfamiliar with the brand name.

If you worry about getting sick away from home, consider purchasing **medical travel insurance** and carry your ID card in your purse or wallet. In most cases, your existing health plan will provide the coverage you need. See "Insurance" in the "Fast Facts" section of appendix A for more information.

We list **hospitals** and **emergency numbers** in the "Fast Facts" section of appendix A.

GENERAL AVAILABILITY OF HEALTH CARE

For travel abroad, you may have to pay all medical costs upfront and be reimbursed later. Medicare and Medicaid do not provide coverage for medical costs outside the U.S. Before leaving home, find out what medical services your health insurance covers. To protect yourself, consider buying medical travel insurance (see "Insurance" in the "Fast Facts" section of appendix A).

Healthy Travels to You

The following government websites offer up-to-date health-related travel advice.
- **Australia:** www.smartraveller.gov.au
- **Canada:** www.hc-sc.gc.ca/index_e.html
- **U.K.:** www.nhs.uk/Healthcareabroad
- **U.S.:** www.cdc.gov/travel

U.K. nationals will need a **European Health Insurance Card (EHIC; ☏ 0845/606-2030;** www.ehic.org.uk) to receive free or reduced-costs health benefits during a visit to a European Economic Area (EEA) country (European Union countries plus Iceland, Liechtenstein, and Norway) or Switzerland.

For conditions such as epilepsy, diabetes, or heart problems, wear a **MedicAlert Identification Tag (☏ 888/633-4298;** www.medicalert.org), which will immediately alert doctors to your condition and give them access to your records through MedicAlert's 24-hour hot line.

The **International Association for Medical Assistance to Travelers (IAMAT;** ☏ 716/754-4883 or 416/652-0137; www.iamat.org) offers tips on travel and health concerns in the countries you're visiting and lists of local, English-speaking doctors. The **Centers for Disease Control and Prevention** (☏ 800/311-3435 or 404/498-1515; www.cdc.gov) in the U.S. has up-to-date information on necessary vaccines and health hazards by region or country.

Travel Health Online (www.tripprep.com), sponsored by a consortium of travel medicine practitioners, may also offer helpful advice on traveling abroad. You can find listings of reliable medical clinics overseas at the **International Society of Travel Medicine** (www.istm.org).

7 SAFETY

Overall, the security risk to travelers to Munich and the Bavarian Alps is low. Germany experiences, however, a number of demonstrations every year on a variety of political and economic themes. These demonstrations have a tendency to spread and turn violent, and anyone in the general area can become the victim of a random attack. Prior police approval is required for public demonstrations in Germany, and police oversight is routinely provided to ensure adequate security for participants and passersby. Nonetheless, situations may develop that could pose a threat to public safety. All foreign visitors are cautioned to avoid the area around protests and demonstrations and to check local media for updates on the situation.

In addition, hooligans, most often young intoxicated "skinheads," have been known to harass or attack people whom they believe to be foreigners or members of rival youth groups. While U.S. citizens have not been specific targets, several Americans have reported that they were assaulted for racial reasons or because they appeared foreign.

Violent crime is rare in Munich, but it can occur, especially high-risk areas such as train stations. Most incidents of street crime consist of theft of unattended items and pickpocketing. There have been a few reports of aggravated assault against U.S. citizens in higher-risk areas. Take the same precautions against becoming a crime victim as you would in any city.

Report the loss or theft abroad of your passport immediately to the local police and the nearest embassy or consulate. If you are the victim of a crime while overseas, in addition to reporting to local police, contact the nearest embassy or consulate for assistance. The embassy/consulate staff can, for example, assist you in finding appropriate medical care, contacting family members or friends, and explaining how funds can be transferred. Although the investigation and prosecution of the crime is solely the responsibility of local authorities, consular officers can help you understand the local criminal justice process and find an attorney if needed.

U.S. citizens may refer to the Department of State's pamphlet, *A Safe Trip Abroad,* for tips on a trouble-free journey. The pamphlet is available by mail from the Superintendent of Documents, U.S. Government Printing Office, Washington, DC 20402, or via the U.S. State Department website at http://travel.state.gov. Click on "International Travel" and then "Travel Brochures" within the "Tips for Traveling Abroad" submenu.

8 SPECIALIZED TRAVEL RESOURCES

TRAVELERS WITH DISABILITIES

Germany is one of the better countries for travelers with disabilities. Munich has excellent facilities. The local tourist offices can issue permits for drivers to allow them access to disabled parking areas. Newer hotels are more sensitive to the needs of those with disabilities, and the more expensive restaurants, in general, are wheelchair accessible.

Older, smaller towns, including those in the Bavarian Alps, may pose more of a problem, however, especially where the streets are cobblestone. Also, because of the Alps' many hills and endless flights of stairs, visitors with disabilities may have difficulty getting around outside of major cities, but conditions are slowly improving. If the areas you wish to visit seem inaccessible or you are not certain, you may want to consider taking an organized tour specifically designed to accommodate travelers with disabilities.

Organizations that offer assistance to travelers with disabilities include **Moss Rehab** (© 800/CALL-MOSS; www.moss resourcenet.org), which provides a library of accessible-travel resources online; **SATH (Society for Accessible Travel and Hospitality;** © 212/447-7284; www.sath. org), which offers a wealth of travel resources for all types of disabilities and informed recommendations on destinations, access guides, travel agents, tour operators, vehicle rentals, and companion services; and the **American Foundation for the Blind (AFB;** © 800/232-5463 or 212/502-7600; www. afb.org), a referral resource for the blind or visually impaired that provides information on traveling with Seeing Eye dogs.

AirAmbulanceCard.com (© 877/424-7633) is now partnered with SATH and allows you to preselect top-notch hospitals in case of an emergency.

Access-Able Travel Source (© 303/232-2979; www.access-able.com) offers a comprehensive database on travel agents from around the world with experience in accessible travel; destination-specific access information; and links to such resources as service animals, equipment rentals, and access guides.

Many travel agencies offer customized tours and itineraries for travelers with disabilities. Among them are **Flying Wheels Travel** (© 507/451-5005; www.flying wheelstravel.com) and **Accessible Journeys** (© 800/846-4537 or 610/521-0339; www.disabilitytravel.com).

Flying with Disability (www.flying-with-disability.org) is a comprehensive information source on airplane travel.

Also check out the magazine *Emerging Horizons* (www.emerginghorizons.com), available by subscription ($17 year; $22 outside U.S.).

The "Accessible Travel" link at **Mobility-Advisor.com** (www.mobility-advisor.com) offers a variety of travel resources to persons with disabilities.

British travelers should contact **Holiday Care** (© 0845-124-9971 in the U.K. only; www.holidaycare.org.uk) to access a wide range of travel information and resources for seniors and those with special needs.

For more on organizations that offer resources to travelers with disabilities, go to Frommers.com.

GAY & LESBIAN TRAVELERS

Although Munich is one of the "gayest" cities of Europe, there is also prejudice and hostility here. Violence against gays and foreigners (especially nonwhite) is not unknown. On the other hand, homosexuality is widely accepted by a vast number of the city's population, especially young people. The legal minimum age for consensual homosexual sex is 18.

The International Gay and Lesbian Travel Association (IGLTA; © 954/630-1637; www.iglta.org) is the trade association for the gay and lesbian travel industry and offers an online directory of gay- and lesbian-friendly travel businesses; go to its website and click on "Members."

Many agencies offer tours and travel itineraries designed specifically for gay and lesbian travelers. **Above and Beyond Tours** (© 800/397-2681; www.abovebeyondtours.com) are gay Australian tour specialists. **Now, Voyager** (© 800/255-6951; www.nowvoyager.com) is a well-known San Francisco–based gay-owned and -operated travel service. **Olivia Cruises & Resorts** (© 800/631-6277; www.olivia.com) charters entire resorts and ships for exclusive lesbian vacations and offers smaller group

experiences for both gay and lesbian travelers. **Gay.com Travel** (© 415/834-6500; www.gay.com/travel or www.outandabout.com), is an excellent online successor to the popular *Out & About* print magazine. It provides regularly updated information about gay-owned, gay-oriented, and gay-friendly lodging, dining, sightseeing, nightlife, and shopping establishments in every important destination worldwide. British travelers should click on the "Travel" link at **www.uk.gay.com** for advice and gay-friendly trip ideas.

The Canadian website **GayTraveler** (gaytraveler.ca) offers ideas and advice for gay travel all over the world.

The following travel guides are available at many bookstores, or you can order them from any online bookseller: *Spartacus International Gay Guide, 35th Edition* (Bruno Gmünder Verlag; www.spartacusworld.com/gayguide); *Odysseus: The International Gay Travel Planner, 17th Edition* (Odysseus Enterprises, Ltd.); and the *Damron* guides (www.damron.com), with separate, annual books for gay men and lesbians.

For more gay and lesbian travel resources, visit Frommers.com.

SENIOR TRAVELERS

Mention that you're a senior when you make your travel reservations. Although all major U.S. airlines have canceled their senior discount and coupon book programs, many hotels still offer discounts for seniors. In most cities, people over the age of 60 qualify for reduced admission to theaters, museums, and other attractions, as well as discounted fares on public transportation.

Members of **AARP** (formerly known as the American Association of Retired Persons), 601 E St. NW, Washington, DC 20049 (© 888/687-2277; www.aarp.org), get discounts on hotels, airfares, and car rentals. AARP offers members a wide range of benefits, including *AARP The Magazine* and a monthly newsletter. Anyone older than 50 can join.

Frommers.com: The Complete Travel Resource

It should go without saying, but we highly recommend **Frommers.com,** voted Best Travel Site by *PC Magazine*. We think you'll find our expert advice and tips; independent reviews of hotels, restaurants, attractions, and preferred shopping and nightlife venues; vacation giveaways; and an online booking tool indispensable before, during, and after your travels. We publish the complete contents of over 128 travel guides in our **Destinations** section covering more than 3,600 places worldwide to help you plan your trip. Each weekday, we publish original articles reporting on **Deals and News** via our free **Frommers.com Newsletter** to help you save time and money and travel smarter. We're betting you'll find our new **Events** listings (http://events.frommers.com) an invaluable resource; it's an up-to-the-minute roster of what's happening in cities everywhere—including concerts, festivals, lectures, and more. We've also added weekly **podcasts, interactive maps,** and hundreds of new images across the site. Check out our **Travel Talk** area featuring **Message Boards** where you can join in conversations with thousands of fellow Frommer's travelers and post your trip report once you return.

Many reliable agencies and organizations target the 50-plus market. **Elderhostel** (© 800/454-5768; www.elderhostel. org) arranges study programs for those ages 55 and over (and a spouse or companion of any age) in the U.S. and in more than 80 countries around the world. Most courses last 5 to 7 days in the U.S. (2–4 weeks abroad), and many include airfare, accommodations in university dormitories or modest inns, meals, and tuition.

Recommended publications offering travel resources and discounts for seniors include the quarterly magazine *Travel 50 & Beyond* (www.travel50andbeyond.com) and the bestselling paperback *Unbelievably Good Deals and Great Adventures That You Absolutely Can't Get Unless You're Over 50 2009–2010, 18th Edition* (McGraw-Hill), by Joan Rattner Heilman.

Frommers.com offers more information and resources on travel for seniors.

9 SUSTAINABLE TOURISM

Sustainable tourism is conscientious travel. It means being careful with the environments you explore, and respecting the communities you visit. The **International Ecotourism Society (TIES)** defines **ecotourism** as responsible travel to natural areas that conserves the environment and improves the well-being of local people. TIES suggests that ecotourists follow these principles:

- Minimize environmental impact.
- Build environmental and cultural awareness and respect.
- Provide positive experiences for both visitors and hosts.
- Provide direct financial benefits for conservation and for local people.
- Raise sensitivity to host countries' political, environmental, and social climates.
- Support international human rights and labor agreements.

You can find some eco-friendly travel tips and statistics, as well as touring companies and associations—listed by destination under "Travel Choice"—at the **TIES** website, www.ecotourism.org. **Ecotravel. com** lets you search for sustainable touring companies in several categories (water-based, land-based, spiritually oriented, and so on).

While much of the focus of ecotourism is about reducing impacts on the natural environment, ethical tourism concentrates

---

(Tips) It's Easy Being Green

Here are a few simple ways you can help conserve fuel and energy when you travel:

- Each time you take a flight or drive a car greenhouse gases release into the atmosphere. You can help neutralize this danger to the planet through "carbon offsetting"—paying someone to invest your money in programs that reduce your greenhouse gas emissions by the same amount you've added. Before buying carbon offset credits, just make sure that you're using a reputable company, one with a proven program that invests in renewable energy. Reliable carbon-offset companies include **Carbonfund** (www.carbonfund.org) and **TerraPass** (www.terrapass.org).
- Whenever possible, choose nonstop flights; they generally require less fuel than indirect flights that stop and take off again. Try to fly during the day—some scientists estimate that nighttime flights are twice as harmful to the environment. And pack light—each 15 pounds of luggage on a 5,000-mile flight adds up to 50 pounds of carbon dioxide emitted.
- Where you stay during your travels can have a major environmental impact. To determine the green credentials of a property, ask about trash disposal and recycling, water conservation, and energy use; also find out whether sustainable materials were used in the property's construction. The website **www.greenhotels.com** recommends green-rated member hotels around the world that fulfill the company's stringent environmental requirements.
- At hotels, request that your sheets and towels not be changed daily. (Many hotels already have programs like this in place.) Turn off the lights and air-conditioner (or heater) when you leave your room.
- Use public transport where possible—trains, buses, and even taxis are more energy-efficient forms of transport than driving. Even better is to walk or cycle; you'll produce zero emissions and stay fit and healthy on your travels.
- If renting a car is necessary, ask the rental agent for a hybrid, or rent the most fuel-efficient car available. You'll use less gas and save money at the tank.
- Eat at locally owned and operated restaurants that use produce grown in the area. This contributes to the local economy and cuts down on greenhouse gas emissions by supporting restaurants where the food is not flown or trucked in across long distances.

on ways to preserve and enhance local economies and communities, regardless of location. You can embrace ethical tourism by staying at a locally owned hotel or shopping at a store that employs local workers and sells local goods. **Responsible Travel** (www.responsible travel.com) is a great source of sustainable travel ideas; the site is run by a spokesperson for ethical tourism in the travel industry. **Sustainable Travel International** (www.sustainabletravelinternational.org) promotes ethical tourism practices, and manages an extensive directory of sustainable properties and tour operators around the world.

In the U.K., **Tourism Concern** (www.tourismconcern.org.uk) works to reduce social and environmental problems connected to tourism. The **Association of Independent Tour Operators** (AITO; www.aito.co.uk) is a group of specialist operators leading the field in making holidays sustainable.

Volunteer travel has become popular among those who want to venture beyond the standard group-tour experience to learn languages, interact with locals, and make a positive difference while on vacation. Volunteer travel usually doesn't require special skills—just a willingness to work hard—and programs vary in length from a few days to a number of weeks. Some programs provide free housing and food, but many require volunteers to pay for travel expenses, which can add up quickly.

For general info on volunteer travel, visit **www.volunteerabroad.org** and **www. idealist.org**.

Before you commit to a volunteer program, it's important to make sure any money you're giving is truly going back to the local community, and that the work you'll be doing will be a good fit for you. **Volunteer International** (www.volunteer international.org) has a helpful list of questions to ask to determine the intentions and the nature of a volunteer program.

10 PACKAGES FOR THE INDEPENDENT TRAVELER

Package tours are simply a way to buy the airfare, accommodations, and other elements of your trip (such as car rentals, airport transfers, and sometimes even activities) at the same time and often at discounted prices.

One good source of package deals is the airlines themselves. Most major airlines offer air/land packages, but among airline packagers, **Lufthansa** (© **800/399-5838** or 01/805-83-84-26 in Germany; www. lufthansa.com) leads the way. You may also wish to try **American Airlines Vacations** (© **800/321-2121;** www.aavacations. com), **Delta Vacations** (© **800/654-6559;** www.deltavacations.com), **Continental Airlines Vacations** (© **800/301-3800;** www.covacations.com), and **United Vacations** (© **888/854-3899;** www.united vacations.com). Several big **online travel agencies**—Expedia, Travelocity, Orbitz, Site59, and Lastminute.com—also do a brisk business in packages.

Travel packages are also listed in the travel section of your local Sunday newspaper. Or check ads in the national travel magazines such as *Arthur Frommer's Budget Travel Magazine, Travel + Leisure, National Geographic Traveler,* and *Condé Nast Traveler.*

11 ESCORTED GENERAL-INTEREST TOURS

Escorted tours are structured group tours, with a group leader. The price usually includes everything from airfare to hotels, meals, tours, admission costs, and local transportation.

American Express Vacations (© 800/335-3342; www.americanexpressvacations. com) is one of the biggest tour operators in the world. Its offerings are comprehensive, and unescorted customized package tours are available, too.

Brendan Tours (© 800/421-8446; www.brendantours.com) has a selection of 7- to 15-day tours. Accommodations are at the better hotels, and rates include everything except airfare. **Collette Vacations** (© 800/340-5158; www.collettevacations. com) has an Alpine Countries tour that covers southern Germany, Austria, and Switzerland. **Abercrombie & Kent** (© 800/554-7016; www.abercrombiekent.com) provides group tours to various areas of Germany and will customize them to suit your needs.

Despite the fact that escorted tours require big deposits and predetermine hotels, restaurants, and itineraries, many people derive security and peace of mind from the structure they offer. Escorted tours—whether they're navigated by bus, motorcoach, train, or boat—let travelers sit back and enjoy the trip without having to drive or worry about details. They take you to the maximum number of sights in the minimum amount of time with the least amount of hassle. They're particularly convenient for people with limited mobility and they can be a great way to make new friends.

On the downside, you'll have little opportunity for serendipitous interactions with locals. The tours can be jam-packed with activities, leaving little room for individual sightseeing, whim, or adventure—plus they often focus on the heavily touristed sites, so you miss out on many a lesser-known gem.

12 SPECIAL-INTEREST TRIPS

Germany is one of the great outdoor destinations of Europe. From its mountains and beaches to its rivers and castles, there is much to see and explore. It has summer attractions galore, plus skiing on its Alpine slopes in winter.

E.E.I. Travel, 19021 120th Ave. NE, Ste. 102, Bothell, WA 98011 (© 800/927-3876; www.eeitravel.com), has a variety of self-guided walking and biking tours as well as cross-country skiing trips in Germany. It covers such areas as the Black Forest and King Ludwig's Trail, and will customize trips.

BIKING

Pedaling through the Bavarian countryside is the way to go for many visitors. You can bike through green valleys and past rivers, such as the Danube, while enjoying rural landscapes and life in German villages. **Allgemeiner Deutscher Fahrrad-Club,** P.O. Box 107747, Hellerallee 23, 28077, Bremen (© 0421/34-62-90; www.adfc.de), offers information on biking in Germany.

Since the mid-1980s, **Classic Adventures,** P.O. Box 143, Hamlin, NY 14464 (© 800/777-8090 or 585/964-8488; www.classicadventures.com), has offered bike tours of such areas as the Romantic

Road. **Euro-Bike and Walking Tours,** P.O. Box 990, DeKalb, IL 60115 (© **800/ 321-6060;** www.eurobike.com), has a full range of bicycling and walking tours of Bavaria, as well as a 9-day biking tour of Germany, Switzerland, and France.

Dozens of companies in Britain offer guided cycling tours. One of the best is the **Cyclists Touring Club,** 69 Meadrow, Godalming, Surrey GU7 3HS (© **0870/ 873-0060;** www.ctc.org.uk). Membership costs £35 ($70) a year.

HIKING & MOUNTAIN CLIMBING

These sports are popular in the German uplands. It's estimated that Germany has more than 80,000 marked hiking and mountain-walking tracks. The **Deutschen Wanderverband,** Wilhelmshöher Alle 157–159, 34121 Kassel (© **0561/938730;** www.wanderverband.de), services the trails and offers details about trails, shelters, huts, and addresses of hiking associations in various regions.

The **Deutsche Alpenverein,** Von-Kahr-Strasse 2–4, 80997 Munich (© **089/14-00-30;** www.alpenverein.de), owns and operates 50 huts in and around the Alps that are open to all mountaineers. This association also maintains a 15,000km (9,320-mile) network of Alpine trails.

The best **Alpine hiking** is in the Bavarian Alps, especially the 1,235m (4,052-ft.) Eckbauer, on the southern fringe of Partenkirchen. The tourist office will supply hiking maps and details (see chapter 12). Another great place for hiking is **Berchtesgaden National Park,** Kurgarten, Maximilianstrasse 1, Berchtesgaden (© **08652/ 64-34-3;** www.nationalpark-berchtesgaden. de), bordering the Austrian province of Salzburg. This park offers the best-organized hikes and will hook you up with various hiking groups.

MOTORCYCLING

Guided motorcycle tours through Bavaria are the specialty of **Beach's Motorcycle Adventures,** 2763 W. River Pkwy., Grand Island, NY 14072 (© **716/773-4960;** www.beaches-mca.com). The 2- to 3-week tours on BMW bikes begin and end in Munich, with accommodations at small hotels and inns. Maps are provided, as well as information and suggestions for sightseeing and independent cruising along the way.

WINTER SPORTS

More than 300 winter-sports resorts operate in the German Alps and wooded hill country such as the Harz Mountains and the Black Forest. In addition to outstanding ski slopes, trails, lifts, jumps, toboggan slides, and skating rinks, many larger resorts also offer ice hockey, ice boating, and bobsledding. Curling is very popular as well, especially in upper Bavaria. The Olympic sports facilities at Garmisch-Partenkirchen enjoy international renown, as do the ski jumps of Oberstdorf and the artificial-ice speed-skating rink at Inzell. More than 250 ski lifts are found in the German Alps, the Black Forest, and the Harz Mountains. Information on winter-sports facilities is available from local tourist bureaus and offices of the German National Tourist Board (see "Visitor Information," earlier in this chapter).

Garmisch-Partenkirchen (see chapter 12) is Germany's most famous winter-sports center. Set in beautiful Alpine scenery, this picturesque resort is close to Zugspitze, Germany's highest mountain. A mountain railway and a cable car can take you to the peak. In the town itself is the Olympic Ice Stadium, built in 1936, and the Ski Stadium, which has two jumps and a slalom course. Skiers of every level will be satisfied with the slopes on the mountain above the town. For information, contact the **Tourist Office** on Richard-Strauss-Platz (© **08821/18-07-00**).

13 STAYING CONNECTED

TELEPHONE

The country code for Germany is 49. To call Germany from the United States, dial the international access code 011, then 49, then the city code (Munich's is 89), then the regular phone number. *Note:* The phone numbers listed in this book are to be used within Germany; when calling from abroad, omit the initial 0 in the city code.

German phone numbers are not standard. In some places, numbers have as few as three digits. In cities, one number may have five digits, whereas the phone next door has nine. Germans also often hyphenate their numbers differently. But since all the area codes are the same, these various configurations should have little effect on your phone usage once you get used to the fact that numbers vary from place to place.

Be careful dialing **toll-free numbers.** Many companies maintain a service line beginning with 0180. However, these lines might appear to be toll free but really aren't, costing 0.12€ (19¢) per minute. Other numbers that begin with 0190 carry a surcharge of 1.85€ ($2.95) per minute—or even more. Don't be misled by calling a 1-800 number in the United States from Germany. This is not a toll-free call but costs about the same as an overseas call.

CELLPHONES

The three letters that define much of the world's wireless capabilities are GSM (Global System for Mobiles), a big, seamless network that makes for easy cross-border cellphone use. In general reception is good. But you'll need a Scriber Identity Module (SIM) card. This is a small chip that gives you a local phone number and plugs you into a regional network. In the U.S., T-Mobile and AT&T Wireless use this quasi-universal system; in Canada, Microcell and some Rogers customers are GSM, and all Europeans and most Australians use GSM. Unfortunately, per-minute charges can be high—usually $1 to $1.50 in western Europe.

For many, **renting** a phone is a good idea. While you can rent a phone from any number of overseas sites, including kiosks at airports and at car-rental agencies, we suggest renting the phone before you leave home. North Americans can rent one before leaving home from **InTouch USA** (*©* **800/872-7626** or 703/222-7161; www.intouchglobal.com) or **RoadPost** (*©* **888/290-1616** or 905/272-5665; www.roadpost.com). InTouch will also, for free, advise you on whether your existing phone will work overseas.

Buying a phone can be economically attractive, as many nations have cheap prepaid phone systems. Once you arrive at your destination, stop by a local cellphone shop and get the cheapest package; you'll probably pay less than $100 (around 60€) for a phone and a starter calling card. Local calls may be as low as 0.06€ (10¢) per minute, and in many countries incoming calls are free.

INTERNET & E-MAIL
With Your Own Computer

More and more hotels, cafes, and retailers are signing on as Wi-Fi (wireless fidelity) "hot spots." Mac owners have their own networking technology: Apple AirPort. **T-Mobile Hotspot** (www.t-mobile.com/hotspot or www.t-mobile.co.uk) serves up wireless connections at coffee shops nationwide. **Boingo** (www.boingo.com) and **Wayport** (www.wayport.com) have set up networks in airports and high-class hotel lobbies. iPass providers (see below) also give you access to a few hundred wireless hotel lobby setups. To locate other hot spots that provide **free wireless networks** in cities in Germany, go to **www.jiwire.com**.

Online Traveler's Toolbox

Veteran travelers usually carry some essential items to make their trips easier. Following is a selection of handy online tools to bookmark and use.

- **Airplane Food** (www.airlinemeals.net)
- **Airplane Seating** (www.seatguru.com and www.airlinequality.com)
- **Foreign Languages for Travelers** (www.travlang.com)
- **Maps** (www.mapquest.com)
- **Subway Navigator** (www.subwaynavigator.com)
- **Time and Date** (www.timeanddate.com)
- **Travel Warnings** (http://travel.state.gov, www.fco.gov.uk/travel, www.voyage.gc.ca, or www.smartraveller.gov.au)
- **Universal Currency Converter** (www.xe.com/ucc)
- **Visa ATM Locator** (www.visa.com), **MasterCard ATM Locator** (www.mastercard.com)
- **Weather** (www.intellicast.com and www.weather.com)

For dial-up access, most business-class hotels offer dataports for laptop modems, and a few thousand hotels in Germany now offer free high-speed Internet access. In addition, major Internet service providers (ISPs) have local access numbers around the world, allowing you to go online by placing a local call. The **iPass** network also has dial-up numbers around the world. You'll have to sign up with an iPass provider, who will then tell you how to set up your computer for your destination(s). For a list of iPass providers, go to www.ipass.com and click on "Individuals Buy Now." One solid provider is **i2Roam** (© 866/811-6209 or 920/233-5863; www.i2roam.com).

Wherever you go, bring a **connection kit** of the right power and phone adapters, a spare phone cord, and a spare Ethernet network cable—or find out whether your hotel has them for guests.

Without Your Own Computer

To find cybercafes check **www.cybercaptive.com** and **www.cybercafe.com**. Cybercafes are found in all large U.K. cities, especially Berlin and Frankfurt. But they do not tend to cluster in any particular neighborhoods because of competition. They are spread out, but can be found on almost every business street in large cities.

Aside from formal cybercafes, most **youth hostels** and **public libraries** have Internet access. Avoid **hotel business centers** unless you're willing to pay exorbitant rates.

Most major airports now have **Internet kiosks** scattered throughout their gates. These give you basic Web access for a per-minute fee that's usually higher than cybercafe prices.

14 TIPS ON ACCOMMODATIONS

In general, Germany has one of the highest standards of innkeeping in the world. Hotels range from five-star palaces of luxury and comfort to plain country inns and simple guesthouses (*Gasthäuser*), with a huge variation in rates. The cheapest accommodations are in pensions *(Fremden-heime)* or rooms in private homes (look for a sign saying ZIMMER FREI, meaning there's a room for rent). Hotels listed as *garni* provide no meals other than breakfast.

Also, tourist offices will often book you into a room for a small charge. Obviously, the earlier you arrive in these offices, the more likely you are to get a good room at the price you want.

SURFING FOR HOTELS

In addition to the online travel booking sites **Travelocity, Expedia, Orbitz, Priceline,** and **Hotwire,** you can book hotels through **Hotels.com; Quikbook** (www.quikbook.com); and **Travelaxe** (www.travelaxe.net).

HotelChatter.com is a daily webzine offering smart coverage and critiques of hotels worldwide. Go to **TripAdvisor.com** or **HotelShark.com** for helpful independent consumer reviews of hotels and resort properties.

It's a good idea to **get a confirmation number** and **make a printout** of any online booking transaction.

Throughout Germany, as in many tourist centers worldwide, hotels routinely overbook, so booking by credit card doesn't automatically hold your room if you arrive later than expected or after 6pm. The hotel clerk always asks when you expect to arrive, and the hotel usually holds the room until that time. Always pad your expected arrival by a few hours to be safe. However, all bets are off after 7pm, and the hotel is likely to give your room away unless you call and specifically ask them to hold it. If you've made a reservation very far in advance, confirm within 24 hours of your expected arrival. If you're experiencing a major travel delay, alert the hotel as soon as you can.

Beware of billing. Readers report that sometimes in Germany they booked a room online at one rate, but were charged a higher rate when they checked out. Keep your online confirmation in case of a dispute.

SAVING ON YOUR HOTEL ROOM

The **rack rate** is the maximum rate that a hotel charges for a room. Hardly anybody pays this price, however, except in high season or on holidays. To lower the cost of your room:

- **Ask about special rates or other discounts.** You may qualify for corporate, student, military, senior, frequent flier, trade union, or other discounts.
- **Dial direct.** When booking a room in a chain hotel, you'll often get a better deal by calling the individual hotel's reservation desk rather than the chain's main number.
- **Book online.** Many hotels offer Internet-only discounts, or supply rooms to Priceline, Hotwire, or Expedia at rates much lower than the ones you can get through the hotel itself.
- **Remember the law of supply and demand.** You can save big on hotel rooms by traveling in a destination's off season or shoulder seasons, when rates typically drop, even at luxury properties.
- **Look into group or long-stay discounts.** If you come as part of a large group, you should be able to negotiate a bargain rate. Likewise, if you're planning a long stay (at least 5 days), you might qualify for a discount. As a general rule, expect 1 night free after a 7-night stay.
- **Sidestep excess surcharges and hidden costs.** Many hotels have adopted the unpleasant practice of nickel-and-diming their guests with opaque surcharges. When you book a room, ask what is included in the rate, and what is extra. Avoid dialing direct from hotel phones, which can have exorbitant rates. And don't be tempted by the room's minibar offerings: Most hotels charge through the nose for water, soda, and snacks. Finally, ask about local taxes and service charges, which can increase the cost of a room by 15% or more.

- Carefully consider your hotel's meal plan. If you enjoy eating out and sampling the local cuisine, it makes sense to choose a **Continental Plan (CP),** which includes breakfast only, or a **European Plan (EP),** which doesn't include any meals and allows you maximum flexibility. If you're more interested in saving money, opt for a **Modified American Plan (MAP),** which includes breakfast and one meal, or the **American Plan (AP),** which includes three meals. If you must choose a MAP, see if you can get a free lunch at your hotel if you decide to do dinner out.
- **Book an efficiency.** A room with a kitchenette allows you to shop for groceries and cook your own meals. This is a big money saver, especially for families on long stays.
- **Consider enrolling in hotel chains' "frequent-stay" programs.** Frequent guests can now accumulate points or credits to earn free hotel nights, airline miles, in-room amenities, merchandise, tickets to concerts and events, discounts on sporting facilities, and more.

For more tips on surfing for hotel deals online, visit Frommers.com.

LANDING THE BEST ROOM

Somebody has to get the best room in the house. It might as well be you. Joining the hotel's frequent-guest program may make you eligible for upgrades. A hotel-branded credit card usually gives its owner "silver" or "gold" status in frequent-guest programs for free. Always ask about a corner room. They're often larger and quieter, with more windows and light, and they often cost the same as standard rooms. When you make your reservation, ask if the hotel is renovating; if it is, request a room away from the construction. Ask about nonsmoking rooms and rooms with views. Be sure to request your choice of twin, queen- or king-size beds. If you're a light sleeper, ask for a room away from vending or ice machines,

elevators, restaurants, bars, and discos. Ask for a room that has been recently renovated or refurbished.

If you aren't happy with your room when you arrive, ask for another one. Most lodgings will be willing to accommodate you.

In resort areas, ask the following questions before you book a room:

- What's the view like? Cost-conscious travelers may be willing to pay less for a back room facing the parking lot, especially if they don't plan to spend much time in their room.
- Does the room have air-conditioning or ceiling fans? Do the windows open? If they do, and the nighttime entertainment takes place alfresco, you may want to find out when showtime is over.
- What's included in the price? Your room may be moderately priced, but if you're charged for beach chairs, towels, sports equipment, and other amenities, you could end up spending more than you bargained for.
- How far is the room from the beach and other amenities? If it's far, is there transportation to and from the beach, and is it free?

B&B STAYS

Many travelers prefer to go the B&B route when touring Bavaria. This can be an inexpensive alternative to pricey hotels. However, some B&Bs, of course, are more luxurious than even a first-class hotel. Naturally, these come with a higher price tag. Breakfast, as promised in the name, is served, and often the staff at a B&B will pack you a picnic lunch if you're staying over in the area and want to go hiking. In some cases, and only if arranged in advance, a home-cooked German dinner might be served.

For reservations, contact **Bed & Breakfast Inns Online** (© **800/215-7365** or 615/868-1945; www.bbonline.com), or **Bn BFinder.com** (© **888/547-8226** or 212/432-7693; www.bnbfinder.com).

BUNGALOW, VILLA & APARTMENT RENTALS

Dozens of agencies handle these kinds of rentals, the best of which are **At Home Abroad, Inc.** (© 212/421-9165; www. athomeabroadinc.com); and **Drawbridge to Europe** (© 888/268-1148; www. drawbridgetoeurope.com), which offers vacation rentals (even a private castle) in *Mittel Europa,* including not only Bavaria but also Switzerland and Austria. **Interhome** (© 800/882-6864 or 954/791-8282; www.interhome.us) offers properties in 21 countries, including Germany.

HOUSE-SWAPPING

House-swapping is becoming a more popular and viable means of travel; you stay in their place, they stay in yours, and you both get a more authentic and personal view of a destination, the opposite of the escapist retreat many hotels offer. Try **HomeLink International** (Homelink.org), the largest and oldest home-swapping organization, founded in 1952, with more than 11,000 listings worldwide ($75/£37.50 yearly membership). **HomeExchange.com** ($50/£25 for 6,000 listings) and **InterVac.com** ($69/£34.50 for more than 10,000 listings) are also reliable.

ROMANTIK HOTELS

Throughout Germany, including Bavaria, you'll encounter "Romantik" hotels, not chains but voluntary associations of small inns and guesthouses that have one element in common: They are usually old and charming, and romantic in architecture. If you like a traditional ambience as opposed to bandbox modern, then a Romantik Hotel might be for you. The requirement is that the hotel be in a historic building (or at least one of vintage date) and personally managed by the owner. Usually you get a regional cuisine and good, personal service, along with an old-fashioned setting and cozy charm. Sometimes the plumbing could be better, and standards of comfort vary widely, but all have been inspected.

For details, contact **Romantik Hotels & Restaurants** (© 800/650-8018 in the U.S. or 069/661-2340 in Germany; www. romantikhotels.com).

Suggested Itineraries

Mad King Ludwig would perhaps scoff at the idea of tackling his once beloved kingdom in just 1 day—or even 2 or 3 days. But what did he know, really?

If that is all the time you have, we want to help you make the most of it by providing a ready-made itinerary that allows you to have a complete, unforgettable trip.

Of course, there is always a hidden section of Munich, or a slice of the Bavarian Alps, that awaits your discovery on your own as you seek out its hidden treasures, but that can wait for another day and another trip.

You can make the most of your short time by fortifying yourself with an old-fashioned Bavarian breakfast of *Weisswurst* (those little finger-size white sausages). Head for *Donisl* (p. 115), which opens at 9am. A true Münchner downs these sausages with a mug of beer.

1 GETTING TO KNOW MUNICH

CITY LAYOUT

Munich's main rail station, **Hauptbahnhof**, lies just west of the town center and opens onto Bahnhofplatz. From there you can take Schützenstrasse to one of the major centers of Munich, **Karlsplatz**, nicknamed Stachus (see p. 154 for the story). Many tram lines converge on this square. From Karlsplatz, you can continue east along the pedestrians-only Neuhauserstrasse and Kaufingerstrasse until you reach **Marienplatz**, which is located deep in the **Altstadt (Old Town)** of Munich.

From Marienplatz you can head north on Dienerstrasse, which will lead you to Residenzstrasse and finally to **Max-Joseph-Platz**, a landmark square, with the Nationaltheater and the former royal palace, the Residenz. East of this square runs **Maximilianstrasse**, the most fashionable shopping and restaurant street of Munich, containing the prestigious Hotel Vier Jahreszeiten Kempinski München. Between Marienplatz and the Nationaltheater is the **Platzl** quarter, where you'll head for nighttime diversions; here are some of the finest (and also some of the worst) restaurants in Munich, along with the landmark Hofbräuhaus, the most famous beer hall in Europe.

North of the Old Town is **Schwabing**, a former bohemian section whose main street is Leopoldstrasse. The large, sprawling municipal park grounds, the **Englischer Garten**, are due east of Schwabing.

Main Arteries & Streets

The best-known street in Munich is **Maximilianstrasse**, the most fashionable shopping avenue and one of the city's busiest east-west arteries. Other major east-west thoroughfares include **Kaufingerstrasse** and **Neuhauserstrasse**. Both are major shopping avenues in the core of the Altstadt's pedestrian zone. Two of Munich's great 19th-century avenues, **Ludwigstrasse** and **Brienner Strasse**, stretch toward the district of Schwabing. Ludwigstrasse was designed to display the greatness of the kingdom of Ludwig I and is bordered on both sides by impressive neoclassical and neo-Romanesque buildings.

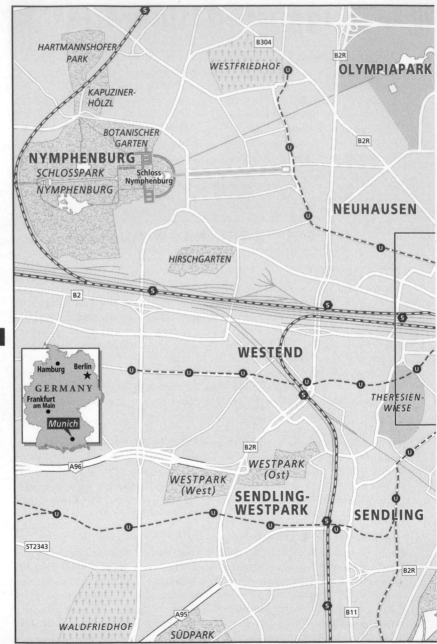

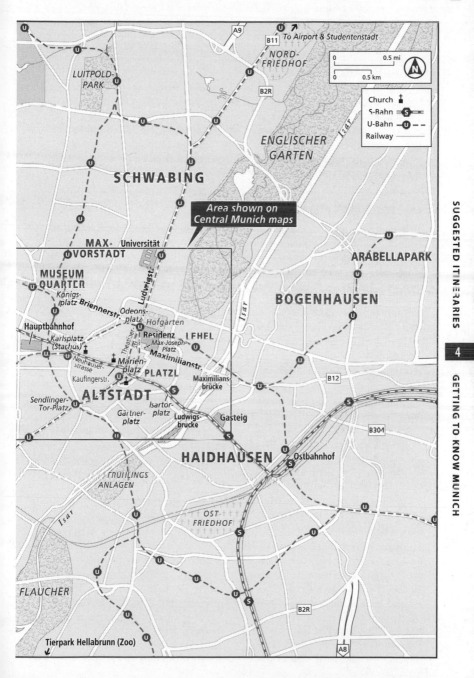

Odeonsplatz, on the southern end of Ludwigstrasse, was established to celebrate the Bavarian kingdom. **Leopoldstrasse** begins on the northern side of Ludwigstrasse and continues through Schwabing. The last of the 19th-century boulevards to be constructed was **Prinzregentstrasse,** lying between Prinz-Carl-Palais and Vogelweide-platz. Along the Prinzregentstrasse at no. 7 is the residence of the prime minister of Bavaria.

Finding an Address/Maps

Locating an address is relatively easy in Munich, because even numbers run up one side of a street and odd numbers down the other. In the Altstadt, "hidden" squares may make finding an address difficult; therefore, you may need a detailed street map, not the more general maps handed out free by the tourist office and many hotels. The best ones (containing a detailed street index) are published by Falk, and they're available at nearly all bookstores and at many newsstands. These pocket-size maps are easy to carry, with a detailed street index.

NEIGHBORHOODS IN BRIEF

Altstadt This is the historic part of Munich, the site of the original medieval city. The Altstadt is bounded by the Odeonsplatz and Sendlinger Tor ("Tor" means gate) to the north and the south, respectively, and by the Isartor and Karlstor to the east and west. You can walk across the district in 15 minutes.

The hub is Marienplatz, the town's primary square, with its Rathaus (Town Hall). In the Middle Ages, Marienplatz was the scene of many jousts and tournaments as well as public entertainment like executions. Today, it is brimming with mimes, musicians, and street performers. The square is also the site of many festivals and political rallies and is the traditional stopping and starting place for parades and processions. Included in the Altstadt district is the Fussgänger (pedestrian) Zone, home to many of Munich's elegant shops.

Haidhausen This district is home to Gasteig, the city's primary cultural, educational, and conference center. The modern complex houses the city library and the Munich Philharmonic Orchestra. Its various theaters and lecture halls play host to a variety of events, principally musical and theatrical performances. The district is also a trendy nightlife center.

Lehel Just east of the Altstadt, this district is part of the original planned expansion of the city that occurred in the latter years of the 19th century. The area is mainly residential and is noted for its fine neo-Renaissance architecture.

Ludwigstrasse One of Munich's great monumental avenues, this street was originally designed for King Ludwig I as a street worthy of his kingdom. The buildings in the southern section of the street adhere to a strict neoclassical style, whereas the architecture in the northern sector is neo-Romanesque. The overall effect is that of uniformity.

Maximilianstrasse The equivalent of New York's Fifth Avenue, Maximilianstrasse is Munich's Golden Mile. Planned as a showcase for King Maximilian II's dominion, it has architecture in what is known as Maximilianic style, an eclectic combination of styles with an emphasis on Gothic. Here you find the city's most elegant and expensive boutiques, restaurants, and hotels. Visitors can browse through stores like Armani, Hermès, and Bulgari. Along with numerous chic hotels and restaurants, the street is also home to the Museum of Ethnology and the overpowering monument to the king, the Maxmonument. The street is the primary connector from the Altstadt to the suburbs of Lehel and Haidhausen.

Olympiapark Host to rock and pop concerts as well as other performances, this residential and recreational area was the site of the 1972 Olympics, which is remembered for the terrorist attack by the Arab "Black September" group against Israeli athletes. The 1972 Munich Olympic Games were meant to show the world the bold new face of a radically rebuilt Munich, showcasing the premises of the innovative Olympic City. The Black September Arab terrorists, however, had different plans. They managed to slip into the compound housing the Israeli athletes and, before the day was over, had slaughtered a total of 11 of Israel's finest athletes. A storm of protest was raised around the world. The Games were virtually ruined, and Munich's bright new image was shattered (their police force seemed to make mistake after mistake); dank memories of the Holocaust were revived at a time when Germany, and Munich specifically, was trying to forget its recent past and show the world that it had moved into a brighter and happier future. For more information, see p. 143.

Located northwest of the city center, this enormous development is practically a city unto itself. It has its own post office, railway station, elementary school, and even its own mayor. The top level of the enormous television tower is the best place to view Munich and its vicinity.

Nymphenburg Located just northwest of the city center is the Nymphenburg Palace and Park, the original home of the Wittelsbach rulers. The baroque palace is home to the famous Nymphenburg porcelain museum and factory. Adjoining the palace is a vast expanse of lakes and gardens.

Schwabing This area, in the city's northern sector, was (in the 1920s and then, again, after World War II and into the 1950s) a center of bohemian life, much like New York's Greenwich Village. Like Greenwich Village, it has gentrified into a locale for lawyers, producers, and other professionals, as well as a hangout for university students and a lively nightlife scene. At the start of the 20th century, it was the place where the city's leading artists, actors, poets, musicians, and writers lived or gathered. Many famous literary figures have called Schwabing home, including Thomas Mann. It has the city's finest examples of Art Nouveau architecture. Leopoldstrasse makes almost a straight axis through its center. The Englischer Garten forms its eastern border, the Studentenstadt is to its north, and Olympiapark and Josephsplatz mark its western border.

Arabellapark The city's ultramodern commercial and industrial quarter, northeast of the city center, is home to several large international companies. Its glass and concrete buildings have become an outstanding feature of Munich's skyline.

Bogenhausen Located just northeast of the city center and near Arabellapark, this area, like Schwabing, has many excellent examples of Art Nouveau architecture. Once the district where the prosperous had their homes, Bogenhausen is now home to numerous galleries, boutiques, and restaurants.

Briennerstrasse Designed as part of the development of the Maxvorstadt during the reign of Maximilian I, this street was home to the aristocratic families and wealthy citizens of Munich. Today it has galleries and luxury shops.

Maxvorstadt Launched as a planned expansion of the city by King Maximilian I, the area today draws its character from the facilities of the University of Munich, and it teems with student bars, bookshops, and galleries.

Westpark This 71-hectare (175-acre) park, laid out for the fourth International Garden Show, has extensive lawns, playgrounds, and ponds. The park is complete with two beer gardens, several cafes, and a lakeside theater that hosts outdoor concerts in summer. Also located in the park is the Rudi Sedlmayer Sports Hall, one of Munich's premier venues for large rock concerts.

2 THE BEST OF MUNICH IN 1 DAY

Touring Munich in 1 day seems ridiculous at first, considering that it is a sprawling metropolis filled with treasures, and has some of Europe's greatest museums and palaces. But it can be done if you get an early start and have a certain discipline, plus a lot of stamina. This "greatest hits" itinerary focuses on the Altstadt, the Old Town, in the heart of Munich. You can begin at the central square, Marienplatz, taking in the carillon *(Glockenspiel)* and walk nearby to an old church, an open-air market, and the most fashionable shopping boulevard in Munich. After lunch, there will be time left for a visit to both the Alte Pinakothek and the Deutsches Museum, the two most important museums in Munich, followed by a late afternoon visit to the Englischer Garten, climaxed by a beer debauch at the Hofbräuhaus am Platzl.

After breakfast, launch your day by heading for the center of town opening onto:

❶ Marienplatz ★

This is the most historic and most scenic square of Altstadt (the Old Town). As you stand here, you'll be in the heart of Munich. Because many of the attractions are nearby, you'll cross this square—perhaps—several times. Try to come back at 11am to watch the greatest show in town, the 43-bell *Glockenspiel* (carillon) on the 8.5m (28-ft.) central spire of the Neues Rathaus (New Town Hall). Brightly painted mechanical figures re-enact famous events in the city's history. This is the fourth largest carillon in Europe. You can climb the steps of the Town Hall (or take an elevator) for one of the most panoramic views of Munich. The Altes Rathaus (Old Town Hall), with a plain Gothic tower, stands to the right of the New Town Hall.

Before you hit the major museums, take a stroll along or by some of the major attractions of the Altstadt, including:

❷ Peterskirche

The oldest church in Munich (p. 139) stands at Rindermarkt. The church can be viewed immediately south of the Neues Rathaus. Its bell tower—known locally as Alter Peter, or "Old Peter"—towers over this 13th-century Gothic church. But since you've already seen a panoramic view, you may resist climbing its 306 steps for another vista.

In the rear of the church, you come to:

❸ Viktualienmarkt

Our favorite place in Munich to get the makings of a picnic, this open-air market (p. 165) with dozens of stalls is called "the stomach of Munich." To the north stands **Heiliggeistkirche,** or the Church of the Holy Ghost, a late Gothic hall–type church with much later baroque ornamentations.

A local told us that the Viktualienmarkt is not just a place to come for cheese, wine, and sausages, but "one can unlock the heart of the Münchner by visiting it," if you can understand what he meant.

Again, delaying your visit to the museums, cut north from the market, heading along Dienerstrasse until you come to Residenzstrasse. Cut east along:

❹ Maximilianstrasse

Just so you don't get the idea that Munich is all "quaintery," walk along its most fashionable street, lined with boutiques and houses of fashion. It is the Fifth Avenue of Munich, its Champs-Elysées, but different from both of those streets. Certainly it is one of the great shopping streets of Europe. Maximilianstrasse also has some of the leading art galleries of Europe. We could spend a day just visiting them to see avant-garde German art, but time is rushing by—and there's still much to see.

The great museum of Munich is the:

❺ Alte Pinakothek ★★★

It really takes 4 hours to see this museum (p. 127)—one of Europe's greatest art galleries—in any depth, but you can do it in an hour and a half by concentrating only on its masterpieces. The collections were started by the ruling Wittelsbachs at the beginning of the 16th century, and they have grown over the centuries with frequent bequests. Albrecht Dürer is remarkably represented, as are the "Three Rs"—Rembrandt, Rubens, and Raphael—plus a host of other old European masters, including one of our favorites, Pieter Brueghel. Promise yourself a more detailed visit on your next trip to Munich.

Time for a lunch break. See our restaurant recommendations in chapter 6.

After lunch, head for the:

❻ Deutsches Museum ★★★

On an island in the Isar River, but still in the heart of Munich, this is the German Museum of Masterpieces of Science and Technology (p. 131). When you see all these vehicles, locomotives, aircraft, and machinery, you'll wish that you'd pursued that career as an engineer. This museum takes up 5.3 hectares (13 acres) and is the largest of its kind in the world, with at least 16,000 artifacts on display. Instead of a day spent, you'll have to settle for a 2-hour preview to keep up with our schedule.

To cap the afternoon, head for the:

❼ Englischer Garten ★

If it's summer, hopefully you won't be offended by a little nudity. Japanese tourists certainly aren't. You'll see them all over the park snapping pictures of Münchners letting it all hang out. Nudity aside, the real reason to come here is to enjoy one of the largest and most beautiful parks in the country (p. 142). With its lakes and pavilions, including a Chinese pagoda, this is an ideal place to take a respite from all that rushed sightseeing. There are also beer gardens if you'd like an early start on the suds.

After you return to your hotel, set out for your wildest and most rollicking evening in Munich by heading for the fabled:

❽ Hofbräuhaus am Platzl ★

No beer garden in all the world is as well known as this sprawling, state-owned brewery (p. 174), holding 4,500 beer drinkers. Oktoberfest is all-year-round here. How are you at downing a liter in a blue-glazed mug in 3 minutes? Münchners do it all the time. The air is overheated, and the smell of sausages, stale tobacco, and beer permeates this massive building constructed at the end of the 19th century. The largest banquet hall you will likely ever see is on the second floor. In case you care, that monster Adolf Hitler used to hang out here. The pounding oompah band and the singing and shouting drinkers contribute to the retro Bavarian atmosphere.

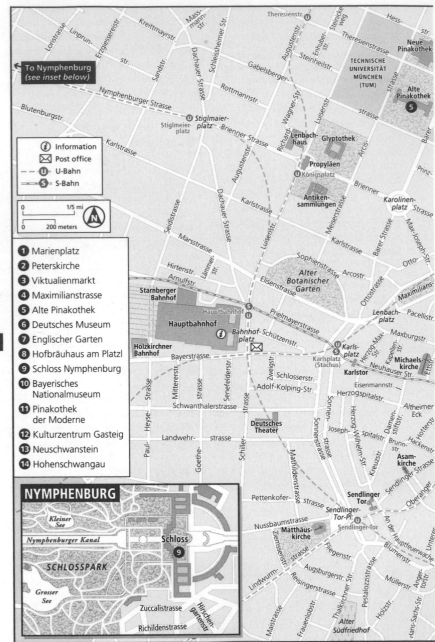

To Nymphenburg
(see inset below)

(i) Information
(⊠) Post office
(U) U-Bahn
(S) S-Bahn

0   1/5 mi
0   200 meters

1 Marienplatz
2 Peterskirche
3 Viktualienmarkt
4 Maximilianstrasse
5 Alte Pinakothek
6 Deutsches Museum
7 Englischer Garten
8 Hofbräuhaus am Platzl
9 Schloss Nymphenburg
10 Bayerisches
   Nationalmuseum
11 Pinakothek
   der Moderne
12 Kulturzentrum Gasteig
13 Neuschwanstein
14 Hohenschwangau

NYMPHENBURG

Kleiner
See

Nymphenburger Kanal

Schloss
9

SCHLOSSPARK

Grosser
See

Zuccalistrasse

Hirsch-
garten-
str.

Richildenstrasse

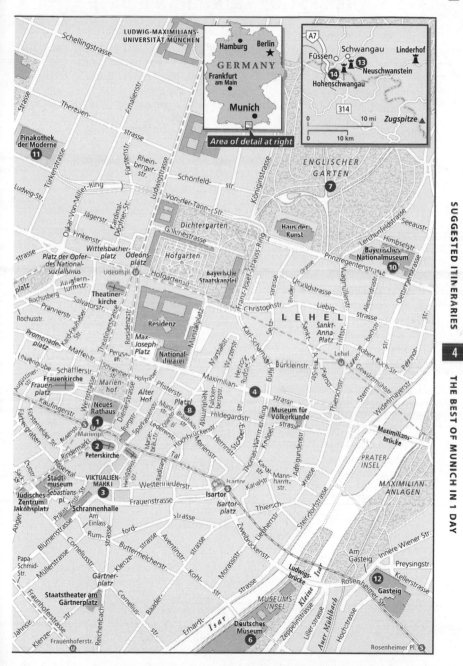

3 THE BEST OF MUNICH IN 2 DAYS

If you've already made your way through "The Best of Munich in 1 Day," you'll find that your second full-day tour takes in a different part of Munich. One of Bavaria's greatest attractions, Schloss Nymphenburg, lies right on the outskirts and is easy to reach by public transportation. Because it's riddled with things to see and do, you'll need to devote an entire morning to it, at least 2 to 3 hours, before lunchtime. In the afternoon, if your time is budgeted properly, you can take in two more of the city's major attractions, both of which are museums—the Bayerisches Nationalmuseum, followed by the Pinakothek der Moderne.

Via U-Bahn station Rotkreuzplatz, head for:

❾ Schloss Nymphenburg ★★★

Begun in 1664, the summer palace of the ruling dynasty, the Wittelsbachs, is one of the most beautiful palaces in Europe (p. 136). The kings of Bavaria always came here for their fair-weather romps, as when Ludwig I chased the famous courtesan, Lola Montez, through the gardens. You can wander at leisure through the spectacular interiors of the palace, pausing in the Great Gallery of Beauties which displays the king's pick of the most beautiful women of yesteryear. If glass coronation coaches are your thing, visit the Marstallmuseum, followed by a leisurely walk through Nymphenburg's park. With your limited time, you can't explore all 200 hectares (494 acres). Allow about 20 minutes to visit Amalienburg, the rococo hunting lodge by François Cuvilliés. Princess Maria Amalia hunted game from the roof, as palace guards drove the poor animals through the yard while she shot them in the head.

After all this, it's time out for lunch. Our recommendations are in chapter 6.

After lunching at the restaurant of your choice, you can take the U-Bahn to Lethel for a visit to:

❿ Bayerisches Nationalmuseum ★★

This gigantic monster (p. 131) sprawls across three floors and covers the history of Bavarian culture, mainly from the Middle Ages to the 19th century. From Christmas nativity cribs to Renaissance jewelry, there is much here to amuse and delight. The medieval and Renaissance woodcarving,

especially from Tilman Riemenschneider, is worth the trip here. Allow at least an hour to cover some of the highlights.

After a visit to this museum, take the U-Bahn to Odeonsplatz for a visit to:

⑪ Pinakothek der Moderne ★★

On the most beautiful square in Munich, this complex is a virtual museum quarter (p. 132). But for those rushed for time, as we are, one gallery, the Staatsgalerie Moderner Kunst (Gallery of Modern Art), is the gem. In an avant-garde glass-and-concrete building, the museum is the largest in Germany—and one of the biggest in Europe—in its collections of modern art. You expect to meet Matisse and Picasso, but there are so many other masters, enough to dazzle the eye for a mile: Kandinsky, Kirchner (our favorite), Max Ernst, Giacometti, de Kooning, Francis Bacon, and even Andy Warhol. We compare this museum favorably to London's Tate Gallery or Paris's Pompidou.

After a rest at your hotel, you might consider an evening at:

⑫ Kulturzentrum Gasteig

On the bluffs of the Isar River, this is one of the greatest performance halls in Germany (p. 169), with five different theaters, including the Philharmonic Hall. Chances are that at the time of your visit, a cultural presentation will be featured according to your liking. It's a great way to spend an evening. Of course, there are always the beer gardens if you're so inclined.

Having sampled the charms of Munich in just 2 days, make your third and final day a little different by skipping out of town and heading south into Bavaria to see Mad Ludwig's two imposing castles. It doesn't take long to visit either Neuschwanstein or Hohenschwangau, but you'll need to allow plenty of time for reaching the castles of "The Fairy-Tale King," plus long waits to gain entrance in summer. Neuschwanstein is the single most visited and popular attraction in all of Germany. Plan on a luncheon stopover in the little town of Hohenschwangau. Our recommendations for dining begin on p. 104.

⓭ Neuschwanstein ★★★

If you have time for only one castle in all of Germany, make it Neuschwanstein (p. 228), which you can see in the morning, saving Hohenschwangau (see below) for the afternoon. Neuschwanstein is like a fantasy castle created by Disney except it's real, complete with battlements, gables, lookouts, spiral stairways, towers, and gates, even courtyards. You're taken on a guided tour, lasting 35 minutes. Keep your eyes wide and your mouth agape. If you have time before lunch after your view of the castle, you can wander through the surrounding forests, enjoying the panoramas. Those with stamina and lots of time can climb the mountain in 2 hours for the photo op of two lifetimes.

⓮ Hohenschwangau

To the sounds of a Wagner opera, loony King Ludwig II designed the fairy-tale kingdom of Neuschwanstein (p. 204), his romantic masterpiece. But he actually grew up at Hohenschwangau down below. In a heavy Romanesque style, the castle dates from the 12th century, when it was the headquarters of the kings of Schwangau. But Hohenschwangau in its present format was constructed between 1832 and 1836 by Ludwig's father, who transformed it into an elegant palace.

After visiting both castles, you'll still have time to make it back to Munich for the night.

5 THE BEST OF BAVARIA IN 1 WEEK

If you budget your time carefully, you can see some of the highlights of Bavaria in just 1 week. Naturally, you will want to visit its capital, Munich. The most important manmade attractions, including some of Europe's greatest museums, are here. But for pure scenic grandeur, the Bavarian Alps rank among Europe's greatest treasures.

One of Europe's most beautiful drives is the **Deutsche Alpenstrasse (German Alpine Road) ★★★**, which stretches for some 480km (298 miles) from Berchtesgaden in the east, all the way to Lindau on Lake Constance in the west. The road goes through mountains, lakes, "black" forests, and "castles in the sky." Where commercial reality hasn't intruded, it's a true fantasy. In winter, driving can be perilous, and mountain passes are often shut down. We always prefer to take the drive in early spring or early autumn.

Day ❶: Hitler's Scenic Retreat at Berchtesgaden ★★

From Munich, head south along Autobahn A8 (and drive in the right lane if you want to avoid the hysterical speeders on the left). Turn south on Rte. B20 for **Berchtesgaden,** 158km (98 miles) southeast of Munich. After settling in and having lunch, take an afternoon excursion to **Obersalzberg** and the **Kehlstein** ★★ (p. 198). The Kehlstein road was blasted from bedrock, and an elevator ascends to the summit, once Hitler's famed Eagles Nest. The panorama is quite spectacular.

While here you can also explore the **National Park Berchtesgaden** (p. 191) and the town of **Berchtesgaden** itself (p. 192). Overnight in Berchtesgaden.

Day ❷: Königssee ★★ & Bad Reichenhall ★

While still based in Berchtesgaden, take the 2-hour boat ride on the **Königssee** (p. 197), 5km (3 miles) to the south. This long, narrow lake, famed for its steep banks and dark waters, is one of Europe's most dramatic and romantic sights. In the afternoon, drive west along the Alpine road and then north on Rte. B20 some 19km (12 miles) to **Bad Reichenhall** (p. 200). This is one of Germany's most famous spas on the Saalach River. The town was built around its *Kurpark* (spa center), and it's filled with both luxury and moderately priced hotels.

Day ❸: Neues Schloss ★★, Another Ludwig Castle

Get back on Autobahn A8 toward Munich, but turn off at Prien am Chiemsee, 85km (53 miles) southeast of Munich. The premier attraction here is the **Neues Schloss** (p. 204), a fantastic castle begun by Ludwig II in 1878 on the island of Herrenchiemsee. You can find food and lodging at Prien.

Day ❹: Bad Tölz to Mittenwald ★

Get back on the autobahn to Munich, but take a cross-country route (472) to **Bad Tölz** (p. 185), one of Bavaria's leading spas. Its spa center (Kurverwaltung) makes a good place to take a break. **Hotel Am Wald,** Austrasse 39 in Bad Tölz (ℂ **08041/ 78830**), is a reasonable place to dine, with meals beginning at 10€ ($16). It serves good Bavarian fare—nothing fancy, but fit

fortification for this breezy part of the country. Standing on its own grounds, the hotel lies about a 10-minute walk from the Altstadt (Old Town).

Leave Bad Tölz and go along Hwy. 472 for another 8km (5 miles) to **Bad Heilbrunn,** another typical Bavarian spa. There's not much to see, but in another 6.5km (4 miles) you reach **Benediktbeuern,** Upper Bavaria's oldest Benedictine monastery. Records trace it back to the year 739. After a look, continue along for 6.5km (4 miles) to Kochel am See, with its Alpine vistas, and from here take B20 for 32km (20 miles) to **Mittenwald** on the Austrian frontier. Plan an overnight stay.

Day ❺: Garmisch-Partenkirchen & the Zugspitze ★★★

You'll want to spend as much time as possible in **Mittenwald,** one of the most beautiful and evocative of all Bavarian villages. It is also a major center for violin making. At least give it a morning before driving northwest for 19km (12 miles) on Rte. 2 to **Garmisch-Partenkirchen,** two towns combined. After checking in, head for the major attraction, the **Zugspitze,** the highest peak in Germany (more about this on p. 216). Wear warm clothing. You can overnight in Garmisch, which has the most hotels and restaurants of all the resorts of Bavaria.

Day ❻: En Route to Oberammergau ★

Leaving Garmisch-Partenkirchen, head north for 19km (12 miles) to Oberammergau. Along the way you'll pass **Kloster Ettal ★,** founded by Ludwig the Bavarian in 1330. Its original 10-sided church is a stunning example of the Bavarian rococo style. See p. 222. Some 9.5km (6 miles) to the west is **Schloss Linderhof ★★**, one of Mad King Ludwig's royal residences, built on the grounds of his hunting lodge between 1874 and 1878. These two attractions will

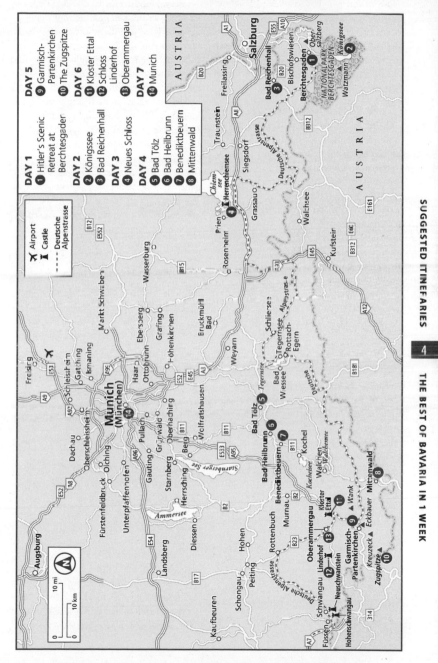

DAY 1
1 Hitler's Scenic Retreat at Berchtesgaden

DAY 2
2 Königssee
3 Bad Reichenhall

DAY 3
4 Neues Schloss

DAY 4
5 Bad Tölz
6 Bad Heilbrunn
7 Benediktbeuern
8 Mittenwald

DAY 5
9 Garmisch-Partenkirchen
10 The Zugspitze

DAY 6
11 Kloster Ettal
12 Schloss Linderhof
13 Oberammergau

DAY 7
14 Munich

Airport
Castle
---- Deutsche Alpenstrasse

take up most of your day, but you'll still arrive in the little old woodcarver's village of **Oberammergau,** 11km (6³/₄ miles) northeast of Linderhof, in time to wander about. Later, enjoy a hearty Bavarian dinner before turning in to your Alpine bed.

Coverage of attractions, hotels, and restaurants begins on p. 219.

Day ⑦: Return to Munich ★★★

The Alpine village of Oberammergau lies 95km (59 miles) southwest of Munich. Most motorists make the run in 1¹/₂ hours. If you leave Oberammergau in the morning, you can easily be in Munich in time to check into a hotel and have lunch. If you arrive in Munich on Day 7, it will be convenient for your takeoff in the morning.

After lunch, you'll still have the afternoon for some of those sights you missed

in your first 2 days in Munich (see above). Try to take in a visit of the **Residenz** ★ (p. 134), the enormous palace of the Wittelsbach family and the official residence of the rulers of Bavaria from 1385 to 1918. It lies at Max-Joseph-Platz 3. You might also try to visit the **Cuvilliés Theater** ★★, one of the most flamboyant in all of Europe. These visits will take at least 2 hours. With the remaining time, visit **Frauenkirche** ★, the "Cathedral of Our Lady" at Frauenplatz (p. 138).

If it's a summer night, you might enjoy a final evening in one of the outdoor beer gardens, a fit farewell to the kingdom of the brew. If you're not big on the suds, you might like to dine in one of the restaurants of **Schwabing** (p. 118), which has been compared to New York's Greenwich Village.

Where to Stay in Munich

Finding a room in Munich is comparatively easy, but tabs tend to be high. Bargains are few and hard to find, but they do exist. If you arrive in town without a hotel reservation, go to the **Munich Tourist Office** on Platform 2 at the Hauptbahnhof (✆ **089/233-96-500;** www.muenchen.de), where general information about Munich and its attractions is also available; it's open Monday to Saturday 9am to 8pm and Sunday 10am to 6pm. The English-speaking personnel, with access to more than 300 hotels (and collectively about 35,000 beds), will come to your rescue. Tell them what you can afford and they'll pick a suitable hotel in that price range. There's no charge for the reservation, but you must make a 10% down payment on the room, an amount that will be deducted from your final hotel bill.

Be sure to get a receipt as well as a map with instructions on how to reach the place they've booked for you. Keep your receipt. If you don't like the room, go back to the tourist office and they'll try to find you other lodging.

Frankly, we find that this reservations service is most appropriate for travelers arriving at Munich's railway station without a reservation—the last-minute arrangements the staff can make, especially during periods when many hotels are full, can be very useful. But they'll also arrange reservations weeks or months in advance of your arrival, without charge, if you want them to.

Written correspondence describing your needs and preferences should be addressed to Landeshauptstadt München, Fremdenverkehrsamt, Sendlingerstrasse 1, 80331 München. The hotel reservation service can also be reached by phone through the tourist office (see above) or through its direct line (✆ **089/233 96 500**), by fax (089/233-30-133), or by e-mail (hotelservice@muenchen.de). *Note:* The hotel reservation service maintains different hours than the main tourist office: Monday to Thursday from 9am to 5pm and Friday 9am to 3pm.

All hotels raise their prices for Oktoberfest and for various trade fairs. Some hotels announce their rates in advance, while others prefer to wait until the last minute to see what the market will bear. In general, prices during the festival rise about 15% or more. Prices listed under hotel reviews below are for non-Oktoberfest stays. For the most up-to-date information, call the specific hotel where you'd like to stay.

1 CENTRAL MUNICH

VERY EXPENSIVE

Bayerischer Hof & Palais Montgelas ★★★ The Bayerischer Hof hotel and the 17th-century Palais Montgelas combine to form a Bavarian version of New York's Waldorf-Astoria. It's been a favorite since King Ludwig I came here to take a bath (the royal palace didn't have bathtubs then). Rooms range from medium to extremely spacious. The

Central Munich Accommodations

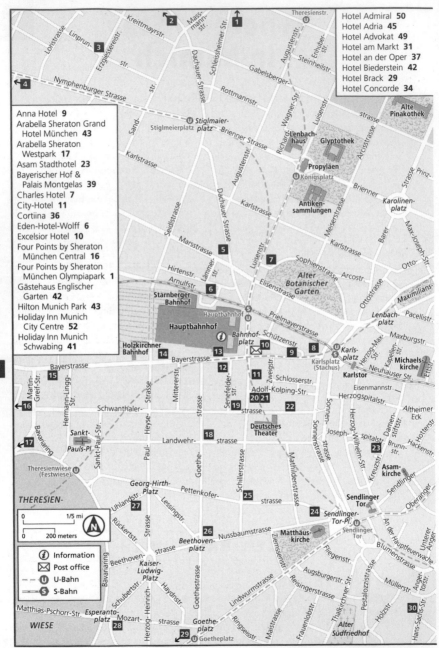

Hotel Admiral **50**
Hotel Adria **45**
Hotel Advokat **49**
Hotel am Markt **31**
Hotel an der Oper **37**
Hotel Biederstein **42**
Hotel Brack **29**
Hotel Concorde **34**

Anna Hotel **9**
Arabella Sheraton Grand
Hotel München **43**
Arabella Sheraton
Westpark **17**
Asam Stadthotel **23**
Bayerischer Hof &
Palais Montgelas **39**
Charles Hotel **7**
City-Hotel **11**
Cortiina **36**
Eden-Hotel-Wolff **6**
Excelsior Hotel **10**
Four Points by Sheraton
München Central **16**
Four Points by Sheraton
München Olympiapark **1**
Gästehaus Englischer
Garten **42**
Hilton Munich Park **43**
Holiday Inn Munich
City Centre **52**
Holiday Inn Munich
Schwabing **41**

Information
Post office
U-Bahn
S-Bahn

Hotel Domus **46**
Hotel Erzgiesserei
 Europe **3**
Hotel Europäischer
 Hof **12**
Hotel Exquisit **24**
Hotel Germania **19**
Hotel Jedermann **15**

Hotel Königshof **8**
Hotel Leopold **41**
Hotel Mirabell **18**
Hotel Monaco **20**
Hotel München Palace **44**
Hotel Olympic **30**
Hotel-Pension
 Am Siegestor **41**

Hotel-Pension Beck **48**
Hotel-Pension Mariandl **26**
Hotel Preysing **51**
Hotel Reinbold **21**
Hotel Rotkreuzplatz **4**
Hotel Schlicker **32**
Hotel Splendid-Dollmann
 im Lehel **47**

Hotel Torbräu **33**
Hotel Uhland **27**
Hotel Vier Jahreszeiten
 Kempinski München **38**
Hotel Wallis **22**
Intercity-Hotel München **13**
King's Hotel First Class **5**
Kraft Hotel **25**
Kurpfalz Hotel **16**
Mandarin Oriental **35**
Mercure Hotel München
 am Olympiapark **2**
München City Hilton **53**
München Marriott Hotel **41**
Pension Westfalia **28**
Renner Hotel Carlton **40**
Sofitel Munich Bayerpost **14**

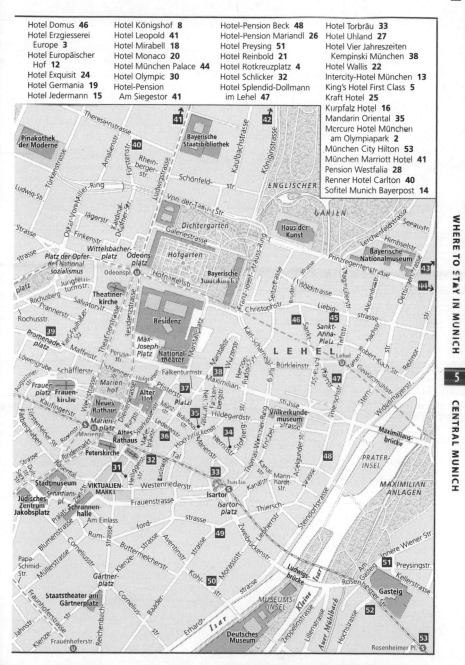

decor ranges from Bavarian provincial to British country-house chintz. Many beds are four-posters. The large bathrooms have a private phone and plenty of shelf space. Palais Montgelas has 20 of the most upscale rooms as well as conference and banquet rooms.

Promenadeplatz 2–6, 80333 München. ℂ **089/21-20-0.** Fax 089/21-20-906. www.bayerischerhof.de. 395 units. 269€–454€ ($430–$726) double; from 1,440€ ($2,304) suite. AE, DC, MC, V. Parking 26€ ($42). Tram: 19. **Amenities:** 3 restaurants; 5 bars; nightclub; spa; rooftop pool and garden; gym; sauna; car rental; room service; massage; babysitting; laundry service; dry cleaning; nonsmoking rooms; sun terrace; 1 room for those w/limited mobility. *In room:* TV, minibar, hair dryer, safe, Wi-Fi.

Charles Hotel ★★★ Set at the edge of the old Botanical Gardens, this luxurious modern hotel is part of the Rocco Forte brand of European hotels. A government-rated five-star hotel, the Charles rose in the historic center of Munich, standing in its own tranquil gardens. The spacious bedrooms, each bright and airy, open onto views of the gardens and the more distant Alps. Sleek, contemporary furnishings grace the rooms, which have soundproof doors and windows. The bathrooms are among Munich's best decorated with original Nymphenburger porcelain.

Sophhienstrasse 28, 80333 München. ℂ **089/544-555-0.** Fax 089/544-555-2000. www.charleshotel.de. 160 units. 390€–530€ ($624–$848) double, 720€ ($1,152) junior suite, from 960€ ($1,536) suite. AE, DC, MC, V. Parking: 24€ ($38). U-Bahn: Karlsplatz. **Amenities:** Restaurant; bar; indoor pool; fitness room; spa; steam bath; sauna; room service; laundry service; dry cleaning; Internet access. *In room:* A/C, TV, minibar, hair dryer, safe.

Hotel Vier Jahreszeiten Kempinski München ★★★ This grand hotel is not only the most elegant in Munich but also Germany's most famous and distinctive, and among the finest in the world. Its tradition stretches back to 1858. Rooms and suites—which have hosted royalty, heads of state, and famed personalities from all over the world—combine the charm of days gone by with modern luxuries. The antique-style beds feature fine linens on sumptuous mattresses. The large bathrooms are equipped with all sorts of special treats, including luxurious robes. The windows opening onto Maximilianstrasse are double-glazed.

Maximilianstrasse 17, 80539 München. ℂ **089/2125-0.** Fax 089/2125-2000. www.kempinski-vier jahreszeiten.de. 308 units. 246€–450€ ($394–$720) double; from 720€ ($1,152) suite. AE, DC, MC, V. Parking 20€ ($32). Tram: 19. **Amenities:** Restaurant; 2 bars; indoor heated pool; fitness center; sauna; Turkish bath; solarium; room service; massage; babysitting; laundry service; dry cleaning; nonsmoking rooms; rooms for those w/limited mobility. *In room:* A/C, TV, minibar, hair dryer, safe, Wi-Fi.

Königshof ★★ In the heart of Munich, the lively, personalized Königshof overlooks the famous Karlsplatz (Stachus) and the old part of the city, where it opened in 1862. The proprietors, the Geisel family, maintain its legend. As a mansion hotel, it attracts an extremely upmarket clientele but does not match the Mandarin Oriental (see below) as a premier address. The hotel offers traditional comforts plus up-to-date facilities. All its sleekly styled rooms have soundproofing and picture windows. Shopping and sightseeing streets are found nearby.

Karlsplatz 25, 80335 München. ℂ **089/55-13-60.** Fax 089/5513-6113. www.koenigshof-hotel.de. 87 units. 310€–475€ ($496–$760) double; from 410€ ($656) suite. AE, DC, MC, V. Parking 22€ ($35). S-Bahn: S3, S7, or S8 to Karlsplatz. Tram: 19. **Amenities:** Restaurant; bar; sauna; limited room service; babysitting; laundry service; dry cleaning; nonsmoking rooms; rooms for those w/limited mobility. *In room:* A/C, TV, minibar, hair dryer, safe, Wi-Fi.

Mandarin Oriental ★ One of Munich's smaller hotels is also one of its most posh. Only the Hotel Vier Jahreszeiten Kempinski München and the Bayerischer Hof (see above) outclass this sophisticated and luxurious winner. The stylish and elegant, wedge-shaped

1880s building combines neo-Renaissance, neoclassical, and Biedermeier touches. It's located within sight of the Frauenkirche at Marienplatz. A marble staircase sweeps upward to the very comfortable, large rooms, each with specially crafted furniture or original antiques. Many of the accommodations contain private terraces opening onto views of Munich.

Neuturmstrasse 1, 80331 München. (℮) **089/290-980.** Fax 089/222-539. www.mandarinoriental.com/ munich. 73 units. 395€–520€ ($632–$832) double; from 630€ ($1,008) suite. AE, DC, MC, V. Parking 20€ ($32). U-Bahn/S-Bahn: Marienplatz. Tram: 19. **Amenities:** 2 restaurants; bar; rooftop pool; fitness room; room service; babysitting; laundry service; dry cleaning; nonsmoking rooms; rooms for those w/limited mobility. *In room:* A/C, TV, minibar, hair dryer, safe, Wi-Fi.

Sofitel Munich Bayerpost ★★   In the heart of Munich, this modern hotel in a traditional building lies near the Hauptbahnhof. It combines the architectural style of yesterday with modern amenities. Built in the Wilhelminian style, the hotel is rated five stars by the government, and it's a bastion of luxury and comfort. The midsize to spacious bedrooms are beautifully furnished with natural materials and tasteful fabrics. The Maisonette suites on the eighth floor are known for their panoramic views over the city and the Alps beyond.

Bayerstrasse 12, 80335 München. (℮) **089/599480.** Fax 089/599481000. www.sofitel.com. 396 units. 149€–179€ ($238–$286) double, 229€–449€ ($366–$718) junior suite, from 564€ ($902) suite. AE, DC, MC, V. Parking: 24€ ($38). U-Bahn: Hauptbahnhof. **Amenities:** Restaurant; bistro; bar; indoor pool; solarium; fitness center; spa; sauna; room service; business center; laundry service; dry cleaning; disco; rooms for those w/limited mobility. *In room:* A/C, TV, minibar, hair dryer, safe, Wi-Fi.

EXPENSIVE

Admiral ★★   In the vicinity of the Deutsches Museum (p. 131) and the Isar River, this is a government-rated four-star deluxe hotel. In a tranquil location, its rooms are spread over six floors. The furnishings are elegant, the comfort top rate. The bedrooms to request are those with a small balcony opening onto the hotel gardens. As a thoughtful touch, each room is supplied with a basket of fresh fruit. The breakfast buffet is one of the most generous we've seen in Munich—even the jams are homemade. In summer, fresh Bavarian fruit is a regular feature.

Kohlstrasse 9, 80469 München. (℮) **089/216-350.** Fax 089/293-674. www.hotel-admiral.de. 33 units. 150€–350€ ($240–$560) double. Rates include buffet breakfast. AE, DC, MC, V. Parking 15€ ($24). S-Bahn: Isartor. Tram: 17, 18. **Amenities:** Bar; room service; babysitting; laundry service; dry cleaning; nonsmoking rooms; rooms for those w/limited mobility. *In room:* TV, free minibar, hair dryer, iron, safe, Wi-Fi.

Arabella Sheraton Westpark ★   A 10-story, government rated four-star member of the Arabella chain, this hotel is personalized and intimate. The midsize to spacious rooms were last renovated in 1996, but are still well maintained. Bedrooms come in three different grades, prices based on altitude (the higher, the more expensive), decor, and the presence of robes. The more expensive rooms evoke a country-house aura in decor. The cheaper rooms are on the lower three floors and are the most timeworn, but are sufficiently comfortable. The location on the western side of Munich is near the fairgrounds where Oktoberfest is staged. The steel-and-glass structure is a bit too institutional for our tastes, attracting E.U. business clients and a lot of tour groups.

Garmischer Strasse 2, 80339 München. (℮) **800/325-3535** in the U.S. and Canada, or 089/5-19-60. Fax 089/5196801. www.starwoodhotels.com. 258 units. 110€–189€ ($176–$302) double; 220€–410€ ($352–$656) suite. AE, DC, MC, V. Parking 20€ ($32). U-Bahn: U4 or U5 to Heimeran Platz. **Amenities:** Restaurant; bar; indoor pool; sauna; steam room; room service; babysitting; laundry service; dry cleaning; nonsmoking rooms; rooms for those w/limited mobility. *In room:* A/C, TV, minibar, beverage maker, hair dryer, safe, Wi-Fi.

Eden Hotel Wolff ★★   If you must stay near the train station, this is your best bet. The hotel is also located across the street from the Munich terminus of the Lufthansa Airport Bus. The austere stone-clad facade of the Eden Hotel Wolff does not reveal the warmth of the interior decoration or the comfort this hotel has. The interior is richly traditional, with chandeliers and dark-wood paneling. A few of the rooms are small, but most are spacious; all are tastefully furnished in a decor that runs the gamut from extremely modern to rustic. Some units are hypoallergenic, with special beds and a private ventilation system. Ask whether special weekend rates are available. The staff is among the best, most efficient, and most helpful in Munich.

Arnulfstrasse 4–8, 80335 München. ℂ **089/55-11-5-0.** Fax 089/55-11-5-555. www.ehw.de. 210 units. 143€–310€ ($229–$496) double; 275€–375€ ($440–$600) suite. 1 child up to age 6 stays free in parent's room. Rates include buffet breakfast. AE, DC, MC, V. Parking 15€ ($24). U-Bahn/S-Bahn: Hauptbahnhof. **Amenities:** Restaurant; bar; spa; fitness room; room service; babysitting; laundry service; nonsmoking rooms. *In room:* TV, minibar, hair dryer, safe.

Hilton Munich Park ★★   This sleek, 15-story tower in verdant Tivoli Park was transformed into a hotel from an office complex at the time of the 1972 Olympics and stays up to date with renovations as needed. A government-rated five-star hotel, it lies between the Englischer Garten (p. 142) and the Isar River, in a neighborhood close to the headquarters of many giant corporations. Because of that, traffic can sometimes make access for motorists a bit difficult. It's one of Munich's two Hiltons (the other, government-rated four-star München City Hilton, is less plush and has no swimming pool). Bedrooms here have floor-to-ceiling picture windows and balconies affording a distant view of the Alps.

Am Tucherpark 7, 80538 München. ℂ **800/445-8667** in the U.S. and Canada, or 089/3-84-50. Fax 089/38-45-25-88. www.hilton.com. 479 units. 139€–260€ ($222–$416) double; from 500€ ($800) suite. Rates include buffet breakfast. AE, DC, MC, V. Parking 16€ ($26). U-Bahn: U3 or U6 to Giselastrasse. Bus: 54 from Schwabing. **Amenities:** 2 restaurants; bar; indoor pool; fitness center; Jacuzzi; sauna; room service; massage; babysitting; laundry service; dry cleaning; nonsmoking rooms; solarium; rooms for those w/limited mobility. *In room:* A/C, TV, minibar, hair dryer, safe, Wi-Fi.

Holiday Inn Munich City Centre ★   After the Arabella Sheraton Grand (p. 99), this is Munich's largest hotel. It's two subway stops east of the Marienplatz in a congested neighborhood near the Isar River, not far from the Kulturzentrum Gasteig (p. 169) and the Deutsches Museum (p. 131). An 11-story concrete structure, it offers a busy and cosmopolitan environment much favored by business travelers and airline personnel. Guest rooms are all well maintained and have bathrooms with shower-tub combinations. Rated four stars by the government, it's the kind of place that shows bustling, international Munich at its most efficient, not its most charming.

Hochstrasse 3, 81669 München. ℂ **877/660-8550** in the U.S. and Canada, or 089/4-80-30. Fax 089/4-48-92-77. www.ichotelsgroup.com. 589 units. 210€–390€ ($336–$624) double; 300€–580€ ($480–$928) suite. AE, DC, MC, V. Parking 17€ ($27). S-Bahn: Rosenheimer Platz. **Amenities:** 2 restaurants; bar; indoor pool; sauna; salon; room service; laundry service; dry cleaning; nonsmoking rooms. *In room:* A/C, TV, beverage maker, minibar, hair dryer, safe, Wi-Fi.

Hotel Concorde ★   Set on a quiet side street, a few minutes' walk from some of the most frequently visited attractions in town, this efficiently managed hotel has six floors and an elevator. Its desirable location and its proximity to both the British and the American consulates draw a large number of diplomats. Bedrooms have modern, somewhat bland styling, with large, comfortable beds, angular contemporary furnishings, and well-kept bathrooms mostly with shower-tub combinations. Although there are no dining or bar facilities on-site, many restaurants are in the neighborhood.

Herrnstrasse 38-40, 80539 München. ℂ **089/22-45-15.** Fax 089/2-28-32-82. www.concorde-muenchen. de. 71 units. 138€ ($221) double; from 166€ ($266) suite. Rates include buffet breakfast. AE, DC, MC, V. Parking 13€ ($21). Closed Dec 22–Jan 7. U-Bahn: Marienplatz. S-Bahn: Isartor. **Amenities:** Lounge; laundry service; dry cleaning; nonsmoking rooms. *In room:* TV, minibar, hair dryer.

Intercity-Hotel München ★

This government-rated four-star hotel was once a late-19th-century Jugendstil showplace at the southern precincts of Munich's main railway station. Blasted apart during World War II and rebuilt in a bland angular style, its modern interior retains only hints of its Art Nouveau origins. If you're a railway buff, you may be disappointed that you won't be able to watch trains arriving or departing, but that's overcome by the bedrooms that are soundproofed against noise, and are comfortable, contemporary, and suited to the needs of international travelers. As a concession to Munich's unending obsession with folklore, a few of the hotel's bedrooms have Bavarian-style rustic furnishings.

Bayerstrasse 10, 80335 München. ℂ **089/444440.** Fax 089/44444-399. www.intercityhotel.de. 198 units. 90€–261€ ($144–$418) double; 225€–359€ ($360–$574) suite. AE, DC, MC, V. Parking 15€ ($24). U-Bahn or S-Bahn: Hauptbahnhof. **Amenities:** Restaurant; bar; room service; babysitting; laundry service; dry cleaning; nonsmoking rooms. *In room:* A/C, TV, minibar, hair dryer, safe, Wi-Fi.

King's Hotel First Class ★

The interior of King's Hotel (a 4 min. walk from the Hauptbahnhof) sports the most traditional Bavarian decor of any of the many government-rated four-star hotels in Munich. The seven-story building looks, from the outside, like a modern town house, but inside, carved headboards, flowered fabrics, and rich paneling offer a pleasant contrast to the 21st-century anonymity of the area around the city's main railway station. Built in 1987, the hotel was named after a German family that prides itself on the English spelling of its name.

Dachauer Strasse 13, 80335 München. ℂ **089/55-18-70.** Fax 089/55-18-73-00. www.kingshotel.de. 90 units. 160€–250€ ($256–$400) double; from 230€ ($368) suite. Some weekends (Fri–Sun) depending on bookings 84€ ($134) double. AE, DC, MC, V. Parking 13€ ($21). U-Bahn: Hauptbahnhof. **Amenities:** Breakfast room; bar; sauna; laundry service; dry cleaning; nonsmoking rooms; rooms for those w/limited mobility. *In room:* A/C, TV, kitchen (in some), beverage maker (in some), minibar, hair dryer, safe, Wi-Fi.

MODERATE

Adria

Adria has an inviting, friendly atmosphere. The lobby sets the stylish contemporary look, and guest rooms are furnished with armchairs or sofas, small desks, and well-kept bathrooms with shower-tub combinations. Breakfast—a buffet with waffles, cakes, homemade rolls, health-food selections, and even sparkling wine—is served in the garden room. On Sunday, smoked salmon is an added treat.

Liebigstrasse 8a, 80538 München. ℂ **089/24-21-170.** Fax 089/24-21-17999. www.adria-muenchen.de. 45 units. 70€–200€ ($112–$320) double. AE, MC, V. Free parking. U-Bahn: Lehel. Tram: 20. **Amenities:** Laundry service; dry cleaning. *In room:* TV, minibar, hair dryer.

Advokat Hotel

This hotel occupies a six-story apartment house originally constructed in the 1930s. Its stripped-down, streamlined interior borrows in discreet ways from Bauhaus and minimalist models. One Munich critic said the rooms look as if Philippe Starck had gone on a shopping binge at Ikea. The result is an aggressively simple, clean-lined, and artfully spartan hotel with few facilities. The German government gives it three stars. The Advokat lies around the corner from its more upscale neighbor, the Admiral, with which it shares management, but whose rooms often cost more.

There's no restaurant on the premises and no particular extras to speak of other than a cozy in-house bar and a delightful rooftop breakfast. But the prices are reasonable, and the staff is helpful.

Baaderstrasse 1, 80469 München. ℭ **089/21-63-10.** Fax 089/21-63-190. www.hotel-advokat.de. 50 units. 160€–280€ ($256–$448) double. Rates include buffet breakfast. AE, DC, MC, V. Parking 12€ ($19). S-Bahn: Isartor. **Amenities:** Breakfast room; nonsmoking rooms. *In room:* TV, minibar, hair dryer, Wi-Fi.

An der Oper   This five-floor hotel, built in 1969, is superbly located for sightseeing or shopping in the traffic-free malls, and it's just steps from the Bavarian State Theater (p. 168). In spite of its basic decor, there are touches of elegance. Rooms, which range from small to medium, have double-glazed windows, a small sitting area with armchairs, and a table for those who want breakfast in their rooms.

Falkenturmstrasse 11, 80331 München. ℭ **089/290-02-70.** Fax 089/290-02-729. www.hotelanderoper. com. 68 units. 180€–270€ ($288–$432) double; 246€–390€ ($394–$624) apt. Rates include buffet breakfast. AE, MC, V. Parking 15€ ($24). Tram: 19. **Amenities:** Nonsmoking rooms; rooms for those w/limited mobility. *In room:* TV, minibar, hair dryer, Wi-Fi.

Anna Hotel   This building was constructed around 1900 as a four-story office block, and when it was converted into this hotel in 2002, the developers had to evict at least one doctor's office. The streamlined and stylish Anna is a clean, charming, well-managed hotel that's loaded with wood paneling and warm tones of ochre and russet, with touches of yellow-and-black marble in the bathrooms. A collection of postmodern sculptures in the lobby is by Stephan Ester, a well-known local artist. Many clients of this hotel are business travelers, who appreciate the well-choreographed service and secure bedrooms. Four suites in a tower afford exceptionally good views over the city.

1 Schützenstrasse, 80335 München. ℭ **089/59-99-4-0.** Fax 089/59-994-333. www.annahotel.de. 73 units. 195€–370€ ($312–$592) double; 370€–550€ ($592–$880) tower suite. Rates include continental breakfast and nonalcoholic minibar contents. MC, V. Parking 22€ ($35). U-Bahn: Karlsplatz or Hauptbahnhof. **Amenities:** Restaurant; bar; free access to health club and sauna a few buildings away; laundry service; dry cleaning; nonsmoking rooms. *In room:* A/C, TV, minibar, hair dryer, Wi-Fi.

Asam Stadthotel ★ ⓕ𝐢𝐧𝐝𝐬   One of Munich's best family-run hotels, Asam lies in a well-restored prewar building. Its bedrooms are large and airy, and each one is nicely appointed with comfortable, modern pieces. We prefer the accommodations facing the rear garden, with its view of the greenery and the steeples of old churches. Some of the bathrooms contain decadently large bathtubs, and each also comes with a shower.

Josephspitalstrasse 3, 80331 München. ℭ **089/230970-0.** Fax 089/230970-97. www.hotel-asam.de. 24 units. 173€–258€ ($277–$413) double; 274€–397€ ($438–$635) junior suite. AE, DC, MC, V. Parking 22€ ($35). U-Bahn: Sendlinger Tor. **Amenities:** Breakfast room; bar; room service; babysitting; laundry service; dry cleaning; all nonsmoking rooms; 1 room for those w/limited mobility. *In room:* TV, minibar, hair dryer, iron, safe, Wi-Fi.

City-Hotel   This six-story hotel was built in 1972, not far from Munich's main railway station. Positioned midway between three- and four-star status by the local tourist authorities, it manages to combine coziness with a modern and efficient design and is a pleasant contrast to the congestion all around it. Bedrooms are unfussy, uncomplicated, and blandly comfortable. No meals are served other than a buffet breakfast, although there's a simple beer hall–style restaurant on the building's street level, which is popular with the crowd from the many nearby offices and businesses.

Schillerstrasse 3a, 80336 München. ℭ **089/51-55-39-0.** Fax 089/550-36-65. www.city-hotel-muenchen. de. 65 units. 120€–250€ ($192–$400) double. AE, DC, MC, V. Parking 12€ ($19). U-Bahn: Hauptbahnhof.

Amenities: Breakfast room; lounge; babysitting; laundry service; dry cleaning; nonsmoking rooms; rooms for those w/limited mobility. *In room:* A/C, TV, minibar, hair dryer, Wi-Fi.

Cortiina ★ (Finds) Built in 2001, this hotel has a foothold with loyal business clients, most of whom hail from Germany, Switzerland, Austria, and Britain. Rising five stories above a centrally located neighborhood in the heart of Munich, its cozy and warm design reminds us of a high Alpine retreat as it might have been reinvented by an aspiring Frank Lloyd Wright. There's a sheathing of intricately crafted, dark-stained oak and exposed flagstones throughout, and a careful allegiance to the Chinese principles of feng shui. This hotel attracts a good number of European architects, including French-born design superstar Andrée Puttman, who seem to feel at home within the artfully rustic, carefully designed venues.

Ledererstrasse 8, 80331 München. ℂ **089/24-22-49-0.** Fax 089/24-22-49-100. www.cortiina.com. 35 units. 196€–266€ ($314–$426) double; 286€–326€ ($458–$522) suite. Rates include continental breakfast. AE, DC, MC, V. Parking 15€ ($24). U-Bahn: Marienplatz. **Amenities:** Breakfast room; bar; honor bar/ lounge; room service; babysitting; laundry service; dry cleaning; nonsmoking rooms. *In room:* TV, minibar, hair dryer, safe, Wi-Fi.

Erzgiesserei Europe This clean, comfortable, and well-managed government-rated three-star hotel is less expensive than it probably could be. It was designed in a postmodern style in 1984, but its mansard roof and arched, balconied windows suggest early-20th-century architecture. It's in a working-class residential neighborhood, a short subway ride from more interesting haunts. Bedrooms are small but comfortable, with modern furniture; some overlook the carefully landscaped inner courtyard that offers cafe service. The on-site restaurant is decorated in a style of German nostalgia.

Erzgiessereistrasse 15, 80335 München. ℂ **089/12-68-2-0.** Fax 089/12-36-198. www.europe-hotels.org. 106 units. 120€–233€ ($192–$373) double; from 280€ ($448) suite. Rates include breakfast. AE, DC, MC, V. Parking 13€ ($21). U-Bahn: U1 to Steiglmaierplatz. **Amenities:** Restaurant; bar; room service; laundry service; dry cleaning; nonsmoking rooms; rooms for those w/limited mobility. *In room:* TV, minibar, hair dryer, Wi-Fi.

Europäischer Hof Opposite the Hauptbahnhof, this nine-story hotel still has the chapel that served its original inhabitants, an order of Catholic nuns, when it was built in 1960. The establishment now offers simple but clean accommodations, some of which overlook an inner courtyard. Most rooms have some built-in furniture; all have double-glazed windows for soundproofing. Despite its dreary location, the hotel is clean and well managed, with cozy touches. Breakfast is the only meal served, although a likable Italian restaurant occupies part of the building's street level.

Bayerstrasse 31, 80335 München. ℂ **089/55-15-10.** Fax 089/55-15-11-444. www.heh.de. 150 units. 92€–262€ ($147–$419) double. Rates include breakfast. AE, DC, MC, V. Parking 10€ ($16). U-Bahn or S-Bahn: Hauptbahnhof. **Amenities:** Bar; laundry service; dry cleaning; all nonsmoking rooms. *In room:* TV, minibar, safe.

Excelsior ★ This solidly comfortable, government-rated four-star hotel near the Hauptbahnhof prides itself on its restored facade, a pale exterior that replicates its original turn-of-the-20th-century design, which was destroyed in wartime bombings. The hotel's bedrooms are quite spacious, outfitted in a tasteful and conservative style. This is a low-key, discreet, highly Europeanized hotel with a resolute lack of glitter.

Schützenstrasse 11, 80335 München. ℂ **089/55-137-0.** Fax 089/55-137-121. www.excelsior-muenchen. de. 114 units. 190€–285€ ($304–$456) double; 315€–355€ ($504–$568) suite. AE, DC, MC, V. Parking 22€ ($35). U-bahn: Hauptbahnhof. **Amenities:** Restaurant; bar; breakfast-only service; laundry service; dry cleaning; nonsmoking rooms. *In room:* A/C, TV, minibar, hair dryer, Wi-Fi.

WHERE TO STAY IN MUNICH

CENTRAL MUNICH

Four Points by Sheraton München Central   Managed by a well-respected middle-bracket German hotel chain, this government-rated three-star, five-floor hotel was built in the 1960s, but has been renovated many times since. It's about a 5-minute walk from the *Messegelände* (trade fair) and the Oktoberfest grounds. Everything is modern, often attractively so, and some rooms have balconies. All units contain well-kept bathrooms with shower-tub combinations. Other than bar snacks and a generous morning buffet, no food is served, but many dining options are nearby.

Schwanthalerstrasse 111, 80339 München. (C) **800/368-7764** in the U.S. and Canada, or 089/51-08-30. Fax 089/51-08-38-00. www.starwoodhotels.com. 102 units. 140€–280€ ($224–$448) double. AE, DC, MC, V. Parking 15€ ($24). Closed 2 weeks at Christmas. Tram: 18 or 19. **Amenities:** Breakfast room; bar; Jacuzzi; sauna; business center; babysitting; laundry service; dry cleaning; nonsmoking rooms; solarium; rooms for those w/limited mobility. *In room:* TV, minibar, hair dryer, trouser press, Wi-Fi.

Hotel Biederstein (Finds)   Near the Englischer Garten, this B&B is a charmer on the Munich hotel scene. Attractively renovated, it is decorated with designer-style modern furnishings in the minimalist style and is operated by the same people who run Gästehaus Englischer Garten, one of the most charming and heavily booked small inns of Munich. The hotel rents bikes to its guests to ride through the Englischer Garten. Bedrooms are spacious and comfortable; the neat tiled bathrooms have tubs with a shower attachment. A first-rate breakfast is served on the terrace.

Keferstrasse 18, 80802 München. (C) **089/38-99-97-0.** Fax 089/38-99-97-389. www.hotel-biederstein.de. 34 units. 103€–275€ ($165–$440) double; 165€–380€ ($264–$608) suite. AE, DC, MC, V. Parking 8€ ($13). U-Bahn: Münchner Freiheit. **Amenities:** Breakfast terrace; room service; babysitting; laundry service; dry cleaning. *In room:* TV, minibar, hair dryer.

Hotel Brack   For Oktoberfest devotees, this hotel is only a 5-minute walk from the festival grounds. It is also a good location at any time of the year, because it lies south of the center but convenient to much of the city's allure. Residing on a broad, tree-lined avenue, it offers small to midsize bedrooms with soundproof windows. The breakfast buffet is rich and varied at this family-run place, and the helpful staff goes out of its way to accommodate you, including arranging tickets for cultural performances.

Lindwurmstrasse 153, 80337 München. (C) **089/747255-0.** Fax 089/72015015. www.hotel-brack.de. 50 units. 99€–169€ ($158–$270) double; 119€–189€ ($190–$302) triple. Rates include breakfast. AE, DC, MC, V. U-Bahn: Poccistrasse. Free parking. **Amenities:** Breakfast room; laundry service; free bikes; Internet access. *In room:* TV.

Hotel Domus   Although this sleekly modern, five-story hotel is rather large, it has some of the aspects of a private home. It's near the Englischer Garten (p. 142), but parking is not a problem, a fact that endears the hotel to many of its regular clients. On weekends, it draws visitors from other parts of Europe on a sightseeing binge; on weekdays, the place has a high percentage of business travelers. Guest rooms are tastefully furnished in appealing monochromatic earth tones, and to help with an undisturbed night's sleep, the hotel pays special attention to the quality of its carpeting and doors. There's also a well-presented breakfast buffet.

St.-Anna-Strasse 31, 80538 München. (C) **089/21-77-73-0.** Fax 089/22-85-359. www.domus-hotel.de. 45 units. 135€–185€ ($216–$296) double; 165€–200€ ($264–$320) suite. Rates include buffet breakfast. AE, DC, MC, V. Parking 15€ ($24). U-Bahn: U4 or U5 to Lehel. **Amenities:** Restaurant; laundry service; dry cleaning; nonsmoking rooms. *In room:* TV, minibar, hair dryer, Wi-Fi.

Hotel Exquisit ★   One of the most appealing hotels in the Sendlinger Tor neighborhood lies behind a wine-colored facade on a quiet residential street that seems far removed from the heavy traffic and bustle of the nearby theater district. Built in 1988, it has a paneled lobby whose focal point is a lounge that gets busy around 6 or 7pm. The pleasant staff offers a genuine welcome, ushering you up to rooms that are spacious and comfortably furnished. About half overlook an ivy-draped garden.

Pettenkoferstrasse 3, 80336 München. ℭ **089/551-99-00.** Fax 089/551-99-499. www.hotel-exquisit. com. 50 units. 180€–285€ ($288–$456) double; 225€–340€ ($360–$544) suite. Rates include buffet breakfast. AE, DC, MC, V. Parking 18€ ($29). U-Bahn: Sendlinger Tor. **Amenities:** Restaurant; bar; sauna; room service; laundry service; dry cleaning; nonsmoking rooms. *In room:* TV, minibar, hair dryer, Wi-Fi.

Hotel Germania (Kids)

This well-run, government-rated three star hotel was built after wartime damage reduced the vicinity of the railway station to rubble. The boxy, sedate building is not a particularly inspired architectural statement—this is very much a functional hotel geared to busy traffic from business travelers and sightseers. The cost is relatively reasonable, and the rooms, although not plush, are superior to those of other comparable three-star hotels in the same neighborhood. The hotel also offers family rooms that consist of two connected rooms where parents and kids are close together yet independent. An Italian restaurant is on the premises.

Schwanthalerstrasse 28, 80336 München. ℭ **089/59046-140.** Fax 089/591171. www.hotel-germania-muenchen.de. 99 units. 100€–180€ ($160–$288) double. Children 11 and under stay free in parent's room. Rates include buffet breakfast. AE, MC, V. Parking 10€ ($16). U-Bahn or S-Bahn: Hauptbahnhof. **Amenities:** Restaurant; bar; nonsmoking rooms. *In room:* TV.

Hotel Monaco ★ (Kids)

This hotel became prominent when it was voted the most popular government-rated hotel in all of Germany in 1998. A member of the Small Elegant Hotels of the World, the Monaco is still as highly regarded as when it first came to prominence. If we judged a hotel by its generous Bavarian breakfast buffet, we'd rate this one a winner. But its bedrooms, which are spacious, modern, and decorated for comfort, make the Monaco appealing as well. Many rooms can be rented for three guests, making it a favorite with families. Personal service is another feature of this family-run hotel only a few steps from the Hauptbahnhof.

Schillerstrasse 9, 80336 Munich. ℭ **089/54-59-94-0.** Fax 089/55-03-70-9. www.hotel-monaco.de. 27 units. 60€–220€ ($96–$352) double; 90€–290€ ($144–$464) triple. Extra bed 20€–50€ ($32–$80). Rates include continental breakfast. AE, MC, V. Parking 15€ ($24). U-Bahn or S-Bahn: Hauptbahnhof. **Amenities:** Breakfast room; room service; nonsmoking rooms. *In room:* TV, Wi-Fi.

Hotel Olympic ★

Built as a private villa around 1900, this hotel represents one of Munich's most appealing conversions of an antique building into a hip and attractive hotel. The lobby occupies a high-ceilinged, Victorian vestibule that retains many of the original details. Breakfast is served in a large, graciously proportioned dining room that invokes memories of the grand bourgeoisie of the Industrial Revolution. Rooms are minimalist and all white, much more modern than the ground-floor reception areas, but comfortable and well engineered. The hotel has an increasing number of gay clients; it's within a neighborhood loaded with gay bars and hangouts.

Hans-Sachs Strasse 4, 80469 München. ℭ **089/23-18-90.** Fax 089/23-18-91-99. www.hotel-olympic.de. 38 units. 155€–200€ ($248–$320) double; 530€–880€ ($848–$1,408) apt. Rates include buffet breakfast. AE, DC, MC, V. Parking 18€ ($29). U-Bahn: Sendlinger Tor. **Amenities:** Breakfast room; lounge; room service; babysitting; laundry service; dry cleaning. *In room:* TV, minibar, hair dryer, Wi-Fi.

Hotel Reinbold

A no-nonsense, no-frills hotel, within a 3-minute walk of the railway station, the Reinbold delivers what it promises: clean, decent rooms and efficient, polite service. It's a boxy-looking structure of six concrete-and-glass stories. Bedrooms are compact, monochromatic, and pleasantly (but not lavishly) furnished, and contain well-kept bathrooms with shower-tub combinations. No meal other than breakfast is served, but there are many restaurants in this busy neighborhood.

Adolf-Kolping-Strasse 11, 80336 München. © **089/59993-902.** Fax 089/5993-994. www.hotel-reinbold. de. 63 units. 69€–249€ ($110–$398) double; 109€–200€ ($174–$320) suite. Rates include breakfast. AE, DC, MC, V. Parking 15€ ($24). U-Bahn or S-Bahn: Hauptbahnhof. **Amenities:** Bar; room service; laundry service; dry cleaning. *In room:* TV, minibar, hair dryer, trouser press, Wi-Fi.

Hotel Schlicker (Finds)

In spite of its location between a McDonald's and a Burger King, this is a hotel of charm and tradition, with a pedigree going back to 1544. The hotel is in the heart of Munich, just steps away from the landmark Marienplatz and around the corner from our favorite food market in Germany, Viktualienmarkt (p. 165). Only the breakfast room suggests that this place was once an ancient inn: The rest of the hotel is modernized. This friendly, inviting hotel is run by the Mayer family, a tradition since 1897. Bedrooms are comfortable and traditional, each midsize.

Tal 8, 80331 München. © **089/24-288-70.** Fax 089/29-60-59. www.hotel-schlicker.de. 69 units. 118€–200€ ($189–$320) double; 240€–270€ ($384–$432) suite. Rates include buffet breakfast. AE, DC, MC, V. Parking 12€ ($19). U-Bahn: Marienplatz. **Amenities:** Breakfast room; room service. *In room:* TV, minibar, safe (in some), Wi-Fi.

Hotel Splendid-Dollmann im Lehel ★ (Finds)

Check in here if you want an up-to-date hotel that's strewn with antiques, fine paintings, good oriental carpets, and a sense of Munich's gracious past. The venue is an elegant 19th-century town house, fronted with chiseled white stone blocks, in the upscale neighborhood known as the Lehel district. Inside, an attentive staff welcomes you into a small, boutique-style hotel replete with a library-style bar and many of the decorative accessories of an upscale private home. Bedrooms are cozy, colorful, and well maintained, each with a different decorative theme and good reproductions of antique furniture. Literary enthusiasts appreciate that these premises, in an earlier incarnation, sheltered the noted (within Germany) writer of novels, poetry, and children's books, Erich Kästner (1899–1974).

Thierschstrasse 49, 80538 München. © **089/23-808-0.** Fax 089/23-808-365. www.hotel-splendid-dollmann. de. 37 units. 170€–210€ ($272–$336) double; 230€–270€ ($368–$432) suite. Parking 8.50€ ($14). AE, DC, MC, V. U-Bahn: Lehel. **Amenities:** Bar; room service. *In room:* TV, Wi-Fi.

Hotel Torbräu ★

The foundations of this government-rated four-star hotel in the heart of historic Munich date from the 15th century. Although many vestiges of its folkloric exterior attest to the hotel's distinguished past, the bedrooms are modern and reasonably comfortable. All units have well-kept bathrooms, mostly with shower-tub combos. In all, it is a lot more charming than many of its bandbox-modern competitors.

Tal 41, 80331 München. © **089/24-234-0.** Fax 089/24-234-235. www.torbraeu.de. 92 units. 185€–258€ ($296–$413) double; 255€–342€ ($408–$547) suite. Rates include buffet breakfast. AE, MC, V. Parking 15€ ($24). Closed 1 week at Christmas. U-Bahn: Isartor. **Amenities:** 2 restaurants; bar; room service; babysitting; laundry service; dry cleaning; nonsmoking rooms. *In room:* A/C, TV, minibar, beverage maker (in some), hair dryer, safe, Wi-Fi.

Kraft Hotel

One of the most appealing things about this simple, government-rated three-star hotel is its location in the heart of the Altstadt, within a few minutes' walk of the Sendlingertorplatz (the southwest corner or junction of the Altstadt) and a 5-minute walk from the main railway station. Architecturally, it's not very appealing, in the style of boxy architecture so widespread in Munich after World War II, but bedrooms are streamlined and efficiently designed, usually with some built-in furniture. There's no restaurant on the premises, but many dining options are within a short walk.

Schillerstrasse 49, 80336 München. ✆ **089/55-059-40.** Fax 089/55-059-479. www.hotel-kraft.com. 33 units. 100€–190€ ($160–$304) double. Rates include breakfast. AE, DC, MC, V. Parking 10€ ($16). U-Bahn: Sendlinger Tor. **Amenities:** Breakfast room; lounge; room service; laundry service; dry cleaning; non-smoking rooms. *In room:* TV, hair dryer, safe, trouser press, Wi-Fi.

Renner Hotel Carlton (Value)

In the heart of Munich near the Schwabing district and the Englischer Garten (p. 142), the Carlton is the premier hotel of a small hotel chain—and one of the city's best deals. Of the three hotels in this chain, the Carlton offers greater comfort; if the Carlton is full, the Savoy or Antare are both well maintained and fairly comfortable. The trio of hotels lies only a block or so from each other. Bedrooms are small and slightly evocative of a luxurious college dormitory room with writing desks, an occasional sofa, and crisp white linens on the beds.

Fürstenstrasse 12, 80333 München. ✆ **089/28-20-61.** Fax 089/287-87-17-05. www.renner-hotel-ag.de. 32 units. 129€ ($206) double; 139€ ($222) triple. AE, MC, V. U-Bahn: Odeonsplatz. **Amenities:** Breakfast room; laundry service; nonsmoking rooms; Wi-Fi (in public areas). *In room:* TV, minibar, hair dryer, safe.

INEXPENSIVE

Am Markt (Value)

This popular, though not luxurious, Bavarian hotel stands in the heart of the older section. Owner Harald Herrler has maintained a nostalgic decor in the lobby. Behind his reception desk is a wall of photographs of friends or former guests, including the late Viennese chanteuse Greta Keller. As Mr. Herrler points out, when you have breakfast here, you're likely to find yourself surrounded by opera and concert artists; the hotel is close to where they perform. Rooms are small, but modern and neat.

Heiliggeistrasse 6, 80331 München. ✆ **089/22-50-14.** Fax 089/22-40-17. www.hotel-am-markt.eu. 32 units. 79€–109€ ($126–$174) double; 149€ ($238) junior suite. Rates include continental breakfast. AE, MC, V. Parking 11€ ($18). S-Bahn: Marienplatz. **Amenities:** Breakfast room; lounge; room service. *In room:* TV, hair dryer, Wi-Fi.

Hotel Jedermann (Value) (Kids)

If you're put off by Munich's high hotel prices, you'll be happy at the Hotel Jedermann. Its central location and good value make it a fine choice, especially for families on a budget (cribs and cots are available). The old-fashioned Bavarian rooms are generally small, but cozy and comfortable, each with a shower-only bathroom. A generous breakfast buffet is served. Staff attitude here, however, needs a major overhaul.

Bayerstrasse 95, 80335 München. ✆ **089/5432-40.** Fax 089/5432-4111. www.hotel-jedermann.de. 55 units. 75€–189€ ($120–$302) double; 90€–219€ ($144–$350) triple. Rates include buffet breakfast. MC, V. Parking 10€ ($16). U-Bahn or S-Bahn: Hauptbahnhof. **Amenities:** Breakfast room. *In room:* A/C (in some units), TV, hair dryer, safe (in most units).

Hotel Mirabell (Kids)

Those seeking a reasonably priced hotel in the center of town might check into this midsize, family-operated hotel near the Hauptbahnhof. It is especially sought out by families because it rents a trio of small apartments. The hotel is frequently renovated as needed and immaculately kept. Bedrooms are midsize and comfortable, spread across six floors. The furnishings are contemporary, most often in pale woods with pastel prints.

Landwehrstrasse 42, 80336 München. ✆ **089/549-17-40.** Fax 089/550-37-01. www.hotelmirabell.de. 65 units, 3 apts. 92€–102€ ($147–$163) double; 130€–155€ ($208–$248) apt. Rates include breakfast. AE, DC, V. Parking 10€ ($16). U-Bahn: Hauptbahnhof. **Amenities:** Bar; room service; babysitting; laundry service; dry cleaning; nonsmoking rooms. *In room:* TV, hair dryer, Wi-Fi.

Hotel-Pension Am Siegestor (Value) Simplicity itself, this little boardinghouse spreads across a trio of floors in a turn-of-the-20th-century town house near the Siegestor (Victory Arch) monument. (The arch was built in the mid–19th century as a monument to honor the Bavarian Army and was based on the architectural concept of Rome's Arch of Constantine.) The location is ideal, in the university sector west of the Englischer Garten (p. 142) and north of the Hofgarten. Take the rickety elevator to the check-in area on the fourth floor. Bedrooms are filled with old-fashioned furnishings, although some are more modernized. Everything depends on your room assignment. Accommodations don't have bathrooms, but the corridor facilities are generally adequate, and you rarely have to wait in line. The most nostalgic bedrooms are on the top floor. These are small, intimate, and cozy rooms resting under beamed ceilings.

Akademeistrasse 5, 80799 München. (C) **089/399-550.** Fax 089/343-050. www.siegestor.com. 20 units. 60€–100€ ($96–$160) double. No credit cards. No parking. U-Bahn: Universität. *In room:* No phone.

Hotel-Pension Beck ★ (Value) In the increasingly chic Lehel district, close to attractions such as the Deutsches Museum (p. 131), this address is shared by in-the-know travelers on a budget. Rooms ranging from midsize to spacious are found in a stately town house. The establishment is filled with fine carpeting, comfortable beds, pinewood pieces of furniture—all in all, a bright Bavarian ambience. Most accommodations don't have private bathrooms, although the hallway bathrooms are more than adequate in most cases. Don't expect a lot of amenities, but there is free Internet access in the reception area if you use your own laptop.

Thierschstrasse 36, 80538 München. (C) **089/220708.** Fax 089/220925. www.pension-beck.de. 44 units, 7 with bathroom. 50€–55€ ($80–$88) double without bathroom; 72€–76€ ($115–$122) double with bathroom. MC, V. Parking: 6€ ($9.60). U-Bahn: Lehel. Tram: 7. **Amenities:** Breakfast room. *In room:* TV, no phone.

Hotel-Pension Mariandl ★ (Finds) Relatively undiscovered, this is a small Bavarian hotel of charm and character. It is housed in a turn-of-the-20th-century neo-Gothic town house that has retained the aura of a bygone age. When the American forces overran Munich in May of 1945, this mansion was commandeered to be hastily converted into the Femina, now part of postwar history as the first nightclub to open after the war. The high-ceilinged bedrooms are spacious and comfortably furnished. The hotel lies about a mile from the main rail station for Munich yet is only a 10-minute walk from the grounds of Oktoberfest. On the ground floor is the Café am Beethovenplatz, where guests order breakfast. That's about it for amenities, however.

Goethestrasse 51, 80336 München. (C) **089/55-29-10-0.** Fax 089/55-29-10-57. www.hotelmariandl.de. 28 units. 70€–165€ ($112–$264) double. Rates include buffet breakfast. AE, DISC, MC, V. No parking. **Amenities:** Restaurant/cafe. *In room:* No phone.

Hotel Wallis Unpretentious, uncomplicated, and comfortable, this government-rated three-star hotel's Bavarian-inspired interior is warmer and cozier than you'd imagine after a look at its angular postwar exterior. Bedrooms are relatively small, but they were renovated in 1995 and are furnished in a simplified version of Alpine-village style. Only breakfast is served, but many worthwhile restaurants are within a short walk. The staff is polite and helpful to newcomers navigating their way around the city.

Schwanthalerstrasse 8, 80336 München. (C) **089/54-90-29-0.** Fax 089/54-90-29-28. www.hotel-wallis.de. 54 units. 88€–249€ ($141–$398) double. Rates include buffet breakfast. AE, DC, MC, V. Parking: 12€ ($19). U-Bahn: Karlsplatz. **Amenities:** Bar; babysitting; laundry service; dry cleaning; nonsmoking rooms. *In room:* TV, minibar, hair dryer, Wi-Fi.

Kurpfalz This family-owned hotel lies in the center of Munich in a 1927 building that has been renovated and altered many times over the years. Twelve minutes by foot from the main rail station, it is very affordable for such a central location. Luxurious it's not, although its rooms are clean, comfortable, and rather functionally furnished, graced in part with reproductions of Bavarian country pieces. Bedrooms are midsize for the most part, each with a shower-tub combination. The fairgrounds for Oktoberfest lie within a 10-minute walk, and many wine taverns, restaurants, and bars are nearby. The breakfast buffet is extensive and varied. The low rates can rise without notice for certain events, certainly for Oktoberfest, so confirm the price before booking.

Schwanthalerstrasse 121, 80339 München. (℃) **089/540-98-60.** Fax 089/540-98-811. www.kurpfalz-hotel. de. 44 units. 62€ ($99) double. Rates include buffet breakfast. AE, MC, V. Parking 8€ ($13). U-Bahn: Theresienwiese. **Amenities:** Bar; laundry service; dry cleaning; nonsmoking rooms. *In room:* TV, hair dryer, Wi-Fi.

Pension Westfalia ★ (Value) This four-story town house (originally built in 1895) near Goetheplatz is one of Munich's best pensions. It faces the meadow where the annual Oktoberfest takes place. Rooms are rather functional and short on extras, but they are well maintained, each with a small shower-only bathroom. The free parking is on the street, when available.

Mozartstrasse 23, 80336 München. (℃) **089/530377.** Fax 089/5439120. www.pension-westfalia.de. 19 units, 14 with bathroom. 50€–60€ ($80–$96) per person double without bathroom; 68€–82€ ($109–$131) per person double with bathroom. Rates include buffet breakfast. AE, MC, V. Free parking. U-Bahn: Goetheplatz. Bus: 58. **Amenities:** Breakfast room; nonsmoking rooms. *In room:* TV.

Uhland Garni ★ Located in a residential area, just a 10-minute walk from the Hauptbahnhof, the Uhland could easily become your home in Munich. The stately town mansion, built in Art Nouveau style, stands in its own small garden. The hotel offers friendly, personal service, and rooms are soundproof, snug, traditional, and cozy. Bathrooms contain showers, and only breakfast is served.

Uhlandstrasse 1, 80336 München. (℃) **089/54335-0.** Fax 089/54335-250. www.hotel-uhland.de. 30 units. 82€–185€ ($131–$296) double. Rates include buffet breakfast. AE, DC, MC, V. Free parking. U-Bahn or S-Bahn: Theresienwiese. Bus: 58. **Amenities:** Breakfast room; nonsmoking rooms. *In room:* TV, minibar, hair dryer, safe, Wi-Fi (in most).

2 SCHWABING

VERY EXPENSIVE

München Marriott Hotel ★★ Marriott's postmodern style fits appropriately into this verdant setting along the northern tier of Schwabing. Built in 1990, about 4km (2½ miles) north of Munich's historic core, it offers a well-designed, Americanized venue whose German staff welcomes travelers from throughout Europe. Bedrooms are standard and identical, but the lobby is one of the most appealing in Schwabing, with blond wood, marble, potted plants, and sunlight streaming in from all sides. The fitness facilities are among the best of any hotel in town. Residents of the Marriott use the health club for free; nonresidents pay 15€ ($17) for a day pass.

Berliner Strasse 93, 80805 München. (℃) **800/228-9290** in the U.S. and Canada, or 089/36-00-20. Fax 089/3600-2200. www.marriott.com. 290 units. 249€–437€ ($398–$699) double, 420€ ($672) junior suite, from 485€ ($776) suite. AE, DC, MC, V. Parking 19€ ($30). U-Bahn: U6 to Nord Friedhof. **Amenities:** 2 restaurants; bar; indoor pool; whirlpool; health club; sauna; room service; babysitting; laundry service; dry cleaning; nonsmoking rooms; rooms for those w/limited mobility. *In room:* A/C, TV, beverage maker, minibar, hair dryer, safe.

MODERATE

Hotel Leopold ★ (Finds) The core of this unusual hotel is a Jugendstil villa that was built in 1924 as a private home. A modern annex is connected to the original house by a glass-sided passageway, and there's a garden area that belonged to the original house. It's close to an exit road from the Autobahn Nürnberg-Würzburg-Berlin, which gives the place the atmosphere of a suburban motel with plentiful parking. Despite the verdant setting, however, the hotel lies only four subway stops from the Marienplatz, and the Englischer Garten (p. 142) is only a few minutes' walk away. Public areas have traditional Bavarian motifs. Rooms in the old section have been modernized to match the rooms in the new section; all have been made as soundproof as possible.

Leopoldstrasse 119, 80804 München-Schwabing. © **089/367061.** Fax 089/3604-3150. www.hotel-leopold. de. 80 units. 132€–215€ ($211–$344) double; 138€–450€ ($221–$720) suite. Rates include buffet break-fast. AE, DC, MC, V. Parking 2.50€ ($4) uncovered or 4.50€ ($7.20) covered. U-Bahn: U3 or U4 to Münchner Freiheit. **Amenities:** Restaurant; bar; health club; sauna; room service; massage; laundry service; dry cleaning. *In room:* TV, minibar, hair dryer, Wi-Fi.

INEXPENSIVE

Gästehaus Englischer Garten ★★ (Kids) This ivy-covered villa oasis of charm and tranquillity, close to the Englischer Garten (p. 142), provides old-fashioned family atmo-sphere and is one of our preferred stopovers in Munich. The decor of the small to medium rooms has been called "Bavarian grandmotherly"; furnishings include genuine antiques, old-fashioned but exceedingly comfortable beds, and Oriental rugs. Bathrooms with showers are small and not one of the hotel's stronger features, but their maintenance is first-rate. In an annex across the street are 15 small apartments, each with a bathroom and a tiny kitchenette. Ask for room nos. 10, 20, 30, or 90; these are bigger and have better views. In fair weather, breakfast is served in a rear garden.

Liebergesellstrasse 8, 80802 München-Schwabing. © **089/3-83-94-10.** Fax 089/3-83-94-133. www. hotelenglischergarten.de. 25 units, 16 with bathroom. 71€–120€ ($114–$192) double without bathroom, 120€–180€ ($192–$288) double with bathroom, 103€–174€ ($165–$278) apt. AE, DC, MC, V. Parking 8€ ($13). U-Bahn: Münchner Freiheit. **Amenities:** Breakfast room; babysitting; laundry service; dry cleaning; nonsmoking rooms. *In room:* TV, minibar.

---

3 OLYMPIAPARK

MODERATE

Four Points by Sheraton München Olympiapark ★★ (Kids) Near the stadium, right at Europe's biggest sports and recreation center, this hotel will appeal to families who want to be near all the major sports action. Its guest rooms are among the most modern and best kept in the city, and sports heroes, both European and American, often stroll casually through the lobby. There's no need to drive into the city center: The U-Bahn will whisk you there in minutes.

Helene-Mayer-Ring 12, 80809 München. © **800/368-7764** in the U.S. and Canada, or 089/357510. Fax 089/35751800. www.starwoodhotels.com. 105 units. 115€–140€ ($184–$224) double; from 250€ ($400) suite. Children 12 and under stay free in parent's room. Rates include breakfast. AE, DC, MC, V. Free park-ing. U-Bahn: U2 or U3 to Olympia Centrum. **Amenities:** Restaurant; bar; room service; laundry service; dry cleaning; nonsmoking rooms. *In room:* TV, minibar, hair dryer, Wi-Fi.

Holiday Inn Munich Schwabing This hotel, with its twin eight-story towers, was built to house visitors to the 1972 Olympics. It's near the Olympic Stadium (p. 143), about 5km (3 miles) north of the historic center. The lobby is stylish, and bedrooms are outfitted with big, carefully soundproofed windows and contemporary, uncontroversial furnishings. Rooms on the upper floor, facing south, benefit from views of the city and the faraway Alps; others overlook the suburbs and the urban sprawl to Munich's north.

Leopoldstrasse 194, 80804 Munich. (C) **800/465-4329** in the U.S., or 089/38-17-90. Fax 089/38-17-98-88. www.ichotelsgroup.com. 362 units. 185€–200€ ($296–$320) double; from 450€ ($720) suite. AE, DC, MC, V. Parking 18€ ($29). U-Bahn: U3 or U6 to Münchner Freiheit. **Amenities:** 2 restaurants; 2 bars; indoor pool; sauna; room service; babysitting; laundry service; dry cleaning; nonsmoking rooms. *In room:* TV, minibar, hair dryer, beverage maker (in some), trouser press, Wi-Fi.

4 HAIDHAUSEN

VERY EXPENSIVE

München City Hilton ★ The München City Hilton lies beside the Deutsches Museum (p. 131) and the performing arts center, Kulturzentrum Gasteig (p. 169). This low-rise hotel, designed with red brick, shimmering glass, and geometric windows, is reminiscent of a Mondrian painting. Munich's historic center is an invigorating 25-minute walk across the river. Rooms contain modern adaptations of Biedermeier furniture and plush carpeting.

Rosenheimerstrasse 15, 81667 München. (C) **800/455-8667** in the U.S. and Canada, or 089/4-80-40. Fax 089/48-04-48-04. www.hilton.com. 480 units. 341€–409€ ($546–$654) double; from 579€ ($926) suite. AE, DC, MC, V. Parking 15€ ($24). S-Bahn: Rosenheimer Platz. **Amenities:** 2 restaurants; bar; cafe; room service; babysitting; laundry service; dry cleaning; nonsmoking rooms; rooms for those w/limited mobility. *In room:* A/C, TV, minibar, hair dryer, Wi Fi.

EXPENSIVE

Hotel Preysing ★ (Finds) If you want a quiet location and don't mind a hotel on the outskirts, consider the Preysing, located across the Isar near the Deutsches Museum (p. 131). (A short tram ride will bring you into the center of the city.) When you first view the building, a seven-story modern structure, you may feel we've misled you. However, if you've gone this far, venture inside for a pleasant surprise. The hotel's style is agreeable, with dozens of little extras to provide homelike comfort. Fresh flowers are everywhere, the furnishings have been carefully selected, and fresh fruit is supplied daily.

Preysingstrasse 1, 81667 München. (C) **089/458450.** Fax 089/45845444. www.hotel preysing.de. 76 units. 155€–245€ ($248–$392) double; from 258€ ($413) suite. Rates include buffet breakfast. AE, DC, MC, V. Parking 12€ ($19). S-Bahn: Rosenheimer Platz. Tram: 18. **Amenities:** Breakfast room; lounge; room service; babysitting; laundry service; dry cleaning. *In room:* A/C, TV, minibar, hair dryer, Wi-Fi.

5 BOGENHAUSEN

EXPENSIVE

Arabella Sheraton Grand Hotel München ★★ This is the largest hotel in Munich, set in the northern suburb of Bogenhausen, about seven subway stops from downtown Munich. This is a hotel that's hard to ignore, towering as it does 22 stories above the surrounding northern suburbs. On the top floor is Munich's most dramatic swimming pool: You get not only panoramic views of the city and the Bavarian countryside but a waterfall as well. Rooms have been recently upgraded and, though still standardized, show a bit of style in their pine furnishing and striped fabrics, and many have balconies opening onto panoramic views.

Arabellastrasse 6, 81925 München. © **800/325-3535** in the U.S. and Canada, or 089/9-26-40. Fax 089/92-64-86-99. www.starwoodhotels.com. 629 units. 165€–314€ ($264–$502) double; from 724€ ($1,158) suite. AE, DC, MC, V. Parking 15€ ($24). U-Bahn: U4 to Arabellapark. **Amenities:** 2 restaurants; bar; indoor pool; health club; sauna; room service; babysitting; laundry service; dry cleaning; nonsmoking rooms; rooms for those w/limited mobility. In room: A/C, TV, minibar, hair dryer, safe, Wi-Fi.

Hotel München Palace ★★ It's tasteful, it's restrained, it's perfectly mannered, and it's very, very aware of how prestigious a stay here can really be. This hotel is sought out by performers at the nearby theaters and concert halls as a peaceful and nurturing address in Bogenhausen, a stylish residential neighborhood east of Munich's medieval core. Originally built in 1986 as an office building, it was later transformed into a hotel. Public areas are streamlined and contemporary, graced with elaborate hypermodern balustrades on travertine-sheathed staircases. Rooms are immaculate and upscale, and each comes with a luxurious bathroom with a tub-and-shower combo.

Trogerstrasse 21, 81675 München. © **089/419-71-0.** Fax 089/419-718-19. www.hotel-palace-muenchen. de. 74 units. 205€–265€ ($328–$424) double; from 430€ ($533) suite. AE, DC, MC, V. Parking 15€ ($24). U-Bahn: Prinzregentumplatz. **Amenities:** Restaurant; bar; health club; sauna; steam room; room service; laundry service; dry cleaning; nonsmoking rooms; rooms for those w/limited mobility. In room: A/C, TV, minibar, hair dryer, safe, Wi-Fi.

6 UNTERMENZING

MODERATE

Romantik Hotel Insel Mühle ★★ (Finds) Until 1985, this 16th-century stone-sided mill in an isolated position beside the Würm (a tributary of the Isar) was left to ruin and decay. The present-day restoration has retained part of the mill's 1506 construction. Although the hotel's reputation is based mainly on its atmospheric restaurant, its guest rooms provide a charming alternative to Munich's many large, modern hotels. The decor and design of each room is different—some have sloping garretlike ceilings—but all have thick carpets, attractive upholstery, and stylish accessories. The real beauty of the place can be seen in the massive beams of the dining room and in the mellow brick vaults of the wine cellar. There's also a plank-covered wharf where parasols shield diners from the midday sun. The cuisine features well-prepared Bavarian and Continental dishes.

Von-Kahr-Strasse 87, 80999 München-Untermenzing. © **089/8-10-10.** Fax 089/8-12-05-71. www.insel-muehle.com. 38 units. 175€–205€ ($280–$328) double; from 250€ ($400) suite. Rates include buffet breakfast. DC, MC, V. Free parking. S-Bahn: Pasing, then bus 76. **Amenities:** Restaurant; lounge; room service; babysitting; laundry service; dry cleaning; nonsmoking rooms. In room: TV, hair dryer, Wi-Fi.

7 OBERMENZING

MODERATE

Jagdschloss ★ (Finds) In the tree-filled tony suburb of Obermenzing, this century-old *Jagdschloss* (hunting lodge) is a delicious retreat that allows you to enjoy Bavarian country life while remaining close to Munich attractions. The country-house aura, enhanced by various Bavarian artifacts, recaptures the flavors of the past, although you'll still find modern comforts. Much of the stucco and original paneling from the former Jagdschloss remain. You open your bedroom window onto a wooden balcony with boxes of geraniums to welcome another day. It's like a setting for a play called *Springtime in Bavaria*. Bedrooms are snug and cozy, with comfortable furnishings and midsize bathrooms with tub and shower. You won't have to go into Munich at night, since you can stay right at the hotel, enjoying its summer beer garden and restaurant. The kitchen serves regional specialties and the waitstaff runs around in lederhosen.

Alte Allee 21, 81245 München-Obermenzing. (C) **089/820-820.** Fax 089/820-82-100. www.weber-gastronomie.de. 30 units. 119€ ($190) double; 130€ ($208) apt. Rates include buffet breakfast. MC, V. Free parking. S-Bahn: Pasing. **Amenities:** Restaurant; beer garden; babysitting; laundry service; dry cleaning; nonsmoking rooms; rooms for those w/limited mobility. *In room:* TV, hair dryer, safe.

8 NEUHAUSEN

MODERATE

Hotel Rotkreuzplatz This is an unheralded little Munich hotel known to some frugal Germans who check in when visiting the capital. Lying only 5 minutes by subway from the heart of Munich, it is easy to reach, opening onto one of the city's landmark squares. An efficient staff operates this little family business, giving you a warm Bavarian welcome. Bedrooms are completely modernized and comfortable, ranging from small to midsize. Breakfast is included in the price of your room, but it's taken at a nearby cafe. Don't expect a lot of special services or amenities. If your needs are not too demanding, you'll get a good bed for the night and much comfort.

Rotkreuzplatz 2, 80634 München. (C) **089/13-99-08-0.** Fax 089/16-64-69. www.hotel-rotkreuzplatz.de. 56 units. 110€–220€ ($176–$352) double; 140€–300€ ($224–$480) triple. Rates include buffet breakfast. AE, DC, MC, V. Parking 10€ ($16). U-Bahn: Rotkreuzplatz. **Amenities:** Nonsmoking rooms. *In room:* TV, hair dryer, safe, Wi-Fi.

Mercure Hotel München Am Olympiapark This is a chain hotel that lies 5 minutes by public transportation from the city center. If you don't demand traditional styling, it has a lot going for it, especially its amenities that range from a bar, as well as a beer garden, to several health club facilities such as a hot tub and steam room. The bedrooms are newly refurbished and medium in size. A hair dryer can be borrowed in the lobby, which also contains a safe for guests. If you don't want to go into the city at night for amusement, you'll find a lively bar on-site. It costs extra, but the hotel's breakfast buffet is one of the most generous in the area.

Leonrodstrasse 79, 80636 München. (C) **089/126-860.** Fax 089/1268-6459. www.mercure.com. 66 units. 100€–249€ ($160–$398) double. Children 11 and under stay free in parent's room. AE, DC, MC, V. Parking 10€ ($16). U-Bahn: Eonrodplatz. **Amenities:** Bar; beer garden; gym; sauna; business services; laundry service; dry cleaning; all nonsmoking rooms. *In room:* TV, minibar, Wi-Fi.

9 NYMPHENBURG

MODERATE

Kriemhild (Kids) This is one of the best choices for visitors with kids in tow, as it lies in the suburb of Nymphenburg, one of the most famous attractions of Munich, known for its beautiful gardens and leafy parks. From the front door of this well-run establishment, you and the children can walk over to the entrance to Schloss Nymphenburg (p. 136). For the adults, there is also nearby Hirschgarten Park, site of the biggest *Biergarten* in Europe. The government-rated three-star hotel is run exceptionally well with an accommodating staff. The more spacious rooms contain a corner sofa, which can be converted for use as a three- or four-bed family room. In the morning, there's an elaborate buffet breakfast, and at night you can drink beer or wine in a cozy Bavarian-styled *Guntherstube* (beer tavern).

Guntherstrasse 16, 80639 München. ✆ **089/171117-0.** Fax 089/171117-55. www.kriemhild.de. 18 units. 102€–170€ ($163–$272) double; 118€–178€ ($189–$285) suite. Rates include buffet breakfast. AE, MC, V. Free parking. Tram: 16 or 17. S-Bahn: Laim. **Amenities:** Breakfast room; bar; nonsmoking rooms. *In room:* TV, minibar, hair dryer, Wi-Fi.

Laimer Hof ★ (Finds) This Renaissance villa is in one of the most tranquil and exclusive sections of Munich. Nymphenburg Palace, with its enchanting park, lies within an easy walk from the hotel. The villa from 1886 was turned into a hotel in 1937, but a young couple, Sebastian and Alexandra Rösch, took over and made substantial improvements and renovations, turning it into one of the most desirable private hotels of Munich. The bedrooms are completely modernized and furnished in a traditional way, exuding comfort and tradition. The hotel is popular with families, and many of the rooms can be connected to form one unit. A lavish breakfast buffet is part of the deal. The hotel is also within a short walk of Hirschgarten, Europe's biggest beer garden. Jogging, walking, and riding a bike are popular in the Nymphenburg Park.

Laimerstrasse 40, 80639 München. ✆ **089/17-80-38-0.** Fax 089/17-82-007. www.laimerhof.de. 23 units. 105€ ($168) double. Rates include buffet breakfast. AE, MC, V. Free parking. U-Bahn: Rotkreuzplatz, then tram no. 17. Bus: 41. **Amenities:** Breakfast room. *In room:* TV, minibar, safe.

TOP Hotel Erzgiesserei Europe ★ (Finds) This undiscovered hotel lies in the suburb of Nymphenburg, site of the famous palace, yet you are only a 5-minute U-Bahn ride from the center of Munich. If you'd like a little entertainment, there's an English-language cinema just around the corner. Rated four stars by the government, it is a first-class hotel with sleek, modern rooms tastefully and comfortably furnished. It's run by an efficient staff who welcome you to their Alt Wuerttemberg restaurant, serving a first-rate international cuisine, tables overflowing into the garden courtyard in summer.

Erzgiessereistrasse 15, Nymphenburg, 80335 München. ✆ **089/12-68-20.** Fax 089/12-36-198. www.topinternational.com. 106 units. 91€–178€ ($146–$285) double. AE, DC, MC, V. Parking 12€ ($19). U-Bahn: Stiglmaierplatz. **Amenities:** Restaurant; bar; room service; laundry service; nonsmoking rooms; rooms for those w/limited mobility. *In room:* TV, hair dryer, minibar, Wi-Fi.

10 NEAR THE AIRPORT

EXPENSIVE

Kempinski Hotel Airport München ★★ When it was built between the runways of Munich's airports in 1993, it was noted as the most architecturally innovative airport hotel in Europe. Partially owned by Lufthansa, it was designed by a Chicago-based architect of German descent, Helmut Jahn, with a four-story shimmering glass-and-steel exterior and an interior design whose colorful, postmodern accents ward off the monochromatic landscape of the surrounding airport. Despite its proximity to runways, the hotel's guest rooms are soothing and silent, the result of effective soundproofing. A soaring lobby contains a subtropical garden with palms and has views over one of Europe's busiest airports.

Terminalstrasse 20, 85356 München. (℃) **800/426-3135** in the U.S., or 089/9-78-20. Fax 089/97-82-26-10. www.kempinski-airport.de. 389 units. 180€–450€ ($288–$720) double; from 395€ ($632) junior suite. AE, DC, MC, V. Parking 18€ ($29). U-Bahn: Airport. **Amenities:** 2 restaurants; bar; indoor pool; health club; Jacuzzi; sauna; room service; massage; laundry service; dry cleaning; nonsmoking rooms; rooms for those w/limited mobility. *In room:* A/C, TV, minibar, hair dryer, safe.

MODERATE

Golden Tulip Hotel Olymp ★
This family-run hotel offers a classic coziness and a degree of Bavarian charm. Its rich ambience comes from its use of woods such as cherry and walnut and its handmade carvings and antique paintings. In warm weather, guests sit on the terrace enjoying drinks, retreating in winter to the snug fireplace. Bedrooms are midsize to spacious and are furnished with smart, modern styling. Under a wood-beamed ceiling, the restaurant serves a blend of Bavarian specialties and international dishes. The hotel is accessible to all major highways such as the A9 (Exit 69) into Munich, and is only a short ride from the international airport.

Wielandstrasse 3, 85386 München-Eching. (℃) **089/327-100.** Fax 089/32710-112. www.goldentulip.com. 96 units. 89€–120€ ($142–$192) double; from 145€ ($232) suite. Rates include buffet breakfast. AE, DC, MC, V. Free parking. **Amenities:** 3 restaurants; bar; indoor pool; sauna; business services; room service; babysitting; laundry service; dry cleaning, nonsmoking rooms; 1 room for those w/limited mobility. *In room:* A/C, TV, kitchenette (in some), minibar, hair dryer, trouser press (in some), safe, Wi-Fi.

Sheraton Munich Airport Hotel ★
Far better than your often-bleak standard airport hotel, this three floor, red-roofed hotel, a 5-minute shuttle-bus ride from the airport, is filled with grace notes such as top-quality tea or coffee for the in-room beverage makers, deluxe toiletries, voice mail, and so on. A first-class hotel surrounded by greenery, it attracts a lot of international business travelers, plus tourists wishing to be near the airport for a fast getaway the following morning. The architect conceived of this hotel as a Bavarian country house. Bedrooms are generous in size and filled with amenities. Because the hotel offers six different types of bedrooms, from the rather simple, functional doubles to the elaborate, spacious executive rooms, the place attracts everybody from the frugal spender to the business client on a fat expense account. The hotel lies 35 minutes by transportation (provided by a hotel van) from Munich's center.

Freisingerstrasse 80, 85445 Schwaig. (℃) **800/325-3535** in the U.S. and Canada, or 089/927-220. Fax 089/9272-2800. www.starwoodhotels.com. 170 units. 149€–189€ ($238–$302) double; from 200€ ($320) suite. Children 12 and under stay free in parent's room. AE, DC, MC, V. Parking 19€ ($30). **Amenities:** Restaurant; bar; indoor pool; fitness center; sauna; room service; babysitting; laundry service; dry cleaning; nonsmoking rooms; rooms for those w/limited mobility. *In room:* A/C, TV, minibar, beverage maker, hair dryer, trouser press, safe.

Where to Dine in Munich

Munich is one of the very few European cities with more than one Michelin-rated three-star restaurant, and some of its sophisticated eating places are among the finest anywhere. This is where to practice *Edelfresswelle* (high-class gluttony), because you'll find many local specialties and first-class international cuisine. The classic local dish, usually consumed before noon, is *Weisswurst,* herb-flavored white-veal sausages blanched in water.

It is said that Münchners consume more beer than people do in any other German city. Bernd Boehle once wrote: "If a man really belongs to Munich, he drinks beer at all times of the day, at breakfast, at midday, at teatime, and in the evening, of course, he just never stops." The place where every first-time visitor heads for at least one eating and drinking fest is the Hofbräuhaus am Platzl (p. 174).

1 CENTRAL MUNICH

VERY EXPENSIVE

Alois Dallmayr ★★ CONTINENTAL   With a history dating from 1700, this is the most famous delicatessen in Germany. After looking at its tempting array of delicacies from around the globe, you'll think you're lost in a millionaire's supermarket—and, in fact, Dallmayr has been a purveyor to many royal courts. Here you'll find Munich's most elegant consumers. The upstairs dining room serves a subtle German version of Continental cuisine, owing a heavy debt to France. The food array is dazzling, ranging from the best herring and sausages we've ever tasted to such rare treats as vine-ripened tomatoes flown in from Morocco and papayas from Brazil. The famous French *poulet de Bresse* (this Bresse chicken is identified throughout Europe as the most flavorful and tender chicken anywhere), beloved of gourmets, is also shipped in. The smoked fish is fabulous, and the soups are superbly flavored, especially the one made with shrimp. If you're dining alone, you may prefer to sit at the counter instead of a table. This bustling restaurant is crowded at lunchtime.

Dienerstrasse 14–15. 🕐 **089/213-51-00.** Reservations recommended. Main courses 35€–44€ ($56–$70); fixed-price 4-course lunch 72€ ($115); fixed-price 7-course dinner 118€ ($189). AE, DC, MC, V. Tues–Sat noon–2pm and 7–10pm. Tram: 19.

Boettner's ★★★ INTERNATIONAL   Long featured in this guide, Boettner's—in business since 1901 when it first opened as a tea and oyster shop—thrives at a newer location where it has kept its old devotees but also gained new and younger fans. The restaurant is housed in Orlandohaus, a Renaissance structure in the heart of Munich. Culinary fans from yesterday will recognize its wood-paneled interior, which was dismantled and moved to the new site. If anything, the cuisine seems better than ever—at least it's lighter and more refined. Try the lobster stew in a cream sauce and almost any

dish with white truffles. Pike balls appear delectably in a Chablis herb sauce, and succulent lamb or venison appear enticingly in a woodsy morel sauce. Desserts are sumptuous. The French influence is very evident in many traditional Bavarian recipes.

Pfisterstrasse 9. ☎ **089/22-12-10.** Reservations required. Main courses 19€–46€ ($30–$74). AE, DC, MC,
V. Mon–Sat 11:30am–3pm and 6pm–midnight. U-Bahn: Marienplatz.

Ederer ★★ MODERN INTERNATIONAL   Noted as one of the poshest and most
desirable addresses in Munich, and the culinary domain of celebrity chef Karl Ederer, this
restaurant occupies an antique building that's noted for its huge windows, several blazing
fireplaces, very high ceilings, and an appealing collection of paintings. Inspiration for
menu items includes cuisines from Bavaria, France, Italy, and the Pacific Rim, among
others. The menu changes with the seasons and the whim of the kitchen staff, but may
include such starters as marinated sweet-and-sour pumpkin served with shiitake mushrooms, parsley roots, and lukewarm chunks of octopus; or terrine of duckling foie gras
with a very fresh brioche and a dollop of pumpkin jelly. Representative main courses
include a delectable roasted breast of duckling with stuffing, glazed baby white cabbage,
mashed potatoes, and gooseliver sauce, or pan-fried anglerfish with a sauce made from
olive oil, lemon grass, and thyme.

Kardinal Faulhaber Strasse 10. ☎ **089/24-23-13-10.** Reservations required. Main courses 22€–33€
($35–$53); fixed-price 2-course lunch 27€ ($43); fixed-price 3-course dinner 48€ ($77), 5-course dinner
85€ ($136). AE, DC, MC, V. Mon–Sat noon–2:30pm and 6:30–10pm. U-Bahn: Marienplatz or Odeonsplatz

Garden Restaurant ★ MEDITERRANEAN/INTERNATIONAL   This showcase
restaurant in one of Munich's showcase hotels looks like a miniature pastel-colored palace. Its solemnly hushed room, off the bustling hotel lobby, is filled with blooming
plants. Upscale food is served to a cosmopolitan crowd. Menu items are about as culti-
vated and esoteric as any in Munich. Examples include thin noodles with strips of quail
and mushroom sauce, and a "land and sea" salad—a bouquet of greens stuffed with
gooseliver and fresh mushrooms. One of the most sought-after dishes is filet of Dover
sole in lemon-butter sauce, served simply but flavorfully with fresh spinach and boiled
potatoes. Desserts are appropriately lavish and imaginative. Ever had baked curd cheese
ravioli with rhubarb and tonka bean ice cream?

In the Bayerischer Hof Hotel, Promenadeplatz 2–6. ☎ **089/21-20-993.** Reservations recommended.
Main courses 18€–35€ ($29–$56). AE, DC, MC, V. Daily noon–3pm and 6–11:30pm. Tram: 19 or 21.

G-Munich ★★ INTERNATIONAL   Arguably the most innovative and avant-garde
restaurant in Munich, this place welcomes you with startling lighting—the candles seem
to float. A far cry from the beer, sausage, and dumpling joints, it serves such divine creations as gooseliver crème brûlée. We urge you to savor such dishes as tartare of suckling
veal with a purée of white beans, followed by glazed quail with potatoes and a purée of
green Mediterranean olives and caper-flavored butter. You can be sure the chefs are in
complete control as you sample such mains as roast rack of venison with a ragout of wild
mushrooms, or mullet from the Breton coast with a tomato and herb ravioli. Among the
luscious desserts is a yogurt terrine with blackberry sorbet and a sugared tomato. Deliv-
ered in labeled paper bags, a selection of breads is served with a carousel of three virgin
olive oils and three kinds of salt.

Geyerstrasse 52. ☎ **089/7474-7999.** Reservations required. Main courses 18€–34€ ($29–$54); fixed-
price menus 76€–98€ ($122–$157). AE, MC, V. Restaurant Tues–Sat 6–11pm. Bar and lounge daily 3pm–
2am. Closed Dec 23–Jan 7 and Mar 21–24. U-Bahn: Südbahnhof.

WHERE TO DINE IN MUNICH

6

CENTRAL MUNICH

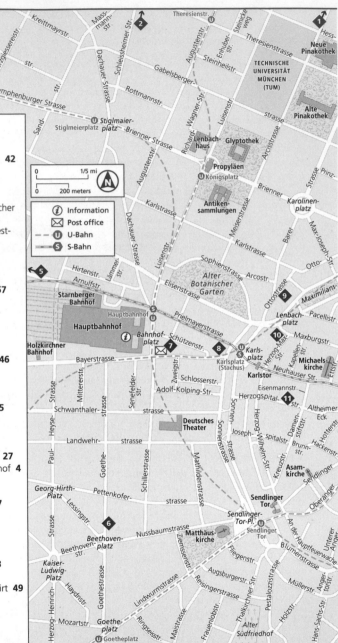

Acquarello **57**
Alba **57**
Alois Dallmayr **41**
Andechser am Dom **42**
Asam Schlössl **18**
Austernkeller **23**
Bibulus **36**
Biergarten Chinesischer
  Turm **37**
Bier- und Oktoberfest-
  museum **21**
Bistro Cézanne **34**
Bistro Terrine **35**
Boettner's **38**
Bogenhauser Hof **57**
Buon Gusto
  (Talamonti) **22**
Café am
  Beethovenplatz **6**
Café Dukatz **26**
Café Glockenspiel **46**
Café Luitpold **30**
Casale **57**
Cohen's **32**
Der Katzlmacher **55**
Deutsche Eiche **15**
Donisl **47**
Ederer **28**
Garden Restaurant **27**
Gasthof Weichandhof **4**
Gaststätte zum
  Flaucher **18**
Geisel's Vinothek **7**
Grüne Gans **14**
Guglhopf **44**
Hackerhaus **13**
Halali **31**
Hard Rock Cafe **53**
Hirschgarten **5**
Hofer – der Stadtwirt **49**
Käfer-Schänke **57**
La Bouille **1**
La Galleria **51**
La Terrazza **2**

To Schloss Nymphenburg

Information
Post office
U-Bahn
S-Bahn

0   1/5 mi
0   200 meters

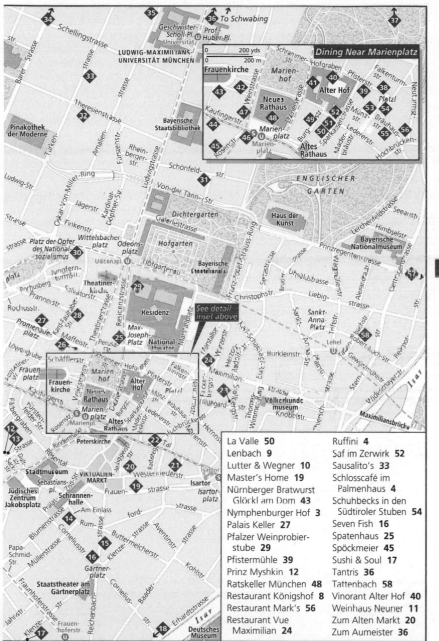

La Valle **50**
Lenbach **9**
Lutter & Wegner **10**
Master's Home **19**
Nürnberger Bratwurst
  Glöckl am Dom **43**
Nymphenburger Hof **3**
Palais Keller **27**
Pfalzer Weinprobier-
  stube **29**
Pfistermühle **39**
Prinz Myshkin **12**
Ratskeller München **48**
Restaurant Königshof **8**
Restaurant Mark's **56**
Restaurant Vue
  Maximilian **24**

Ruffini **4**
Saf im Zerwirk **52**
Sausalito's **33**
Schlosscafé im
  Palmenhaus **4**
Schuhbecks in den
  Südtiroler Stuben **54**
Seven Fish **16**
Spatenhaus **25**
Spöckmeier **45**
Sushi & Soul **17**
Tantris **36**
Tattenbach **58**
Vinorant Alter Hof **40**
Weinhaus Neuner **11**
Zum Alten Markt **20**
Zum Aumeister **36**

Restaurant Königshof ★★★ INTERNATIONAL/FRENCH   This is one of Munich's grand hotel dining rooms, with oyster-white oak panels, polished bronze chandeliers, silver candelabra, and porcelain. The waiters are polite and skilled, the chefs highly inventive. This venerated restaurant just seems to get better and better. The cuisine is dazzling, light, full of flavor, and prepared with only the finest of ingredients. For the most discerning foodies in Germany, this restaurant is a must on their gastronomic itineraries. Sit back and succumb to the exquisite and varied pleasures of the intelligent, graceful cuisine that emerges from the kitchen. Among the favorite dishes we've sampled are sautéed anglerfish with wild garlic and vine-ripened cherry tomatoes, or turbot with fresh morels. Especially delectable is a saddle of bison with sautéed polenta, eggplant, and young onions. Lobster appears with a delightful vanilla butter, and loin of lamb is aromatically seasoned with fresh herbs.

In the Hotel Königshof, Karlsplatz 25 (Am Stachus). ℂ **089/55-136-0.** Reservations required. Main courses 36€–46€ ($58–$74); fixed-price menus 90€–130€ ($144–$208). AE, DC, MC, V. Tues–Sat noon–2:30pm and 7–10pm. S-Bahn: Karlsplatz. Tram: 19, 20, or 21.

Restaurant Vue Maximilian ★ FRENCH/INTERNATIONAL   Restaurant Vue Maximilian is in a quiet and elegant location within walking distance of the opera house. The atmosphere is dignified and refined, the service extremely competent, and the food prepared along classic French lines with imaginative variations, including Asian influences. The menu changes every 4 to 6 weeks. You may begin with crayfish with asparagus and a green parsley mousse, or a terrine of boiled beef and horseradish. For a main course, try pan-fried filet of char with fresh vegetables or a filet of Bavarian beef with roasted wood mushrooms and truffled celery.

In the Hotel Vier Jahreszeiten Kempinski München, Maximilianstrasse 17. ℂ **089/2125-0.** Reservations required. Main courses 20€–32€ ($32–$51); fixed-price 4-course menu 82€ ($131). AE, DC, MC, V. Daily noon–3:30pm and 6–11:30pm. Tram: 19.

Schuhbecks in den Südtiroler Stuben ★★★ BAVARIAN/INTERNA-TIONAL   This luxe restaurant is at the very top of all the restaurants of Bavaria, given serious competition only by Tantris (p. 118). Chef Alfons Schuhbeck enjoys well-deserved celebrity. East meets West in his fusion cuisine, which some critics liken to "California freestyle." At the top of his menu, the chef welcomes you with "modest greetings," but there is nothing modest about the cuisine. The menu is forever changing, based on the freshest and best ingredients in any season. Some of our favorite starters include fish soup made with freshwater fish and crayfish, given added zest with a touch of curry; marinated tuna fish with caviar and vegetable jelly; and the truffle-infused pasta with Parmesan and summer vegetables. We also adore such main dishes as saddle and tongue of veal with pan-fried asparagus and a carrot and celery purée, or the combination stuffed rabbit shank and grilled duck breast with Roman flour dumplings.

An Platzl 6–8. ℂ **089/21-66-900.** Reservations required. Fixed-price menus 78€–123€ ($125–$197). AE, DC, MC, V. Tues–Sat 11am–3pm; Mon–Sat 6–11pm. U-Bahn/S-Bahn: Marienplatz.

EXPENSIVE

Austernkeller ★ SEAFOOD   This "oyster cellar" is a delight to both visitors and locals, with the largest selection of oysters in town. Many gourmands make an entire meal just of Austernkeller's raw oysters; others prefer them elaborately prepared—for example, oysters Rockefeller. A delectable dish to start is the shellfish platter with fresh oysters, mussels, clams, scampi, and sea snails. Or you might begin with a richly stocked fish soup or cold hors d'oeuvres. French meat specialties are offered, but most guests prefer the fish dishes—no other chef in Munich can make a lobster Thermidor as good as that served here. The restaurant, under a vaulted ceiling, has a refined atmosphere, and it makes successful attempts at genuine elegance; but because of a collection of everything from plastic lobsters to old porcelain, the decor comes off as a bit kitschy. However, the service is attentive, and you'll enjoy your meal.

Stollbergstrasse 11. (℃) **089/298-787.** Reservations required. Main courses 20€–32€ ($32–$51). AE, DC, MC, V. Daily 5pm–1am. Closed Dec 23–26. U-Bahn: Isartor.

Buon Gusto (Talamonti) ★ ITALIAN/TUSCAN   This is among the finer Italian restaurants in Munich. Its interior features two dining areas, a simple, rustic-looking bistro overlooking an open kitchen, and a more formal dining room. Menu items and prices are identical in both areas. Owned and managed by an extended family, the Talamontis, whose members are likely not to speak English, the place emphasizes fresh ingredients, strong and savory flavors, and food items inspired by the Italian provinces of the Marches and Tuscany. Delectable examples include ravioli stuffed with mushrooms and herbs, roasted lamb with potatoes, lots of different forms of scaloppine, and fresh fish served simply, with oil or butter and lemon. The risottos are especially flavorful. During Oktoberfest and trade fairs, the place is mobbed.

Hochbrückenstrasse 3. (℃) **089/29-63-83.** Reservations recommended. Main courses 19€–35€ ($30–$56). AE, MC, V. Mon–Sat 11am–1am. Closed Dec 23–Jan 3. U-Bahn or S-Bahn: Marienplatz.

Restaurant Mark's ★★★ FRENCH/CONTINENTAL   This restaurant in the Mandarin Oriental hotel is appropriately elegant with an impeccably trained staff. Lunch is served in a small, cozy enclave off the lobby, Mark's Corner, and is usually limited to a fixed-price menu favored by businesspeople. Dinners are more elaborate, served one floor above street level in a formal dining room that overlooks a monumental staircase and the lobby. On Sunday and Monday nights only, the formal dining room is closed, and dinner is served in Mark's Corner. Menus change monthly and according to the whim of the chef. Many dishes are somewhat experimental but still succeed beautifully, such as filet of beef with a ragout of artichokes and potatoes and deep-fried baby garlic buds; sea wolf with green lentils, bacon, and gooseliver; and filet of beef with horseradish, served with dumplings and Savoy cabbage.

In the Mandarin Oriental, Neuturmstrasse 1. (℃) **089/29098-875.** Reservations recommended. Main courses 29€–32€ ($46–$51); fixed-price lunch 79€ ($126); fixed-price dinner 100€ ($160). AE, DC, MC, V. Daily noon–2pm and 7–11pm. U-Bahn or S-Bahn: Marienplatz.

Seven Fish ★ SEAFOOD   Some of the best and freshest fish dishes are served at this first-class restaurant lying a short walk from the famous Munich open-air market, Viktualienmarkt. Based on the freshest catch of the day, the menu is forever changing. The smartly executed cuisine was created by two Greek brothers who know their fish. At a small bar, you can enjoy Japanese-style sushi or else sit at one of the main tables, some of which overflow onto the square out front in fair weather.

Gärtnerplatz 6. (℃) **089/23-00-02-19.** Reservations recommended. Main courses 20€–30€ ($32–$48). AE, MC, V. Daily 10am–11pm. U-Bahn: Marienplatz.

MODERATE

Der Katzlmacher ★ (Finds) ITALIAN   Few Italian restaurants would have had the nerve to adopt as their name a pejorative German term referring to Italians. This one did, however, and its sense of humor has helped make it beloved by loyal local fans. The setting is a postwar building near the university, with dining rooms that are evocative of an elegant and rustic mountain lodge high in the Italian Alps. Stylish and theatrical, and filled with well-dressed, prosperous-looking clients, it contains lavishly carved paneling, masses of artfully arranged flowers, and huge amounts of charm. The cooking is based on the culinary traditions of the Marches, Friuli, and Emilia-Romagna, all known for their fine cuisines and agrarian bounty. The owner is Claudio Zanuttigh, who supervises specialties that might include calzone stuffed with spinach and pine nuts, carpaccio of duck breast, a commendable grilled swordfish with red-wine vinaigrette, eel with champagne sauce, and a succulent version of *fritto misto del pesce* (mixed fried fish) based on whatever is in season.

Bräuhausstrasse 6. ✆ **089/333360.** Reservations recommended. Main courses 18€–28€ ($29–$45); fixed-price lunch menus 16€–27€ ($26–$43); fixed-price dinner menus 41€–54€ ($66–$86). MC, V. Mon–Sat noon–3pm and 6:30–11pm. U-Bahn: Marienplatz.

Dukatz ★ INTERNATIONAL/FRENCH Our hangout in Munich is this cafe/restaurant that pays tribute to the writer Oskar Maria Graf (1894–1967) and is decorated with Graf memorabilia. Jenny Holzer, the New York artist, was called in to carry out the Graf theme. She took sentences from Graf's writings and inscribed them on the cafe's leather benches and on the plates. You'll have to finish your meal to see what Graf had to say. A typical remark: "It must soon be that I am famous." Munich is the center of publishing in Germany, and writers, editors, and readers drop in throughout the day for coffee and cake.

This is no mere coffeehouse, however. The restaurant serves full-fledged meals with some of the Bavarian countryside's finest ingredients. At lunch, try a sandwich such as the baguette with rabbit or the pastrami with sauerkraut. At dinner, we have enjoyed salmon in champagne sauce with fresh oysters. The *Blutwurst* in pastry, with diced apples, was better than the typical *boudin noir* in a French bistro. For dessert, try the pear tart with almond cream.

Maffeistrasse 3. ✆ **089/71040737-3.** Reservations not needed. Main courses 15€–28€ ($24–$45). No credit cards. Mon–Sat noon–2:30pm and 6:30–10:30pm; Sun 10am–7pm. U-Bahn: Marienplatz.

Geisel's Vinothek ★ ITALIAN/INTERNATIONAL This hotel eatery is a cozy enclave of rustic charm that evokes an unpretentious trattoria high in the Italian Alps. It's known for its assortment of Italian, French, Austrian, and German wines, dispensed by the glass. You can sit at the bar or, if you want a meal, at one of about a dozen tables. The menu is meant to be a savory foil for the wine: Some of the best examples include anglerfish medallion with avocado, mint, and crispy bacon; cold sliced roast beef with a rémoulade sauce; or a delectable breast of duck with broccoli, apricots, and almond cream.

In the Hotel Excelsior, Schützenstrasse 11. ✆ **089/55-13-71-40.** Reservations recommended for dining, not necessary for wine tasting. Main courses 14€–22€ ($22–$35). Glass of wine 3€–8€ ($4.80–$13). AE, DC, MC, V. Restaurant daily noon–2:30pm and 6:30pm–midnight; wine tasting on Mon once a month noon–1am. U-Bahn: Hauptbahnhof.

Grüne Gans BAVARIAN/CHINESE/INTERNATIONAL If you're visiting Viktualienmarkt (p. 165)—and we suggest that you do—this small and intimate dining room is a good reliable choice in the area. After looking at all the delectable foodstuffs that Münchners purchase, you will have whetted your appetite. "The Green Goose" tempts you with a range of dishes, most of which are Bavarian. The chefs dip less successfully into international cuisine, with a selection of Chinese dishes tossed in for fun. The Bavarian pork dishes are the most recommendable, although you may want to begin with one of the fresh salads purchased directly from the market nearby. The soups are excellent, especially the cream of chervil soup we sampled. Many good sausages are offered along with some beef specialties. They also do excellent calf's kidneys in a velvety smooth sauce made with freshly chopped tarragon. Many people in show business patronize this bustling little tavern, as the pictures on the walls testify.

Am Einglass 4. © **089/266-228.** Reservations recommended. Main courses 19€–28€ ($30–$45). No credit cards. Mon–Sat 5pm–1am. U-Bahn: Marienplatz.

Halali BAVARIAN Little has changed since this place was first decorated around 1900, and very few of the staff or its clients would ever want change. The setting is baronial, devoted to a Teutonic version of the Hunt, as its name (which translates into something akin to "Tally-Ho") suggests. Amid high ceilings, solid archways, and a collection of stags' horns, you can order flavorful traditional dishes, including the specialties of the house, terrine of venison and *Blutwurst* (blood sausage). These may be followed by filet of venison in wine sauce and succulent versions of grilled Bavarian duck, guinea fowl, or pheasant served in either Beaujolais or cranberry sauce, depending on the whim of the chef. A traditional, popular dessert is a warm apple tart with vanilla sauce. Everything is prepared with a definite style and flair. You get very good value here.

Schönfeldstrasse 22. © **089/28 59 09.** Reservations recommended. Main courses 20€–24€ ($32–$38), fixed-price dinner 52€ ($83). AE, MC, V. Mon–Fri noon–3pm and 6pm–midnight. U-Bahn: Odeonsplatz.

Hard Rock Cafe (Kids) AMERICAN This international chain member packs them in for its bar grub. Like all Hard Rocks around the world, it's filled with memorabilia, with artifacts or representations of everybody from Eric Clapton to Madonna. If you've ever dined at a Hard Rock, expect the same here, the usual array of juicy burgers, fajitas, and steaks served with tasty sides in giant portions. Their homemade-style meatloaf will make you think you're back in Kansas, though their pasta Bolognese could use a lot of improvement. You come here for the fun, the diversion, and the amusement more than the food, however.

Platz 1. © **089/242-9490.** Reservations required Fri and Sat. Main courses 10€–22€ ($16–$35). AE, MC, V. Sun–Thurs noon–1am; Fri–Sat noon–2am. S-Bahn: Marienplatz.

La Galleria ★ ITALIAN This is one of the most appealing of the several Italian restaurants in Munich's center. It provides gracious service and a roster of dishes that change with the availability of ingredients and the inspiration of the chefs. Examples are poached sea wolf with fresh vegetables in fennel sauce, an aromatic guinea fowl scented with lavender, homemade spaghetti with white Italian truffles, herb-flavored risotto with chunks of lobster and braised radicchio (the best we've had in Munich), and roasted soft-shell crabs with a light onion sauce.

Sparkassenstrasse 11. © **089/297995.** Reservations recommended. Main courses 18€–25€ ($29–$40); fixed-price dinners 40€–55€ ($64–$88). AE, DC, MC, V. Mon–Sat noon–2:30pm and 6:30–11:30pm. U-Bahn or S-Bahn: Marienplatz.

Lenbach ★ CONTINENTAL/ASIAN Aggressively hip and aesthetically striking, this is one of the most sought-after and iconoclastic restaurants in Munich. It occupies a landmark brick-and-stone building, erected in 1887, that originally functioned as the home and sales outlet for the era's most flamboyant antiques dealer, who frescoed its interior with Renaissance murals. An unusual blend of hypermodern and Renaissance motifs greets clients here, whose path to their table is along a slightly elevated catwalk that evokes a runway where supermodels might strut their stuff before a phalanx of photographers.

Delectable menu items include a rack of Iberian pork with garlic or boiled veal with risotto and fresh vegetables. Thai curry appears with tiger prawns, or you might order the sea bass with an unusual potato-and-pomegranate risotto. For starters, try beef steak tartare with homemade walnut hash browns or grilled octopus with fresh grapefruit.

Ottostrasse 6. ℂ **089/549130-0.** Reservations recommended. Lunch main courses 8.50€–15€ ($14–$24); dinner main courses 20€–29€ ($32–$46). AE, DC, MC, V. Mon–Sat 11:30am–2:30pm and 6pm–midnight. U-Bahn: Stachus.

Lutter & Wegner INTERNATIONAL/MEDITERRANEAN   The elaborate baroque styling of the building that contains this restaurant was completed in 1898 as the headquarters of a publicly funded association of artists. In the 1980s, it was adapted into a network of dining rooms. Today it's been taken over by a restaurant chain (Lutter & Wegner) that's well known within Germany and Austria. Dining areas range from functional and contemporary looking to lush. Favorite spots include the lavishly baroque Venezia Room or the Weinhandlung. The Kunstler Lounge evokes the decorative flair used in other parts of Bavarian by Mad Ludwig. Menu items include a creamy fennel and orange soup; curried wurst or schnitzels with potatoes; entrecôte steaks with potato salad; zanderfish with a purée of celery; saltimbocca with mango chutney; rack of veal stuffed with pesto, tomato ragout, and baked Parmesan; and a creamy veal *gulasch* with *spatzle* and mushrooms.

Im Künstlerhaus, Lenbachplatz 8. ℂ **089/54-59-49-0.** Reservations recommended. Main courses 16€–22€ ($26–$35). AE, MC, V. Daily 11am–midnight. U-Bahn: U4 or U5 to Stachus.

Master's Home ITALIAN   If you like the idea of dining in a place that looks like a flea market, head here. Opened in 1988, the restaurant resides in a former private home, and dining areas include tables placed in a former bathroom or in the living room. The singles bar here is one of the hottest in town (p. 172), and many people come just to drink. The bar, filled with antique wood furnishings, evokes a gentlemen's club in London's Edwardian era. The menu is forever changing, so we can't recommend specialties. Past delights—and likely to be featured again—include grilled filet of ostrich, with buttery potatoes and a mixed salad; carpaccio of salmon with an arugula salad; a delectable fettuccine with black truffles; and baked breast of duck.

Frauenstrasse 11. ℂ **089/22-99-09.** Reservations recommended. Main courses 8€–20€ ($13–$32); 8-course fixed-price menu 45€ ($72). AE, DC, MC, V. Restaurant daily 6pm–1am. Bar daily 6pm–4am. S-Bahn: Isartor.

Pfistermühle BAVARIAN   The country comes right into the heart of Munich at this authentic and old-fashioned place, a series of charmingly decorated dining rooms in a converted old mill. A warm welcome and a refreshing cuisine await you here. Many of the dishes would be familiar to your Bavarian grandmother, and portions are generous and satisfying. Come here for some of the most perfectly prepared roasts in the city, always served with a selection of fresh vegetables. Or you can opt for a fine array of simply prepared fresh fish from the lakes and rivers of Bavaria, especially the delectable salmon trout or brown trout. Most fish dishes come with chive-flecked sour cream and a potato pancake. Finish with a pyramid of vanilla custard served with a fresh berry sauce followed by a glass of wild-cherry schnapps.

In the Platz Hotel, Pfistermühle 4. ℂ **089/23-703-865.** Reservations recommended. Main courses 13€–20€ ($21–$32). AE, DC, MC, V. Mon–Sat noon–11pm. U-Bahn: Marienplatz.

Ratskeller München BAVARIAN   Throughout Germany, you'll find Ratskellers, traditional cellar restaurants in Rathaus (city hall) basements, serving decent and inexpensive food and wine. The decor is typical: dark wood and carved chairs. The coziest tables are in the semiprivate dining nooks in the rear, under the vaulted painted ceilings. Bavarian music adds to the ambience. The menu, generally a showcase of regional fare, includes some international dishes, many of them vegetarian or lighter in content than the usual German fare served in town cellars. Delectable menu items include ocean filet of cod sautéed in butter and served with a German potato salad or *Schweinshaxe* (roast pork shank), baked with a crunchy crust and served with potato dumplings and red cabbage.

In Rathaus, Marienplatz 8. © **089/21-99-89-0.** Reservations required. Main courses 10€–24€ ($16–$38). AE, MC, V. Daily 10am–midnight. U-Bahn or S-Bahn: Marienplatz.

Spatenhaus BAVARIAN/INTERNATIONAL The Spatenhaus, one of Munich's best-known beer restaurants, has wide windows overlooking the opera house on Max-Joseph-Platz. You can sit in an intimate, semiprivate dining nook or at a big table. Spatenhaus has traditional Bavarian food and generous portions at reasonable prices. If you're curious about the fabled Bavarian gluttony, order the Bavarian plate, which is loaded with various meats, including pork and sausages. (After that, you'll have to go to a spa.) Other fine choices include grilled filets of lemon sole with a creamy lobster sauce, roast pork with potato dumplings and red cabbage, and grilled salmon with ricotta-stuffed ravioli. Of course, to be loyal, you should order the restaurant's own beer, Spaten-Franziskaner-Bier. A dining annex on the second floor, open daily from 11:30am to 1am, specializes in international cuisine, including brook trout or roast salmon steak with noodles in a lobster sauce, as well as Angus beef with a red-wine sauce with fried potatoes. Main courses in the annex cost 18€ to 24€ ($29–$38).

Residenzstrasse 12. © **089/290706-0.** Reservations recommended. Main courses 9.20€–28€ ($15–$45). AE, MC, V. Daily 9:30am–12:30am. U-Bahn: Odeonsplatz or Marienplatz.

Vinorant Alter Hof ★ (Value FRANCONIAN In a castle in the heart of the city, this restaurant serves the best Franconian regional cuisine in Munich. In the basement is a wine bar where you can enjoy inexpensive snacks and the best of regional wines. Upstairs a more formal cuisine is served, including an excellently prepared fixed-price menu. This old favorite adjusts its menus to take advantage of the best ingredients in any season—game in autumn, fresh asparagus in the spring. Although cooking for the masses, the chefs manage to create distinctive flavor in their dishes. Desserts are yummy and made fresh daily, great on flavor, and heavy on calories.

Alter Hof 3. © **089/24-24-37-33.** Reservations recommended in main restaurant. Main courses 16€–22€ ($26–$35). DC, MC, V. Mon–Sat 11:30am–11:30pm. U-Bahn or S-Bahn: Marienplatz.

Weinhaus Neuner BAVARIAN/INTERNATIONAL This is an *Ältestes Weinhaus Münchens* (Old Munich Wine House), one of the city's landmark taverns. Dating from the late 15th century, it's the only building in Munich with its original Tyrolean vaults. The place brims with warmth and charm. Once young priests were educated here, but after Napoleon brought secularization, it became a wine tavern and a rendezvous for artists, writers, and composers, including Richard Wagner. The casual *Weinstube* is the less formal section and has lots of local atmosphere. New dishes on the menu include mussels with braised lemons and fresh asparagus in a basil sauce. The filet of turbot with fresh mushrooms in a champagne sauce is sublime, as is the carpaccio of filet of beef with fresh herbs and truffle-flavored vinaigrette. Finish with a homemade sorbet with a pineapple ragout.

Herzogspitalstrasse 8. © **089/2-60-39-54.** Reservations recommended. Main courses 18€–24€ ($29–$38); fixed-price lunch 18€–23€ ($29–$37); fixed-price dinner 37€ ($59). AE, MC, V. Mon–Sat 11:30am–3pm and 5:30–midnight. U-Bahn or S-Bahn: Karlsplatz/Stachus.

Zum Alten Markt (Value BAVARIAN/INTERNATIONAL Snug and cozy, Zum Alten Markt serves beautifully presented fresh cuisine. Located on a tiny square off Munich's large outdoor food market (Viktualienmarkt), the restaurant has a mellow charm and a welcoming host, Josef Lehner. The interior decor, with its intricately coffered wooden ceiling, came from a 400-year-old Tyrolean castle. In summer, tables are set up outside. Fish and fresh vegetables come from the nearby market. You may begin with a tasty homemade soup, such as cream of carrot or perhaps black-truffle tortellini in cream sauce with young onions and tomatoes. The chef makes a great Tafelspitz (boiled beef). You can also order classic dishes such as roast duck with applesauce or a savory roast suckling pig.

Am Viktualienmarkt, Dreifaltigkeitsplatz 3. ⓒ **089/29-99-95.** Reservations recommended. Main courses 13€–18€ ($21–$29). No credit cards. Mon–Sat noon–midnight. U-Bahn or S-Bahn: Marienplatz. Bus: 53.

INEXPENSIVE

Andechser am Dom GERMAN/BAVARIAN   This restaurant and beer hall is set on two floors of a postwar building adjacent to the rear of the Frauenkirche. It serves beer brewed in a monastery near Munich (Andechser) and generous portions of German food. You're welcome to order a snack, a full meal, or just a beer. Menu items are often accompanied with German-style potato salad and green salad and include such dishes as veal schnitzels, steaks, turkey croquettes, roasted lamb, fish, and several kinds of sausages that taste best with tangy mustard. In clement weather, tables are set up on the roof and on the sidewalk in front, both of which overlook the back of one of the city's finest churches.

Weinstrasse 7A. ⓒ **089/298481.** Reservations recommended. Main courses 6.50€–15€ ($10–$24). AE, DC, MC, V. Daily 10am–1am. U-Bahn or S-Bahn: Marienplatz.

Bier- und Oktoberfest Museum ★ ⓕ Finds BAVARIAN   Nothing in Munich is this authentically Bavarian. The Augustiner Brewery operates this museum and restaurant as a non-profit organization in one of Munich's oldest buildings, going back to 1327. You can visit the museum and learn a lot about beer and even Oktoberfest. After the tour, you're given a voucher for a Bavarian snack and a glass of brew for only 4€ ($6.40). The snack includes the famous Camembert-like cheese of Munich, *Obatzda*, as well as *Leberwurst* (liver sausage). Your doctor may not like it, but to go Bavarian all the way you can spread *Schmalz* (chicken fat) over your freshly baked rye bread. After 6pm, stick around for the regional Bavarian fare, starting perhaps with a beer-infused goulash and noodles and following with sausage salads or schnitzels and the like. Naturally, everything is washed down with the Augustiner brew.

Sterneckstrasse 2. ⓒ **089/2423-1607.** Reservations not needed. Main courses 4€–6.90€ ($6.40–$11). No credit cards. Museum Tues–Sat 1–5pm. Beer Hall Tues–Sat 6pm–midnight. U-Bahn or S-Bahn: Isartor.

Café am Beethovenplatz BAVARIAN/INTERNATIONAL/VEGETARIAN   This eatery can be patronized as either a cafe or a full-fledged restaurant at its location between Pettenkoferstrasse and Beethovenplatz. It's a bit of a charmer and relatively unnoticed by visitors. A grand piano takes up one section of the spacious dining room. At night, the works of many composers—not just Ludwig—are performed here. It's sort of old-fashioned and a bit corny, very Middle Europe, and that's why it's so beloved locally. In addition to the classics, you can also hear jazz. Many patrons drop in for breakfast from a large menu, especially recommended on a Sunday when live classical music is heard. Many in-the-know guests come here for the pork dishes, and roast pig *(Schweinebraten)* is the specialty. The restaurant has a deal with a farmer in Bavaria who is said to raise free-range pigs that are fed an excellent diet. In addition to the pork, an array of international dishes and even some vegetarian specialties are offered as well.

Goethestrasse 51. ⓒ **089/552-9100.** Reservations not needed. Main courses 8€–21€ ($13–$34). AE, MC, V. Daily 9am–1am. U-Bahn: Goetheplatz.

Cohen's JEWISH/CENTRAL EUROPEAN   This joint serves food like that available in Munich before the war and the dreaded Holocaust. Come here for the tastes and flavors of another era, everything washed down with Golan wines imported from Israel. We'd visit just to eat Cohen's potato salad, but you can have so much more, including gefilte fish, latkes, and wonderful goulash dishes. Roast hen appears with couscous, and a delicious green split pea soup is also served. Naturally the matzo ball and noodle soup is delectable. Singers perform on Friday evenings.

Theresienstrasse 31, Maxvorstadt. ✆ **089/280-9545.** Reservations recommended. Main courses 9€–12€ ($14–$19). AE, MC, V. Mon–Sat noon–3pm and 6–10:30pm. U-Bahn: Theresienstrasse.

Deutsche Eiche GERMAN   The building was constructed in 1864, and there's been a restaurant with a mostly gay, or at least arts-oriented, clientele since its debut. In the 1970s, Fassbinder, the noteworthy film director, hung out here, usually dressed in chains and leather. In the 1990s, the place was renovated into a less evocative, more streamlined-looking beer hall, still with a healthy percentage of gay clients, with direct access to a 26-room hotel and one of the busiest gay saunas in Munich. Rooms in the hotel are relatively affordable at 110€ to 135€ ($176–$216) for a double. Each has a TV and telephone and an all-white, efficient-looking collection of furnishings.

However, we recommend the place as a restaurant/bar. Simple beer hall–style food includes escalope of pork with french fries, turkey steak with mushrooms in cream and homemade noodles, and a filet of pork with roasted potatoes and fresh vegetables.

Reichenbachstrasse 13. ✆ **089/23-11-66-0.** Reservations not necessary. Main courses 10€ 16€ ($16–$26). AE, MC, V. Daily 7am–1am. U-Bahn: Fraunhoferstrasse

Donisl BAVARIAN/INTERNATIONAL   Donisl is one of Munich's oldest beer halls, dating from 1715. Readers have praised this restaurant as *gemütlich* (cozy, pleasant), with its relaxed and comfortable atmosphere, although the seating capacity is about 550. In summer, you can enjoy the hum and bustle of the Marienplatz by dining in the garden area out front. The restaurant has two levels, the second of which is a gallery. Most of the staff speaks English. The standard menu offers traditional Bavarian food as well as a menu of weekly changing specials. A specialty is *Weisswurste*, the little white sausage that has been a decades-long tradition of this place. Select beers from Munich's own Hacker-Pschorr Brewery top the evening. A zither player at noon and an accordion player in the evening entertain diners.

Weinstrasse 1. ✆ **089/22-01-84.** Reservations recommended. Main courses 6€–8€ ($9.60–$13). AE, DC, MC, V. Daily 9am–midnight. U-Bahn or S-Bahn: Marienplatz.

Hackerhaus BAVARIAN   Back in the 1400s, Bavarian beer drinkers flocked here to celebrate the opening of yet another brewery, Hacker-Pschorr. It's still going strong today. We have Bavarian friends who maintain that Pschorr is their favorite beer even to this day. If Josef Pschorr, who was born in 1770 and was a famous brewery king of Bavaria, were by some miracle to pay a visit today, he wouldn't be surprised at the offerings of the kitchen, especially at the specialty, "Josef Pschorr's own roast beef with rémoulade sauce" and fried potatoes. The list of Bavarian specialties here reads like a classic from Grandmother Bavarian's kitchen, including calf's lungs and bread dumplings or Bavarian ravioli on sauerkraut with onions. Of course, there are more familiar regional dishes such as pork knuckle with potato dumplings and a cabbage salad. Other favorites include pork cutlets stuffed with ham and cheese or filet of beef in a green-pepper-and-cream sauce. Wood-paneled dining rooms spread over three floors. In summer, beer drinkers spill into an inner courtyard. The restaurant's beer tavern, the Bürgerstube, houses what is reportedly the world's largest mug.

Sendlingerstrasse 14. $\copyright$ **089/260-5026.** Main courses 7€–30€ ($11–$48). AE, MC, V. Daily 9am–midnight. U-Bahn: Marienplatz.

Hofer—der Stadtwirt BAVARIAN A restaurant called Weinstadl has stood here longer than anyone remembers. Its origins, in fact, go back to 1551. For some reason, this tavern has recently undergone a name change, although it remains its historic self. At least it didn't become a McDonald's! Right off the Marienplatz, it is a good place to wind down and cool off in summer as you settle into its beer garden. The fountain depicts a Bavarian burgher enjoying a glass of wine and is much photographed. In winter, the place changes, as drinkers and diners retreat inside to a vaulted room, sitting at tables fronted with benches. These tables are freely shared, and there is a convivial, fun-loving atmosphere. The menu is predictable, but the food is quite good. The Vienna goulash is good and spicy. The boiled beef is another favorite, and is well done, as is the roast chicken salad with potatoes. Every day there are 15 to 20 specials.

Burgstrasse 5. $\copyright$ **089/242-10-444.** Main courses 8.50€–23€ ($14–$37). AE, DC, MC. Mon–Sat 10am–12:30am; Sun 10am–4pm. U-Bahn: Marienplatz.

La Valle ★ (Kids) ITALIAN Right off the Marienplatz in the heart of Munich, this is one of the best restaurants and pizzerias in town. There's an elegant bar for a pre-dinner drink, the interior is decorated in a classic Italian style, and the service from the largely "south of the border" staff is among the finest in the area. Luigi, the owner, is always on hand to provide menu advice, especially about the day's creations of fish, pasta, or meat specialties. For starters, the minestrone is about the best in Munich, as are the pastas, especially the rigatoni with onions and bacon in a hot tomato sauce. Pizzas come with toppings ranging from cheese and mushrooms to salami. There's always a grilled fish of the day, perhaps king prawns with fresh herbs, each with fresh vegetables. The best meat dish is the tender veal in a white wine–and–lemon sauce.

Sparkassenstreet 5. $\copyright$ **089/29-16-06-76.** Reservations recommended. Small main courses and pizzas 6.80€–13€ ($11–$21); main courses 13€–18€ ($21–$29). AE, MC, V. Daily 11am–12:30am. U-Bahn or S-Bahn: Marienplatz.

Nürnberger Bratwurst Glöckl am Dom ★ (Value) BAVARIAN The homesick Nürnberger comes here just for one dish with those delectable little sausages: *Nürnberger Schweinwurst mit Kraut.* You can also find such items as crispy roast pork with bread dumplings and cabbage salad, veal breast stuffed with a potato-and-cucumber salad, or boiled ox with diced vegetables and fried potatoes. This restaurant first opened in 1893. It was rebuilt after World War II, and it is now the coziest and warmest of all local restaurants. Chairs look almost as if they were hand-carved, and upstairs, reached through a hidden stairway, is a dining room hung with reproductions of Dürer prints. Tables are shared, and food is served on tin plates. Last food orders go in at midnight. A short walk from Marienplatz, the restaurant faces the Frauenkirche.

Frauenplatz 9. $\copyright$ **089/291945-0.** Reservations recommended. Main courses 10€–20€ ($16–$32). MC, V. Daily 10am–1am. U-Bahn: U2 or U3 to Marienplatz.

Palais Keller ★★ (Value) BAVARIAN/GERMAN Massive, with a high turnover and a sense of bustling energy, this richly folkloric restaurant is down a flight of stone steps, deep in the cellar of one of Munich's finest hotels. Despite its elegant associations, its prices are competitive with those of Munich's many beer halls. Waitresses speak English and wear frilly aprons and genuine smiles. There is a tempting array of such German dishes as veal in sour cream sauce with glazed turnips, cabbage, and carrots; pike balls on buttery leaf spinach with shrimp sauce; and Tafelspitz with horseradish and vinaigrette sauce. Some diners, especially those who make the place a regular stopover, order whatever *Tagsteller* (platter of the day) is served, with a foaming mug of beer or one of the many German wines.

In the Hotel Bayerischer Hof (Palais Montgelas), Promenadeplatz 2. ℂ **089/2-12-09-90.** Reservations recommended. Main courses 6€–20€ ($9.60–$32). AE, DC, MC, V. Daily 10am–midnight. Tram 19.

Pfalzer Weinprobierstube ★ GERMAN/PALATINATE   Former chancellor Helmut Kohl used to patronize this place for one dish: *Saumagen*, which is an herb-infused meatloaf baked in a pig's stomach. This time-honored favorite has earned the *Stube* (old-country home-style Bavarian restaurant) its culinary reputation—that and other dishes such as original Palatinate-style (from a region of Germany bordering France) grilled sausage and vintner's spicy roast pork. The chef is big on bellies here (and you'd get one too if you dined here every day), including grilled pork belly. For more modern tastes, there is baked filet of white fish. Every morning the cooks prepare soups that Bavarians have eaten for centuries, including liver dumpling soup Palatinate-style and goulash soup. If you'd like an assortment of Palatinate specialties, including liver sausage and baked ham, you can order a farmhouse platter. There is one of the best cheese selections in town here, including old-fashioned favorites. There is also a large selection of good wines.

Residenzstrasse 1. ℂ **089/225-628.** Reservations not taken. Main courses 8€–13€ ($13–$21). DC, MC, V. Daily 10am–11:30pm. U-Bahn: Odeonsplatz.

Prinz Myshkin VEGETARIAN   This popular vegetarian restaurant near the Marienplatz offers freshly made salads, some macrobiotic selections, Indian and Thai vegetarian dishes, as well as vegetarian *involtini* (stuffed roll-ups) and casseroles, soups, and zesty pizzas, many of which are excellent. You can sample such dishes as a potato-zucchini truffle gratin with lamb's lettuce and a honeynut dressing or else homemade buckwheat crepes filled with spinach, ricotta, and Parmesan cheese in an herb-laced cream sauce. Roulettes of Swiss chard come with roasted nuts, fresh mushrooms, and tofu in an herb-flavored cream sauce, and you can also order tofu stroganoff with steamed broccoli and carrots.

Hackenstrasse 2. ℂ **089/265596.** Reservations recommended. Main courses 8€–16€ ($13–$26). AE, MC, V. Daily 11am–12:30am. U-Bahn or S-Bahn: Marienplatz.

Saf im Zerwirk ★ Finds VEGAN   How times have changed around here. In a building some 7 centuries old, wild game used to be skinned and butchered around the corner from the Hofbräuhaus, that famous beer palace. Today this vegan, part raw food establishment serves a plant-based cuisine created by Chad Sarno, who uses organic produce. Most dishes are cooked at a very low temperature to preserve optimal flavor and nutrition. The claim is that such uncooked vegan food cleanses the body of destructive toxins. Try such innovative dishes as lasagna with black truffles and macadamia nuts or beetroot ricotta ravioli with a cashew filling. A cauliflower risotto comes with a seared sage polenta with tempura shiitake mushrooms drizzled in truffle oil. Desserts are spectacular, including "drunken fruits" in a bitter cocoa syrup with a passion fruit crème with kiwi relish and hemp brittle. For your drink of choice, have you ever had a tarragon-laced gin tonic?

Lederstrasse 3. ℂ **089/2323-9191.** Reservations recommended. Main courses 5.50€–19€ ($8.80–$30). AE, MC, V. Mon–Sat 11:30am–4pm and 6pm–midnight. U-Bahn or S-Bahn: Marienplatz.

Spöckmeier BAVARIAN *Weisswurst,* those little white sausages of Munich, are king here. Locals flock here to devour them in the early morning, along with mugs of beer, of course. Both breakfast and beer drinking start early, as the waitresses bring out fat breakfast sausages. Some diners, mainly men, start their pretzel consumption at breakfast as well. You can drop in anytime until late at night, ordering as little or as much as you want. The draft beers, a selection of four, flow throughout the day. Lunch might be a simple affair, including roast beef with a salad and freshly baked bread. One favorite among locals is *Eintopf,* a rich flavored broth of slivers of pork and homemade noodles. If you like hearty fare, you can sample such main dishes as cabbage and minced meat roll with bacon sauce and boiled potatoes or else Wiener schnitzel with cranberry sauce. This is a true Bavarian beer restaurant, with tables placed on three floors. For a true Bavarian atmosphere, retreat to the intimate *Keller* (cellar).

Rosenstrasse 9. (℃) **089/268-088.** Reservations not needed. Main courses 12€–30€ ($19–$48). AE, DC, MC, V. Daily 9:30am–midnight. U-Bahn: Marienplatz.

Sushi & Soul JAPANESE Huge windows open onto a quiet residential street. Expect big airy spaces, flickering candles, and a minimalist decor whose main ornamentation derives from a hip and stylish crowd of good-looking singles and couples. The menu is based on sushi, salads, and hot Japanese food. Fresh ingredients go into the tasty fare, a refreshing change of pace from the typical Bavarian diet.

Klenzestrasse 71. (℃) **089/20-10-992.** Reservations recommended. Main courses 9€–40€ ($14–$64). AE, MC, V. Daily 6pm–1am. U-Bahn: Fraunhoferstrasse.

Tattenbach BAVARIAN Cozy and accommodating, this restaurant offers a dark-paneled, German-traditional decor, and a youthful counterculture clientele. Menu items are *gutbürgerlich* (traditional) and flavorful, with emphasis on Italian-style pastas, gnocchi, salads, sauerbraten, and beef filets in pepper sauce. Don't expect grandeur or spit-and-polish formality, because the venue is relatively unpretentious and low-key. In summer, a beer garden opens.

Tattenbachstrasse 6. (℃) **089/22-52-68.** Reservations recommended. Main courses 11€–19€ ($18–$30). No credit cards. Mon–Fri 11am–1am; Sat–Sun 5pm–1am. U-Bahn: Lehel.

2 NEAR THE ISAR, SOUTH OF THE CENTER

INEXPENSIVE

Asam Schlössl BAVARIAN/INTERNATIONAL This Augustiner brewery restaurant offers a relaxed, relatively informal hideaway amid the congestion of Munich. The building was built as a private villa in 1724. Some of the original castlelike design remains, though the structure has been expanded and renovated over the years. All brews offered are products of Augustiner, including both pale and dark versions of *Weissebier,* beer fermented from wheat. Menu items include such typical Bavarian fare as *Böffla-mott* (beef braised in red wine) with *Semmelknödel* (bread dumplings), and a dish beloved by Emperor Franz Josef of Austria, *gesottener Tafelspitz mit frischen Kren,* a savory form of the familiar boiled beef with horseradish.

Maria-Einsiedel-Strasse 45. (℃) **089/723-63-73.** Reservations not needed. Main courses 7.50€–20€ ($12–$32). AE, MC, V. Daily noon–1am. U-Bahn: Thalkirchen.

3 SCHWABING

This district, which was called "bohemian" in the 1940s, overflows with restaurants. Many of them are awful, but there are several good ones, some of which attract a youthful clientele. The evening is the best time for a visit.

VERY EXPENSIVE

Tantris ★★★ MEDITERRANEAN/INTERNATIONAL   Tantris serves Munich's finest cuisine. Chef Hans Haas was once voted the top chef in Germany, and he has refined and sharpened his culinary technique since. The setting is unlikely: a drab commercial area, with bare concrete walls and a garish decor. But inside, you're transported by the fine service and excellent food that's a treat for the eye as well as the palate. The choice of dishes is wisely limited, and the cooking is subtle and original. You may begin with a terrine of smoked fish served with a green cucumber sauce and follow with classic roast duck on mustard-seed sauce or a delightful concoction of lobster medallions on black noodles.

Johann-Fichte-Strasse 7, Schwabing. (*C*) **089/36-19-59-0.** Reservations required. Fixed-price 4-course lunch 96€ ($154); fixed price 5-course dinner 125€ ($200), 8-course dinner 145€ ($232). AE, DC, MC, V. Tues–Sat noon–3pm and 6:30–10:30pm. Closed public holidays, annual holidays in Jan and May. U-Bahn: Dietlindenstrasse.

EXPENSIVE

Bistro Terrine ★★ FRENCH   The restaurant looks like an Art Nouveau French bistro, and its nouvelle cuisine is based on traditional recipes as authentic and savory as anything you'd find in Lyon or Paris. The dining room is arranged, with banquettes and wood and glass dividers, in a way that makes it seem bigger than it is. During clement weather, there's additional seating on an outdoor terrace. Menu items are innovative, and may include tartar of herring with freshly made potato chips and salad, watercress salad with sweetbreads, cream of paprika soup, an autumn fantasy of nuggets of venison served with hazelnut-flavored gnocchi in port wine sauce, zander baked in an herb-and-potato crust, or an alluring specialty salmon with a chanterelle-studded risotto. The most satisfying desserts may include a traditional *tarte tatin* (a tart filled with, usually, apples) or even an old-fashioned crème brûlée.

Amalienstrasse 89. (*C*) **089/28-17-80.** Reservations recommended. Main courses 23€–32€ ($37–$51); fixed-price dinner menus 75€–85€ ($120–$136). AE, MC, V. Tues–Fri noon–3pm; Mon–Sat 6:30–11:30pm. U-Bahn: U3 or U6 to Universität.

MODERATE

Bibulus ★ ITALIAN   If you come here in the summer and sit on the outdoor terrace with its garden view, it's easy to believe that you've suddenly been transported to the Mediterranean. The interior is full of streamlined furnishings and dramatic, oversize modern paintings. Menu items come from all over Italy, but the favorites are those from the owner's native Friuli, near Venice. In season there's lavish use of asparagus, arugula, shellfish, rabbit, wild mushrooms, and venison in such alluring preparations as ravioli stuffed with lobster, tagliatelle, rotini, linguini with braised radicchio and shellfish, and, when available, saltimbocca (veal with prosciutto).

Siegfriedstrasse 11. (*C*) **089/396447.** Reservations recommended. Main courses 16€–23€ ($26–$37); fixed-price lunch menus 12€–17€ ($19–$27); fixed-price dinner 37€ ($59). AE, DC, MC, V. Mon–Fri noon–2:30pm; daily 6:30–11pm. U-Bahn: Münchner Freiheit.

Bistro Cézanne ★ (Finds) FRENCH   Chef and owner Patrick Geay operates this undiscovered little Parisian-style bistro, which has glamour, charm, and flair. On his blackboard menu, he chalks his specialties of the day, based on that morning's market-fresh ingredients. We'd dine here for his vegetable preparations alone—they're that good. Although his menu is forever changing, we have enjoyed his delightful scallops, cooked just right, and served in a sauce of truffles. His masterpiece is pigeon served with fresh goat cheese. Other succulent menu choices include a risotto of rabbit with flap mushrooms; foie gras with an eggplant-flavored vinaigrette; stingray with capers and lemon; and calves' liver with sage butter. The bistro is lined with copies of paintings by mostly impressionists, including Van Gogh and (of course) Cézanne.

Konradstrasse 1. (C) **089/391-805.** Reservations required. Main courses 16€–22€ ($26–$35). AE, MC, V. Tues–Sun 6pm–1am. U-Bahn: Giselastrasse. Tram: 27.

La Bouille FRENCH/MEDITERRANEAN   Sunny Provence is celebrated at this restaurant, which opened in 2004 to immediate success. In elegant surroundings, you're welcomed with a smile. Friendly service, fine French wines, and, most of all, the flavor-filled cooking redolent of olive oil and the aromas of Provence prevail here. Recommended are perfectly prepared dishes that included pigeon with green cabbage, rack of lamb with a fresh olive crust, and a tender and beautifully flavored breast of duck. Save room for one of the artfully crafted desserts.

Neureutherstrasse 15, at Arcisstrasse. (C) **089/399936.** Reservations recommended. Main courses 18€–23€ ($29–$37); fixed-price menus 48€–58€ ($77–$93). DC, MC, V. Mon–Fri 12:30–2:30pm and 7pm–midnight; Sat 7pm–midnight; Sun 6:30–11pm. U-Bahn: Josephsplatz or Universität.

INEXPENSIVE

Sausalito's MEXICAN   Imagine a sprawling labyrinth of rooms whose layout and lighting suggest a German beer hall. Then imagine that instead of boozy, middle-aged clients swilling beer, it's loaded with young, nubile students from the nearby university. Add to that a heady blend of tequila-based party-colored drinks and tacos, and you'll have the equivalent of spring break in Daytona Beach with a German accent. Come here to drink, dialogue, mingle, and chow down on fajitas, enchiladas, quesadillas, steaks, burritos, and burgers.

Türkenstrasse 50. (C) **089/28-15-94.** Main courses 12€–18€ ($19–$29). AE, MC, V. Daily 5pm–12:30am. U-Bahn: Universität.

4 BOGENHAUSEN/PRIELHOF

VERY EXPENSIVE

Acquarello ★★★ ITALIAN/MEDITERRANEAN   One of Bavaria's greatest Italian restaurants pursues a cuisine so classical and sublime, it may cause gourmets to want to drive south for the sunny flavors of Italy. Large wall murals and soft classical music set the stage for perfectly prepared and imaginative specialties. The owner and host, Mario Gamba, sums up a dining experience here this way: "We're like a perfume that one associates with a lovely experience and whose fragrance is remembered for a lifetime." A bit of overstatement, but the chefs are really skilled. Among the light yet earthy repertoire of dishes is a lobster carpaccio with orange mayonnaise and basil oil. The ravioli is stuffed with ricotta and served with walnuts on melted butter. An especially good dish is John

Dory under a leek crust with a mustard-seed sauce with beet gnocchi. For dessert nothing tops the chocolate ravioli with mint ice cream served with an orange sauce.

Muelbauerstrasse 36. ℂ **089/470-4848.** Reservations required. Main courses 22€–38€ ($35–$61). Fixed-price menus 39€–98€ ($62–$157). AE, MC, V. Mon–Fri noon–2pm; daily 6:30–10:30pm. U-Bahn: Bohmer-wald-Platz.

EXPENSIVE

Alba ★ ITALIAN   In the upscale neighborhood of Prielhof, this is one of Munich's most glamorous bistros. It was once a sophisticated French-Austrian restaurant, and the decor remains Austrian and urbane; a green ceramic *Kachelofen* (porcelain stove) dominates one side of the dining room. Menu items are influenced by a lighter Italian cuisine and are based on whatever is good, fresh, and of high quality at the market. Savor the subtle balance of flavors and plan to make an evening of it, because it's a convivial place for food and drink. The tortellini *di patate* (made with potatoes) is a succulent starter or else you may opt for spaghetti *à la diabla* (with hot sauce) with fiery red peppers. The sea bass with fresh asparagus is delicate and savory. At meal's end, a *gelato à la limon* (ice cream made from fresh lemons) is soothing.

Oberföhringer Strasse 44. ℂ **089/985353.** Reservations required. Main courses 16€–30€ ($26–$48). No credit cards. Mon–Fri noon–2:30pm; Mon–Sat 6–11pm. U-Bahn: U-4 to Arabellapark.

Bogenhauser Hof GERMAN/INTERNATIONAL   In the verdant residential suburb of Bogenhausen, 5km (3 miles) east of the Marienplatz, this stylish and well-liked restaurant occupies a stately looking villa that was built as a hunting lodge in 1825. With its reputation for well-conceived food and intelligent, sensitive service, the restaurant has flourished since it was established in the mid-1980s. You'll dine in a high-ceilinged dining room decorated in a wood-paneled style, or in good weather, outside in a manicured garden beneath the spreading limbs of massive chestnut trees. The cuisine is as elegantly prepared as the decor; only market-fresh ingredients are used, deftly handled by the skilled chefs. The menu changes seasonally, but is likely to include a salad of fresh wild greens garnished with grilled scampi and rock lobster; or carpaccio of venison with fresh herbs and olive oil. Filet of turbot is prepared any way you like. The chef usually suggests champagne sauce and white truffles, or perhaps with lobster sauce, depending on the season. Equally appealing is rack of young lamb with turmeric sauce, served with fresh green beans and gratin of potatoes.

Ismaninger Strasse 85, Bogenhausen. ℂ **089/985586.** Reservations recommended. Main courses 26€–36€ ($42–$58). AE, DC, MC, V. Mon–Sat noon–2:30pm and 6–10:30pm. Closed Dec 24–Jan 6 and 10 days at Easter. U-Bahn: U5 to Max-Weber-Platz, then tram 18 to Essnerplatz or Sternbadstrasse.

Käfer-Schänke GERMAN/INTERNATIONAL   This is a great spot for casual dining with elegant style, in a setting that evokes a chalet. It's located on the second floor of a famous gourmet shop called Käfer. The cuisine roams the world for inspiration—from Lombardy to Asia. You select your hors d'oeuvres from the most dazzling display in Munich. Often Käfer-Schänke devotes a week to a particular country's cuisine. On one visit, we enjoyed the classic soup of the French Riviera (sea bass with fennel). From a cold table, you can choose smoked salmon or smoked eel. Venison, quail, and guinea hen are also regularly featured.

Prinzregentenstrasse 73. ℂ **089/41-68-247.** Reservations required. Main courses 25€–42€ ($40–$67). AE, DC, MC, V. Mon–Sat noon–11pm. Closed holidays. U-Bahn: Prinzregentenplatz. Bus: 53 or 54.

MODERATE

Casale ★ ITALIAN   One of the more restrained, discreet, and formal of Munich's many Italian restaurants, with an upscale decor more self-consciously "expensive" than many of its competitors, this restaurant is north of the city center, near the megahotels of the Bogenhausen district. It works hard on such tours de force as a nine-course *menu dégustazione* that requires several hours to consume gracefully. Menu items are savory and stylish and usually served with flair: sea bass prepared with rosemary in a salt crust, filet of beef with Barolo sauce, and an array of pastas that include ravioli stuffed with pulverized veal and spices and an excellent linguine with fresh asparagus or exotic seasonal mushrooms.

Ostpreussenstrasse 42. ☎ **089/936268.** Reservations recommended. Main courses 17€–28€ ($27–$45); fixed-price menus 41€ ($66). AE, MC, V. Daily noon–2:30pm and 6–10:30pm. U-Bahn: U4 to Arabellapark.

6 NYMPHENBURG

EXPENSIVE

Nymphenburger Hof AUSTRIAN   Many Münchners consider an outing to this restaurant's verdant outdoor terrace, about 9.5km (6 miles) west of the Marienplatz and about 5km (3 miles) from Schloss Nymphenburg (p. 136), the next best thing to a week in the country. Although the modern blue-and-white interior is attractive in any season, the place is especially appealing in summer when the terrace, separated from the busy avenue by a screen of trees, is open. Don't expect even a hint of tradition, because everything here is streamlined and modern. The only nostalgic thing about the place is the courtly but amused service and the cuisine, inspired by what used to be known as the Austro-Hungarian Empire. Examples include Wiener schnitzel, Tafelspitz (the favorite of Austrian Emperor Franz Josef), *Kaiserschmarr* (a sweet dessert made with apples), a variety of Czech pastries made with honey and plums, and the gooey, sticky dessert beloved across the border, *Salzburger nockerl* (a light and creamy dessert made from eggs, vanilla, sugar, and butter).

Nymphenburger Strasse 24. ☎ **089/1-23-38-30.** Reservations recommended in summer. Main courses 17€–25€ ($27–$40); fixed-price menus 55€–73€ ($88–$117). AE, MC, V. Mon–Sat noon–2:30pm and 6–11pm. U-Bahn: U1 to Steiglmaierplatz.

7 OBERMENZING

INEXPENSIVE

Gasthof Weichandhof ★ (Finds) BAVARIAN   If you'd like to escape from the hordes in the center of Munich, a traditional favorite among the city residents is this old farmhouse restaurant at the beginning of the autobahn to Stuttgart. It lies in one of Munich's better suburbs, Obermenzing. Every night seems a festival here; the food is good and affordable, and patrons come here to relax, converse, and drink as much as to devour the food. When the weather turns warm in spring, a terrace covered in vines opens to diners and stays open until there's a bite to the autumn wind. With the tiled stoves giving off heat and ambience, it's a mellow and pleasurable choice even in December and January. You are served regional fare here—and plenty of it. Some of the best and most typical dishes are inspired by both Bavarian and Viennese kitchens. Boiled beef, flavored with herbs, is the eternal favorite and a dish said to have been ordered nightly by Franz Josef, the Austrian emperor. You're also served large pork knuckles, roast suckling pig, and any number of other dishes, including liver. A fish soup, made with zander, is served daily. The chefs are experts at making strudels.

Betzenweg 81. (✆) **089/891-1600.** Reservations recommended. Main courses 7.50€–20€ ($12–$32). AE, MC, V. Sun–Fri 11am–midnight; Sat 5pm–midnight. S-Bahn: Obermenzing.

---

8 CAFES

Many Münchners take a break during the day to relax over coffee or a beer, read the newspaper, or meet friends.

CENTRAL MUNICH

Café Glockenspiel (Kids) PASTRIES/INTERNATIONAL   This is the most frequented cafe in Munich. It's across from the Rathaus, and a crowd gathers here every day at 10:30am to watch the miniature tournament staged by the clock on the Rathaus facade. In addition to the view, the cafe has strong coffee and freshly made pastries with a limited menu of hot dishes. It also makes a fine place to end your day tour of Munich and to fortify yourself for Munich after dark. Arrive around 5pm for a drink and watch the square morph from daytime to night. It's an ideal place for people-watching, too.

Marienplatz 28. (✆) **089/26-42-56.** Main courses 11€–18€ ($18–$29); fixed-price 3-course dinner 31€ ($50), 4-course dinner 38€ ($61). MC, V. Mon–Sat 10am–1am, Sun 10am 7pm. U-Bahn or S-Bahn: Marienplatz.

Café Luitpold   Opened in 1888 and rebuilt in a blandly modern style after the ravages of World War II, this cafe once attracted such notables as Ibsen, Kandinsky, Johann Strauss the Younger, and other musicians, artists, and authors, as well as members of the royal court of Bavaria. What you'll find today, however, is mainstream workaday Munich stopping in for a pastry, a platter of food, coffee, or beer. There's a more formal restaurant associated with the place, but we tend to prefer the cafe section. A large beer costs 3€ to 4€ ($4.80–$6.40); coffee starts at 3€ ($4.80).

Briennerstrasse 11. (✆) **089/24-28-750.** MC, V. Mon–Fri 9am–7:30pm; Sat 8am–6:30pm. U-Bahn: Königsplatz or Odeonsplatz.

Guglhopf   Though it opened in the 1970s, this cafe's old-fashioned ambience and Bavarian rusticity make it seem older than it really is. It's named for the closest thing to a Bavarian "national pastry," the *Guglhopf*. Made with flour, eggs, and sugar, the pastry comes in at least four different variations, including chocolate and/or nuts. Equally nationalistic is the *Apfelstrudel* (apple strudel) served with vanilla sauce. If you're craving more than just dessert, try the pan-fried mushrooms with cream and herb sauce, served over a bed of homemade noodles. Borrow any of a half-dozen newspapers while eating your pastry and drinking your coffee or beer. A slice of the namesake pastry costs 2.50€ ($4); beer or *Weissebeer* is 3€ ($4.80); platters are 7€ to 13€ ($11–$21).

Kaufingerstrasse 5. (✆) **089/260-8868.** No credit cards. Mon–Sat 8am–8pm; Sun 10am–7pm. U-Bahn: Marienplatz.

Schlosscafé im Palmenhaus   This cafe is in a historical reconstruction of a 17th-century building that once functioned as a conservatory for palm trees. The original building, older than the *Schloss* itself, was destroyed in World War II. Here you can have your coffee capped with whipped cream or drink your beer in the garden, weather permitting. Coffee costs from 2€ ($3.20), and beer goes for 3€ ($4.80). Luncheon platters of unpretentious food include rice curries, schnitzels with french fries, and salads from 8€ to 25€ ($13–$40).

In the gardens of Schloss Nymphenburg, near entrance 43 and the rose gardens. © **089/175309.** No credit cards. Daily 10am–7pm. S-Bahn: Lain. Tram: 17.

NEUHAUSEN

Ruffini   Münchners head for this turn-of-the-20th-century former residence for a respite from the pressures of the inner city. It offers everything you'd expect from a traditional cafe. You can relax over your coffee or beer with the most recent edition of several different newspapers, or view the cafe's current painting exhibition (most are for sale). The cafe maintains its own bakery in the cellar, and a wine shop and delicatessen on a corner nearby. Coffee costs 2€ to 3.50€ ($3.20–$5.60); snacks such as cheese platters go for 6€ ($9.60). Warm platters are 8.50€ to 15€ ($14–$24). The cafe offers natural food, free from artificial fertilizers, flavors, or coloring.

Orffstrasse 22–24. © **089/161160.** No credit cards. Tues–Sun 10am–11:30pm. U-Bahn: U1 to Rotkreuzplatz.

10 BEER GARDENS

If you're in Munich between the first sunny spring day and the last fading light of a Bavarian-style autumn, you should head for one of the city's celebrated beer gardens *(Biergartens)*. Traditionally, beer gardens were simply tables placed under chestnut trees planted above the storage cellars to keep beer cool in summer. People, naturally, started to drink close to the source of their pleasure, and the tradition has remained. (Lids on beer steins, incidentally, were meant to keep out flies.) It's estimated that today Munich has at least 400 beer gardens and cellars. Food, drink, and atmosphere are much the same in all of them: Solid citizens in feathered hats, *Schicki-Mickies* (club-going Bavarian yuppies), grandmothers, students, and tourists rub shoulders as they down their hefty liter mugs of beer. And as you drink, it's a tradition to complain about anything and everything. Linguists have even coined a word for the local habit of mumbling into a stein of beer—*guanteln*. And why not? It's a therapeutic, relatively inexpensive way to let off steam.

CENTRAL MUNICH

Biergarten Chinesischer Turm ★ BAVARIAN   Our favorite beer garden is in the Englischer Garten (p. 142), the park lying between the Isar River and Schwabing. The biggest city-owned park in Europe, it has several beer gardens, of which the Biergarten Chinesischer Turm is the best. The largest and most popular of its kind in Europe, it takes its name from its location at the foot of a pagoda-like tower, a landmark that's easy to find. Beer and Bavarian food, and plenty of it, are what you get here. For a large glass or mug of beer, ask for *ein mass Bier,* which is enough to bathe in. It will likely be slammed down, still foaming, by a server carrying 12 other tall steins. Homemade dumplings are a specialty, as are all kinds of tasty sausage. You can get a first-rate *Schweinebraten* (braised loin of pork served with potato dumpling and rich brown gravy), which is Bavaria's answer to the better-known sauerbraten of the north. Huge baskets of pretzels are passed around, and they're eaten with Radi, the large, tasty white radishes famous from these parts. Oompah bands often play, adding to the festive atmosphere. It's open March to November until 1am, but from December to February, its closing depends on the weather and the number of patrons.

Englischer Garten 3. (℃) **089/3-83-87-30.** Main courses 13€–20€ ($21–$32). AE, MC, V. Mar–Nov daily 10am–midnight; Dec–Feb daily but hrs. vary. U-Bahn: Universität.

Gaststätte zum Flaucher BAVARIAN If you're going to the zoo (p. 143), you might want to stop close by at the nearby Gaststätte zum Flaucher for fun and food. The word *Gaststätte* tells you that it's a typical Bavarian inn. This one is mellow and traditional, with tables set in a tree-shaded garden overlooking the river. You can order the local specialty, *Leberkäse*, a large sausage loaf eaten with freshly baked pretzels and plenty of mustard, a deli delight. Beer costs from 7€ ($11) for a liter mug.

Isarauen 8. (℃) **089/7-23-26-77.** Main courses 7.50€–10€ ($12–$16). No credit cards. May–Oct daily 10am–midnight; Nov–Apr Sat–Sun 10am–9pm. Bus: 52.

SCHWABING

La Terrazza BAVARIAN/INTERNATIONAL In a century-old house northwest of Schwabing at the edge of Luitpold Park, this hall is noted for mass consumption of beer. Most visitors head for the street-level restaurant. Bavarian and international specialties include well-seasoned soups, grilled steak, veal, pork, and sausages. If you just want to drink, visit the rowdier and less expensive beer hall in the cellar. A large beer costs 4€ ($6.40).

Brunnerstrasse 2. (℃) **089/3-08-89-66.** Main courses 7€–20€ ($11–$32). AE, MC, V. Restaurant daily 11am–11pm. Beer hall daily 11am–1am. U-Bahn: Scheidplatz.

NYMPHENBURG

Hirschgarten ★ BAVARIAN In the Nymphenburg Park sector (near one of Munich's leading sightseeing attractions, Schloss Nymphenburg; p. 136), west of the heart of town, this beer garden is part of a 200-hectare (494-acre) park with hunting lodges and lakes. The largest open-air restaurant in Munich, it seats some 8,000 beer drinkers and Bavarian merrymakers.

Hirschgartenstrasse 1. (℃) **089/1799-9199.** Meals 7.50€–15€ ($12–$24); large beer 10€ ($16). MC, V. Daily 9am–midnight. S-Bahn: Laim. Tram: Romanplatz.

FREIMANN

Zum Aumeister BAVARIAN If you have a car, and have a nostalgic streak, you'll enjoy dining and drinking beer in the historic and evocative atmosphere of Zum Aumeister. Few places so authentically recapture the life gone by—surely the Bavarian royals, if they could miraculously return, would be delighted to see that their old hunting lodge is still around, and not much changed. It lies off the Frankfurter Ring at München-Freimann, a 20-minute drive north of the center. It offers a daily list of seasonal Bavarian specialties. Especially enjoyable is the cream of cauliflower soup and the rich oxtail soup.

Sondermeierstrasse 1. (℃) **089/325224.** Main courses 9.50€–17€ ($15–$27); large beer 3.20€–7€ ($5.10–$11). MC, V. Daily 10am–midnight. From central Munich, follow the signs for the Autobahn A8, and follow it in the direction of Nürnberg. Exit at the "Freimann" exit, turning left onto the blvd. it funnels into, and then note the signs pointing to Zum Aumeister.

Exploring Munich

Munich is a city of art and culture, with innumerable monuments and more museums than any other German city. In quality, its collections surpass those of Berlin. The Wittelsbachs (the ruling family of Europe from approximately the 13th to early 20th c.) were great collectors—some say pillagers—and left behind a city full of treasures.

Go to Munich to have fun and to enjoy the relaxed lifestyle, friendly ambience, and wealth of activities, sightseeing, and cultural events. Munich is stocked with so many treasures that any visitor who plans to "do" the city in a day or two will not only miss out on many major sights, but also fail to grasp the city's spirit and absorb its special flavor.

1 EXPLORING THE CITY CENTER

Marienplatz ★, dedicated to the patron of the city, whose golden statue atop a huge column (the Mariensäule) stands in the center of the square, is the heart of the Altstadt, or Old Town. On its north side is the **Neues Rathaus (New Town Hall)**, built in 19th-century Gothic style. Each day at 11am, and also at noon and 5pm in the summer, the Glockenspiel on the facade stages an elaborate performance, including a miniature tournament, with enameled copper figures moving in and out of the archways. Because you're already at the Rathaus, you may wish to climb the 55 steps to the top of its tower (an elevator is available) for a good overall view of the city center. **Altes Rathaus (Old Town Hall)**, with its plain Gothic tower, is to the right. It was reconstructed in the 15th century, after being destroyed by fire.

South of the square you can see the oldest church in Munich, **Peterskirche (St. Peter's Church)**. The **Viktualienmarkt,** just off Marienplatz and around the corner from St. Peter's Church, has been a gathering place since 1807. Here, people gossip, browse, snack, and buy fresh country produce, wines, meats, and cheese.

To the north lies **Odeonsplatz**, Munich's most beautiful square. The **Residenz (Royal Palace)** is just to the east, and the **Theatinerkirche** is to the south. Adjoining the Residenz is the restored **Nationaltheater,** home of the acclaimed Bavarian State Opera and Bavarian National Ballet.

Running west from Odeonsplatz is the wide shopping avenue, Briennerstrasse, leading to **Königsplatz.** Flanking this large Grecian square are three classical buildings constructed by Ludwig I—the **Propyläen,** the **Glyptothek,** and the **Antikensammlungen.** The busy Ludwigstrasse runs north from Odeonsplatz to the section of Munich known as **Schwabing.** This is the Greenwich Village or Latin Quarter of Munich, proud of its artistic and literary heritage. Ibsen and Rilke lived here, as well as members of the Blue Rider group, which influenced abstract art in the early 20th century. Today, Schwabing's sidewalk tables are filled with young people from all over the world.

> (Tips) **Saving on Sightseeing**
>
> - Visit the Alte Pinakothek, Neue Pinakothek, Glyptothek, Antikensammlungen, Bayerisches Nationalmuseum, or Münchner Stadtmuseum on Sunday—when admission to the permanent exhibitions is free (you'll have to brave the crowds).
> - Buy combination tickets wherever possible, such as the combination ticket for the Alte Pinakothek and the Neue Pinakothek costing 12€ ($19) adults, 7€ ($11) students and seniors, good for 1 day and cheaper than buying a separate ticket for each.
> - Note that some museums and attractions, such as the Deutsches Museum, the Münchner Stadtmuseum, and the BMW Museum, offer a family ticket that's cheaper than buying individual tickets for adults and children.

Isartor (Isar Gate) is one of the most-photographed Munich landmarks. It's located east of Marienplatz at Isartorplatz. Take the S-Bahn to Isartor. This is the only tower left from the wall that once encircled Munich, forming part of the city's fortifications against invaders.

The other major gate of Munich is the **Karlstor,** once known as Neuhauser Tor, lying northeast of Karlsplatz (nicknamed Stachus; see explanation on p. 154). Take Tram 18 to Karlsplatz. Karlstor lies at the end of Neuhauser Strasse, which formed part of the town's second circuit of walls, dating from the 1500s. The Karlstor takes its official name from Elector of Bavaria Karl Theodor, who had the Karlsplatz laid out and also commissioned to alter the gate. The Karlstor, built in 1302, lost its main tower in an 1857 explosion.

2 PALACES & MAJOR MUSEUMS

Alte Pinakothek ★★★ This is not only Munich's most important art museum but also one of the most significant collections in Europe. The nearly 900 paintings on display (many thousands more are in storage) in this huge neoclassical building represent the greatest European artists from the 14th to the 18th century. Begun as a small court collection by the royal Wittelsbach family in the early 1500s, the artistic treasure-trove grew and grew. There are only two floors with exhibits, but the museum is immense; we do not recommend that you try to cover it all in 1 day.

The landscape painter par excellence of the Danube school, Albrecht Altdorfer, is represented by six monumental works. Works of Albrecht Dürer include his final, and greatest, *Self-Portrait* (1500). Here the artist has portrayed himself with almost Christ-like solemnity. Also displayed is Dürer's two-paneled work called *The Four Apostles* (1526). Several galleries are given over to works by Dutch and Flemish masters. The St. Columba Altarpiece (1460–62), by Roger van der Weyden, is the most important of

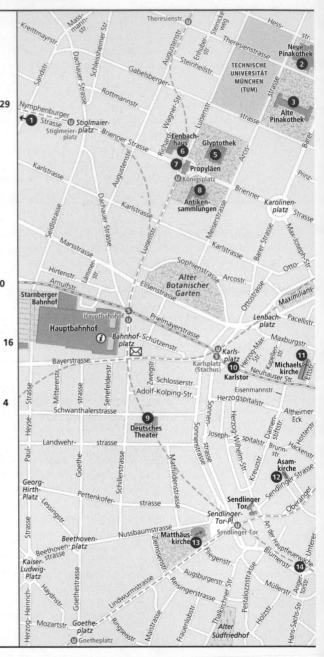

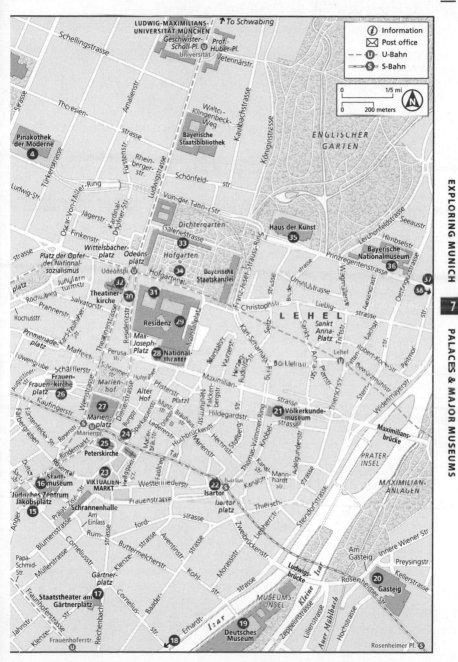

LUDWIG-MAXIMILIANS-
UNIVERSITÄT MÜNCHEN

Geschwister-
Scholl-Pl. Ⓤ   Prof.-
Universität   Huber-Pl.
                Veterinärstr.

↑ To Schwabing

Ⓘ Information
☒ Post office
- Ⓤ - U-Bahn
═Ⓢ═ S-Bahn

0   1/5 mi
0   200 meters

N

Schellingstrasse

Walter-
Klingenbeck-
Weg

Bayerische
Staatsbibliothek

Pinakothek
der Moderne
④

Thelesien-strasse

Amalienstr.

Ludwigstrasse

Kaulbachstrasse

Königinstrasse

ENGLISCHER
GARTEN

Türkenstrasse

Fürstenstr.

Rhein-
berger-
str.

Schönfeld-   str.

Ludwig-Str.

Oskar-von-Miller-Ring

Jägerstr.

Kardinal-
Döpfner-Str.

Von-der-Tann-(Str.

Dichtergarten

Galeriestrasse

Haus der Kunst
㉟

Platz der Opfer
des National-
sozialismus

Wittelsbacher-
platz

Odeons-
platz

Hofgarten

Bayerische
Nationalmuseum
㊱

Lerchenfeldstrasse

Prinzregentenstrasse

Seeaustr.

Hirnbelstr.

Oettingenstrasse

㊲

strasse

Finkenstr.

platz

Rochusberg

Jungfern-
turmstr.

Udeonspl. Ⓤ

㉜

Theatiner-
kirche

Hofgarten str.

Bayerische
Staatskanzlei

Franz-Josef-Strauss-Ring

Christophstr.

Unsöllstrasse

Bruder-

str.

Liebig-
strasse

L E H E L

㊳

Prannersstr.

Salvatorstr.

㉚

Residenz
㉙

Max-
Joseph-
Platz

Marstallplatz

Karl-Scharnagl-

Sankt
Anna-
Platz

Theatinerstr.

Residenzstr.

㉛

Kochusstr.

Promenade-
platz

Karl-Trautloff-Str.

Maffeistr.

Löwengrube

Schäfflerstr.

㉘ National-
theater

Perusa-
str.

Schrammer-
str.

Hofstatt

Marstallstr.

Wurzerstr.

Herzog-
Rudolf-
Str.

Anna-Str.

Seitzstr.

Peter-str.

Bürkleinstr.

Lehel

Robert-Koch-Str.

Gewürzmühlstr.

Seitzstr.

Sterr-str.

Karl-

Zeittnor.

Augustiner-
str.

Frauen-
platz

Frauen-kirche
㉖

Kaufingerstr.

Färbergraben

Marien-
hof

Dienerstrasse

Alter
Hof

Pfisterstr.

Platzl

Münz-
str.

Falckenbergstr.

Neuturmstr.

Maximilian-
strasse

Hildegardstr.

Maximilian-
strasse

㉑ Völkerkunde-
museum

Thomas-Wimmer-Ring

Widenmayerstr.

Maximilians-
brücke

Fürstenfelder-Str.

Rosenstr.

㉗

Marien-
platz
Ⓤ
Marienpl.

㉔

Sparkassenstr.

Burgstr.

Oberanger

Ledererstr.

Mazerstr.

Sebastiansplatz

Hochbrückenstr.

Marienstr.

Thomas-Wimmer-Ring

Knöbel-
strasse

Mann-
hardt-
str.

Adelgundenstr.

Sterndorfstrasse

PRATER-
INSEL

MAXIMILIAN-
ANLAGEN

Rindermarkt

㉕
Peterskirche

Tal

㉓

Heiliggeist-str.

Falkturmstr.

Westenriederstr.

Isartor

㉒
Isartor
Ⓢ

Isartor
platz

Thierschstr.

Liebherrstr.

Innere Wiener Str.

Stadt-
museum
⑯

Jüdisches Zentrum
Jakobsplatz
⑮

Oberanger

Anger

Prälat-Zistl-Str.

VIKTUALIEN-
MARKT

Schrannenhalle

Am
Einlass

Frauenstrasse

Reichenbachstr.

strasse

Zweibrückenstr.

Ludwigs-
brücke

Am
Gasteig

Preysingstr.

Kellerstrasse

Rosenheimer Str.

⑳ Gasteig

Papa-
Schmid-
Str.

Müllerstrasse

Blumenstrasse

Corneliusstr.

Rum-

Buttermelcherstr.

Aventinstr.

Klenze-str.

Kohl-str.

Morasistr.

Liebherrstr.

Steinsdorfstrasse

Gärtner-
platz

Staatstheater am
Gärtnerplatz
⑰

Cornelius-
str.

Baader-str.

strasse

MUSEUMS-
INSEL

Kleine Isar

Zeppelinstrasse

Lilienstrasse

Auer Mühlbach

Hochstrasse

Jahnstr.

Klenze-str.

Fraunhoferstr.

⑱

Erhardt-str.

Isar

⑲
Deutsches
Museum

Rosenheimer Pl. Ⓢ

EXPLORING MUNICH

7

PALACES & MAJOR MUSEUMS

François Cuvilliés: Dwarf with a Big Talent

In the 17th and 18th centuries, Bavaria's rulers were determined to rival Rome itself. In the cutthroat competition for commissions that followed, an unlikely candidate emerged for the role of Munich's most brilliant master of the rococo style.

François Cuvilliés (1695–1768) was a dwarf born in Belgium. Like many of his peers, he was first a pageboy and later court jester to Max Emanuel, elector of Bavaria. When the elector was exiled, François accompanied him; in St-Cloud near Paris, he absorbed his patron's interest in the aesthetics of French baroque architecture. Ambitious and witty, he won Max Emanuel's friendship and support. When the elector was reinstated with pomp and ceremony as ruler of Bavaria, François became a craftsman for the court's chief architect.

Cuvilliés proved himself so talented that in 1720 Max Emanuel sent him for a 4-year apprenticeship to one of the leading architects of Paris, Jacques-François Blondel. After his return to Munich, his work soon eclipsed that of his master. By 1745, the former jester had been elevated to chief architect to the Bavarian court.

His commissions between 1726 and his death in 1768 include some of southern Germany's most important rococo monuments, such as the interior of the **Amalienburg Pavilion** in the park of Nymphenburg Palace and the facade of the **Theatinerkirche.** His most famous creation is the remarkable **Altes Residenztheater,** familiarly called by his name. All his work is notable for a flamboyant sinuousness.

Cuvilliés's son, François Cuvilliés the Younger (1731–77), also became an architect, although he never achieved the greatness of his father. Most notably, he put the finishing touches on the facade of the **Theatinerkirche,** which his father had left unfinished at his death.

these, in size and significance. Measuring nearly 3m (10 ft.) across, it is a triumph of Van der Weyden's subtle linear style and one of his last works (he died in 1464).

The numerous works by Rembrandt, Rubens (there are more Rubens works here than in any other museum in Europe), and Van Dyck include a series of religious panels painted by Rembrandt for Prince Frederick Hendrick of the Netherlands. A variety of French, Spanish, and Italian artists are found in both the larger galleries and the small rooms lining the outer wall. The Italian masters are well represented by Fra Filippo Lippi, Giotto, Botticelli, Raphael *(Holy Family),* and Titian.

You'll also see a *Madonna* by Leonardo da Vinci, a famous self-portrait by the young Rembrandt (1629), and works by Lucas Cranach, including his *Venus.* In the *Land of Cockaigne,* Pieter Brueghel has satirized a popular subject of European folk literature: the place where no work has to be done and where food simply falls into one's mouth. Note the little egg on legs running up to be eaten and the plucked and cooked chicken laying its neck on a plate. In the background, a knight lies under a roof with his mouth open, waiting for the pies to slip off the eaves over his head.

Important works are always on display, but exhibits also change. You'd be wise to buy a map of the gallery to guide you through the dozens of rooms.

Barer Strasse 27. ℂ **089/23-80-52-16.** www.alte-pinakothek.de. Admission 5.50€ ($8.80) adults, 4€
($6.40) students and seniors, free for children 15 and under; 1€ ($1.60) for all on Sun. Wed–Sun 10am–
6pm; Tues 10am–8pm. U-Bahn: Theresienstrasse. Tram: 27. Bus: 53.

Bayerisches Nationalmuseum (Bavarian National Museum) ★★

In 1855, King Maximilian II began an institution to preserve Bavaria's historic and artistic treasures. The collection grew so rapidly that it had to be moved to larger quarters several times over the past 100 years. Its current building, near the Haus der Kunst, contains three vast floors of sculpture, painting, folk art, ceramics, furniture, and textiles, as well as clocks and scientific instruments.

After entering the museum, turn right into the first large gallery, the **Wessobrunn Room,** devoted to early church art from the 5th through the 13th centuries. This room holds some of the museum's oldest and most valuable works. The desk case contains medieval ivories, including the so-called Munich ivory from about A.D. 400. The carving shows the women weeping at the tomb of Christ while the resurrected Lord is gingerly stepping up into the clouds and heaven. At the crossing to the adjoining room is the stone figure *Virgin with the Rose Bush,* from Straubing (ca. 1300), one of the few old Bavarian pieces of church art influenced by the spirit of mysticism.

The **Riemenschneider Room** is devoted to the works of the great sculptor Tilman Riemenschneider (1460–1531) and his contemporaries. Characteristic of the sculptor's works is the natural, unpainted wood of his carvings and statuary. Note especially the *12 Apostles from the Marienkapelle in Würzburg* (1510), the figures of St. Mary Magdalene (1490–92) and St. Sebastian (1490), and the central group from the high altar in the parish church of Münnerstadt (1490–92).

The second floor contains a fine collection of stained and painted glass—an art in which medieval Germany excelled. Other rooms on this floor include baroque ivory carvings, Meissen porcelain, and ceramics. Also on display are famous collections of 16th- to 18th-century arms and armor, and the collection of antique clocks, some dating from the 16th century.

In the east wing of the basement level are many Christmas cribs (a highly decorated crèche representing the Nativity scene) from Germany, Austria, Italy, and Moravia. The variety of styles competes with the variety of materials—wood, amber, gold, terra cotta, and even wax were used in making these nativity scenes. Also on this level is a display of Bavarian folk art, including many woodcarvings.

Prinzregentenstrasse 3. ℂ **089/21-12-401.** www.bayerisches-nationalmuseum.de. Admission 5€ ($8) adults, 4€ ($6.40) students and seniors, free for children 14 and under. Tues–Wed and Fri–Sun 10am–5pm; Thurs 10am–8pm. U-Bahn: Lehel. Tram: 17. Bus: 53.

Deutsches Museum (German Museum of Masterpieces of Science and Technology) ★★★ (Kids)

On an island in the Isar River, in the heart of Munich, this is the largest technological museum of its kind in the world. Its huge collection of priceless artifacts and historic originals includes the first electric dynamo (Siemens, 1866), the first automobile (Benz, 1886), the first diesel engine (1897), and the laboratory bench at which the atom was first split (Hahn, Strassmann, 1938). There are hundreds of buttons to push, levers to crank, and gears to turn, as well as a knowledgeable, English-speaking staff to answer questions and demonstrate how steam engines, pumps, or historical musical instruments work.

The most popular displays are a series of model coal, salt, and iron mines, as well as the electric power hall, with high-voltage displays that actually produce lightning. There are also exhibits on transportation, printing, photography, textiles, and many activities, including glass-blowing and papermaking demonstrations. The air-and-space hall is the largest in the museum. A hall for high-tech exhibits, computer science, automation, microelectronics, and telecommunications is also very intriguing. The museum's astronomy exhibition shows how this science developed from its earliest beginnings to its current status and is the largest permanent astronomy exhibition in Europe. A good restaurant and a museum shop are on the premises.

Museumsinsel 1 (on an island in the Isar River). (C) **089/21-791.** www.deutsches-museum.de. Admission 8.50€ ($14) adults, 7€ ($11) seniors, 3€ ($4.80) students and children 7–12, free for children 6 and under. Daily 9am–5pm. Closed major holidays. S-Bahn: Isator. Tram: 18.

Neue Pinakothek ★   This museum offers a survey of 18th- and 19th-century art, including paintings by Gainsborough, Goya, David, Manet, Van Gogh, and Monet. Among the more popular German artists represented are Wilhelm Leibl and Gustav Klimt; you'll also encounter a host of others whose art is less well known. Note particularly the genre works by Carl Spitzweg, whose paintings poke gentle fun at everyday life in Munich. Across Theresienstrasse from the Alte Pinakothek, the museum was reconstructed after its destruction in World War II, reopening in 1981.

Barer Strasse 29 (across Theresienstrasse from the Alte Pinakothek). (C) **089/23-80-51-95.** www. pinakothek.de. Admission 5.50€ ($8.80) adults, 4€ ($6.40) students and seniors; free for children 15 and under. Thurs–Mon 10am–6pm; Wed 10am–8pm. U-Bahn: Theresienstrasse. Tram: 27. Bus: 53.

Pinakothek der Moderne ★★   In 2002, one of the world's largest museums devoted to the visual arts of the 19th and 20th centuries opened in Munich, just minutes from the Alte and Neue Pinakothek. This is the country's vastest display of fine and applied arts as, for the first time, four major collections came together under one roof. This is Munich's version of the Tate Gallery in London or the Pompidou in Paris.

Wander where your interest dictates: the **Staatsgalerie Moderner Kunst (State Gallery of Modern Art)** ★★★, with paintings, sculpture, photography, and video; **Die Neue Sammlung,** the national museum of applied art featuring design and craftwork; the **Architekturmuseum der Technischen Universität (University of Architecture museum),** with architectural drawings, photographs, and models; and the **Staatliche Grapische Sammlung,** with its outstanding collection of prints and drawings.

Whenever we visit, we spend most of our time in the modern art collection, lost in a world of our favorite artists such as Picasso, Magritte, Klee, Kandinsky, and even Francis Bacon, de Kooning, and Warhol. The museum also owns 400,000 drawings and prints from Leonardo da Vinci to Cézanne up to contemporary artists. They are presented at alternating exhibits.

The architectural galleries hold the largest specialist collection of its kind in Germany, comprising some 350,000 drawings, 100,000 photographs, and 500 models. The applied arts section features more than 50,000 items. You go from the beginnings of the Industrial Revolution up to today's computer culture, with exhibitions of Art Nouveau and Bauhaus along the way.

Barer Strasse 40. (C) **089/23805-360.** www.pinakothek.de. Admission 9.50€ ($15) adults; 6€ ($9.60) students, seniors, and ages 17 and under. 1€ ($1.60) for all on Sun. Fri–Sun and Wed 10am–6pm; Thurs 10am–8pm. U-Bahn: Odeonsplatz.

The Deutsches Museum

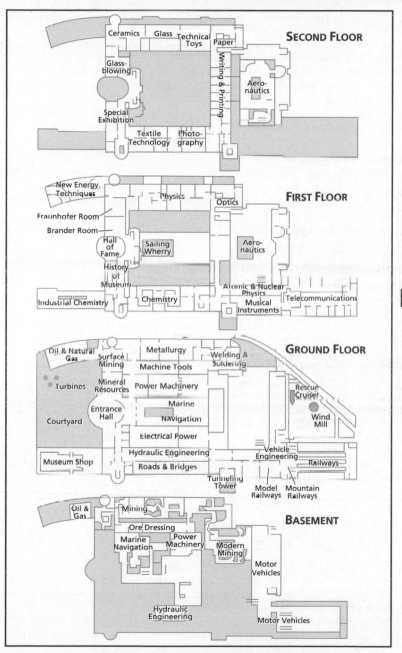

Ceramics
Glass
Technical Toys
Paper
Glass-blowing
Writing & Printing
Aero-nautics
Special Exhibition
Textile Technology
Photo-graphy

FIRST FLOOR

New Energy Techniques
Physics
Optics
Fraunhofer Room
Brander Room
Hall of Fame
Sailing Wherry
Aero-nautics
History of Museum
Atomic & Nuclear Physics
Industrial Chemistry
Chemistry
Musical Instruments
Telecommunications

GROUND FLOOR

Oil & Natural Gas
Surface Mining
Metallurgy
Welding & Soldering
Machine Tools
Turbines
Mineral Resources
Power Machinery
Rescue Cruiser
Entrance Hall
Marine
Wind Mill
Courtyard
Navigation
Electrical Power
Museum Shop
Hydraulic Engineering
Vehicle Engineering
Railways
Roads & Bridges
Tunneling Tower
Model Railways
Mountain Railways

BASEMENT

Oil & Gas
Mining
Ore Dressing
Marine Navigation
Power Machinery
Modern Mining
Motor Vehicles
Hydraulic Engineering
Motor Vehicles

PALACES & MAJOR MUSEUMS

Residenz ★ When one of the Bavarian royals said that he was going to the castle, he could have meant any number of places, especially if he was Ludwig II. But if he said that he was going home, he could only be referring to the Residenz. This enormous palace, with a history almost as long as that of the Wittelsbach family, was the official residence of the rulers of Bavaria from 1385 to 1918. Added to and rebuilt over the centuries, the complex is a conglomerate of various styles. Depending on how you approach the Residenz, you might first see a German Renaissance hall (the western facade), a Palladian palace (on the north), or a Florentine Renaissance palace (on the south facing Max-Joseph-Platz).

The Residenz was restored after its almost total destruction in World War II and now houses the Residenz Museum, a concert hall, the Cuvilliés Theater, and the Residenz Treasury. The **Residenz Museum** (✆ **089/29-06-71**), the southwestern section of the palace, has some 120 rooms of art and furnishings collected by centuries of Wittelsbachs. To see the entire collection, you'll have to take two tours, one in the morning and one in the afternoon. You may also visit the rooms on your own.

The **Ancestral Gallery** is designed like a hall of mirrors, except that instead of mirrors, there are portraits of the Wittelsbach family, set into gilded, carved paneling. The largest room in the museum section is the **Antiquarium,** possibly the finest example of interior Renaissance secular styling in Germany. Frescoes, painted by dozens of 16th- and 17th-century artists, adorn nearly every inch of space on the walls and ceilings. The room is broken into sections by pilasters and niches, each with its own bust of a Roman emperor or a Greek hero. The central attraction is the two-story chimney piece of red stucco and marble, completed in 1600. It's adorned with Tuscan pillars and the coat of arms of the dukes of Bavaria.

On the second floor of the palace, directly over the Antiquarium, is an enormous collection of Far Eastern porcelain. Note also the fine assemblage of Oriental rugs in the long, narrow **Porcelain Gallery.**

If you have time to view only one item in the **Schatzkammer (Treasury)** ★★, make it the 16th-century Renaissance statue of *St. George Slaying the Dragon.* This equestrian statue is made of gold, but you can barely see the precious metal for the thousands of diamonds, rubies, emeralds, sapphires, and semiprecious stones embedded in it. Both the Residenz Museum and the Schatzkammer are entered from Max-Joseph-Platz on the south side of the palace.

From the Brunnenhof, you can visit the Altes Residenztheater, better known as the **Cuvilliés Theater** ★★, whose rococo tiers of boxes are supported by seven bacchants. Directly over the huge center box, where the royal family sat, is a crest in white and gold topped by a jewel-bedecked crown of Bavaria held in place by cherubs in flight. In summer, this theater is the scene of frequent concert and opera performances. Mozart's *Idomeneo* was first performed here in 1781.

The Italianate **Hofgarten,** or Court Garden, is one of the special "green lungs" of Munich. To the north of the Residenz, it's enclosed on two sides by arcades; the garden dates from the time of Duke Maximilian I and was laid out between 1613 and 1617. In the center is the Hofgarten temple, a 12-sided pavilion dating from 1615. Also see the listing for the **Staatliche Museum Ägyptischer Kunst (State Museum of Egyptian Art)** on p. 141, which is located in the Residenz.

Max-Joseph-Platz 3. ✆ **089/29-06-71.** Combination ticket for Residenzmuseum and Schatzkammer 9€ ($14) adults, 8€ ($13) students and seniors, free for ages 15 and under. Ticket for either Schatzkammer or Residenzmuseum 6€ ($9.60) adults, 5€ ($8) seniors and students, free for 16 and under. Apr to mid-Oct daily 9am–6pm; mid-Oct to Mar daily 10am–4pm. U-Bahn: Odeonsplatz.

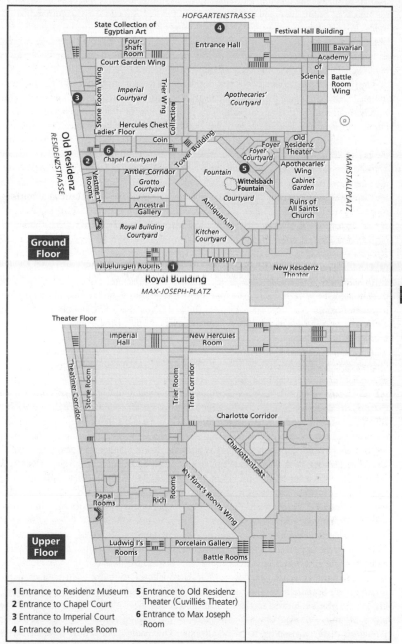

EXPLORING MUNICH

7

PALACES & MAJOR MUSEUMS

HOFGARTENSTRASSE

State Collection of Egyptian Art

Four-shaft Room

Entrance Hall ④

Festival Hall Building

Bavarian Academy of Science

Battle Room Wing

Court Garden Wing

Imperial Courtyard

Trier Wing

Apothecaries' Courtyard

Stone Room Wing

Hercules Chest

Ladies' Floor

Coin Collection

③

Old Residenz

RESIDENZSTRASSE

② Chapel Courtyard ⑥

Antler Corridor

Grotto Courtyard

Vestment Rooms

Ancestral Gallery

Royal Building Courtyard

Kitchen Courtyard

Tower Building

Foyer Foyer Courtyard

Old Residenz Theater

Fountain

⑤

Wittelsbach Fountain

Courtyard

Apothecarles' Wing

Cabinet Garden

Ruins of All Saints Church

Antiquarium

MARSTALLPLATZ

Ground Floor

Nibelungen Rooms ①

Treasury

New Residenz Theater

Royal Building

MAX-JOSEPH-PLATZ

Theater Floor

Imperial Hall

New Hercules Room

Teatiner Corridor

Stone Room

Trier Room

Trier Corridor

Charlotte Corridor

Charlottentrakt

Papal Rooms

Rooms

Rich

Kurfürst's Rooms Wing

Upper Floor

Ludwig I's Rooms

Porcelain Gallery

Battle Rooms

---

1 Entrance to Residenz Museum
2 Entrance to Chapel Court
3 Entrance to Imperial Court
4 Entrance to Hercules Room

5 Entrance to Old Residenz Theater (Cuvilliés Theater)
6 Entrance to Max Joseph Room

Schloss Nymphenburg ★★★ In summer, the Wittelsbachs would pack up their bags and head for their country house, Schloss Nymphenburg. A more complete, more sophisticated palace than the Residenz, it was begun in 1664 by Elector Ferdinand Maria in Italian-villa style and took more than 150 years to complete. The final palace plan was created mainly by Elector Max Emanuel, who in 1702 decided to enlarge the villa by adding four large pavilions connected by arcaded passageways. Gradually the French style took over, and today the facade is a subdued baroque.

The palace interior is less subtle, however. Upon entering the main building, you're in the great hall, decorated in rococo colors and stuccos. The frescoes by Johann Baptist Zimmermann (1756) depict incidents from mythology, especially those dealing with Flora, goddess of spring, and her nymphs, for whom the palace was named. This hall was used for both banquets and concerts during the reign of Max Joseph III, elector during the mid–18th century. Concerts are still presented here in summer.

From the main building, turn left and head for the arcaded gallery connecting the northern pavilions. The first room in the arcade is the Great Gallery of Beauties, painted for Elector Max Emanuel in 1710. More provocative, however, is King Ludwig I's Gallery of Beauties in the south pavilion (the apartments of Queen Caroline). Ludwig commissioned no fewer than 36 portraits of the most beautiful women of his day. The paintings by J. Stieler (created 1827–50) include the *Schöne Münchenerin* (lovely Munich girl) and a portrait of Lola Montez, the dancer whose "friendship" with Ludwig caused a scandal that factored into the Revolution of 1848.

To the south of the palace buildings, in the rectangular block of low structures that once housed the court stables, is the **Marstallmuseum.** In the first hall, look for the glass coronation coach of Elector Karl Albrecht, built in Paris in 1740. From the same period comes the hunting sleigh of Electress Amalia, with the statue of Diana, goddess of the hunt; even the runners are decorated with shellwork and hunting trophies.

The coaches and sleighs of Ludwig II are displayed in the **third hall.** His constant longing for the grandeur of the past is reflected in the ornately designed state coach, meant for his marriage to Duchess Sophie of Bavaria, a royal wedding that never came off. The fairy-tale coach wasn't wasted, however, since Ludwig often used it to ride through the countryside at night, and from castle to castle, creating quite a picture. The coach is completely gilded, inside and out; rococo carvings cover every inch of space except for the panels faced with paintings on copper. In winter, the king would ride in his state sleigh (also on display), nearly as elaborate as the Cinderella coach.

Nymphenburg Park ★ stretches for 200 hectares (494 acres). A canal runs through it from the pool at the foot of the staircase to the cascade at the far end of the English-style gardens. Within the park are a number of pavilions. The guided tour begins with the **Amalienburg** ★★, whose plain exterior belies the rococo decoration inside, designed by Cuvilliés. Built as a hunting lodge for Electress Amalia (in 1734), the pavilion carries the hunting theme through the first few rooms and then bursts into salons of flamboyant colors, rich carvings, and wall paintings. Most impressive is the Hall of Mirrors, a symphony of silver ornaments on a faint blue background.

The **Badenburg** sits at the edge of the large lake of the same name. As its name implies, it was built as a bathing pavilion, although it's difficult to visualize Ludwig dashing from the water in a dripping swimsuit and across those elegant floors. A trip to the basement, however, will help you appreciate the pavilion's practical side. Here you'll see the unique bath, surrounded by blue-and-white Dutch tiles. The ceiling is painted with frescoes of mythological bathing scenes.

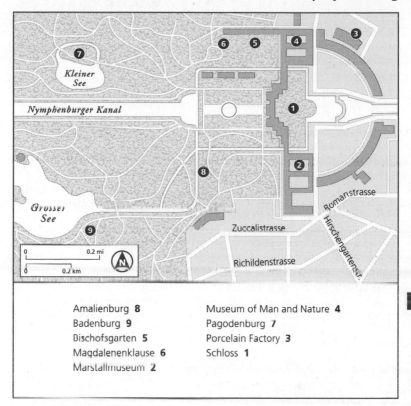

Amalienburg **8**

Badenburg **9**

Bischofsgarten **5**

Magdalenenklause **6**

Marstallmuseum **2**

Museum of Man and Nature **4**

Pagodenburg **7**

Porcelain Factory **3**

Schloss **1**

The octagonal **Pagodenburg,** on the smaller lake on the other side of the canal, looks like a Chinese pagoda from the outside. The interior, however, is decorated with pseudo-Chinese motifs, often using Dutch tiles in place of Chinese ones.

Magdalenenklause may look like a ruin, but that was the intention when it was built in 1725. Also called the Hermitage, it was planned as a retreat for prayer and solitude. The four main rooms of the one-story structure are paneled with uncarved stained oak, with simple furnishings and a few religious paintings—a really drastic change from the other buildings.

Other attractions include the **Porzellansammlung (Porcelain Museum),** which is above the stables of the Marstallmuseum. Some of the finest pieces of porcelain in the world, executed in the 18th century, are displayed here, along with an absolute gem—miniature copies in porcelain, done in extraordinary detail, of some of the grand masterpieces in the Old Pinakothek. Each was commissioned by Ludwig I.

Schloss Nymphenburg 1. ℰ **089/179-080.** www.schloesser.bayern.de. Admission to all attractions 10€ ($16) adults, free for children 6 and under. Separate admissions: 5€ ($8) Schloss Nymphenburg, 4€ ($6.40) to Marstallmuseum, Amalienburg, or Porzellansammlung porcelain. Oct–Mar daily 10am–4pm; Apr–Sept daily 9am–6pm. Free parking beside the Marstallmuseum. U-Bahn: Rotkreuzplatz, then tram 17 to Botanischergarten. Bus: 41.

3 THE GREAT CHURCHES

In addition to the historic churches described below, you may also want to visit the **Matthäuskirche,** Nussbaumstrasse 1 (U-Bahn: Sendlinger Tor), an Evangelical cathedral built between 1953 and 1955.

Asamkirche   St.-Johann-Nepomuk-Kirche, commonly referred to as the *Asamkirche* after its builders, was constructed by the Asam brothers, Cosmas Damian and Egid Quirin. Although modest on the outside, the interior of this small 18th-century church is a baroque fantasy. Above the entrance stands a statue of the church's patron, St. Nepomuk, a 14th-century monk (said to have performed many noble deeds and known for helping the poor) who drowned in the Danube. Entering the chapel, visitors are greeted with a burst of frescoes surrounded by rich red stucco and lavishly gilded woodwork, superbly illustrating the Bavarian passion for ornamentation.

Sendlingerstrasse 62. ⓒ **089/23-68-79-89.** Free admission. Daily 9am–5pm. U-Bahn: Sendlinger Tor.

Frauenkirche (Cathedral of Our Lady) ★   When the smoke cleared from the 1945 bombings, only a fragile shell remained of Munich's largest church, which is affectionately known as Liebfrauenkirche. Workmen and architects who restored the 15th-century Gothic cathedral used whatever remains they could find in the rubble, along with modern innovations. The overall effect of the rebuilt Frauenkirche is strikingly simple, yet dignified.

The twin towers, or Liebfrauendom, which remained intact with their strange early Gothic onion domes, have been the city's landmark since they were added to the church in 1525. Instead of the typical flying buttresses, huge props on the inside support the edifice and separate the side chapels. Twenty-two simple octagonal pillars support the Gothic vaulting over the nave and chancel.

Entering the main doors at the cathedral's west end, you first notice no windows (actually, except for the tall chancel window, they're hidden by the enormous pillars). According to legend, the devil was delighted at the notion of hidden windows and stamped in glee at the stupidity of the architect—you can still see the strange footlike mark called "the devil's step" in the entrance hall.

In the chapel directly behind the high altar is the cathedral's most interesting painting: *The Protecting Cloak,* a 1510 work by Jan Polack, showing the Virgin holding out her majestic robes to shelter all humankind. The collection of tiny figures beneath the cloak includes everyone from the pope to peasants.

Frauenplatz. ⓒ **089/29-00-82-0.** Free admission. Sat–Thurs 7am–7pm; Fri 7am–6pm. U-Bahn or S-Bahn: Marienplatz.

Michaelskirche   The largest Renaissance church north of the Alps, Michaelskirche was constructed by Duke Wilhelm the Pious in 1583. Seven years into construction, the tower collapsed. The duke took this as divine portent that the church was not large enough. During the second phase of construction, the size of the church was dramatically increased, making it not only the largest one north of the Alps, but also the possessor of the world's second-largest barrel-vaulted roof. Among those who have been laid to rest in the crypt are Duke Wilhelm himself and more than 40 Wittelsbachs, including "Mad" King Ludwig II, perhaps the family's most notorious member.

Neuhauser Strasse 52. ⓒ **089/2-31-70-60.** Free admission. Church daily 7am–7pm; crypt Mon–Fri 9:30am–1pm and 3–4:30pm, Sat 10am–3pm. U-Bahn or S-Bahn: Marienplatz.

Peterskirche (St. Peter's Church)   Munich's oldest church (1180), known locally as Old Peter, has turned over a new leaf, and it's a gold one at that. The white-and-gray interior has been decorated with gilded baroque accents and *trompe l'oeil* medallions. It contains a series of murals by Johann Baptist Zimmermann, but nothing tops the attraction of the bizarre relic in the second chapel on the left: the gilt-covered and gem-studded skeleton of St. Mundita. From its resting place on a cushion, it stares at you with two false eyes in its skull. Jewels cover the mouth of its rotten teeth, quite a contrast to the fresh roses usually kept in front of the black-and-silver coffin. The church also has a tall steeple that you can climb. Colored circles on the lower platform tell you whether the climb is worthwhile: If the circle is white, you can see the Alps.

Rindermarkt 1 (near the Rathaus). (℃ **089/2-60-48-28.** Church free; tower 2.50€ ($4) adults, 1.50€ ($2.40) students, 0.50€ (80¢) children. Mon–Sat 9am–6pm; Sun 10am–7pm. U-Bahn or S-Bahn: Marienplatz.

Theatinerkirche   Named for a group of Roman Catholic clergy (the Theatines), this church, dedicated to Saint Kajetan, is Munich's finest example of Italian baroque. Two Italian architects, Barelli and Zucalli, began building it in 1662. François Cuvilliés added the facade a century later, and his son completed the structure in 1768. Fluted columns that line the center aisle support the arched ceiling of the nave. Above the transept, dividing the nave from the choir, the ceiling breaks into an open dome, with an ornate gallery decorated with large but graceful statues. Nothing detracts from the whiteness of the interior except the dark wooden pews and canopied pulpit. Since 1954 the church has been under the care of the Dominican Friars.

Theatinerstrasse 22. (℃ **089/21-06-96-0.** Free admission. Church Mon–Fri 10am–1pm and 1:30–4:30pm; Sat 10am–3pm. U-Bahn: Odeonsplatz.

---

4 MORE ATTRACTIONS

MUSEUMS

Antikensammlungen (Museum of Antiquities) ★   After 100 years of floating from one museum to another, the Museum of Antiquities finally found a home in the 19th-century neoclassical hall on the south side of Königsplatz. This collection grew around the vase collection of Ludwig I, who had fantasies of transforming Munich into a second Athens. It was originally called the Museum Antiker Kleinkunst (Museum of Small Works of Ancient Art). Many pieces are small in size but not in value or artistic significance.

Entering the museum, you're in the large central hall. The five main-floor halls house more than 650 Greek vases, collected from all parts of the Mediterranean. The pottery has been restored to near-perfect condition; much of it dates as far back as 500 B.C. The oldest piece here, "the goddess from Aegina," dates from 3000 B.C. This pre-Mycenaean figure, carved from a mussel shell, is on display with the Mycenaean pottery exhibits in Room I. The upper level of the Central Hall is devoted to large Greek vases discovered in Sicily and to Etruscan art.

Returning to the Central Hall, take the stairs down to the lower level to see the collection of Greek, Roman, and Etruscan jewelry. Note the similarities to today's design fashions. Included on this level, as well, are rooms devoted to ancient colored glass, Etruscan bronzes, and Greek terra cottas.

Königsplatz 1. ℭ **089/59-98-88-30.** Admission 3.50€ ($5.60) adults, 2.50€ ($4) students and seniors, free for children 15 and under. Joint ticket to the Museum of Antiquities and the Glyptothek 5.50€ ($8.80) adults, 3.50€ ($5.60) students and seniors; free for all on Sun. Tues–Sun 10am–5pm (Thurs until 8pm). U-Bahn: U2 to Königsplatz.

Bavaria Film Studios This is Europe's largest filmmaking center. Production was begun here as early as 1920. In the 1970s, Fassbinder, Wim Wenders, and Herzog worked here; Stanley Kubrick shot his interiors for *Paths of Glory;* and Bob Fosse produced *Cabaret.* Tours take you through the sets of famous films like *Das Boot* and *The Neverending Story,* and you can watch films on the Showscan, a superwide movie screen. Children enjoy the Action Show, a demonstration of movie stunts.

Bavariafilmplatz 7, Geiselgasteig. ℭ **089/64-990.** Admission 10€ ($16) adults, 9€ ($14) students and seniors, 7€ ($11) children 4–14. Tours Mar–early Nov daily 9am–4pm, early Nov–Feb daily 10am–3pm; show Mar–Oct daily noon and 1:30pm, additional shows Sat–Sun 2:30pm. Tram: 25.

Deutsches Theatermuseum Founded in 1910, the German Theatermuseum is a haven for theater fans from all over the world. Its collection includes theater plans and stage sets, as well as various props, costumes, and masks used in productions around the world. The archive contains thousands of manuscripts, programs, and revues. The museum's library houses additional manuscripts, scores, and journals. Available here is the *Münchner Spielplan,* a service providing information on all current theatrical performances in the Munich area. The museum is open only for special exhibitions.

Galerie Strasse 4a. ℭ **089/2-10-69-10.** Free admission to the library. For special exhibitions, Tues–Sun 10am–5pm; library Tues–Fri 10am–noon and 1–5pm. U-Bahn: Odeonsplatz.

Glyptothek ★ The ideal neighbor for the Museum of Antiquities, the Glyptothek supplements the pottery and smaller pieces of the main museum with the country's largest collection of ancient Greek and Roman sculpture. Included are the famous pediments from the temple of Aegina, two marvelous statues of *kouroi* (youths) from the 6th century B.C., the colossal figure of a *Sleeping Satyr* from the Hellenistic period, and a splendid collection of Roman portraits. In all, the collection is the country's largest assemblage of classical art. King Ludwig I, who had fantasies of transforming Munich into another Athens, ordered it built.

Königsplatz 3. ℭ **089/28-61-00.** Admission 3.50€ ($5.60) adults; 2.50€ ($4) students, seniors, and children. Tues–Sun 10am–5pm (Thurs until 8pm). U-Bahn: Königsplatz.

Jüdisches Museum München Conceived in the 1920s, a Jewish museum is now a reality. The collection of permanent and temporary exhibits is part of a municipal building project in the center of Munich. It is a repository of Jewish culture in the city. On three exhibition floors, visitors can gain insights into Jewish life and culture as lived in Munich. On each floor is a study area or learning center and library where visitors can explore issues of interest. Adjacent to Marienplatz and Viktualienmarkt, the complex is part of a large Jewish community center that includes a new synagogue with a cornerstone that was laid in 2003, 65 years after the pogrom and the destruction of Munich's synagogues. On the site of the museum are a bookstore and a cafe/bar. The permanent exhibition of artifacts is located on the lower level.

St. Jakobsplatz 16. ℭ **089/233-96096.** www.juedisches-museum.muenchen.de. Admission 8€ ($13) adults, 4€ ($6.40) students and children. Tues–Sun 10am–6pm. U-Bahn or S-Bahn: Marienplatz.

Münchner Stadtmuseum (Municipal Museum) ★ Munich's Municipal Museum is to the city what the Bavarian National Museum is to the whole state. Housed in the former armory building, the museum offers insight into the city's history and the daily lives of its people. Special exhibitions about popular arts and traditions are frequently presented. A wooden model shows Munich in 1572. The extensive furniture collection is changed annually so that visitors have a chance to see various periods from the vast storehouse.

The museum's most important exhibit is its Morris dancers *(Moriskentanzer)* on the ground floor. These 10 figures, each 60cm (2 ft.) high, carved in wood, and painted in bright colors by Erasmus Grasser in 1480, are among the best examples of secular Gothic art in Germany. In the large Gothic hall on the ground floor, you can admire an important collection of armor and weapons from the 14th to the 18th century.

The second-floor photo museum traces the early history of the camera back to 1839. The historical collection of musical instruments on the fourth floor is one of the greatest of its kind in the world. It includes an ethnological collection. Daily at 6 and 9pm, the film museum shows two films from its extensive archives.

St. Jacobs-Platz 1. (C) **089/233-22370.** www.stadtmuseum-online.de. Admission 4€ ($6.40) adults, 2€ ($3.20) students and children 6–15, free for children 5 and under; 6€ ($9.60) family ticket; free for all on Sun. Tues–Sun 10am–6pm. U-Bahn or S-Bahn: Marienplatz.

Schack-Galerie To appreciate this florid and romantic overdose of sentimental German paintings of the 19th century, you've got to enjoy fauns and elves at play in picturesque, even magical, landscapes. Such art has its devotees. This once-private collection adheres to the baroque tastes of Count Adolf Friedrich von Schack of Schwerin (1815–94), who spent a rich life acquiring works by the likes of Spitzweg, Schwind, Feuerbach, and others, many others, some of whom would have been appropriately assigned to the dustbin of art history.

Prinzregentenstrasse 9. (C) **089/23805-224.** Admission 3€ ($4.80) adults, 2€ ($3.20) children. Wed–Sun 10am–5pm. Bus: 100.

Staatliche Museum Agyptischer Kunst (State Museum of Egyptian Art) The Egyptian collection is located in the Residenz (p. 134). The museum evolved from the collections made by Duke Albrecht V and King Ludwig I and contains pieces from every period of Egyptian history, from the predynastic period (4500–3000 B.C.) to the Coptic period (4th–9th c. A.D.). On exhibit are sculptures, reliefs, jewelry, tools, and weapons, as well as sarcophagi.

Hofgartenstrasse 1. (C) **089/29-85-46.** Admission 5€ ($8) adults, 4€ ($6.40) children. Tues 9am–5pm; Sat–Sun 10am–5pm. U-Bahn: Odeonsplatz. Bus: 53.

Staatliches Museum für Völkerkunde (Ethnology Museum) This museum, housed in an imposing building completed in 1865, has an extensive collection of art and artifacts from all over the world and is one of the principal museums of its kind in Europe. Particularly interesting is the Peruvian collection; the museum also has exhibitions from other parts of South America, East Asia, and West and Central Africa.

Maximilianstrasse 42. (C) **089/21-01-36-100.** Admission 3.50€ ($5.60) adults, 2.50€ ($4) students and seniors, free for children 14 and under. Thurs–Sun 9:30am–5:15pm. Tram: 17 or 19.

Städtische Galerie im Lenbachhaus ★ This gallery is in the ancient gold-colored villa of portrait painter Franz von Lenbach (1836–1904). It's devoted to both his work and that of other artists. Enter through the gardens. You'll first be greeted by a large collection of early pieces by Paul Klee (1879–1940). There's also an outstanding group of works by Kandinsky, leader of the Blue Rider movement in the early 20th century, and many 19th- and 20th-century paintings throughout the villa. The enclosed patio is pleasant for a coffee break.

Luisenstrasse 33. (☎ **089/23-33-20-00**. www.lenbachhaus.de. Admission 6€ ($9.60) adults, 3.50€ ($5.60) students and children 6–12, free for children 5 and under. Tues–Sun 10am–6pm. U-Bahn: Königsplatz.

Stuck-Villa (Jugendstil Museum)   This splendid house was designed by painter Franz von Stuck (1863–1928) for himself and mingles Art Nouveau style with elements of the late neoclassical. The ground-floor living rooms contain frescoes by the artist himself, and many of his paintings are on display. On the first floor is a permanent collection of Jugendstil (German Art Nouveau).

Prinzregentenstrasse 60. (☎ **089/45-55-511**. Free admission. Thurs–Sun 11am–6pm. U-Bahn: U4 to Prinzregentenplatz or Max-Weber-Platz.

5 PARKS, GARDENS & THE ZOO

Munich's city park, the 18th-century **Englischer Garten** ★, borders Schwabing on the east and extends almost to the Isar River. This is one of the largest and most beautiful city parks in Germany. It was the brainchild of Sir Benjamin Thompson, the English scientist who spent most of his life in the service of the Bavarian government. You can wander for hours along the walks and among the trees, flowers, and sunbathers. Nude sunbathing is permitted in certain areas of the park (some claim these areas are Munich's most popular tourist attraction). For a break, stop for tea on the plaza near the Chinese pagoda, or have a beer at the nearby beer garden. You might also take along a picnic put together at the elegant shop of **Alois Dallmayr,** or less expensive fare from **Hertie,** across from the Hauptbahnhof, from **Kaufhof** at Marienplatz, or from Munich's famous open-air market, the **Viktualienmarkt.**

Bordering Nymphenburg Park to the north is the **Botanischer Garten.** The garden is composed of 22 hectares (54 acres) of land, and has more than 15,000 varieties of flora. Each subdivision is devoted to a particular plant variety. The highlight is the Alpine garden, laid out according to geographic region and altitude. It's at its peak during the summer months. Another favored attraction is the heather garden; visitors to the garden during the late summer months are treated to an explosion of vibrant violets and purples. Other attractions include the rose garden, the fern gorge, and the series of hothouses that are home to numerous exotic tropical plants. To reach the Botanischer Garten, located on Menzingerstrasse 67 (☎ **089/17-86-13-10**; www.botmuc.de), take tram 17. The garden is open November to January daily from 9am to 5pm; February and March daily from 10am to 5pm; April, September, and October daily from 8am to 5pm; and May to August daily from 9am to 7pm. The hothouses open a half-hour before the garden. Admission is 3€ ($4.80) for adults and 2€ ($3.20) for children.

In west Munich, between Schloss Nymphenburg and the main railway line, stands the **Hirschgarten.** Designated by Elector Karl Theodor as a deer park in 1791, this 27-hectare (67-acre) tract of land is home to one of Munich's most tranquil stretches of greenery. In the 19th century, Münchners would visit the meadow to view the protected game as they grazed. The head huntsman secured the right to sell beer, which prompted the Hirschgarten to soar in popularity. Eventually a beer garden was established, now the largest in the world, with a capacity for 8,000 thirsty patrons. To reach the park, you can take the S-Bahn to Laim, or you can catch bus no. 32 or 83 from Steubenplatz. Although no longer a wildlife preserve, the Hirschgarten still draws the citizens of Munich for picnics, barbecues, or afternoon chess games.

Hellabrunn Zoo stands in Tierpark Hellabrunn, about 6km (3³/₄ miles) south of the city center, at Tierparkstrasse 30 (℃ **089/62-50-80;** www.zoo-munich.de; U-Bahn: Thalkirchen; bus: no. 52). It's one of the largest zoos in the world, with hundreds of animals roaming in a natural habitat. A walk through the attractive park is recommended even if you're not a zoo buff. There's a big children's zoo, as well as a large aviary. You can visit the zoo daily 8am to 6pm (in winter 9am–5pm); admission is 9€ ($14) for adults, 6€ ($9.60) for students and seniors, 4.50€ ($7.20) for children ages 4 to 14, and free for children 3 and under. To reach the park, you can take bus no. 52, leaving the Marienplatz, or U-Bahn U3 to Thalkirchen.

---

6 THE OLYMPIC GROUNDS

Olympiapark (℃ **089/30-67-0;** www.olympiapark-muenchen.de; U-Bahn: Olympiazentrum), site of the 1972 Olympic Games, occupies 300 hectares (741 acres) at the city's northern edge. More than 15,000 workers from 18 countries transformed the site into a park of nearly 5,000 trees, 43km (27 miles) of roads, 32 bridges, and a lake. Olympiapark is a city in itself: It has its own railway station, U-Bahn line, mayor, post office, churches, and elementary school. The planners even broke the city skyline by adding a 293m (961-ft.) television tower in the center of the park.

The area's showpiece is a huge **Olympic Stadium,** capable of seating 69,300 spectators, and topped by the largest roof in the world—nearly 67,000 sq. m. (721,182 sq. ft.) of tinted acrylic glass. The roof serves the additional purpose of collecting rainwater and draining it into the nearby Olympic lake.

Olympia Tower, Olympiapark (℃ **089/30-67-27-50),** is open daily 9am to midnight. A ride up the tower (on the speediest elevator on the continent, no less) costs 4.50€ ($7.20) for adults and 2.80€ ($4.50) for children 15 and under. An exclusive dining spot in the tower is the **Tower Restaurant** (℃ **089/30668585),** with a selection of international and German dishes; it's open daily 11am to 5pm and 6.30 to 11pm. A complete dinner costs 30€ to 60€ ($48–$96). The food is good and fresh, but of secondary consideration—most come here for the extraordinary view, which reaches to the Alps. Four observation platforms look out over Olympiapark. The Tower Restaurant revolves around its axis in 60 minutes, giving guests who linger a changing vista of Munich. Diners Club, MasterCard, and Visa are accepted.

At the base of the tower is the **Restaurant Olympiasee,** Spiridon-Louis-Ring 7 (℃ **089/30-67-28-22),** serving genuine Bavarian specialties, with meals costing 12€ ($19) and up. Favored items include half a roast chicken and various hearty soups. Food is served daily 10am to 7pm (8:30pm in summer). The restaurant is popular in summer because of its terrace. No credit cards are accepted.

The **BMW Museum,** Olympiapark 2 (℃ **0180/21-18-822;** www.bmw-museum.de), is open Tuesday to Friday 9am to 6pm, Saturday and Sunday 10am to 8pm. Admission is 12€ ($19) for adults and 6€ ($9.60) for children. The museum presents more than 90 years of BMW heritage, including a large range of BMW Roadsters plus the BMW Art Car Collection—called "rolling masterpieces." You can also see exhibitions of how the company is researching alternative forms of engine and energy resources, with a focus on hydrogen as a fuel. The circular building of the BMW Museum is called the "Bowl," and is the venue for temporary exhibitions.

Black September for the Olympics

The 1972 Munich Olympics was meant to celebrate peace among nations, and for the first 10 days, they did. However, on September 5, eight Palestinian terrorists, later claiming to be part of the "Black September" terrorist group, entered Olympic Village. Within a few minutes of entering the quarters of the sleeping Israeli athletes, they had already killed two Israelis and taken nine others hostage.

As the ensuing siege played out on TV sets around the world, the terrorists demanded the release of 200 Arab guerrillas jailed in Israel, and safe passage for themselves and their hostages. Few novelists could have conceived the plot (and mistakes by German law enforcement) that ensued, as negotiations helplessly and hopelessly dragged on between the terrorists and the West German security officials. In Israel, Golda Meir firmly stood by her government's policy of "not dealing with terrorists." That job fell clearly upon the shoulders of the West Germans.

On the evening of the day of the attack, helicopters transported the terrorists and their hostages from Olympic Village to the military air base at Fürstenfeldbruck, 24km (15 miles) away, landing at 10:30pm. The negotiations suddenly collapsed when a West German sharpshooter hidden in the darkness fired unexpectedly at the terrorists. The Palestinians quickly responded by unleashing automatic fire at the tied and bound Israelis; one tossed a hand grenade into a helicopter, killing the remaining hostages. In response, the West Germans unleashed their firepower, killing five of the terrorists before capturing the others.

Mark Spitz, an American Jew and winner of seven gold medals, was flown out of Germany for his own safety as the Olympic Games were suspended for the first time ever. The world mourned, and in a controversial decision, the Games resumed 34 hours later. The presiding officer of the games, Avery Brundage, issued a famous pronouncement, "The Games must go on!" and so they did.

7 ESPECIALLY FOR KIDS

From the Deutsches Museum to the Münchner Marionettentheater to the Bavaria Film Studio, kids love Munich.

On the third floor of the **Münchner Stadtmuseum** (p. 140) is an array of puppets from around the world, with star billing going to the puppeteer's art. The comical and grotesque figures include both marionettes and hand puppets. The collection also includes detailed puppet theaters and miniature scenery, a Lilliputian version of the world of the stage. A special department is devoted to fairground art, including carousel animals, shooting galleries, roller-coaster models, and wax and museum figures. The main exhibit contains the oldest-known carousel horses, dating from 1820.

If children have a favorite museum in Munich, it's the **Deutsches Museum** (p. 131), which has many interactive exhibits.

Spielzeugmuseum, in the Altes Rathaus, Marienplatz 15 (© **089/29-40-01;** U-Bahn or S-Bahn: Marienplatz), is a historical toy collection. It's open daily 10am to 5:30pm.

Admission is 3.50€ ($5.60) for adults, 1.50€ ($2.40) for children, and 6€ ($9.60) for a family.

At the **Münchner Marionettentheater,** Blumenstrasse 32 (© **089/26-57-12;** U-Bahn: Marienplatz), puppet shows delight adults as well as children; many productions are of Mozart operas. Performances are on Wednesday, Thursday, Saturday, and Sunday at 3pm. Admission is 8€ ($13) for adults and 6.50€ ($10) for children.

At the **Bavaria Film Studios** (p. 140), Europe's largest filmmaking center and Munich's version of Hollywood, children enjoy the film presentations and the Bavaria Action Show, which features a stunt team demonstrating fistfights and fire stunts, tumbling down staircases, and even taking a 28m-high (92-ft.) plunge. Guided 1¹/₂-hour tours (book 4 weeks in advance for a tour in English) are given March to October daily 9am to 4pm (off season 10am–3pm). Admission is 10€ ($16) for adults, 9€ ($14) for students and seniors, 7€ ($11) for children ages 4 to 14, and free for children 3 and under.

Hellabrunn Zoo has a large children's zoo where children can pet the animals. For details, see "Parks, Gardens & the Zoo," above.

Not to be ignored is the **Circus Krone,** Marsstrasse 43 (© **089/55-81-66;** U-Bahn: Hackerbrüke). It might be compared to London's Albert Hall, because its productions are so varied. Matinee performances are held daily. Tickets are 15€ to 36€ ($24–$58) adults, and 9€ to 30€ ($14–$48) seniors and children.

---

8 SIGHTSEEING TOURS

BY BUS

City tours encompass aspects of both modern and medieval Munich, and depart from the main railway station aboard blue-sided buses. Departures, depending on the season and the tour, occur between two and eight times a day, and tours are conducted in both German and English. Most tours last no more than 2¹/₂ hours, with the exception of a scientific odyssey that focuses on the technological triumphs of Munich as witnessed by various museums that include the Deutsches Museum. That experience usually lasts for a minimum of 4 hours, plus the time you spend wandering through museums at the end of your tour.

Tours cost 11€ to 60€ ($18–$96) adults, 6€ to 14€ ($9.60–$22) children 13 and under. Advance reservations for most city tours aren't required, and you can buy your ticket from the bus driver at the time you board. Tours leave from the square in front of the Hauptbahnhof, at Hertie's.

To go farther afield and visit major attractions in the environs (such as Berchtesgaden or Ludwig II's castles), contact **Sightseeing Gray Line,** Schützenstrasse 9 (© **089/549-075-60;** U-Bahn or S-Bahn: Hauptbahnhof), open year-round Monday to Friday 9am to 6pm and Saturday 9am to 1pm. (Travel agents in Munich, as well as the concierge or reception staff at your hotel, can also book these tours.) At least a half-dozen touring options are available, ranging from a 1-hour overview of the city to full-day excursions to such outlying sites as Berchtesgaden, Oberammergau, and Hohenschwangau, all covered in chapter 12. To participate in tours that go outside the city limits, advance reservations are required, especially if you want the bus to pick you up at any of Munich's hotels.

BY BIKE

Pedal pushers will want to try the popular **Mike's Bike Tour,** Hochbrückenstrasse (© **089/255-43-988;** www.mikesbiketours.com). Bike-rental services include maps, locks, child and infant seats, and helmets at no extra charge. English and bilingual tours of central Munich run from March 16 to April 15 and September 1 to November 10 daily at 12:30pm and from April 16 to August 31 daily at 4pm. Participants meet under the tower of the Old Town Hall, a gray building on the east end of Marienplatz. The tour veers from the bike paths only long enough for a lunch stop at a beer garden. Fear not, fainthearted: The bikes are new, and the rides are easy, with plenty of time for historical explanations, photo opportunities, and question-and-answer sessions. The cost for a tour, including the bike, is 24€ ($38). It is also possible to rent a bike for 12€ ($19) for same-day return or 21€ ($34) overnight.

ON FOOT

Munich Walk Tours, in English (© **0171/2740204;** www.munichwalktours.de), is a fun way to get to know the city. Munich is shared from various expert points of view; these range from a straight City Walk, taking in the highlights, to a Beer and Brewery Tour. The City Walk is offered only from January 2 to April 30 and October 17 to November 30 daily at 10:45am, lasting $2^1/_4$ hours and costing 10€ ($16). The Beer and Brewery tour departs January 2 to April 30 and October 2 to December 31, Monday, Wednesday, and Saturday at 5:30pm; May 1 to September 15 daily 6:15pm; and September 16 to October 1 daily 2:30pm. It lasts 3 hours and costs 18€ ($29). Hitler's Munich—Third Reich Tour, an intriguing sojourn, is conducted only January 2 to March 31 and November 1 to December 31 Monday and Wednesday to Sunday at 10:30am; April 1 to June 30 daily 10am. It lasts $2^1/_2$ hours and costs 12€ ($19). Children 13 and under with an adult go free on these tours. The meeting point for all tours is at the main entrance of the New Gothic Rathaus on Marienplatz. Call to confirm starting times and places to meet or to ask about other tours.

9 ACTIVITIES & OUTDOOR PURSUITS

BEACHES, POOLS & WATERSPORTS   On hot weekends, Münchners travel to nearby lakes, the **Ammersee** and the **Starnberger See,** where bathing facilities are clearly marked. Both are a short drive from the city and are favorites for sailing, windsurfing, and other watersports (see chapter 11 for more information). Visitors can also go for a dip at **Maria-Einsiedel,** in the frigid, snow-fed waters of the Isar River.

The city has several public swimming pools. The largest of these is the giant competition-size pool in the Olympiapark, the **Olympia-Schwimmhalle** (© **089/30-67-22-90;** U-Bahn: Olympiazentrum). Admission is 5€ ($8). Information on both sailing and windsurfing is available from the **Bayerischer Landes-Sportverbund,** Georg-Brauchle-Ring 93 (© **089/15-70-23-66**).

BIKING   The city is full of bike paths. Most major streets have bike lanes, and the many parks and gardens scattered throughout Munich allow for hours of riding. The tourist office provides suggested tours in its *Radi Touren*. Although printed in German, the excellent maps are easily followed. You can rent bikes at **Mike's Bike Tour** (© **089/255-43-988;** see above).

EXPLORING MUNICH

7

ACTIVITIES & OUTDOOR PURSUITS

(Tips) **Munich's Soccer Craze**

Like Italy, England, and Brazil, Germany is crazed over soccer. Munich's famous soccer team (and one of Europe's most outstanding) is the **Bayern München.** However, it's a matter of civic pride to many Münchners, especially when they're soaked with beer, to root enthusiastically for a less-well-rated local team, **T.S.V. 1860 München.** This team was around about 40 years before Bayern München was founded, and it still arouses local loyalty—something like the Chicago White Sox as opposed to the much beloved and beleaguered Chicago Cubs. Both teams call the Olympic Stadium in Olympiapark their home.

If you want to attend a match, chances are good there'll be one in Munich's enormous Olympic Stadium (p. 143). For more information, call the Soccer League Association at **089/69-93-10.** To get tickets for any sports event, call (✆) **089/54-81-81-81,** Monday to Friday 10am to 8pm, and Saturday 10am to 5pm.

BOATING Rowboats add to the charm of the lakes in the **Englischer Garten.** (There's also a kiosk located at the edge of the Kleinhesseloher See for rentals during clement weather.) There are rowboat rentals on the southern bank of the **Olympiasee,** in the Olympiapark.

Raft trips on the Isar River, between the town of Wolfrathausen and Munich, are offered from early May until late September. A raft may contain up to 60 other passengers, but if the idea appeals to you, contact **Franz and Sebastian Seitner,** Heideweg 9, D-82515 Wolfrathausen (✆ **08171/18-320**).

GOLF One of the best courses is **Golf-Club Feldafing,** Tutzingerstrasse 15, D-82340 Feldafing (✆ **08157/9-33-40**), situated beside a clear Bavarian lake, the Starnberger See. It's open from April to mid-November every day from 8am to 7pm (closed in winter). Depending on the day of the week you arrive, greens fees for 18 holes cost 70€ ($112) on weekdays and 90€ ($144) on weekends and holidays. Be warned in advance that although you can play without a reservation every Monday to Friday (if you have a handicap of 34 or less), on Saturday and Sunday you'll need to be accompanied by a club member. **Golfclub Strasslach** (also known as the Munich Golf Club), Tölserstrasse 95 (✆ **08170/929-1811**), requires visitors to reserve their tee times in advance. The course charges greens fees of 60€ ($96). From April to October only, this course is open to the general public Monday to Friday 8am to 7pm; weekends are reserved for members only. Both clubs are a 45-minute drive south of Munich's center.

JOGGING Regardless of the season, the most lushly landscaped place in Munich is the **Englischer Garten** (U-Bahn: Münchner Freiheit), which has an 11km (6³/₄-mile) circumference and an array of dirt and asphalt tracks. Also appropriate are the grounds of the **Olympiapark** (U-Bahn: Olympiazentrum) or the park surrounding **Schloss Nymphenburg** (U-Bahn: Rotkreuzplatz, then tram 17 toward Amalienburgstrasse; bus: 41).

148 More convenient to the center of the city's commercial district is a jog along the embankments of the Isar River.

TENNIS   At least 200 indoor and outdoor tennis courts are scattered around greater Munich. Many can be booked in advance by calling 🄲 **089/54-81-81-81.** For information on Munich's many tennis tournaments and competitions, contact the **Bayerischer Tennis Verbund,** Georg-Brauchle-Ring 93, D-80992 München ((🄲 **089/15-70-23-66**).

Strolling in Munich

A walk through Munich is the only true way to get to know it. The Altstadt (Old Town/historic center) is the traditional walking tour for most visitors; however, travelers with more time may enjoy visiting some of the lesser known but equally interesting sights near this historic city center. A walk through Schwabing is also a must for those who want to have a more offbeat experience.

WALKING TOUR 1 THE HISTORIC CENTER

START:	Frauenkirche.
FINISH:	Königsplatz.
TIME:	2¹/₂ hours, not counting shopping or any visits inside places mentioned here.
BEST TIMES:	Daylight hours during clement weather.
WORST TIMES:	Monday to Friday from 7:30 to 9am and 4:30 to 6pm, because of heavy traffic.

With a history spanning centuries of building and rebuilding, Munich is one of Europe's most architecturally interesting cities. Postwar developments have marred Munich's once-homogeneous look, but in rebuilding their city after the war, Münchners tried to respect tradition as much as possible. If you, like the ordinary visitor, have time for only one walking tour, make it the historic center, the point where the city began before it branched out in all directions.

First take either the U-Bahn or the S-Bahn to Marienplatz. After leaving the subway stop, the tour of the historic center begins to the immediate west, where you'll see a dignified cathedral with impressive brickwork.

❶ Frauenkirche

This cathedral was begun in 1468 on the site of a much older church and was completed after 20 years. The majestically somber building is capped with twin towers. In spite of massive bombings, these towers escaped Allied bombardments during World War II. They now serve as landmarks on Munich's skyline and have also become a symbol of the city.

Walk southeast along any of the pedestrian alleyways radiating away from the rear of the church. In a couple of minutes, you're in the most famous medieval square of Munich.

❷ Marienplatz

In the center of this square, a golden statue of the Virgin Mary (the **Mariensäule**) rises above pavement that was first laid in the 1300s when the rest of the city's streets were a morass of mud and sewage. On the square's northern boundary sits the richly ornamented, neo-Gothic **Neues Rathaus (New City Hall),** built between 1867 and 1908 as a symbol of Munich's power. On its facade is the famous **Glockenspiel,** the mechanical clock that performs a miniature tournament several times a day. At the square's eastern border, beyond a stream of traffic, is the simpler and smaller **Altes Rathaus (Old City Hall),** which was rebuilt in its present form in 1470 after fire destroyed an even earlier version.

From the square, walk south along Rindermarkt, encircling the masonry bulk of:

❸ Peterskirche

This church's interior is a sun-flooded fantasy of baroque stucco and gilt. Completed in 1180, the church was built on the foundations of a Romanesque basilica erected around 1000. St. Peter's is the oldest parish church in Munich, and for many years, it was the only one. Explore the richly decorated interior, if you have time. If not, settle for a view of the impressive Gothic facade, which was constructed between 1379 and 1386 after a fire destroyed the church in 1327.

Walk around the outside of the church to the back, where you'll find the sprawling premises of one of the best-stocked food emporiums in Europe, the:

❹ Viktualienmarkt

Known as "Munich's stomach," this is where you can snack, have a beer, pick up makings for a picnic, or just observe the ritual of European grocery shopping.

At the northern end, at the corner where streets Rosen Tal and Im Tal meet, rises the richly ornate baroque walls of the:

❺ Heiliggeist (Holy Ghost) Church

This Gothic "Hall Church" originally belonged to the 14th-century Hospice of the Holy Ghost, a medieval order flourishing in the 1300s. It was built on foundations laid by another structure in the 12th century, and the church was completed in 1730. After other hospice buildings were demolished in 1885, three bays were added to the western facade of the church, giving it a neobaroque facade. World War II bombs brought much destruction, and only the original choir, buttresses, and north wall of the nave remain intact. The rest of the building is a reconstruction.

Cross the busy boulevard identified as Im Tal and walk north along Maderbraustrasse (within a block it changes to Orlandostrasse). Here, look for the entrance to the most famous beer hall in Europe, the state-owned:

❻ Hofbräuhaus

For a description, see p. 174. For now, note its location for an eventual return.

Now, walk northwest along Pfisterstrasse. To your left are the walls of the:

❼ Alter Hof

This palace was originally built in 1255, and once served as the palace of the Wittelsbachs, although it was later eclipsed by even grander palaces. Since 1816, it has housed the colorless offices of Munich's financial bureaucracies.

On the opposite (northern) edge of Pfisterstrasse rise the walls of the:

❽ Münzhof

Built between 1563 and 1567, this building has, during its lifetime, housed, in turn, the imperial stables, the first museum north of the Alps, and (1809–1986) a branch of the government mint. Today, it's headquarters for Munich's Landmark Preservation office (Landesamt für Denkmalschutz). If it's open, the double tiers and massive stone columns of the building's Bavarian Renaissance courtyard are worth a visit.

Pfisterstrasse funnels into a broader street, Hofgraben. Walk west for 1 block, and then turn right (north) along Residenzstrasse. The first building on your right is the main post office (Hauptpost), and a few paces on is:

❾ Max-Joseph-Platz

Designed as a focal point for the monumental Maximilianstrasse that radiates east, the plaza was built in the 19th century on the site of a Franciscan convent in honor of Bavaria's first king.

At the north edge of the plaza lie the vast exhibition space and labyrinthine corridors of one of Munich's finest museums, the:

❿ Residenz

Constructed in different stages and styles from 1500 to 1850, the Residenz was the official home of Bavarian rulers until 1918. Restored and rebuilt in its original form after World War II, the complicated

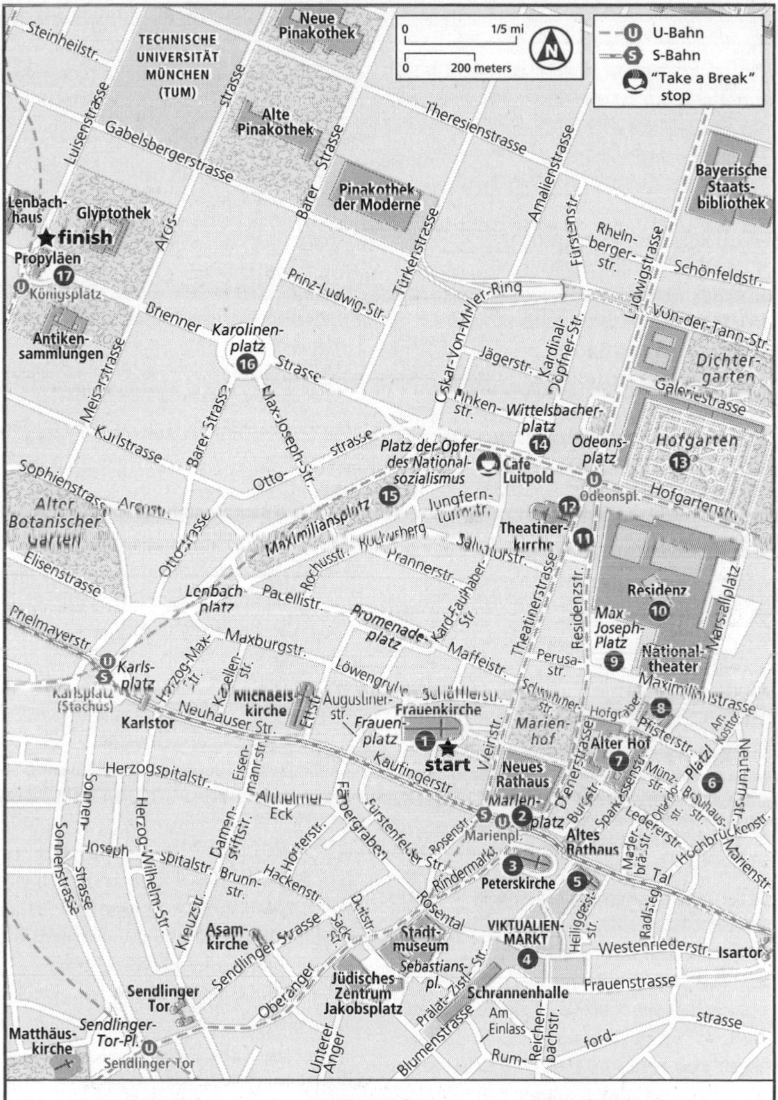

0
1/5 mi
0
200 meters
N
U-Bahn
S-Bahn
"Take a Break" stop
Neue Pinakothek
TECHNISCHE UNIVERSITÄT MÜNCHEN (TUM)
Alte Pinakothek
Pinakothek der Moderne
Bayerische Staats-bibliothek
Lenbach-haus
Glyptothek
finish
Propyläen
Königsplatz
Antiken-sammlungen
Karolinen-platz
Platz der Opfer des National-sozialismus
Cafe Luitpold
Wittelsbacher-platz
Odeons-platz
Odeonspl.
Hofgarten
Dichter-garten
Theatiner-kirche
Residenz
Max Joseph-Platz
National-theater
Alter Botanischer Garten
Lenbach-platz
Maximiliansplatz
Promenade-platz
Karls-platz
Karlsplatz (Stachus)
Karlstor
Michaels-kirche
Frauenkirche
Frauen-platz
start
Marien-hof
Neues Rathaus
Marien-platz
Marienpl.
Alter Hof
Altes Rathaus
Peterskirche
Altheimer Eck
Asam-kirche
Stadt-museum
VIKTUALIEN-MARKT
Jüdisches Zentrum Jakobsplatz
Schrannenhalle
Sendlinger Tor
Sendlinger-Tor-Pl.
Sendlinger Tor
Matthäus-kirche
Isartor
Steinheilstr.
Gabelsbergerstrasse
Theresienstrasse
Luisenstrasse
Arcisstrasse
Barer Strasse
Amalienstrasse
Türkenstrasse
Fürstenstr.
Rheinberger-str.
Ludwigstrasse
Schönfeldstr.
Von-der-Tann-Str.
Prinz-Ludwig-Str.
Oskar-Von-Miller-Ring
Brienner Strasse
Jägerstr.
Kardinal-Döpfner-Str.
Finken-str.
Galeriestrasse
Hofgartenstr.
Meiserstrasse
Karlstrasse
Max-Joseph-Str.
Ottostrasse
Sophienstrasse
Elisenstrasse
Prielmayerstr.
Pacellistr.
Rochusstr.
Prannerstr.
Salvatorstr.
Maxburgstr.
Löwengrube
Maffeistr.
Theatinerstrasse
Residenzstr.
Perusa-str.
Maximilianstrasse
Neuhauser Str.
Augustiner-str.
Kaufingerstr.
Weinstr.
Herzogspitalstr.
Sonnenstrasse
Herzog-Wilhelm-Str.
Josephspitalstr.
Damenstiftstr.
Hackenstr.
Hotterstr.
Färbergraben
Fürstenfelder Str.
Rosenstr.
Rindermarkt
Rosental
Kreuzstr.
Sendlinger Strasse
Oberanger
Unterer Anger
Sebastians-pl.
Prälat-Zistl-Str.
Blumenstrasse
Am Einlass
Reichenbachstr.
Frauenstrasse
Westenriederstr.
Heiliggeiststr.
Radlsteg
Tal
Pfisterstr.
Ledererstr.
Hochbrückenstr.
Neuturmstr.
Marienstr.
Platzl

1 Frauenkirche
2 Marienplatz
3 Peterskirche
4 Viktualienmarkt
5 Heiliggeist Church
6 Hofbräuhaus
7 Alter Hof
8 Münzhof
9 Max-Joseph-Platz
10 Residenz
11 Feldherrnhalle
12 Theatinerkirche
13 Hofgarten
14 Wittelsbacher-Platz
15 Maximiliansplatz
16 Karolinenplatz
17 Königsplatz

site has seven semiconcealed courtyards, lavish apartments that have housed foreign visitors like Elizabeth II and Charles de Gaulle, and museums that include the Residenz Museum, the Treasure House of the Residenz, the richly gilded rococo **Cuvilliés Theater** (1753), and the Herkulessaal, a concert hall noted for its baroque decorations.

Walk from Max-Joseph-Platz north along Residenzstrasse. Make the first left and walk west on Salvatorstrasse. Within another block, turn right (north) along Theatinerstrasse. On your right you'll immediately notice an important Munich landmark, the:

⓫ Feldherrnhalle

This open-air loggia was designed by Friedrich von Gärtner and constructed between 1841 and 1844. Von Gärtner's model was the Loggia dei Lanzi in Florence. King Ludwig I commissioned the construction of the loggia as a tribute to the Bavarian army. The bronze figures honoring Bavarian generals Tilly (1559–1632) and Wrede (1767–1838) are based on drawings by Ludwig Schwanthaler.

The two lions on the steps are the work of a sculptor, Ruemann, in 1906. Although Hitler's attempted putsch in Munich failed, along with the subsequent march to the Feldherrnhalle, the loggia later became a Nazi rallying point. Today, the Brown Shirts are replaced by street singers and musicians.

On the western (opposite) side of the same street (Theatinerstrasse) is the:

⓬ Theatinerkirche (Church of St. Kajetan)

Completed in 1690, this church's tripledomed, Italian-baroque facade was added about a century later by the Cuvilliés team of father and son. Its crypt contains the tombs of many of the Wittelsbachs.

Continue north, passing through Odeonsplatz, below which several subway lines converge. On the northeastern side of this square lie the flowers, fountains, and cafes of one of Munich's most pleasant small parks, the:

⓭ Hofgarten

Originally laid out for members of the royal court in 1613, this garden was opened to the public in 1780. Here, as well as along the avenues radiating away from it, lie many opportunities for you to:

> **☕ TAKE A BREAK**
> Do as the Münchners do and enjoy the panorama of Odeonsplatz and the nearby Hofgarten. One attractive choice is **Café Luitpold**, Briennerstrasse 11 (☎ **089/24-28-750**). Rebuilt in a streamlined design after World War II, it has, in the past, welcomed such cafe-loving habitués as Ibsen, Johann Strauss the Younger, and Kandinsky.

Walk west along Briennerstrasse, through a neighborhood lined with impressive buildings. On your right, notice the heroic statue of Maximilian I, the Great Elector (1597–1651), rising from the center of:

⓮ Wittelsbacher-Platz

One of the most famous squares of Munich, Wittelsbacher-Platz evokes, for some, a grand hall. It's enveloped by palaces, most of which were designed by Leo von Klenze, including the 1820 Palais Arco-Zinneberg on the square's western side. The 1825 Wittelsbacher-Palais rises on the north side of the square. Today, it is the head office of Siemens. The impressive neoclassical equestrian statue in the center is much photographed. Bertel Thorvaldsen, one of Denmark's leading sculptors, created this statue in 1830. Also in the center is Wittelsbacher-Brunnen, or Wittelsbach Fountain, the most celebrated in the city. It is another neoclassical work, created in the last decade of the late 1800s by Adolf von Hildebrand, the noted sculptor.

Continue on Briennerstrasse until you see the gentle fork to your left, Sonnenstrasse. This leads into the verdant and stylish perimeter of:

⓯ Maximiliansplatz

This leafy square begins at Max-Joseph-Platz and runs to the east. Maximilian II wanted a platz and a street more loosely defined than the rigidly designed Ludwig-strasse. Maximiliansplatz and Maximilian-strasse were conceived and designed so that shops, hotels, gardens, restaurants, offices, and public buildings could coexist side by side. Thus, the "Maximilianic style" was created, which is a medley of various styles with many elements from past architectural movements, such as Gothic. Shop at your leisure or plan to return later.

For the moment, return to Briennerstrasse, turn left (west), and head toward the 26m (85-ft.) obelisk (erected in 1833) that soars above:

⑯ Karolinenplatz

This was the city's first star-shaped open space. Based on his model for the Place de l'Etoile in Paris, Karl von Fisher mapped out this square from 1809 to 1812. Although it doesn't match the radiance of its inspiration, it is nonetheless an impressive landmark. But don't judge Von Fischer too harshly when you see the square today. His uniform neoclassical look has been regrettably altered in the postwar era

by buildings no longer in harmony with his original design. In the center of the square, Leo von Klenze placed an obelisk commemorating the 30,000 (or more) Bavarian soldiers who were lost in the ill-fated Russian campaign of 1812.

To the northwest, Karolinenplatz is linked by Briennerstrasse to:

⑰ Königsplatz

In the early 19th century, Crown Prince Ludwig (later Ludwig I) selected this formal neoclassical design from an architectural competition. Its perimeter is ringed with some of Germany's most impressive museum buildings, the Doric-inspired Propyläen monument (west side), the Antikensammlungen (south side), and the Ionic-fronted Glyptothek (north side).

At Königsplatz, you will be at one of the major subway stops of Munich, a 5 minute ride south to the Hauptbahnhof, where you can catch subways to most of the major sightseeing attractions of Munich, or even to attractions in Bavaria or in the suburbs of Munich.

EXPLORING WEST OF MARIENPLATZ

WALKING TOUR 2   EXPLORING WEST OF MARIENPLATZ

START:	Marienplatz.
FINISH:	Münchner Stadtmuseum.
TIME:	2 hours, not counting shopping or any visits inside places mentioned here.
BEST TIMES:	Daylight hours during clement weather.
WORST TIMES:	Monday to Friday from 7:30 to 9am and 4:30 to 6pm, because of heavy traffic.

Those walkers with more time who would like a more penetrating look at the Altstadt (Old Town) can take yet a second tour, this one lying west of the heart of Munich, the Marienplatz. Among other attractions, such as monuments and fountains, this tour passes by some of Munich's best-known churches.

To reach the starting point of this tour from the Marienplatz, walk west down the shop-lined Koffingerstrasse to Liebfrauenstrasse and past the Frauenkirche (visited on the previous tour) and continue west to:

❶ Michaelskirche (St. Michael's)

This is the largest Renaissance church north of the Alps. The ruler, Duke William the

Pious (1583–97), made the church the spiritual center of the Counter-Reformation. Resting under a barrel-vaulted roof (the second largest in the world after St. Peter's in Rome), the church (architect unknown) houses the tombs of King Ludwig II and other Wittelsbach rulers. The facade is graced with a large sculpture of the Archangel Michael, a splendid bronze figure made by Hubert Gerhard in 1588.

Continue west on Neuhauser Strasse to the:

❷ Richard Strauss Fountain

The fountain's central column has scenes from Strauss's *Salome* (1905) interpreted, with flair, in bas-relief.

Continue west on Neuhauser Strasse to the:

❸ Bürgersaal

Dating from 1710, this "Citizens' Hall" was the meeting place and house of worship for the Marian Congregation, a Jesuit branch. Designed by Giovanni Antonio Viscardi, the hall became a fully consecrated church in 1778 but was mostly destroyed by Allied air raids in World War II. Immediately rebuilt in 1945 and 1946, it looks like it used to, and many visitors assume it is much older. The facade, with its double pilasters, is the original, as is the figure of Madonna and Child on a crescent moon seen in the double staircase. The lower floor contains the tomb of Rupert Mayer (1876–1945), a Jesuit who bravely resisted the Nazi regime.

Continue to the end of the pedestrian mall, where you'll see the fountain of the little boy at the medieval Karlstor. You've come to the:

❹ Stachus (Karlsplatz)

This busy intersection was designed and constructed when the old town walls of Munich were demolished in 1791. The official name of the square is Karlsplatz, in honor of the Elector Karl Theodor. Because he was viewed as an unfair ruler, however, the townspeople defiantly refused to call the square Karlsplatz. Instead, they came up with the nickname "Stachus." The exact meaning has never been established, and no one seems to agree. "Stachus" may have referred to a local eatery that stood on this square in the 18th century, or it could even refer to a marksman who practiced nearby.

Diagonally and to the right is the 19th-century Palace of Justice. Directly in front of you, at a distance, is the main train station. Turn 180 degrees and walk back to the Richard Strauss fountain. You will enjoy one of the finest views in Munich as the silhouette and facade of Michaelskirche appear on the skyline. Turn right at Eisenmannstrasse and head for:

❺ St.-Anna-Damenstift

This beautiful late-baroque church was once attached to a convent and is today a secondary school for girls. The architect, Johann Baptist Gunetzhainer, constructed the church between 1732 and 1735, and the Asam brothers, Egid Quirin and Cosmas Damian, did notable stucco and fresco work inside. Destroyed in part by World War II bombs, the church was reconstructed in its original style in the early 1950s. Miraculously, the facade escaped the bombing unscathed. Amidst the debris of war, many statues and figures were discovered that were incorporated into the reconstructed altars, giving them an antique look.

The street name changes to Damenstiftstrasse as you go south for the duration of the block and you pass number 4, a pretty old house, and the 18th-century Palais Lerchenfeld. Although you've not made a turn, the street is now named Kreuzstrasse, home of the:

❻ Allerheiligenkirche am Kreuz

Jorg von Halspach, popularly known as Ganghofer, not only designed the more famous Frauenkirche but also created this parish church in 1478. Today, its parishioners are primarily Ukrainian Catholics. In 1620, the church received a heavy baroque overlay, and many major artists from the 17th century contributed to its present look, including Johan Rottenhammer, who painted *The Madonna Appearing Before St. Augustine* on the High Altar.

Continue directly south along Kreuzstrasse until you come to the junction with Herzog-Wilhelm-Strasse. Across this street lies:

❼ Sendlingertorplatz

The Sendlinger Tor, once a medieval fortification, was built in 1318, about the same time as the Karlstor (one of the town gates

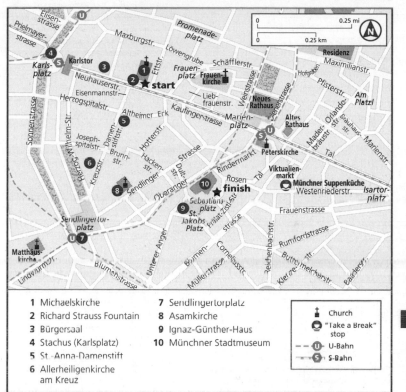

1 Michaelskirche
2 Richard Strauss Fountain
3 Bürgersaal
4 Stachus (Karlsplatz)
5 St.-Anna-Damenstift
6 Allerheiligenkirche
  am Kreuz
7 Sendlingertorplatz
8 Asamkirche
9 Ignaz-Günther-Haus
10 Münchner Stadtmuseum

✝ Church
☕ "Take a Break" stop
--Ⓤ-- U-Bahn
--Ⓢ-- S-Bahn

to the Altstadt). The two side towers of the gates are all that remain.

Sendlinger Strasse, a lengthy, brightly colored avenue of small commercial outlets, leads back to Marienplatz. Walking northeast, stand back on the right side of the street admiring the facade of the:

⑧ Asamkirche

The Asam brothers created this church building in 1746 as a sort of monument to themselves. Be sure to step inside to see the extravagant Bavarian rococo interior, courtesy of Egid Quirin Asam, along with frescoes and paintings by his brother, Cosmas Damian. A figure of St. John of

Nepomuk, to whom the building is dedicated, is above the door. Next door to the church is the Asam brothers' private house; note the graceful facade with its many allusions to art and poetry.

After viewing Asamkirche, continue northeast along Sendlinger Strasse, taking the second right southeast along Dultstrasse, cross the Oberanger Rinder, and head into St. Jakobsplatz, where you'll see the:

⑨ Ignaz-Günther-Haus

This memorial house is a tribute to the 18th-century Bavarian rococo artist who lived and worked out of the edifice during his lifetime. Restoration was completed in 1977, and the Münchner Stadtmuseum (see below) now maintains it. The Madonna out front is a Günther replica, and an exhibit inside displays some of his other works.

On the same block is the:

⑩ Münchner Stadtmuseum

Housed in the old, 15th-century city arsenal, this museum is turreted in front. Exhibits vary seasonally, often featuring one of the countless local artists in Munich's cultural history. Several displays, however, are permanent and are reviewed on p. 140.

WINDING DOWN
You've finished! If you want to take a break, continue down Sendlinger Strasse, veering left into Sebastiansplatz, and admire the old houses lining the street. Exit the Sebastiansplatz from its eastern edge and walk for 3 blocks along the meandering length of the Prälat-Zistl-Strasse until you reach the Viktualienmarkt. The **Münchner Suppenküche** (no phone) is a Munich legend, a true soup kitchen at what is called "the stomach of the city." On the coldest days, join the Münchners devouring hearty soups such as *Gulaschsuppe* (goulash soup), sausage and sauerkraut, and *Krustis* (sandwiches). Or buy some bread and fruit at one of the many stands, sit back, and enjoy the fountains and statues that surround you.

WALKING TOUR 3 SCHWABING

START:	Wedekindplatz.
FINISH:	Englischer Garten.
TIME:	2½ hours with minimal stopovers.
BEST TIMES:	Morning to mid-afternoon while students bustle to and from class.
WORST TIMES:	Monday to Friday from 7:30 to 9am and 4:30 to 6pm.

Schwabing was incorporated into the city in 1890. Its golden era as an artists' center was from 1890 to 1914. Novelists Thomas Mann and Herman Hesse, the poet Rainer Maria Rilke, satirist Karl Kraus, and playwright Franz Wedekind were some of the better-known authors who lived in the area. For a short period after World War II, it became legendary as Germany's hip center. The days of *vie de bohème* (bohemian life) are long gone, and Schwabing has lost most of its distinctive character. In many ways, its situation is comparable to that of New York's Greenwich Village, which is hardly the haven for artists, writers, and poets that it once was. Rents have soared to ridiculous highs, and the artists in Schwabing long ago retreated to cheaper areas. A more monied crowd occupies Schwabing today, as it has become the "in" place to live in Munich.

The tour begins in the section of Schwabing behind the Münchner Freiheit station known as Old Schwabing. Movie theaters, music clubs, and even a handful of cabarets give it the markings of cosmopolitanism.

❶ Wedekindplatz

Once the community market, the Wedekindplatz is the neighborhood's focal point. It is named for Franz Wedekind, whose "Lulu" plays about a *femme fatale* provided the basis for the 1929 Louise Brooks film, *Pandora's Box,* and for Alban Berg's opera *Lulu.*

Head west down Fellitzschstrasse past the Münchner Freiheit rail station, and cross the:

❷ Leopoldstrasse

The most famous street in Schwabing is also the most fun to walk down and to take in scenes of local life. It is a favorite

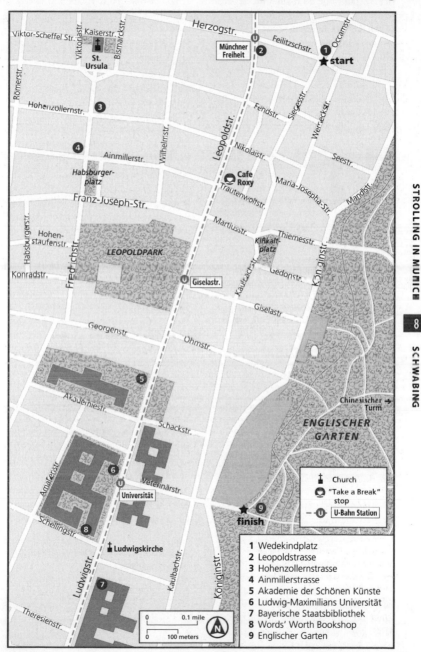

STROLLING IN MUNICH

8

SCHWABING

Legend:

- ♱ Church
- ☕ "Take a Break" stop
- Ⓤ U-Bahn Station

1 Wedekindplatz
2 Leopoldstrasse
3 Hohenzollernstrasse
4 Ainmillerstrasse
5 Akademie der Schönen Künste
6 Ludwig-Maximilians Universität
7 Bayerische Staatsbibliothek
8 Words' Worth Bookshop
9 Englischer Garten

promenade for both visitors and local residents. Cafes line both sides of the street, and there are many restaurants and bars to enjoy. On a summer evening, Leopoldstrasse is the place to be. Students, struggling artists, whatever, fill the streets hawking their wares, usually arts and crafts—often trash. The street becomes like an outdoor souk, with vendors selling everything from carvings to leather items, some of dubious quality.

> ### TAKE A BREAK
> The cafe/bar, **Café Roxy**, Leopoldstrasse 48 (℡ **089/34-92-92**), is a good place for a refreshing cold drink, perhaps a beer, which seems to be the choice for most patrons. If you're hungry, you can also order some Bavarian or Italian dishes. An urbane crowd is attracted to this hip cafe, the best place to relax in the neighborhood.

A block farther on, take a left on Wilhelmstrasse, travel south for 2 blocks, and then take a right on:

❸ Hohenzollernstrasse

Here you can further study Jugendstil. The facades that adorn the buildings lining this street are fine examples of the bright and geometric decorations that typify that style. Look also for the little quirky fashion boutiques that give the street its fame.

Continue west to the junction with Römerstrasse. Once here, head south along Römerstrasse until you come to Ainmillerstrasse, at which point you walk east.

❹ Ainmillerstrasse

The artistic unshackling of the Jugendstil movement laid the foundation for further development of an artistic consciousness that was the basis for many of the eager manifestos set forth by the *Blaue Reiter* (Blue Rider) school. Appropriately, Wassily Kandinsky, the premier artist associated with the Blue Rider movement, once lived down the street. You will find many of the finest examples of Jugendstil on the

east end of the street—including the facade at no. 22 that sports Adam and Eve lying at the base of the tree of knowledge. Continue east to Leopoldstrasse, where Kandinsky once lived in a building long gone.

Head south down Leopoldstrasse until you approach the:

❺ Akademie der Schönen Künste (Academy of Fine Arts)

This building, erected at the end of the 19th century, enthusiastically recalls the Italian Renaissance. The academy is best known for the "Secession" movement that was spearheaded by its students in the 1890s. This protest against traditional aesthetics and a call for a new creativity in the arts led quickly to the growth of Jugendstil and helped define Munich as a centerpiece of the Art Nouveau movement.

Continue south on Leopoldstrasse and you will enter the:

❻ Ludwig-Maximilians Universität (University of Munich) campus

Frederich von Gärtner engineered the construction of the edifice, one of the most aesthetically fine in all of Munich. Gärtner relieved Leo von Klenze (who designed the Alte Pinakothek) as Bavaria's court architect, and the relative flamboyance of this structure is compared favorably with Von Klenze's more staid approach. It was here that the student society, the White Rose, made a last effort to resist Hitler in 1942 to 1943. Its leaders, Sophie and Hans Scholl, were brutally executed for "civil disobedience." (A memorial to the movement is located in the lower mezzanine at Geschwister-Scholl-Platz 1; open weekdays 10am–4pm.)

A 2-minute walk south is the twin-spired university church of St. Ludwig's and the:

❼ Bayerische Staatsbibliothek (Bavarian State Library)

This mammoth library is one of the largest in all of Europe. It stands where the Schwabing Gate of medieval Munich once cast its shadow.

Before leaving campus, duck down Schellingstrasse and drop in at:

❽ Words' Worth Bookshop

This shop is located at Schellingstrasse 3. The student district's liveliest street is south of the university in a suburb of Schwabing known as Maxvorstadt. Munich is Germany's publishing center, and the bookstores throughout Schwabing will satisfy the most avid reader. Formerly the Anglia English Bookshop, this Words' Worth branch is our favorite bookstore along this street. As the name suggests, this store specializes in English-language titles, and it's a hangout for visiting Americans and English-speaking expatriates living in Munich.

Head back north up Leopoldstrasse, returning to the university's center. Take a right on Veterinärstrasse, directly across the street from Gärtner's famed building. Those without inhibition may want to begin disrobing. You're being routed to the:

❾ Englischer Garten

Munich's most famous park is full of nude sunbathers. The Chinese Tower is the most recognizable landmark of the gardens. The wooden tower, trimmed with gold leaf, was destroyed during World War II but reemerged in the 1950s to the delight of its beer-garden devotees—revered even by upstart Schwabingers, and a good place to take a break and end your walk.

Shopping in Munich

Visitors to Munich usually come for the fun, the beer gardens, the cultural scene, or the nightlife—not for the shopping. However, Munich is full of beautiful and elegant (and expensive) shops and has a number of really intriguing retailers.

1 THE SHOPPING SCENE

In the historic city center, you'll find an extensive pedestrian-only shopping area. **Kaufingerstrasse** and **Neuhauser Strasse,** the principal shopping streets, extend from the Hauptbahnhof to Marienplatz, then north to Odeonsplatz. For even more upscale shopping, head to **Maximilianstrasse,** where you'll discover numerous chic boutiques and fashion houses that rival any on Fifth Avenue. For funkier wares, head to Schwabing, the former bohemian quarter. **Schellingstrasse** and **Hohenzollernstrasse** are home to many unusual galleries and hip boutiques.

2 SHOPPING A TO Z

ART

Bayerischer Kunstgewerbe-Verein ★★ This is the largest, most visible, and most historic art gallery of its type in Germany, established by the Bavarian government in the 1840s as a showcase for local artists. One of its two interconnected buildings is a Jugendstil monument, the other of no artistic importance. Works by more than 400 artists are displayed and sold in the art gallery. In a sales outlet, the Ladengeschäft, crafts in all kinds of media, textiles, and woven objects are sold at prices that begin at 25€ ($40). It's open Monday to Friday 9:30am to 6pm, and Saturday 9:30am to 2pm. Pacellistrasse 6–8. ℂ 089/2-90-14-70. U-Bahn: Karlsplatz.

BOOKS

Hugendubel Not only is this Munich's biggest bookstore, but it also enjoys a central location. It sells a number of English-language titles, both fiction and nonfiction, and also offers travel books and helpful maps. Open Monday to Friday from 9am to 7pm, and Saturday from 9am to 2pm. Marienplatz 22. ℂ 089/48-44-84. www.hugendubel.de. U-Bahn or S-Bahn: Marienplatz.

Words' Worth The stock runs from 19th-century English and American classics to recent releases, with art books and offbeat modern literature thrown in as well. One corner is devoted to a display of English tea caddies and marmalades, profits from which go to Britain's National Trust. The store is open Monday, Tuesday, and Friday from 9am to 6:30pm, Wednesday and Thursday 9am to 8pm, and Saturday 10am to 3pm. Schellingstrasse 31. ℂ 089/2-80-91-41. U-Bahn: U3 or U6 to Universität.

CHINA, SILVER & GLASS

Kunstring Meissen ★ This establishment's close links to the porcelain factories of Meissen and Dresden in what was then East Germany stretch back to the coldest days of the Cold War. It was then Munich's exclusive distributor of Meissen and Dresden (Germany's most famous styles of porcelain). Though exclusive access is a thing of the past, Kunstring's still carries one of Munich's largest selections of elegant porcelain. *Note:* With two of Europe's most impeccable pedigrees in porcelain, neither Meissen nor Dresden has adopted the assembly-line methods used by many of their more industrialized competitors. Anything you buy can be shipped, although if you're looking for the more esoteric objects, there might be a delay if Kunstring doesn't have the object in stock. Kunstring is open Monday to Friday 9:30am to 5pm, and Saturday 9:30am to 2pm. Briennerstrasse 4. ✆ **089/28-15-32.** U-Bahn: Odeonsplatz.

Nymphenburger Porzellanmanufaktur ★★ About 8km (5 miles) northwest of the heart of Munich, you'll find one of Germany's most famous porcelain factories on the grounds of Schloss Nymphenburg. You can visit its exhibition and sales rooms Monday to Friday from 10am to 5pm. Shipments can be arranged if you make purchases (This is a bit of a trek, but you'll probably be taking a sightseeing trip to Schloss Nymphenburg anyway.) There's also a more central branch in Munich's center at Odeonsplatz 1 (✆ **089/ 282428;** U-Bahn: U6 to Odeonsplatz). Nördliches Schlossrondell 8. ✆ **089/1-79-19-70.** Bus: 41.

Rosenthal Studio-Haus ★★★ Established in 1879 in the Bavarian town of Selb near the Czech border, Rosenthal is one of the most prestigious names in German porcelain. Although traditional patterns are still made, most of the line now focuses on contemporary designs. Prices for Rosenthal designs are preestablished by the manufacturer, and there are no price breaks at this factory outlet. The outlet is owned and operated by Rosenthal itself, so you will find the widest selection of Rosenthal patterns available in Germany here. In addition to porcelain, the line includes furniture, glass, and cutlery, all scattered over two floors of spotlessly maintained showrooms. It's open Monday to Friday 9:30am to 8pm, and Saturday 9:30am to 2pm. Dienerstrasse 17. ✆ **089/22- 26-17.** U-Bahn or S-Bahn: Marienplatz.

CRAFTS & FOLKLORIC GOODS

Bayerischer Kunstgewerbeverein (Bavarian Association of Arts & Crafts) This showcase for Bavarian artisans has excellent handicrafts: ceramics, glasses, jewelry, woodcarvings, pewter, and seasonal Christmas decorations. Open Monday to Friday 9am to 6pm, and Saturday 9am to 1pm. Pacellistrasse 6–8. ✆ **089/29-01-47-0.** U-Bahn: Karlsplatz.

Ludwig Mory This is a famous place to buy traditional Bavarian beer steins. It's near the cathedral, its one-room setting is folkloric, and it basks in a reputation that has been building since the 1830s. After seeing this place, you'll never want to drink Budweiser from a can again. Fashioned from pewter, and to a lesser degree, ceramic, sometimes lidded, sometimes not, the steins range from the honest but unpretentious to richly decorative works of art that might round off a private collection. It's open Monday to Friday from 9am to 6pm, and Saturday from 9am to 1pm. Amalienstrasse 16. ✆ **089/22- 45-42.** U-Bahn or S-Bahn: Odeonsplatz.

Prinoth ★ Ⓕ Finds Most of the woodcarvings sold here are produced in small workshops in South Tirol, that folklore-rich part of Austria that was annexed to Italy after

World War I. The selection is wide-ranging and broad, and since the setting lies 5.5km (3¹/₂ miles) west of Munich's tourist zones, prices are reasonable compared to those of shops closer to the Marienplatz. It's open Monday to Friday 9am to 6pm. Guido Schneblestrasse 9A. ✆ **089/56-03-78.** U-Bahn: U4 or U5 to Laimerplatz.

Wallach ★★ Established more than a century ago, Wallach is the largest emporium in Munich for Bavarian handcrafts, both new and antique, as well as the evocative, sometimes kitschy folk art. You'll find antique butter churns, hand-painted wooden boxes and trays, painted porcelain clocks, wooden wall or mantelpiece clocks, and doilies whose use faded along with that of antimacassars (the cloth covers, sometimes embroidered, used to protect the back or arms of upholstered furniture), but which are charming nonetheless. The store is open Monday to Friday from 10:30am to 6pm (Thurs until 8:30pm), and Saturday from 10:30am to 4pm. Residenzstrasse 3. ✆ **089/22-08-710.** U-Bahn or S-Bahn: Odeonsplatz.

DEPARTMENT STORES

Kaufhof This is the Munich branch of the upscale department store chain that was established in Cologne during the late 19th century. It came to Munich in 1972 and is one of the largest stores in town, on five floors in a building on the city's historic square. Wander freely among displays that are art forms in their own right. You'll find men's, women's, and children's clothing; housewares; groceries; and virtually everything else you might think of. It's open Monday to Friday 9am to 6:30pm (Thurs until 8:30pm), and Saturday 8:30am to 2pm. There's a smaller branch of this emporium at Karlsplatz 2 (✆ **089/5-12-50;** U-Bahn: Karlsplatz) that maintains the same hours. Marienplatz. ✆ **089/23-18-51.** U-Bahn or S-Bahn: Marienplatz.

Ludwig Beck am Rathauseck This is Munich's major department store. Most merchandise is intended for local residents; however, visitors may be interested in this four-floor shopping bazaar, which sells handmade crafts, both old and new, from all over Germany. Items include decorative pottery and dishes, etched-glass beer steins and vases, painted wall plaques depicting rural scenes, and decorative flower arrangements. There's unusual kitchenware, colored flatware, calico hot pads and towels, and a collection of casually chic leather-trimmed canvas purses. The shop also offers fashions, textiles, and even jazz recordings. Within the same block, the store has opened two more outlets: Wäsche-Beck, selling lingerie, linens, and curtains, and Strumpf-Beck, featuring the town's largest selection of stockings and hosiery. All three locations are open Monday to Friday from 10am to 8pm, and Saturday from 9:30am to 4pm. Marienplatz 11. ✆ **089/23-69-10.** U-Bahn or S-Bahn: Marienplatz.

ELECTRONICS

Saturn Electro Technocenter Anyone interested in electronics will enjoy comparing what's available at home to what's widespread and selling like gangbusters in Germany. For insight into design, speed, capabilities, and accessories, head for Munich's two superstores that deal exclusively in computers, cameras, DVD players, sound systems, and all kinds of electronics. If it's sold anywhere in Europe, you'll almost certainly find it here. Open Monday to Friday 10am to 7pm, and Saturday 10am to 8pm. Schwanenthaler Strasse 115. ✆ **089/51-08-50.** U-Bahn: Theresienwiese.

ENGRAVINGS & POSTCARDS

Philatelie und Ansichtskarten It doesn't really look like a shop, but rather like a dusty storeroom at a museum. It's the rendezvous for academics and collectors throughout Germany, who phone in special requests for antique engravings and post- cards that depict specific settings, personalities, and places. Merchandise, each piece carefully filed and stored in cardboard boxes that are arranged by subject, ranges from the sober to the schmaltzy. Open Monday to Friday 9am to 6pm, and Saturday 9am to 1pm. Bahnhofplatz 2. *℃* **089/59-67-57.** U-Bahn: Bahnhofplatz.

EYEWEAR

Pupille   Germans have long been known for their first-class eyewear. Here you will find the most stylish, sophisticated, and also practical eyewear in Munich. In all shades and colors, enough to please even Michael Jackson, the outlet in the center of town displays glass shelf after glass shelf of the most fetching glasses and all the accessories you'll need. Open Monday to Friday 10am to 7pm, and Saturday 10am to 6pm. Theatinerstrasse 8. *℃* **089/24-24-38-38.** Metro: Odeonsplatz or Marienplatz.

FASHION
Men & Women
Bogner Haus   Founded by Willy Bogner, former Olympic champion downhill racer, this store stocks well-made women's clothing upstairs, men's clothing on the street level, and clothing suited for whatever sport happens to be seasonal at the time of your visit in the cellar. Somewhere in the store, you'll find whatever you need to be appropriately clad for any occasion. One of its best is the Fire & Ice Department in the cellar, where garments for young men and women have the kind of flair that might please some of the most demanding people in your life—your teenage children. The store is open Monday to Wednesday and Friday 9:30am to 6:30pm, Thursday 9:30am to 7:30pm, and Saturday 9:30am to 3pm. Residenzstrasse 15. *℃* **089/2-90-70-40.** U-Bahn or S-Bahn: Marienplatz or Odeonsplatz.

Frankonia   This store carries Munich's most prestigious collection of traditional Bavarian dress (called *Tracht*). If you see yourself dressed in a hunter style, this place can outfit you well. There's a fine collection of wool cardigan jackets with silvery buttons. It's open Monday to Friday 9am to 6:30pm, and Saturday 9am to 2pm. Maximiliansplatz 10. *℃* **089/2-90-00-20.** U-Bahn: Odeonsplatz.

Loden-Frey   You can see the twin domes of the Frauenkirche above the soaring glass-enclosed atrium of this shop's showroom. Go here for the world's largest selection of *Loden* clothing and traditional costumes, as well as for international fashions from top European designers such as Armani, Valentino, and Ungaro. Open Monday to Friday 9am to 6:30pm, and Saturday 9am to 2pm. Maffeistrasse 7. *℃* **089/210390.** U-Bahn/S-Bahn: Marienplatz.

Men
Hirmer   This shop has the best collection in town of German-made men's clothing. The staff here is especially helpful in outfitting you with something that looks good on you, the selection coming from such brand names as Boss, Barbour, Rene Lezard, and Van Laak. Both business and leisure suits are sold at middle- to upper-bracket prices. They even cater to "big beer bellies." Open Monday to Friday 9am to 6pm, and Saturday 9am to 2pm. Kaufingerstrasse 28. *℃* **089/236-830.** U-Bahn: Marienplatz.

Women
Maendler   With a series of boutiques scattered over two floors, this store caters to the well-dressed woman. You may prefer to just wander around, appreciating the creative

vision of Joop, Claude Montana, New York New York, and Jil Sander, but a quick consultation with any of the staff poised near the store's entrance can point you in the right direction. Looking for that special something for your dinner with the city's mayor or the president of Germany? Ask to see the formal eveningwear of English designer David Fielden. Looking for something more daring and avant-garde? Head for this outfit's other branch, **Rosy Maendler,** Maximiliansplatz 12 (same phone). Here you'll find a youthful version of the same store and garments by Madonna's favorite designer, Jean-Paul Gaultier, whose exhibitionistic and/or erotic leather and rubber clothing will cause a stir on either side of the Atlantic. Both shops are open Monday to Friday 9:30am to 6pm, and Saturday 9:30am to 2pm. Theatinerstrasse 7. (C) 089/24-22-88-50. U-Bahn: Marienplatz.

Wies'n Tracht & mehr ★ (Finds) The milkmaid-style dress, the dirndl, has been making a comeback. In spite of its low-cut bodice, it is considered as wholesome. The best selection of dirndls in Munich is offered at this outlet, but prices are not cheap, starting at 400€ ($640). Both new and vintage dirndls are sold here. They are worn with the traditional off-the-shoulder white blouse and often an apron. Open Monday to Friday 9:30am to 6pm, and Saturday 9:30am to 2pm. Six locations in total are scattered around Munich. Tal 19. No phone. www.wiesn-tracht-mehr.de. U-Bahn or S-Bahn: Marienplatz.

FOOD

Dallmayr ★ What Fauchon is to Paris, and Fortnum & Mason is to London, the venerable firm of Dallmayr is to Munich. Gastronomes as far away as Hamburg and Berlin sometimes telephone orders for exotica not readily available anywhere else, and its list of prestigious clients reads like a who's who of German industry and letters. Wander freely among racks of foodstuffs, some of which are too delicate to survive shipment abroad, others that can be shipped anywhere. The shop is open Monday to Friday 9am to 6:30pm, and Saturday 9am to 1pm. The restaurant associated with this store is reviewed on p. 104. Dienerstrasse 14–15. (C) 089/2-13-50. Tram: 19.

JEWELRY & WATCHES

CADA-Schmuck ★ The handmade, unique pieces of jewelry designed by Herbert Kopp, and on sale here, are hard to resist. His jewelry comes in 18-karat gold or sterling silver. There is also a first-class selection of watches, including such designer names as Dior. Open Monday to Friday 10am to 7pm, and Saturday 10am to 6pm. Maffeistrasse 8. (C) 089/25-54-270. U-Bahn: Odeonsplatz.

Hemmerle ★★★ This is *the* place in Munich for jewelry. The founders of this stylish shop created bejeweled fantasies for the Royal Bavarian Court of Ludwig II. Today, in a setting of southern baroque–style pastel-painted paneling, you can buy some of the area's most exciting jewelry. All pieces are limited editions, designed and made in-house by Bavarian craftspeople. The company also designs its own wristwatch, the Hemmerle, and distributes what is said to be one of the world's finest watches, the Breguet. The store is open Monday to Friday 9am to 6pm, and Saturday 9:30am to 1pm. Maximilianstrasse 14. (C) 089/2-42-26-00. U-Bahn: Marienplatz.

MARKETS

In addition to those markets listed below, a traditional market, **Auer Dult,** is held three times a year in the Mariahilfplatz. Dates vary but the months are April, July, and October (see also the "Munich Calendar of Events," in chapter 3). Antiques dealers, food, and Bavarian bands are present; it's a great place for bargains. Take tram 7, 15, 25, or 27.

Christkindlmarkt One of the most visible and traditional in Munich, this December Christmas market attracts visitors from all over Germany and Europe—only the Christmas market in Nürnberg is more famous. Hundreds of stalls offer Christmas ornaments, handmade children's toys, carved figures, and nativity scenes. The square is full of local color; the stall keepers are picturesque in their woolen coats, hats, and gloves; and the scene is enhanced by frequent snowfalls. Opening hours vary with the enthusiasm of the merchants. In most cases, stalls are open 10am to 8pm Monday to Saturday, although as Christmas approaches, many open on Sunday as well, until 7pm. Marienplatz. U-Bahn: Marienplatz.

Elisabethmarkt This is Schwabing's smaller and less dramatic version of Munich's premier outdoor market, the Viktualienmarkt (see below). It's held every Monday to Saturday from 7 to about 11am, although some die-hard merchants manage to hold out until 1:30pm. Completely decentralized, each individual vendor operates exclusively on his or her own account. Stalls tend to be more laden with bounty in spring, summer, and fall, but a few hardy souls maintain a presence here even in the depths of winter. Elisabethplatz. Tram: 18.

Grossmarkthalle ★ This is Munich's equivalent of Paris's Rungis (formerly Les Halles). Buyers from virtually every restaurant in Munich make an early morning pilgrimage to this industrial-looking complex in the city's southern suburbs. Purveyors arrive with lorries from as far away as Italy; buyers congregate from throughout Bavaria and beyond. Be warned, though, an entrance fee of 3€ ($3.60) allows you only to browse and admire the way business is conducted; buying is wholesale only—homemakers who do show up usually bring bushel baskets or wheeled carts to haul away impressive quantities of peaches, apples, or whatever. It's open Monday to Saturday from 5 to 10:30am. Thalkirchen. U-Bahn: U3 to Fürstenried West.

Viktualienmarkt Unless you happen to be staying in a place where you have access to a kitchen, it's doubtful that you'll want to be hauling groceries back to your hotel room during your stay in Munich. That doesn't detract, however, from the allure of wandering through the open-air stalls of the city's most prominent food market, a few minutes' walk south of the Marienplatz (there is no specific address, but the market sprawls over a wide area and can't be missed). It's composed of hundreds of independently operated merchants who maintain whatever hours they want, often closing up their cramped premises whenever the day's inventory is sold out. Most economy-minded shoppers, however, show up, shopping basket in hand, around 8am, to stock their larders before noon. By 5pm, only the hardiest of merchants remain in place, and by early evening, the kiosks are locked up tight. On the premises is a worthy collection of wine, meats, cheeses, and all the other bounty of the Bavarian agrarian world. Marienplatz. U-Bahn or S-Bahn: Marienplatz.

PEWTER

Sebastian Wesely This is one of the best sites in Munich for the acquisition of everybody's favorite utilitarian metal, pewter. Favored throughout the 16th and 17th centuries because of the ease with which it can be crafted into baroque forms, it burnishes to a low luster that's still prized today. This shop carries an impressive array of reproductions, any of which would make a valuable addition to your home. It's open Monday to Friday 9am to 6pm, and Saturday 10am to 6:30pm. Rindermarkt 1. © **089/26-45-19.** U-Bahn: Marienplatz.

Behringer   One of the best shoe selections in Munich is found at this chic store that also sells an extensive array of bags, belts, and accessories. The staff is low-key so there is no pressure to buy, although you might want to check out the new, casual, and laid-back look. All in all, evolution in footwear rather than revolution is the watchword here. Open Monday to Friday 10am to 7pm, and Saturday 10am to 6pm. Salvatorplatz 4. ☎ **089/29-59-55.** U-Bahn: Odeonsplatz.

SOUVENIRS

Max Krug   Dating from 1925, this is the most famous store in Munich, selling Bavarian memorabilia and all types of souvenirs. From cuckoo clocks to music boxes, it's all here, including enough beer tankards to restage *The Student Prince.* Most of the souvenirs, such as nutcrackers, originate in the Black Forest. Open Monday to Saturday from 9:30am to 8pm. Neuhauser Strasse 2. ☎ **089/22-45-01.** U-Bahn or S-Bahn: Marienplatz.

TOYS

Münchner Poupenstuben und Zinnfiguren Kabinette   This is the kind of store you either thrill to or find impossibly claustrophobic. Here is a miniature world where houses, furniture, birdcages, and people are cunningly crafted from pewter or carved wood. Many of the items look deceptively realistic. Famous throughout Germany, the shop has been managed for 150 years by women of the same family, and some of the figures are still made from the original 150-year-old molds that are collectors' items in their own right. Anything in this place would make a great gift not only for a child but also for an adult with a nostalgic bent. It's open Monday to Friday 10am to 6pm, and Saturday 10am to 1pm. Maxburgstrasse 4. ☎ **089/29-37-97.** U-Bahn: Karlsplatz.

Obletter's ★   Established in the 1880s, this is one of the largest emporiums of children's toys in Munich, with five floors that contain everything from folkloric dolls to computer games. Some of the most charming toys are replicas of middle European antique dolls and toys; they often look suspiciously capable of coming alive beneath someone's Christmas tree, like in the *Nutcracker* ballet. It's open Monday to Friday 9am to 7:30pm, and Saturday 9am to 4pm. Karlsplatz 11. ☎ **089/55-08-95-10.** U-Bahn: Karlsplatz.

WINE

Geisel's Vinothek ★   Other than Dallmayr, which does this kind of thing on a much bigger scale, this is the most sophisticated wine shop in Munich. Its inventory includes wines from Germany, Austria, Italy, and France. Because the chef here is a passionate advocate of wines from western France, there's an especially strong selection of bordeaux. Most of the selections offered by the glass at the restaurant's bar are sold by the bottle in the wine shop, allowing you to taste before you buy the whole bottle. The shop is open daily 10am to 1am. In Hotel Königshof, Karlsplatz 25. ☎ **089/55-13-60.** U-Bahn or S-Bahn: Hauptbahnhof.

Munich After Dark

Munich is a major performing-arts center and has a lively nightlife. The city is home to major orchestras, a world-class opera company, and a ballet company. Many theaters are scattered throughout the city, offering everything from classic to modern German drama.

Munich's nightlife varies with the weather. When the weather is fair and the night air balmy, the *Biergartens* and *Biersteins* are brimming. During winter, patrons of the beer gardens turn to Munich's beer halls, such as the illustrious Hofbräuhaus (p. 174), to quaff brews and share in the typical Bavarian songfest. Beer gardens and beer halls usually empty around midnight; then the club scene cranks up. Munich's club scene is quite eclectic. It is possible to find almost any type of club, from country-and-western bars to ultratechno dance halls. Many clubs rave until the wee hours of the morning. Haidhausen and Schwabing vie as the place to go, with the trendiest clubs and nightlife.

To find out what's happening in the Bavarian capital, go to the tourist office outside the Hauptbahnhof and request a copy of *Monatsprogramm* (a monthly program guide), for 1.65€ ($2.65). It contains a complete cultural guide, telling you not only what's being presented—from concerts to opera, from special exhibits to museum hours—but also how to purchase tickets. (The *Monatsprogramm* is in German, but it's a simple German, with lots of emphasis on addresses, dates, and listings; as such, even people without a firm grasp of German get a lot of information from it.)

1 THE PERFORMING ARTS

Nowhere else in Europe, other than London and Paris, will you find so many musical and theatrical performances. The good news is the low cost of seats—so count on indulging yourself and going to several concerts. You'll get good tickets if you're willing to pay anywhere from 10€ to 45€ ($16–$72). Pick up a *Monatsprogramm* (see above) for information and schedules.

For events that sell out and popular events for which the number of available tickets is reduced by season tickets and long-term subscriptions (such as the opera's summer festival performances), you'll have to go to the box office—organizers of these events tend not to cooperate with outside ticket agencies. But for virtually everything else in Munich, you'd be well advised to head for **München Tickets** (*(C)* **089/54-81-81-81**), where you can purchase tickets to cultural, entertainment, or sporting events.

OPERA & CLASSICAL MUSIC

Besides the organizations listed below, Munich is home to the **Munich Radio Orchestra (Münchner Rundfunkorchester)** and the **Bavarian Radio Orchestra (Symphonieorchester des Bayerischen Rundfunks).** For ticket information, contact the events office of the Bayerischer Rundfunk-Veranstaltungsbüro, Arnulfstrasse 44, Rundfunkplatz 1 (*(C)* **089/55-80-80;** fax 089/59-00-23-26), open Monday to Friday from 8:30am to 6pm.

Bayerische Staatsoper (Bavarian State Opera) ★★★ The Bavarians give their hearts and souls to opera, and this is one of the world's great opera companies. Its productions are beautifully mounted and presented, and the company's roster includes some of the world's greatest singers. Hard-to-get tickets may be purchased at the box office Monday to Friday 10am to 6pm and Saturday 10am to 1pm, plus 1 hour before each performance. The Nationaltheater is also the home of the **Bavarian State Ballet.** Performing in the Nationaltheater, Max-Joseph-Platz 2. ✆ **089/2185-1920.** www.bayerische. staatsoper.de. Tickets 15€–243€ ($24–$389), including standing room. U-Bahn or S-Bahn: Marienplatz.

Münchner Philharmoniker (Munich Philharmonic) ★★ This famous orchestra was founded in 1893. James Levine is its music director. It performs in Philharmonic Hall at the Gasteig Cultural Center, which also shelters the Richard Strauss Conservatory and the Munich Municipal Library, and has five performance halls. You can purchase tickets at the ground-level Glashalle, Monday to Friday from 9am to 6pm and on Saturday from 9am to 2pm; these hours frequently change, so call before you go. The season begins in mid-September and runs to July. Performing in the **Gasteig Kulturzentrum,** in the Haidhausen district, at Rosenheimerstrasse 5. ✆ **089/480985500.** www.muenchnerphilharmoniker.de. Tickets 10€–51€ ($16–$82). S-Bahn: Rosenheimer Platz. Tram: 18 to Gasteig. Bus: 51.

MAJOR THEATERS & CONCERT HALLS

There are theaters and performance halls all over town. Concerts are given in the **Herkulessaal** (in the Residenz, Hofgarten; ✆ **089/29-06-71**). The **Staatstheater am Gärtnerplatz** (✆ **089/20-24-11**) offers a varied program of opera, operetta, ballet, and musicals.

Altes Residenztheater (Cuvilliés Theater) ★★ A part of the Residenz (p. 134), this theater is a sightseeing attraction in its own right. The Bavarian State Opera and the State Theater perform small-scale works here in keeping with the tiny theater's intimate character (it seats 550). It was designed by court architect François Cuvilliés in the mid–18th century and is celebrated as Germany's most outstanding example of a rococo tier-boxed theater. During World War II, the interior was dismantled and stored. After the war, it was reassembled in the reconstructed building. For admission of 5€ ($8), visitors can view the theater daily 9am to 6pm. Box-office hours are Monday through Friday from 10am to 6pm, Saturday from 10am to 1pm, and 1 hour before the beginning of every performance. Residenzstrasse 1. ✆ **089/2185-1940.** Opera tickets 26€–155€ ($42–$248); play tickets 16€–65€ ($26–$104). U-Bahn: U3, U4, U5, or U6 to Odeonsplatz.

Bayerisches Staatsschauspiel (Bavarian State Theater) This repertory company is known for its performances of the classics: Shakespeare, Goethe, Schiller, and others. The box office, around the corner on Maximilianstrasse, is open Monday to Friday 10am to 6pm, Saturday 10am to 1pm, and 1 hour before performances. Max-Joseph-Platz. ✆ **089/21-85-19-20.** Tickets 15€–60€ ($24–$96). U-Bahn or S-Bahn: Marienplatz.

Deutsches Theater The regular season of the Deutsches Theater lasts throughout the year. Musicals are popular, but operettas, ballets, and international shows are performed as well. It's the only theater in Germany that's also a ballroom. During Carnival in January and February, the seats are removed and stored, replaced by tables and chairs for more than 2,000 guests. Handmade decorations by artists combined with lighting effects create an enchanting ambience. Waiters serve wine, champagne, and food. The costume balls and official black-tie festivities here are famous throughout Europe.

Kulturzentrum Gasteig   This huge brick-and-glass complex stands on the bluffs of
the Isar River in the Haidhausen District. The center, which opened in 1985, has five
performance halls, including the Philharmonic Hall. It also shelters the Richard Strauss
Conservatory and the Munich Municipal Library. Two other concert halls of interest to
most visitors are the Kleiner Konzertsaal and the Richard Strauss Musikschule. Rosenheimerstrasse 5. *(C)* **089/48-49-76.** S-Bahn: Rosenheimer Platz. Tram: 18 to Gasteig. Bus: 51.

Münchner Kammerspiele (Munich Studio Theater)   Contemporary plays as
well as classics from German or international playwrights, ranging from Goethe to
Brecht and Shakespeare to Goldoni, are performed by the company here. The season lasts
from early October to the end of July. You can reserve tickets by phone Monday to Friday
from 10am to 6pm, but you must pick them up at least 2 days before the performance.
The box office is open Monday to Friday from 10am to 6pm and on Saturday from
10am to 1pm, plus 1 hour before performances.

   The theater also has a second smaller venue called **Werkraum,** where new produc
tions—mainly by younger authors and directors—are presented. The location is at
Hildegardstrasse 1 (call the number below for more information). Maximilianstrasse 28.
(C) **089/233-966-01.** Tickets 6€–39€ ($9.60–$62). U-Bahn: Marienplatz. S-Bahn: Isartorplatz. Tram: 19.

---

2 THE CLUB & MUSIC SCENE

NIGHTCLUBS

Bayerischer Hof Night Club   This sophisticated club is in a large room in the extensive cellars of the Bayerischer Hof (p. 83). Between 7 and 10pm every night (except
Mon), the club is a piano bar. Behind a partition that disappears after 10pm is a bandstand for live orchestras, which play to a crowd of dancing patrons every night from
10pm to 3 or 4am, depending on business. Entrance to the piano bar is free, but there's
a cover charge to the nightclub on Friday and Saturday nights. Drinks begin at 8€ ($13).
The club and bar are open daily 8pm to 3 or 4am. Daily happy hour is 7 to 8:30pm,
with drinks starting at 5€ ($8). In the Hotel Bayerischer Hof, Promenadeplatz 2–6.
(C) **089/21200.** Cover 5€–50€ ($8–$80). No cover for hotel guests. Tram: 19.

Café am Hochhaus   On any given night the scene shifts here. One night might be
boogie and soulful reggae; another night retro and disco. On Sunday there is a gay
T-dance, and on Monday night management promises "anything can happen." Open
Monday to Saturday 8pm to 3am. Blumenstrasse 29. *(C)* **089/890-581-52.** U-Bahn: Sendlinger
Tor.

Nachtgalerie   This night gallery contains two dance halls rocking to party music and
hip-hop along with house, electro, or even rhythm and blues. The club attracts largely
intoxicated crowds in their 20s and 30s. International student parties are often staged
here. Expect various theme nights, perhaps one devoted to the sounds of a Caribbean
summer. Girls dance with girls, boys with boys, and sometimes boys with girls. The cover
is 10€ ($16), but once inside, drinks are cheap—beginning at 2€ ($3.20). Open Friday
and Saturday 10pm to 5am. Amulfstrasse 17. *(C)* **089/32455595.** S-Bahn: Hackerbrücke. (At the
end of the bridge, veer right and descend the steps.)

Night Flight (Finds) This nightclub is designed to highlight the visual effect of airplane departures and arrivals. To get here, you'll have to drive 40km (25 miles) north of the city or take a 30-minute ride on the S-Bahn. The site is on the periphery of the Munich Airport, in an industrial-looking building midway between three enormous hangars. You can drink at five different bars, dance, and listen to the loud music that changes according to the night of the week. There's even a restaurant. In summer, there's an outside terrace where virtually everything at the airport can be seen with eerie clarity. Friday nights, with techno-rap as the theme, draw the youngest audience. Other nights, the crowd ranges from 25 to a youthful 40. It's open Tuesday to Saturday 10pm to 6am. Franz Josef Strauss Airport, Wartungsallee 9. (✆) **089/97-59-79-99.** Cover 10€ ($16). S-Bahn: Flughafen.

JAZZ

Jazzclub Unterfahrt This is Munich's leading jazz club, attracting artists from throughout Europe and North America. It is not only the city's best, but also one of Europe's 10 best jazz clubs, according to *Wire*, a leading music magazine in Europe. Reaching it requires wandering down a labyrinth of underground cement-sided corridors that might remind you of a bomb shelter during the Cold War. Inside, the space opens to reveal flickering candles, a convivial bar, high ceilings, and clusters of smallish tables facing a stage and whatever singers and musicians happen to be emoting at the time. Off to one corner is an art gallery. The bar here opens daily at 8pm; live music is Tuesday to Sunday 8:30pm until 1am, Friday and Saturday 7:30pm to 3am. Einsteinstrasse 42. (✆) **089/448-2794.** Cover 10€–14€ ($16–$22). U-Bahn: Max-Weber-Platz.

Mister B's Small, dark, and popular with blues and jazz aficionados, this club hosts a slightly older, mellower crowd than the rock and dance clubs. Blues, jazz, and rhythm-and-blues combos take the stage Thursday to Saturday. Hours are Tuesday to Sunday 8pm to 3am. Herzog-Heinrichstrasse 38. (✆) **089/53-49-01.** Cover 5€–9€ ($8–$14). U-Bahn: Goetheplatz.

COUNTRY

Oklahoma File under "surreal." German and European bands decked out in cowboy hats and boots struggle with the nuances of an extremely foreign musical form. Even when the results are dead-on mimicry, there's something strange about watching German "cowboys" line dance or lean on the bar while guzzling Spaten. The cover is usually at the low end of the scale, rising when English and American acts hit the stage. Depending on your mood, this place can be a lot of fun. Pull on your jeans and come on in Tuesday to Saturday 7pm to 1am. Schäftlarnstrasse 156. (✆) **089/7-23-43-27.** Cover 10€–12€ ($16–$19). U-Bahn: Thalkirchen.

Rattlesnake Saloon One of Munich's two country-western saloons, this is a down-home homage to the redneck charms of hound dogs, battered pickup trucks, and cowboy hats and boots. Rib-sticking platters (rib-eye steaks, barbecued pork, and chili) can be ordered to wash down with the steins of Spaten beer that go so well with the live country music. Performers come from Munich, England, Canada, and, in some cases, even Nashville, Tennessee. Regardless of how authentic the twang in the music might be, you'll have a fun evening here, and someone will invariably rise to the challenge of conducting a rodeo-style line dance lesson for anyone who's interested in learning. Rattlesnake is open Tuesday to Sunday 7pm to 1am. The location is 5km (3 miles) north of the Marienplatz. Schneeglöckchenstrasse 91. (✆) **089/1-50-40-35.** Cover 7€–12€ ($11–$19). S-Bahn: Fasanerie.

> **(Moments)** **Wenches, Knaves & Medieval Delicacies**
>
> **Welser-Kuche,** Residenzstrasse 27 (℃ **089/29-65-65**), re-creates a hearty medieval feast every night, beginning at 8pm. Guests must be prepared to stick around for 3 hours. In many ways, this is a takeoff on the Tudor banquets that are popular with tourists in London. *Magde* and *Knechte* (wenches and knaves) wearing 16th-century costumes serve food in hand-thrown pottery, and guests eat the medieval delicacies with their fingers, aided only by a stiletto-like dagger. Many recipes are authentic, based on a 16th-century cookbook. You can order a 6-course or 10-course menu called a *Welser Feast* that costs 45€ ($72) and 50€ ($80), respectively. The place can be good fun if you're in the mood; but it's likely to be overflowing with tourists, so reservations are recommended. It's open daily from 7pm to 1am. To get there, take the U3 U-Bahn to Odeonsplatz.

DANCE CLUBS & DISCOS

Max Emanuel Brauerei Beer hasn't been brewed here since the 1920s, when the place was transformed into a showcase/beer hall for Löwenbräu beer. It still serves steins of beer and platters of filling German grub. On Wednesday and Friday, the cavernous floor above street level reverberates with salsa music (beginning at 9pm) or 1950s-style rock 'n' roll (Sun beginning at 8pm). During salsa nights, most of Munich's Latino population, from the Dominican Republic to southern Chile, makes it a point of honor to show up to show off their merengue steps. On Sunday nights, the site can also be fun in a convertible-Chevy and saddle shoes kind of way. There is a cover of 8€ to 15€ ($13–$24) if you want to be in one of the rooms offering special live music such as salsa, swing, or rock 'n' roll. Hours in summer when they have a beer garden are daily from 11am to 1am. In winter, hours are daily from 5pm to 1am. Adalbertstrasse 33. ℃ **089/2-71-51-58.** U-Bahn: Universität.

Parkcafé Who'd ever guess this home to chic freaks was a Nazi hangout in the 1930s? The place contains five lively bars, two of them outfitted like the inside of a ship, plus a strident color scheme using oranges and reds, among other colors. Many nights are themed, ranging from "Black Beat" music on Wednesdays to "gay Sundays." It's open daily 10am to midnight. Sophienstrasse 7. ℃ **089/5161-7980.** Cover 8€–11€ ($13–$18). U-Bahn: Königsplatz or Lenbachplatz.

Schwabinger Podium This place is loud, urban, underground, smoky, crowded, and often raucous, but its fans wouldn't change it even if they could. There's live music every night, and a crowd that is up on the musical scenes in London and Los Angeles. It's open Sunday to Thursday from 8pm to 1am, and Friday and Saturday from 8pm to 3am. Wagnerstrasse 1. ℃ **089/39-94-82.** U-Bahn: Münchner Freiheit.

3 THE BAR & CAFE SCENE

Alter Simpl Once a literary cafe, Alter Simpl takes its name from a satirical review of 1903. Lale Andersen, who popularized the song "Lili Marlene," frequented this cafe/bar when she was in Munich. (She also maintained, as she pointed out repeatedly in her autobiography, that the correct spelling of the song was "Lili Marleen.") Today it attracts locals, including young people, counterculturists, and *Gastarbeiter* (foreign workers). The real fun begins at 11pm, when the artistic ferment becomes more reminiscent of iconoclastic Berlin than Bavaria. It's open Sunday to Thursday 11am to 3am, Friday and Saturday 11am to 4am. Türkenstrasse 57. ✆ **089/2-72-30-83.** U-Bahn: Universität.

Café Puck A dark-paneled retreat for students, artists, and workers, this cafe plays a variety of roles for its diverse crowd. It's a bar to students; a restaurant to the locals, who like the German, American, and Asian dishes; and a hangover cure for artists and young people who creep in after midday for a big American breakfast. You'll find German- and English-language newspapers, plenty of conversation, and often someone who wants to practice English. Most of the staff speak fluent English. Open daily 9am to 1am. Türkenstrasse 33. ✆ **089/280-22-80.** U-Bahn: Universität.

Havana Club This is not the spicy Cuban club you might expect. Employees may tell you about the bar's brush with fame, when Gloria Estefan made an appearance, but its day-to-day function is as a lively singles bar fueled by rum-based cocktails. Open Monday to Thursday 6pm to 1am, Friday and Saturday 6pm to 3am, and Sunday 7pm to 1am. Herrnstrasse 30. ✆ **089/291884.** S-Bahn: Isartor.

Holy Home Close to Gärtnerplatz, this cozy hideaway is home to Munich's coterie of artists and designers. Patrons in their 20s and 30s often spend hours listening to the home-grown DJs spin their magic. Fresh Augustiner beer is on tap, beginning at 3.20€ ($5.10); mixed drinks cost around 8€ ($13). Open Monday to Wednesday and Sunday 7pm to 1am, Thursday to Saturday 7pm to 3am. Reichenbachstrasse 21. ✆ **089/2014546.** U-Bahn: Sendinger Tor.

K&K Klub This basement dive looks dirty and grungy. Graffiti artists have decorated its main door. But a mixed crowd often begins their nighttime prowl of Munich by using this place as a launch pad. Some of the best DJs in Munich play electro and house music to the demimonde who show up here. At an adjoining table, we heard a group of young guys organizing a sex party for later in the evening. This *klub* is not for the faint of heart. Open Monday to Wednesday and Sunday 8pm to 2am, Thursday and Saturday 8pm to 5am. Reichenbachstrasse 22. ✆ **089/20207463.** U-Bahn: Frauenhofer.

Killians Irish Pub/Ned Kelly's Australian Bar This is a two-in-one venue. If you grow tired of Irish music, you can take a trip Down Under in the adjoining bar. Behind the Frauenkirche, these bars are among the liveliest in Munich, with Irish and Australian beer and food, live music, and broadcasts of major sports events. In one bar, Irish bands play on weekdays, giving way on Saturday and Sunday to rock 'n' roll or rhythm and blues. The Australian menu is more exotic than the more familiar Irish grub. Ever had ostrich curry? Only a minute's walk from the Marienplatz, the location of the bars is in the exact center of Munich. Both bars are open Monday to Thursday 4pm to 1am, Friday and Saturday 11am to 2 or 3am, and Sunday noon to 1am. Frauenplatz 11. ✆ **089/24219899.** U-Bahn or S-Bahn: Marienplatz.

Master's Home This is one of the historic core's most animated and convivial bars. It seems to attract a wider range of clients than most other watering holes in Munich. The setting is the ground floor of an imposing, 19th-century building close to the Marienplatz. The large room, outfitted with antiques and warm colors, is in the style of an Edwardian-era club in London and suggests a living room in a comfortably battered

but upscale private home. There's also a restaurant (p. 112). The bar is open nightly from **173**
6pm to 3am. Frauenstrasse 11. ✆ **089/22-99-09.** S-Bahn: Isartor.

Pusser's New York Bar   This is the only European franchise of a well-run chain of restaurant-bars based in Tortola, British Virgin Islands. Its nostalgic decor celebrates the British navy of the 18th and 19th centuries. The specialties are Caribbean-inspired dishes and rum-based drinks, such as Pusser's Painkiller (rum, coconut, fresh orange juice, pineapple, and grated nutmeg). The cellar houses a piano bar. Open daily 6pm to 3am. Falkenturmstrasse 9. ✆ **089/220500.** U-Bahn or S-Bahn: Marienplatz.

Sausalitos   For the best margaritas in town, head to this welcoming Mexican cantina. If you're in your 20s, you'll fit right in. You never know what to expect: perhaps a young man walking around in a leather jockstrap or a blonde beauty showing off her latest nipple piercings. If you're ravenous, order the generous platters of main dishes ranging from 9€ to 13€ ($14–$21), or else opt for drinks costing from 6€ to 9€ ($9.60–$14). During happy hour daily from 5 to 8pm, mixed drinks are half-price. Open Monday to Thursday and Sunday 11am to 1am, Friday and Saturday 11am to 2:30am. Im Tal 16. ✆ **089/24295494.** U-Bahn or S-Bahn: Marienplatz.

Schumann's Bar am Hofgarten   This is the most legendary bar of Munich with an international fan club, lots of pizzazz, a long history, and a layout, with its ample use of green marble and wooden paneling, that evokes the inside of a church. When the drinks begin to flow and the crowd gets animated, however, it's a rip-roaring affair that gets very crowded. There's a simple roster of menu items that change with the season and the outside temperature. Open Monday to Friday 5pm to 3am, Saturday and Sunday 6pm to 3am. Odeonsplatz 6–7, at the corner of Galerie Strasse. ✆ **089/22-90-60.** U-Bahn: Odeonsplatz.

Shamrock   At this beer lover's bar, you can compare the great brews of Germany with the best of the Irish exports. A modest assortment of food is served (nothing to write home about), such as baguette-style sandwiches and stuffed pita pockets, but most clients come to drink. There's free entertainment every night between 9pm and midnight, when a mixed bag of Irish, rock, country, folk, funk, or blues musicians take to the stage. Located near the university, Shamrock sees its fair share of students. It's open Sunday to Thursday from 6pm to 1am, Friday and Saturday from 6pm to 2am. Trautenwolfstrasse 4–6. ✆ **089/33-10-81.** U-Bahn: Giselastrasse.

Stadtcafé   This virtual communications center of hip Munich attracts creative, artsy people. By Munich standards, it closes relatively early. Expect lots of chitchat from table to table, and someone is sure to be scribbling away at his or her unfinished life story (or novel). Open Monday to Saturday 11am to midnight, and Sunday 10:30am to 1am. St. Jakobsplatz 1. ✆ **089/26-69-49.** U-Bahn: Marienplatz.

---

4 BEER HALLS

The *Bierhalle* is a traditional Munich institution, offering food, entertainment, and, of course, beer.

Augustinerbrau   On the principal pedestrian-only street of Munich, this beer hall offers generous helpings of food, good beer, and a mellow atmosphere. Dark-wood panels and ceilings in carved plaster make the place look even older than it is. It's been around for less than a century, but beer was first brewed on this spot in 1328, as the literature about the establishment claims. The long menu changes daily, and the cuisine is not for dieters: It's hearty, heavy, and starchy, but that's what customers want. It's open daily from 11am to 11pm. Neuhauserstrasse 27. (℃) **089/23-18-32-57.** U-Bahn or S-Bahn: Karlsplatz/Stachus. Tram: 19.

Hofbräuhaus am Platzl ★   The state-owned Hofbräuhaus is the world's most famous beer hall. Visitors with only 1 night in Munich usually come here. The present Hofbräuhaus was built in 1897, but the tradition of a beer house on this spot dates from 1589. In the 19th century, it attracted artists, students, and civil servants, and was called the Blue Hall because of its dim lights and smoky atmosphere. When it grew too small to contain all the patrons who wanted to visit, architects designed another, in 1897.

Today, 4,000 beer drinkers can crowd in here on any given night. Several rooms, including a top-floor room for dancing, are spread over three floors. With its brass band (which starts playing at 11am), the ground-floor Schwemme is most typical of what you probably expected—here it's eternal Oktoberfest. In the second-floor restaurant, strolling musicians entertain, and dirndl-clad servers offer mugs of beer between singalongs. Every night the Hofbräuhaus presents a typical Bavarian show in its Fest-Hall, starting at 7:45pm and lasting until midnight. (This was also the 1920 setting for the notorious meeting of Hitler's newly launched German Workers Party, when a brawl erupted between the Nazis and their Bavarian enemies.) The hall is open daily 9am to midnight. Am Platzl 9. (℃) **089/22-16-76.** U-Bahn or S-Bahn: Marienplatz.

5 GAY & LESBIAN CLUBS

Much of Munich's gay and lesbian scene takes place in the blocks between the Viktualienmarkt and Gärtnerplatz, particularly on Hans-Sachs-Strasse.

Bau   Macho and swaggering, this gay bar encourages leather, denim, and as many uniforms as can be crammed onto the bodies that surround its street-level bar. Dimly lit and international, it's not as scary as it might look at first. Don't be surprised if you spot several New York City cop uniforms on either level. It's open nightly 8pm to 3am. Müllerstrasse 41. (℃) **089/269208.** U-Bahn: Sendlinger Tor.

Bei Carla (Finds)   Although little known among visitors, this is one of the best women's bars in Munich, attracting a crowd in their late 20s to early 40s. Women come here to meet other women, enjoy the friendly ambience, make conversation, or perhaps toss off a round or two of darts. Open Tuesday to Friday 4pm to 2am, Saturday and Sunday 6pm to 1:30am. Buttermelcherstrasse 9. (℃) **089/227901.** S-Bahn: Isartor.

Inges Karotte   This is one of the major gathering places for lesbians in Munich, both foreign and domestic. One patron called the clients "a female jungle," a widely diverse group of ages, professions, and interests. Many stylish lesbians show up here escorted by their girlfriends. It's a good atmosphere for drinking and mating. Cocktails begin at 5€ ($8), and happy hour is only from 4 to 6pm. Disco music sometimes rules the night. Open Monday to Saturday 6pm to 1am, and Sunday 4pm to 1am. Baaderstrasse 13. (℃) **089/2010669.** U-Bahn: Frauenhofer Strasse.

Kr@ftakt   As might be suggested by its name, this is an Internet cafe and the only gay one in Munich. Its clientele, looking for that Internet connection, is both gay and lesbian. Although we've put this listing in the nightlife section because of its late hours, it even serves a late breakfast costing from 4€ ($6.40). If you arrive late enough, you might even call it brunch. There's a happy hour on Wednesday from 7 to 9pm when a beer goes for only 1€ ($1.60). You can also order food here throughout the day, including pasta dishes costing from 6.90€ to 10€ ($11–$16). We get the impression that more gays go here to socialize in a convivial atmosphere than search the Web. Open Sunday to Thursday 10am to 1am, Friday and Saturday 10am to 3am. Thalkirchenstrasse 4. ✆ 089/21588881. U-Bahn: Sendlinger Tor.

Nil It's fun, it's convivial, and it has a clientele somewhat younger than the one at Teddy-Bar across the street (see below). In addition to fit and youthful German men hanging with one another at the octagon-shaped bar, you're likely to see faded stars from German stage and screen, sipping drinks with their men friends, reflecting on the glory days of their youth. Most of the clients come here to drink and mingle, but if you're hungry, platters of food are well prepared and relatively inexpensive at 6€ to 8€ ($9.60–$13). Open daily 3pm to 3am. Hans-Sach-Strasse 2. ✆ 089/265545. U-Bahn: Sendlinger Tor.

NY Club ★★ Known as New York Discotheque for nearly 2 decades, this club has reinvented itself. Attracting male *fashionistas*, it is now the most stylish and modern gay dance club in town. Guests enjoy two different areas, a beautifully designed lounge or a high-tech dance floor with lots of room for dancing and cruising. Both pastimes are pursued most eagerly here. Look for special events and gay parties by searching the Web at www.nyclub.de. Sonnenstrasse 25. ✆ 089/62232152. U-Bahn: Sendlinger Tor. Cover from 5€ ($8); higher for special events.

Teddy-Bar Gay and neighborly, and ringed with varnished pine and a collection of teddy bears, this is a congenial bar patronized by gay men over 30. It's relatively easy to strike up a conversation, and if you're hungry, there are platters of Bavarian and German food. It's open nightly 6pm to 4am. October to April it opens for brunch at 11am on Sunday. Hans-Sachs-Strasse 1. ✆ 089/2603359. U-Bahn: Sendlinger Tor.

Side Trips from Munich

Mountains, lakes, spas, and medieval towns lie within an hour of Munich, and the landscape is dotted with castles, villas, and Alpine resorts (see chapter 12).

A short drive from Munich delivers visitors to the heart of Starnberg's Five Lakes Region. The **Starnberger See** and **Ammersee** are weekend destinations that afford an enormous assortment of sports. The **Tegernsee** region is also a popular destination. The spa town of **Bad Tölz** is known for its healing waters and clear mountain air.

The environs of Munich are as rich in culture and history as in natural beauty. However, in the midst of all this serenity, the former concentration camp at **Dachau** sounds an ominous note. Before Hitler and the Holocaust, it was a little artists' community, but it's now visited mainly as a symbol of the great horror of the Nazi regime.

1 DACHAU CONCENTRATION CAMP

16km (10 miles) NW of Munich

In 1933, what had once been a quiet little artists' community just 16km (10 miles) from Munich became a tragic symbol of the Nazi era. Shortly after Hitler became chancellor, Himmler and the SS (Nazi special police) set up the first German concentration camp on the grounds of a former ammunitions factory here. The list of prisoners at the camp included enemies of the Third Reich, including everyone from communists and Social Democrats to Jews, homosexuals, gypsies, Jehovah's Witnesses, clergymen, political opponents, trade union members, and others.

During its notorious history, between 1933 and 1945, more than 206,000 prisoners from 30 countries were imprisoned at Dachau, perhaps a lot more. Some were forced into slave labor, manufacturing Nazi armaments for the war and helping to build roads, and so on. Others fell victim to SS doctors, who conducted grotesque medical experiments on them. Still others were killed after Dachau became a center for mass murder: Starvation, illness, beatings, and torture killed thousands who were not otherwise hanged, shot by firing squads, or lethally injected. The death toll was then compounded in December 1944 when a typhus epidemic took thousands of lives within and around the camp, and forced marches in and out of the camp claimed thousands of others as well. At least 30,000 people were registered as dead while in Dachau between 1933 and 1945. However, there are many other thousands who were also murdered there, even if they weren't registered as dead.

The SS abandoned the camp on April 28, 1945, and the liberating U.S. Army moved in to take charge the following day. In all, a total of 67,000 living prisoners—all of them on the verge of death—were discovered at Dachau and its subsidiary camps.

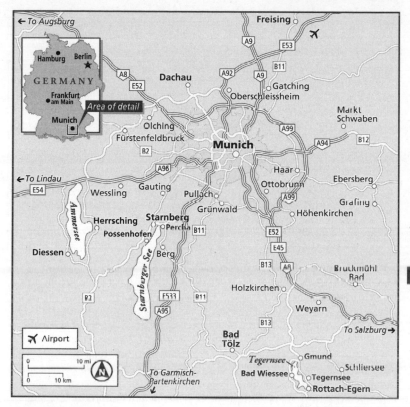

ESSENTIALS
Getting There

BY TRAIN   The frequent suburban train (S-Bahn S2) to Dachau is a 20-minute ride from Marienplatz or Hauptbahnhof in the heart of Munich (direction: Petershausen). From the station, take bus no. 724 or 726 to the camp.

BY CAR   The best road for motorists is a country road, B12. Motorists can also take the Stuttgart Autobahn, exiting at the signposted Dachau turnoff.

TOURING THE CAMP ★

Upon entering the camp, **KZ-Gedenkstätte Dachau,** Alte-Roemar-Strasse 75 (© 08131/ 66-99-70; www.kz-gedenkstaette-dachau.de), you are faced by three memorial chapels— Catholic, Protestant, and Jewish—built in the early 1960s. Immediately behind the Catholic chapel is the "Lagerstrasse," the main camp road lined with poplar trees, once flanked by 32 barracks, each housing 208 prisoners. Two barracks have been rebuilt to give visitors insight into the horrible conditions endured by prisoners.

Before Hitler, a Beloved Artists' Colony

Unknown to many, Dachau had a glorious history long before it became infamous in the annals of human cruelty. At the end of the 19th century, it was one of the leading artists' colonies of Germany, and landscape painting was virtually developed in the Dachau moorlands. Women were not yet allowed in the Munich Art Academy but they were educated in the town's private art schools.

If you have time to spare, you can explore Dachau's historic core, including its **Schloss Dachau,** a hilltop Renaissance castle that dominates the town at Schlossplatz (© **08131/87923**). All that's left of a much larger palace is a wing from 1715. Stand in the east terrace for a panoramic view of Munich in the distance. The highlight is the grand Renaissance hall, with its scenes of figures from ancient mythology. Chamber concerts are staged here. The on-site brewery hosts the town's beer and music festival annually during the first 2 weeks of August. Charging 2€ ($3.20) for admission, the castle is open April to September Tuesday to Sunday 9am to 6pm; October to March Tuesday to Sunday 10am to 4pm.

Many paintings from the artists who settled here in the 1800s are still in town, especially the works on display in **Gemäldegalerie,** Konrad-Adenauer-Strasse 3 (© **08131/567516**), open Tuesday to Friday 11am to 5pm, Saturday and Sunday 1 to 5pm, charging an admission of 4€ ($6.40).

The museum is housed in the large building that once contained the kitchen, laundry, and shower bathrooms, where the SS often brought prisoners for torture. Photographs and documents show the rise of the Nazi regime and the SS. There are also exhibits depicting the persecution of Jews and other prisoners. Every effort has been made to present the facts. The tour of Dachau is a truly moving experience.

The camp is open Tuesday to Sunday 9am to 5pm; admission is free. The English version of a 22-minute documentary film, *KZ-Dachau,* is shown at 11:30am and 3:30pm. All documents are translated in the catalog, which is available at the museum entrance. Visitors are requested to wear appropriate attire (walking shorts and a T-shirt are acceptable).

2 STARNBERGER SEE ★

27km (17 miles) SW of Munich

This large lake, southwest of Munich, is a favorite with Münchners on holiday. If you take a cruise on the lake, you can observe how the terrain changes from low-lying marshlands on the north to Alpine ranges towering above the lake to the south. The town of Starnberg is the best-equipped holiday resort on the lake, with beaches, pools, and lakefront promenades.

ESSENTIALS
Getting There
BY TRAIN   The suburban train (S6) is a 40-minute ride from Marienplatz in the heart of Munich to the town of Starnberg, at the top of Starnberger See.

BY CAR   From Munich, motorists can follow Autobahn 95 toward Garmisch to the Starnberg exit.

Visitor Information
For information, contact the **tourist office** (© **08151/9-06-00**) at Wittelsbacher Strasse 2C, in the city of Berg, open year-round, Monday to Friday 8am to 6pm; May to October, the office also has hours on Saturdays 9am to 1pm.

EXPLORING THE LAKE
Around the 64km (40-mile) shoreline, you can see no fewer than six castles, including the Schloss Berg, where Ludwig II was sent after he was certified as insane in 1886. Across the lake from Berg, the unofficial capital of the lake, stands the castle of Possenhofen, the home of Ludwig's favorite cousin, Sisi. It was in this lake that the king drowned under mysterious circumstances—local legend asserts that he was trying to swim to Possenhofen to ask his cousin's help in making an escape from Schloss Berg, since he was under house arrest. Many historians suggest he was murdered. A cross on the water marks the spot where his body was found. A *Votivkapelle* (memorial chapel) dedicated to Ludwig is on the shore above the cross. It is reached by walking up the hill from the village of Berg, into the Hofgarten, and along the wall of Schloss Berg (no connection with the hotel of the same name recommended below), which lies 5km (3 miles) southeast of Starnberg (the Schloss is not open to the public).

What, exactly, happened to King Ludwig the day his body and that of his doctor (attending physician Doctor Gudden) were found floating on the waters of Starnberg See may never be known. It is believed that relevant documents could shed some light on Ludwig's fate, but they are held privately in the Archives of the Bavarian State and by the Wittelsbach family, who have never made them public. Because Ludwig had practically bankrupted the Bavarian treasury and was a disgrace and a "menace to the throne," Prince Luitpold, who took over from the king as regent, may have wanted the insane former king removed from the picture so that he could have all the power and glory of the kingdom.

Lying on the eastern shore of Lake Starnberg, the small town of **Berg** is 4km (2½ miles) south of the larger town of Starnberg. **Schloss Berg,** Wittelsbacher Strasse 27–29 in Berg, has been owned by the ruling house of Wittelsbach since 1669. Its fame stems from the fact that it was the final residence of King Ludwig II of Bavaria. All the Gothic details added to the castle by King Ludwig in the mid–19th century have been removed, the Schloss returned to its appearance as it would have looked in the 17th and 18th centuries. The castle is still privately owned and not open to the public, and a gatehouse blocks a view of its facade. From the lake, summer foliage blocks the view, though it can be seen from the lake in winter. Although you can't go inside, you can wander through the former grounds of the castle, which have been turned into a public park.

The town of **Possenhofen** lies on the western shore of the lake. This was the summer retreat for Ludwig's favorite cousin, the Empress Elisabeth, nicknamed "Sisi." She was married to Franz Joseph I, the emperor of Austria and the king of Hungary. Sisi spent about 20 summers at this retreat, sending affectionate notes by boatmen across the lake to her cousin, Ludwig. Schloss Possenhofen still stands at Karl-Theodor-Strasse 14 in Possenhofen. Though once owned by royalty, such as Duke Max of Bavaria in 1834, the castle had become derelict by 1920, having been used for everything from a military hospital to a motorcycle repair workshop. In the early 1980s, it was converted into privately owned condos. Although the castle is not open to the public, a wooded park surrounding the Schloss can be visited anytime.

CRUISES & OUTDOOR PURSUITS   The main attractions here are sunshine and watersports. Speedboats, paddle boats, and windsurfers crowd the lake. All of these can be rented from **Surf Tools** (ⓒ **08178/909611**).

Two of the most appealing beaches on the lake include **Possenhofen Strand,** at the lakefront in the village of Possenhofen, and **Perchen Strand,** at the village of Perchen. Access to the beaches is free, but parking costs 5€ ($8). Lifeguards are on duty between May and September 9:30am to 6pm.

For information on cruises around the lake, contact the **Staatliche Schiffahrt** (ⓒ **08151/80-61**) at Dampfschiffstrasse 5, in Starnberg. Cruises are frequent in the summer months.

WHERE TO STAY & DINE

Hotel Leoni ★   This hotel rises three stories between the edge of the lake and a rolling Bavarian hillside. Built in the early 1970s, it has a cozy, country-cousin decor, and the public rooms offer big-windowed views of the lake with its swimmers and sailboats. The midsize bedrooms are outfitted in a tasteful Bavarian manor-house style. A swimming pier owned by the hotel juts out into the lake. In summer, a *Biergarten* serves frothy mugs of beer in a setting a few feet from the edge of the water.

Ortsteil Leoni, Assenbucher Strasse 44, 82335 Berg. ⓒ **08151/50-60.** Fax 08151/50-61-40. www.see hotel-leoni.com. 64 units. 138€–200€ ($221–$320) double; 210€–240€ ($336–$384) suite. Rates include buffet breakfast. AE, DC, MC, V. Free parking. **Amenities:** Restaurant; bar; lounge; indoor heated pool; sauna; babysitting; nonsmoking rooms. *In room:* TV, minibar, hair dryer, Wi-Fi.

Hotel Schloss Berg ★★   This hotel is within half a kilometer (⅓ mile) of the town's famous Schloss and is the most luxurious and comfortable hotel in town. It occupies two buildings, one a 1994 remake of an older building, the other an all-new, chalet-style structure. They are separated from one another by a parking lot and copses of trees. Rooms on the upper end of the price scale are in the older building, whose windows overlook the lake. Bedrooms are comfortable, conservatively decorated, and eminently appropriate for weekend getaways from Munich. Our favorite hangout here is the bar, an atmospheric prelude to a Bavarian-style restaurant.

Seestrasse 17, 82335 Berg. ⓒ **08151/96-30.** Fax 08151/9-63-52. www.hotelschlossberg.de. 60 units. 85€–250€ ($136–$400) double; 133€–280€ ($213–$448) suite. Rates include buffet breakfast. AE, MC, V. Free parking. **Amenities:** Restaurant; bar; Jacuzzi; sauna; laundry service. *In room:* TV, minibar, hair dryer, safe.

3 TEGERNSEE ★

48km (30 miles) SE of Munich

This Alpine lake and the resort town on its eastern shore have the same name. Although small, this is one of the loveliest of the Bavarian lakes, with huge peaks reaching to 1,890m (6,200 ft.), seemingly rising right out of the water, and a circumference of 22km

(14 miles). The lake has four major towns around its edges: Tegernsee (on the east side), Rottach-Egern (ritziest of the four, loaded with the private second homes of wealthy Münchners, on the south side), Gmund (a small village composed only of houses, on the north side, marking the entrance up the valley of the Tegernseetal), and Bad Wiessee (on the west side). For more about Bad Wiessee, see chapter 12.

ESSENTIALS
Getting There
BY TRAIN The station of Tegernsee is an 80-minute ride from Munich's Hauptbahnhof. To reach hotels in Rottach-Egern, you must take a taxi from the station. The trains make stops only in the town of Tegernsee and (less frequently) in the village of Gmund. The distance from the town of Tegernsee to the hamlet of Rottach-Egern is about 2km (1¼ miles). Only a small stream separates the two towns. Taxis make runs all the time between them, charging 7€ to 13€ ($11–$21) per trip.

BY CAR From Munich, take the A8/A9 Autobahn toward Salzburg. At exit 97 (Holzkirchen) veer south and follow the signs to Tegernsee.

Visitor Information
For information, contact the tourist office (© 08022/18-01-40) at Haus de Gastes, Hauptstrasse 2, Tegernsee, open April to October, Monday to Friday 8am to 6pm and Saturday and Sunday 10am to noon and 3 to 5pm; November to March, Monday to Friday 8am to noon and 1 to 5pm and Saturday and Sunday 10am to noon and 3 to 5pm.

EXPLORING THE LAKE
One of the most scenic routes in Bavaria is around the tiny Tegernsee, an easy morning drive. Surrounding the lake is a string of resort towns, including the elegant Rottach-Egern with its ritzy health clinics. Bad Wiessee (see chapter 12) is a year-round resort with curative springs, used in the treatment of rheumatism and heart and respiratory conditions.

A contemporary church is a fine example of modern German church architecture, designed by Olaf Gulbransson of Munich. There's also an **Olaf Gulbransson Museum** (in Kurgarten; © 08022/3338). Open Tuesday to Sunday noon to 5pm, it charges 6€ ($9.60) for adults, 5€ ($8) for seniors, and 1€ ($1.60) for students and persons 17 and under, free for children 5 and under. It's loaded with the cartoons and political satires of Norwegian-born caricaturist Olaf Gulbransson (1873–1958), who lived in Tegernsee and satirized many of Bavaria's and Germany's leaders. He was also editor of a satirical newspaper covering arts and politics, *Simplicissimus.*

CRUISES & OUTDOOR PURSUITS Sailing and windsurfing are the most popular sports here. Both can be arranged (June–Sept) at **Segel Surfschule** (© 08022/75472) near the town of Gmund, 9.5km (6 miles) north of Rottach-Egern. Windsurfers cost from 45€ ($72) for a 3-hour rental.

You can take a 1-hour cruise around the lake on one of the ferryboats operated by **Bayerischer Zehnschiffart GmbH** (© 08022/9-33-11). Boats operate about every 90 minutes from 8am to 8pm, and a circular tour from Tegernsee costs 16€ ($26).

In summer, you can walk and hike along the lakeshore. In winter, because of its small size, the lake freezes over, making it an attraction for skaters.

WHERE TO STAY IN ROTTACH-EGERN

Very Expensive

Bachmair Hotel am See ★★ This posh resort is the most elegant beside the Tegernsee and is set in the heart of town. Today, eight additional buildings supplement the original, generously proportioned *Gartenhaus*, which was constructed in 1827 as a farmhouse. It is almost like a village of minihotels, ringed with terraced gardens. Bedrooms are outfitted with lots of varnished pine and country-baroque pieces. On-site restaurants include two folkloric bistros, a main dining room, and the upscale Gourmet Restaurant.

Seestrasse 47, 83700 Rottach-Egern. ✆ **08022/27-20.** Fax 08022/27-27-90. www.bachmair.de. 288 units. 200€–315€ ($320–$504) double; 550€–1,310€ ($880–$2,096) suite. Rates include half board and buffet breakfast. AE, DC, MC. Free parking. **Amenities:** 3 restaurants; 2 bars; nightclub; 2 pools (1 heated indoor); whirlpool; health club; spa; Jacuzzi; sauna; salon; room service; babysitting; laundry service; dry cleaning; boutiques. *In room:* TV, minibar, hair dryer, safe.

Expensive

Bachmair-Alpina ★ This is the government-rated three-star sibling of the more glamorous, better-located Bachmair Hotel am See (see above). It has a pleasant but uninspired modern Swiss-chalet style and is inland from the lake, in a quiet residential neighborhood. Bedrooms are simple but comfortable and contain well-maintained bathrooms. The Alpina serves breakfast daily. However, if guests want dinner, they arrange for it in advance.

Valepper Strasse 24, 83700 Rottach-Egern. ✆ **08022/928880.** Fax 08022/95793. www.bachmair-alpina. de. 22 units. 120€–165€ ($192–$264) double; 160€–330€ ($256–$528) suite. Rates include buffet breakfast. AE, DC, MC. Parking 5€ ($8). **Amenities:** Breakfast room; bar; indoor heated pool; sauna; room service; babysitting; laundry service; dry cleaning. *In room:* TV, minibar, hair dryer, safe.

Parkhotel Egerner Hof ★ This hotel's detractors suggest that this modern hotel maintains a constant struggle to become a more up-to-date version of the town's government-rated five-star aristocrat, the Bachmair Hotel am See (see above). Despite that, many urbanites from Munich actually prefer the Parkhotel's four-star comfort and alert staff, even though there's no lake view—the hotel is surrounded by meadows and trees—and the establishment is a 20-minute walk south of the town center. Bedrooms are traditionally cozy and warm and come equipped with tidily kept bathrooms. Three excellent restaurants are on-site. The hotel's main dining room, the Sankt-Florian, accommodates guests on half board. Most nonguests, however, opt for a meal in the Dichterstube (dinner only) or the Hubertus-Stüberl (lunch and dinner); see separate review below.

Aribostrasse 19–25, 83700 Rottach-Egern. ✆ **08022/66-60.** Fax 08022/66-62-00. www.egernerhof.de. 93 units. 180€–205€ ($288–$328) double; 270€–355€ ($432–$568) suite. Half board 35€ ($56) supplement per person per day. AE, DC, MC, V. Free parking. **Amenities:** 3 restaurants; bar; indoor heated pool; fitness center; sauna; salon; room service; babysitting; rooms for those w/limited mobility. *In room:* TV, minibar, hair dryer, safe.

Moderate

Haltmair am See Unpretentious, this hotel was expanded in the mid-1970s from a 100-year-old architectural core. The decoration is almost obsessively Bavarian, with lots of Alpine accessories and dark wood paneling in the bedrooms. Suites are equipped with kitchenettes. It's near the center of the town, across the street from the edge of the lake. Other than a worthy buffet breakfast, no meals are served here.

Seestrasse 33–35. 83700 Rottach-Egern. © **08022/27-50.** Fax 08022/2-75-64. www.haltmair.de. 42 units. 95€–120€ ($152–$192) double; 195€–230€ ($312–$368) suite. Rates include buffet breakfast. No credit cards. Free parking. **Amenities:** Breakfast room; lounge; sauna; room service; babysitting; fitness room. *In room:* TV, minibar, hair dryer, safe.

Inexpensive

Gästhaus Maier zum Kirschner am See ★ (Finds)   This is one of the best bets in town for comfortable, reasonably priced accommodations with a personal touch. A farmhouse is recorded to have been here as early as 1350. Some of the remaining antique architectural details date from 1870, when the site was a local farmer's homestead. Bedrooms contain simplified reproductions of antique baroque furniture, comfortable armchairs, and well-maintained bathrooms. No meals, other than breakfast and mid-afternoon coffee and snacks, are served. Only the street separates this hotel from the edge of the lake.

Seestrasse 23, 83700 Rottach-Egern. © **08022/6-71-10.** Fax 08022/67-11-37. www.hotel-maier-kirschner.de. 41 units. 90€–110€ ($144–$176) double; 125€–150€ ($200–$240) apt. Rates include buffet breakfast. No credit cards. Free parking. **Amenities:** Restaurant; bar; spa; sauna; Jacuzzi; outdoor pool; salon. *In room:* TV, minibar, hair dryer, safe.

WHERE TO DINE

Dichterstube/Hubertus-Stüberl ★ (Finds) CONTINENTAL (in Dichterstube)/ BAVARIAN (in Hubertus-Stüberl)   Reaching these two restaurants requires a 20-minute trek on foot or a brief drive south of the town center. It's worth the effort, considering the quality of the food. The less expensive of the two, Hubertus-Stüberl is outfitted like the interior of a hunting lodge, with all the requisite references to "the hunt." Here, menu items include cream of garlic soup with croutons, goulash soup, carpaccio of bonito with a paprika-flavored vinaigrette, smoked filet of trout with horseradish sauce, and such main courses as ragout of venison with chive-flavored polenta, and veal schnitzel "in the style of the Tegernsee" with roasted potatoes.

Meals are more formal, more ambitious, and more expensive in the Dichterstube, site of the best cuisine in town. The eight-course, fixed-price menu is a veritable banquet that requires serious gastronomic attention. Ordering a la carte might be wise for those with less hearty appetites. Depending on the season, menu items may include a galette of wild rice with tartare of salmon and caviar, braised zander with a ragout of crabs, glazed John Dory with chicory sauce, lobster salad with avocados and orange-pepper marmalade, and such desserts as stuffed chocolate cake with champagne-flavored mousse and lemon-flavored sorbet.

In the Parkhotel Egerner Hof, Aribostrasse 19. © **08022/66-60.** Reservations recommended. In the Dichterstube, main courses 29€–35€ ($46–$56); fixed-price menus 90€–100€ ($144–$160). In the Hubertus-Stüberl, main courses 17€–30€ ($27–$48). AE, DC, MC, V. Daily noon–2pm (Hubertus-Stüberl only) and 6–10pm (both restaurants).

ROTTACH-EGERN AFTER DARK

The most convivial tavern in town is the **Weinhaus Moschner,** Kisslinger Strasse 2 (© **08022/55-22**), at the edge of this resort, an old, time-mellowed tavern where not only regional wine but also a hearty dark brew made by a monastery in Tegernsee is served. This is a place for a real Bavarian hoedown, and many of the local men do show up in lederhosen, dancing in the disco on the second floor. An older crowd stays downstairs sampling Franconian wine or else ordering hearty Bavarian fare, especially a wide variety of thick sausages with sauerkraut.

4 AMMERSEE ★

39km (24 miles) SW of Munich

Smaller and less popular than Starnberger See, Ammersee is a bit more rustic and wilder than its cousin. In the past, Ammersee was considered too far from the city for excursions. For that reason, it was never overdeveloped and it retains much of its natural splendor. Although it does have its share of summer homes and hotels, its shores are not quite as saturated or overcrowded as those at Starnberger See.

ESSENTIALS
Getting There
BY TRAIN The suburban train (S-Bahn 5) is a 45-minute ride from Marienplatz in the heart of Munich to Herrsching.

BY CAR Take Autobahn A96 west toward Lindau. Get off at the Herrsching/Wessling exit (Hwy. 2068) and follow signs to Herrsching.

EXPLORING THE LAKE
The village of **Herrsching,** with a population of 10,000, is home to the **Kurpark Schlösschen** (© 08152/42-50), an enormous villa with fabulous turrets, facades, and pagoda roofing. It was constructed in the late 19th century as a summer getaway for the artist Ludwig Scheuermann. It is now home to the municipal cultural center and is the venue for occasional summer concerts.

The small fishing village of **Diessen,** popular for its pottery and its church, the Marienmünster, is a short ferry ride from Herrsching. Ferries depart about nine times a day from the Seepromenade; the ride takes 20 minutes, and the fare to Diessen is 6.80€ ($11) each way. For information, call **Seenschiffahrt Ammersee** (© 08143/9-40-21) at Landsberger Strasse 81 in Ammersee.

Also a short journey from Herrsching, and well worth the time, is the ancient monastery of **Andechs** (© 08152/376-0; www.andechs.de). Set high on a mountain, the Heiliger Berg, this Benedictine monastery (daily 7am–7pm) draws multitudes of pilgrims and beer aficionados. The pilgrims visit to venerate the religious relics from the Holy Land; the less devout make the journey for the stupendous beers and cheeses produced by the monks. Buses depart from the front of Herrshing's railway station every hour year-round. Contact Omnibusverhehr Rauner (© 08152/34-57) for information. You can also hike the 5km (3 miles) uphill to the monastery—head east along the trails marked from the center of Herrsching.

CRUISES & OUTDOOR PURSUITS For a magnificent tour of the lake, take a steamship cruise. Boats depart hourly 9am to 6pm. For information on various trips, contact **Seenschiffahrt Ammersee** (© 08143/9-40-21) at Landsberger Strasse 81 in Ammersee. You can also circumnavigate the lake by taking one of the ferryboats (see above) that depart seven times a day, making stops at seven lakefront towns. For 15€ ($24), you can get on and off all day, boarding the next boat to continue the tour (visitors average two or three stops during the day).

You can rent a paddle boat, rowboat, or electric motorboat at **Stumbaum** (© 08152/ 13-75) at Summerstrasse 22, in Herrsching.

Ammersee-Hotel This well-maintained and unpretentious, government-rated three-star hotel sits behind a turn-of-the-20th-century facade in the heart of town. It has three floors of conservatively modern guest rooms, all renovated and upgraded in the late 1990s. Most have views over the lake. On the premises is a simple, *Weinstube* (wine tavern) style restaurant, plus a bar.

Summerstrasse 32, 82211 Herrsching. © **08152/96-870.** Fax 08152/53-74. www.ammersee-hotel.de. 40 units. 54€–87€ ($86–$139) per person double. Rates include buffet breakfast. AE, DC, MC, V. Free parking. **Amenities:** Restaurant; bar; health spa; sauna; room service; nonsmoking rooms. *In room:* TV, minibar, hair dryer, safe.

Hotel Promenade This is a small, businesslike hotel that occupies a site directly in the center of town. Built in 1988, and with fewer than a dozen guest rooms, it has a blandly modern decor, a bar, and a restaurant that serves Croatian and international food (see below). Some of the units come equipped with a hydromassage shower. Its position directly beside the lake permits sweeping views from the balconies of some rooms, and there's also a lakeside terrace.

Summerstrasse 6, 82211 Herrsching. © **08152/9-18-50.** Fax 08152/59-81. www.hotel-promena.de. 11 units. 90€–165€ ($144–$264) double. Rates include buffet breakfast. DC, MC, V. Parking 13€ ($21). Closed Dec 20–Jan 10. **Amenities:** Restaurant; bar; lounge. *In room:* TV, minibar, hair dryer, Wi-Fi.

WHERE TO DINE

Andechser Hof BAVARIAN This popular dining spot is the kind of place that offers beer and snacks throughout the afternoon and substantial platters of Bavarian food at dinner. The setting is a 1905 building with a decor full of references to the Bavarian experience and style. A *Biergarten* adjacent to the hotel offers such specialties as trout meunière grilled in melted butter or grilled filet of pork with pepper sauce and potato pancakes.

Don't overlook the possibility of an overnight stopover here. There's a total of 23 clean units, full of nostalgic charm, all with private bathrooms, phones, and TVs, renting for 89€ to 120€ ($142–$192) for a double, including breakfast.

Zum Landungssteg 1, 82211 Herrsching. © **08152/9-68-10.** Fax 08152/96-81-44. Main courses 14€–18€ ($22–$29). AE, DC, MC, V. Daily 11am–10pm.

Restaurant Promenade CROATIAN/GERMAN If you've never had Croatian food, this is your chance. This 80-seat dining room has a view over the lake. Croatian food places lots of emphasis on grilled meats and fish, seasoned with herbs, which emerge crisp and seared on the outside, tender on the inside, in the form of grilled lake fish, calf's liver, lamb and pork cutlets, and all kinds of steaks, invariably served with vegetables braised in butter. Also tempting is the marinated rumpsteak, usually a tough cut of meat that, thanks to long marinades and slow cooking, comes up tender and steaming.

In the Hotel Promenade, Summerstrasse 6. © **08152/9-18-50.** Main courses 17€–25€ ($27–$40). AE, MC, V. Sept–June Thurs–Tues noon–3pm and 6:30–9:30pm; July–Aug daily noon–3pm and 6:30–10pm. Closed Dec 20–Jan 10.

---

5 BAD TÖLZ ★

50km (31 miles) S of Munich

The historic spa town of Bad Tölz offers something for every traveler. Situated where the rolling foothills become the mountains of the Alps, the town flanks both sides of the Isar

River, which divides it into two distinct sectors. On the eastern side of the river stands the historic medieval town, complete with chapels, turrets, and walls. Older than Munich, this section offers fine examples of medieval and baroque art and architecture. The major attraction here is **Stadtpfarrkirche,** a church built in 1466—it's an exquisite example of German late-Gothic architecture.

On the western bank of the Isar lies the *Kurverwaltung,* or modern spa, whose iodine-rich waters are known for their soothing and healing powers.

ESSENTIALS
Getting There
BY TRAIN   The train ride takes 1¹/₂ hours from Munich's Hauptbahnhof.

BY CAR   From Munich, motorists can take the Autobahn A8 or A9 toward Salzburg. Exit at Holzkirchen and follow signs southward toward Bad Tölz.

Visitor Information
For information, contact the **Kurverwaltung** (✆ **08041/7-86-70**), at Max-Höforplatz 1, Monday to Friday 9am to 6pm, Saturday 9am to 3pm, and Sunday 10am to noon (May to Oct).

SPORTS & OUTDOOR PURSUITS
Anyone interested in sports will never be bored in Bad Tölz. Golfers have access to two 9-hole courses. **Golf Club Isarwinkel** (✆ **08041/7-78-77**), on the town's northern tier, was built for U.S. military officers when there was a local military base here. Greens fees are 50€ ($80) Monday to Friday and 70€ ($112) Saturday and Sunday. On the western tier, **Golfplatz am Buchberg,** Strasse 124 (✆ **08041/99-94**), is a challenging but less prestigious course. It charges greens fees of 39€ ($62) Monday to Friday and 50€ ($80) Saturday and Sunday. Both courses are open April to October daily 9am to 6:30pm. Advance reservations are a good idea.

Alpamare, Ludwigstrasse 14 (✆ **08041/50-99-99;** www.alpamare.com), is one of the most up-to-date swimming pools in the region, complete with water slides, waterfalls, kiddie pools, and saunas. Admission is 20€ to 33€ ($32–$53), and it's open Monday to Thursday 9am to 9pm, and Friday to Sunday 9am to 10pm. You can also swim in the Isar, but at your own risk. There are no official sites for swimming, and the river is both cold and swift.

The clear, cold, and swift waters of the Isar are well suited for white-water canoeing, kayaking, and rafting between the months of late May and early September. If you have the time and inclination to test your riverine skills, contact **Kajakschule Oberland,** Ganghoferstrasse 7, 83661 Lenggries/Fall (✆ **08045/916-916**), an outfitter that specializes in these wet and sometimes wild diversions. Most visitors opt for a 4-hour downriver ride in a rubber-sided raft, priced at around 40€ ($64) per person. It also offers longer treks that include up to 4 back-to-back days of white-water rafting at prices that begin at 300€ ($480) per person.

The nearest skiing slopes are on the Brauneck mountain. For information, contact **Ski-Centrum,** Berg Brauneck (✆ **08042/89-10**), in the nearby hamlet of Lenggries, a 20-minute drive east of Bad Tölz. A day pass on any of the 30 lifts is 40€ ($64).

Expensive

Jodquellenhof-Alpamare ★   This is Bad Tölz's equivalent of a "grand hotel," with a longer history than any other hotel in town. Originally built in 1860, and modernized inside and out many times since then, it helped launch Bad Tölz into the full-fledged resort you see today. If you opt to stay here, however, don't expect 19th-century authenticity: The hotel has, both commercially and architecturally, kept up with the times. Unlike some spa hotels that appeal to older, more staid clients, Jodquellenhof attracts a family clientele on yearly vacations. On the premises is an array of spa facilities. There's a pleasant hotel bar, and a dining room whose main function is feeding hotel guests on meal plans. Bedrooms are outfitted in a neutral, rather bland style.

Ludwigstrasse 13–15, 83646 Bad Tölz. ℗ **08041/50-90.** Fax 08041/50-95-55. www.jodquellenhof.com. 90 units. 173€–283€ ($277–$453) double; 293€–323€ ($469–$517) junior suite. AE, DC, MC, V. Free parking. **Amenities:** Restaurant; bar; 2 pools (1 heated indoor); health spa; room service; massage; babysitting; laundry service; dry cleaning; nonsmoking rooms. *In room:* TV, hair dryer, safe.

Moderate

Kurhotel Eberl ★   Set in a meadow about half a kilometer (⅓ mile) west of the resort's center, this is a white fronted, timber-studded replica of the kind of modern chalet you're likely to see a lot in Switzerland. Public rooms are lavishly finished with rough-textured beams and timber for a look that, at least from the inside, might make you think that the hotel is older than it is. Guest rooms are conservatively and comfortably outfitted with pale colors and exposed wood, and many have balconies. This is the kind of hotel where guests (mostly German) expect to eat all their evening meals on-site. Only residents are allowed in the *Stube* (beer hall–like) dining room and the hotel's lounges (the hotel is closed to nonguests). Although the town's more superior public spa facilities are nearby, the hotel has an all-inclusive health-and-rest regime package.

Buchenerstrasse 17, 83646 Bad Tölz. ℗ **08041/78-720.** Fax 08041/78-72-78. www.kurhotel-eberl.de. 32 units. 64€–102€ ($102–$163) double; 76€–114€ ($122–$182) suite. Rates include buffet breakfast. MC, V. Parking 5€ ($8). Closed Nov 15–Dec 24. **Amenities:** Breakfast room; bar; indoor heated pool; fitness center; health spa; sauna; salon; massage; all nonsmoking rooms. *In room:* TV, hair dryer, safe.

Inexpensive

Alexandra   This modern hotel has a facade of traditional dark-stained wood, lavishly accented with flower boxes. It's near the town center, on the opposite side of the riverfront promenade from the banks of the Isar. Rooms are unpretentious and outfitted with reproductions of Bavarian furniture. Other than breakfast, no meals are served. Overall, it's a worthwhile and reasonably priced hotel choice.

Kyreinstrasse 33, 83646 Bad Tölz. ℗ **08041/78430.** Fax 08041/784399. www.alexandrahotel.de. 20 units. 40€–69€ ($64–$110) double; 55€–65€ ($88–$104) junior suite. Rates include buffet breakfast. MC, V. Free parking. **Amenities:** Breakfast room; bar; room service; massage; laundry service; dry cleaning; nonsmoking rooms. *In room:* TV, hair dryer, safe.

Kolbergarten ★★   The finest and most lavish in Bad Tölz, this hotel is set in a historic zone on the east bank of the Isar, which sometimes is used for outdoor concerts and parades. It was built in 1905 by the famous Jugendstil architect, Gabriel von Seidel, who added many more folkloric touches, including lavishly ornate eaves, than are usual in his work. Guest rooms are as authentic and antiques-laden as anything you'll find in the area. The hotel's restaurant, Kolbergarten, is an upscale oasis of well-prepared cuisine dedicated to the traditions of South Tirol, a German-speaking Alpine region annexed by

Italy from Austria after World War I. Dinner is served Tuesday to Saturday from 6:30 to 11pm. Because of its limited number of bedrooms, management funnels the overflow to the larger and slightly less expensive sibling hotel, the Posthotel Kolberbräu, which is separately recommended below.

Fröhlichgasse 5, 83646 Bad Tölz. ✆ **08041/78920.** Fax 08041/90-69. www.hotel-kolbergarten.de. 15 units. 41€–64€ ($66–$102) per person double. AE, DC, MC, V. Free parking. **Amenities:** Restaurant; lounge; room service; babysitting; laundry service; dry cleaning. *In room:* TV, hair dryer, safe.

Posthotel Kolberbräu This is a cozy, old-fashioned, urban hotel that belongs to the same owner as the Kolbergarten (see above) but is in a less congested setting. It has an imposing neoclassical facade whose foundations date from the 1600s. Its popular bistro is recommended below. Guest rooms are more prosaic than those at the more aristocratic Kolbergarten and have the kind of cozy, traditional decor that nobody dislikes, but nobody thrills to either. Ten rooms have private balconies.

Marktstrasse 29, 83646 Bad Tölz. ✆ **08041/76880.** Fax 08041/7-68-82-00. www.kolberbraeu.de. 45 units. 78€–98€ ($125–$157) double. Rates include buffet breakfast. Half board 18€ ($29) supplement per person per day. AE, DC, MC, V. Free parking. **Amenities:** All rooms are nonsmoking; units for those w/limited mobility. *In room:* TV, hair dryer.

WHERE TO DINE
Moderate

Altes Fahrhaus ★ CONTINENTAL This is a *restaurant avec chambres* where the pleasant overnight accommodations are less significant than the restaurant. Three kilometers (1³/₄ miles) south of the resort's center, adjacent to the right bank of the Isar River, it's in a 75-hectare (185-acre) compound. The owner is Ely Reiser, who closely supervises (or prepares herself) everything coming out of her kitchens. The food is the best in the region, and Munich-based gastronomes often come here just to have a meal. Menu items change with the seasons but might include a salad of green asparagus with strips of braised gooseliver; bouillon of venison with ravioli or a filet of venison baked in herbs with a pepper-flavored cream sauce; filet of turbot in champagne sauce; or filet of veal with red-wine sauce, noodles, and exotic mushrooms. Because the menu changes almost every day, even the owner is reluctant to name a particular house specialty, although one superb dish that's usually available is a well-seasoned rack of lamb served with eggplant, gratin of potatoes, and zucchini in a mustard sauce. Dessert might be a Grand Marnier soufflé with rhubarb.

On the premises are five bedrooms, each with its own terrace overlooking the river. With breakfast included, doubles cost 100€ to 118€ ($160–$189).

An der Isarlust 1, 83646 Bad Tölz. ✆ **08041/60-30.** Reservations recommended. Main courses 15€–30€ ($24–$48). No credit cards. Wed–Sun noon–2pm and 6–10pm. Closed 1 week in Nov and 1 week in Feb (dates vary).

Inexpensive

Restaurant Posthotel Kolberbräu GERMAN/BAVARIAN This is the kind of no-nonsense, high-volume restaurant that virtually everyone in town has visited at least once in his or her lifetime. A labyrinth of small dining areas, it's a civic rendezvous point. The place is always crowded during the lunch and dinner hours, but throughout the afternoon, it remains open for coffee, pastries, beer, wine, and an abbreviated roster of warm food and platters.

Marktstrasse 29. ✆ **08041/76880.** Main courses 12€–23€ ($19–$37); fixed-price menus 18€ ($29). AE, DC, MC, V. Daily 7–10am, 11am–2pm, and 5–10pm.

A SIDE TRIP TO BENEDIKTBEUREN

This 8th-century monastery (a flourishing cultural center in the Middle Ages) is the oldest Benedictine site north of the Alps. The frescoes in the monastery's baroque church were painted by the father of the famous Asam brothers. It was here, in this ecclesiastical enclave, that the 12th-century secular musical work *Carmina Burana* (the Goliardic songs) first appeared, later to become a popular 20th-century work by Bavarian composer Carl Orff.

Benediktbeuren is 14.5km (9 miles) southeast of Bad Tölz. Admission is free anytime during opening hours of the compounds (daily 9am–6pm), but if you want to participate in a guided tour, you'll pay 3.50€ ($5.60) per person. These guided tours last for about 90 minutes, and they're conducted mostly in German, with occasional bits of translation thrown in. With frequent alterations based on availability of guides and other events scheduled within the monastery, they follow this schedule: Year-round, tours are offered every Saturday and Sunday at 2:30pm. During May and June, a tour is also offered every Wednesday at 2:30pm. During July and August, additional tours are every Monday to Friday at 2:30pm. For information about the monastery and concerts, call © **08857/8-80**.

6 FREISING

32km (20 miles) N of Munich

Freising, one of Bavaria's oldest towns, grew up around a bishopric founded in the 8th century. By the 12th century, under Bishop Otto von Freising, the area had begun a spiritual and cultural boom. Freising, however, was caught in a bitter rivalry with Munich that had repercussions lasting from the 12th century until the beginning of the 19th century. Bishop Otto owned a profitable toll bridge (which was not good for other areas) over the Isar until 1156, when Henry the Lion destroyed it and built his own bridge, wresting control of the lucrative salt route from the bishop and founding his settlement, München. It was Freising that went into decline then as Munich prospered. As a result of the quarrel, up until 1803, Munich was forced to pay compensation to Freising for Henry's action. We do list one restaurant below. However, if you're looking for a place to stay, we recommend going back to Munich (see chapter 5).

ESSENTIALS
Getting There
BY TRAIN   Take S1 of the S-Bahn to Freising, a 25-minute ride.

BY CAR   Freising is northeast of Munich on the B11.

Visitor Information
The **tourist information office** is at Marienplatz 7 (© **08161/5-41-22**). Hours are Monday to Friday 9am to 6pm, and Saturday 9am to 1pm.

SEEING THE SIGHTS
All the main sights are within walking distance of the Bahnhof. The Altstadt contains a number of restored canons' houses (the house occupied by a canon, which is a clergyman belonging to the chapter or the staff, a cathedral, or collegiate church) with fine baroque facades along the Hauptstrasse and in the Marienplatz-Rindermarkt area. The Gothic

St. George's Parish Church, with its lovely baroque tower, was built by the same architect who designed Munich's Frauenkirche. Opposite, in the former Lyceum of the prince-bishops, is the **Asamsaal,** a room decorated by the father of the famous Asam brothers, with a fine stucco and fresco ceiling. Tours are offered occasionally; check the tourist office for information.

A 5-minute walk southwest of the Altstadt, at Weihenstephansberg 9, is the Staatsbrauerei Weihenstephan (✆ **01861/5360**), the world's oldest brewery. The monks of the Benedictine monastery of Weihenstephan were granted the privilege of brewing and serving their own beer in 1040, a tradition that, in a much-modernized form, still continues today. If you want to see how the beer is brewed, you can participate in a guided tour that is conducted Monday at 10am, Tuesday at 10am and 1:30pm, and Wednesday at 10am, costing 9€ ($14), including a beer tasting. Many visitors, however, prefer to skip the brewery tour and head directly for the restaurant across the street (it's owned and operated by the brewery), the **Bräustuben Weihenstephan,** Weihenstephansberg 10 (✆ **01861/13004**). Open daily from 12:30 to 10:30pm, and charging from 11€ to 22€ ($18–$35) for main courses designed to go well with the beer, it's a cozy and folkloric place for a meal. American Express, MasterCard, and Visa are accepted.

Located on the Domberg, a low hill above the Altstadt, **Mariendom** is a twin-towered Romanesque basilica, constructed between 1160 and 1205. The building is rather plain on the outside, but the interior was lavishly ornamented in the baroque style by the Asam brothers in 1723–24. Egid Quirin Asam designed the interior, and Cosmas Damian Asam created the ceiling fresco of the *Second Coming,* with its floating figures and swirling clouds. A notable early medieval sculpture is the famous *Bestiensäule* (Beast Column), an entwined mass of men and monsters. The church's principal feature is the large Romanesque crypt, one of the oldest in Germany, which has survived in its original form.

The 15th-century **cloister** on the east side of the cathedral was decorated with frescoes and stucco by Johann Baptist Zimmerman. To the west of the church is the **Dombibliothek,** a library that dates from the 8th century. In the 18th century, the library acquired a lively ceiling fresco designed by François Cuvilliés.

The **Diözesanmuseum** (Domberg 1; ✆ **08161/4879-0**) is the largest diocesan museum in Germany and contains a comprehensive collection of religious art, including the famous *Lukasbild,* an exceptional Byzantine icon. The museum's exhibits document the history of the Catholic Church over 9 centuries. It's open Tuesday to Sunday 10am to 5pm; admission is 4€ ($6.40).

WHERE TO DINE

Gästhaus Landbrecht BAVARIAN   Small-scale and family-run, this 1860s inn prepares food in the old-fashioned Bavarian style. In a country-rustic dining room, you can begin with the filet of beef soup, one of the richest we've ever tasted, or a delicate cream of celery soup with fresh herbs. Main courses include roast suckling pig, roast rack of venison with red-wine sauce, a main dish of mushrooms, and fresh pikeperch in butter and parsley sauce.

Freisinger Strasse 1, Freising-Handlfinig. ✆ **08167/8926.** Reservations recommended. Main courses 11€–20€ ($18–$32). No credit cards. Sat–Sun 12:30–4pm; Wed–Sun 6–11pm. 5km (3 miles) NW of the town center; follow signs to Freising-Handlfinig.

The Bavarian Alps

If you walk into a rustic Alpine inn along the German-Austrian border and ask the innkeeper if he or she is German, you'll most likely get the indignant response, "Of course not! I'm Bavarian." Some older inhabitants can still remember when Bavaria was a kingdom with its own prerogatives, even while a part of the German Reich (1871–1918).

The huge province of Bavaria includes not only the Alps but also Franconia, Lake Constance, and the capital city of Munich. However, we'll take this opportunity to explore separately the mountains along the Austrian frontier, a world unto itself. The area's hospitality is famous, and the picture of the plump, rosy-cheeked innkeeper who has a constant smile on his or her face is no myth. Many travelers think of the Alps as a winter vacationland, but you'll find that nearly all the Bavarian resorts and villages boast year-round attractions.

Munich is the gateway to the region for those arriving by plane. From Munich, autobahns lead directly to the Bavarian Alps. Frequent trains also connect the region to Munich. If you're beginning your tour in Garmisch-Partenkirchen in the west, you should fly to Munich. However, if you'd like to begin your tour in the east, at Berchtesgaden, then Salzburg in Austria has better plane connections.

1 OUTDOORS IN THE BAVARIAN ALPS

The Bavarian Alps are both a winter wonderland and a summer playground.

In summer, **Alpine hiking** is a major attraction that includes climbing mountains, enjoying nature, and watching animals in the forest. Hikers are able, at times, to observe endangered species firsthand. One of the best areas for hiking is the 1,218m (3,996-ft.) **Eckbauer**, lying on the southern fringe of Partenkirchen (the tourist office at Garmisch-Partenkirchen will supply maps and details).

From Garmisch-Partenkirchen, serious hikers can embark on full-day or overnight Alpine treks, following clearly marked footpaths and staying in mountain huts. Some huts are staffed and serve meals; others are remote and unsupervised. For information, inquire at the local tourist office or write to the government-subsidized **German Alpine Association,** Am Franciscanalplatz 7, 83471 Berchtesgaden (**(**✆**) 08652/64343;** www. alpenverein.de).

If you're a true outdoorsperson, you'll briefly savor the somewhat touristy facilities of Garmisch-Partenkirchen, and then use it as a base for explorations of the rugged **Berchtesgaden National Park,** an easy commute from Garmisch. Many visitors come to the Alps in summer just to hike through the national park, which borders the Austrian province of Salzburg. The 2,427m (7,963-ft.) Watzmann Mountain, clear Alpine lakes like the Königssee, and parts of Mount Jenner are within the park's boundaries, and well-mapped trails cut through protected areas that lead the hiker through spectacular natural beauty. For information about hiking in the park, contact **Nationalparkhaus,** Franziskanerplatz 7, 83471 Berchtesgaden (**(**✆**) 08652/6-43-43**).

You can also stay at one of the inns in Mittenwald or Oberammergau and take advantage of a wide roster of outdoor diversions there. Any of the outfitters below will provide directions and linkups with their sports programs from wherever you decide to stay. Street maps of Berchtesgaden and its environs are usually available for free from the **Kurdirektion des Berchtesgadener Landes** (the local tourist office), Königsseer Strasse 2, Berchtesgaden (*© **08652/96-70**), and intricately detailed maps of the surrounding Alpine topography are available for a fee.

Anglers will find plenty of **fishing** opportunities (especially salmon, pikeperch, and trout) at the lake Hintersee and the rivers Ramsauer Ache and Königsseer Ache. To acquire a fishing permit, contact the **Kurdirektion** (tourist office; see above) at Berchtesgaden, which will direct you to any of four different authorities, based on where you want to fish. For fishing specifically on the Hintersee, contact tourist officials or Hotel Gamsboch in Ramsau (*© **08657/9670**).

You can also practice your **kayaking** or **white-water rafting** techniques on one of the area's many rivers (water level permitting), such as the Ramsauer, Königsseer, Bischofswiesener, and Berchtesgadener Aches. For information and options, contact the abovementioned **Outdoor Club Berchtesgaden.**

If you would like to go **swimming** in an Alpine lake—which is not to everyone's body temperature—there are many bathing areas found along sandy shores of lakes in the Bavarian Forest.

In winter, you'll find some of the greatest **Alpine** and **cross-country skiing** in all of Europe. A regular winter snowfall in January and February usually measures from 12 to 20 inches. This leaves about 2m (6½ ft.) of snow in the areas served by ski lifts. The great **Zugspitzplatt** snowfield can be reached in spring or autumn by a rack railway. The Zugspitze, at 2,962m (9,718 ft.) above sea level, is the tallest mountain peak in Germany. Ski slopes begin at a height of 2,610m (8,561 ft.).

The second great ski district in the Alps is **Berchtesgadener Land,** with Alpine skiing centered on Jenner, Rossfeld, Götschen, and Hochschwarzeck. Snow conditions are consistently good until March. Call the local "Snow-Telefon" at *© **08652/96-72-97** for current snow conditions.

Visitors will also find a cross-country skiing center with tracks kept in first-class condition, natural toboggan runs, an artificial ice run for toboggan and skibob runs, and artificial ice-skating and curling rinks. There's skating between October and February at the world-class ice-skating rink in Berchtesgaden. Less reliable, but more picturesque, is skating on the surface of the Hintersee, once it's sufficiently frozen.

2 BERCHTESGADEN ★★

158km (98 miles) SE of Munich, 18km (11 miles) SE of Bad Reichenhall, 23km (14 miles) S of Salzburg

Ever since Ludwig I of Bavaria chose this resort as a favorite hideaway, the tourist business in Berchtesgaden has been booming. According to legend, the many summits of Watzmann Mountain that tower over the village were once a king and his family who were so evil that God punished them by turning them into rocks. The evil king has evidently not been completely silenced, because the Watzmann has been responsible for the deaths of many mountain climbers on the mile-high cliff on its eastern wall.

Berchtesgaden is an old Alpine village with ancient winding streets and a medieval marketplace and castle square. Because the name of the village has often been linked with

Hitler and the Nazi hierarchy, many visitors believe they are seeing one of the *Führer's*
favorite haunts. This impression is erroneous. Hitler's playground was actually at Obersalzberg (p. 197), on a wooded plateau about a half-kilometer ($^1/_3$ mile) up the mountain.
Berchtesgaden is simply a quiet Bavarian town.

ESSENTIALS
Getting There
BY AIR The nearest airport is **Salzburg Airport** (*©* **0662/85800;** http://engl.
salzburg-airport.com). It has regularly scheduled air service to Frankfurt, Amsterdam,
Brussels, Berlin, Dresden, Dusseldorf, Hamburg, London, Paris, and Zürich. Major
airlines serving the Salzburg airport are **Austrian Airlines** (*©* **0662/854511;** www.aua.
com), **Lauda Air** (*©* **0662/854511;** www.laudaair.com), **Lufthansa** (*©* **0180/58384267;**
www.lufthansa.com), and **Tyrolean** (*©* **0662/854511;** www.tyrolean.at). From Salzburg
you can take a 1-hour train ride to Berchtesgaden, although you'll have to change trains
at Freilassing.

BY TRAIN The Berchtesgaden Bahnhof lies on the Munich-Freilassing rail line. Twelve
trains a day arrive from Munich (trip time: $1^1/_2$ hr.). For rail information and schedules,
call Deutsche Bahn (*©* **01805/99-66-33;** www.bahn.de). Berchtesgaden has three
mountain rail lines—the Obersalzbergbahn, the Jennerbahn, and the Hirscheckbahn—
that connect the mountain plateaus around the resorts. For more information on any of
the three rail lines, contact **Berchtesgadener Bergbahn AG** (*©* **08652/9 58 10**) or
Obersalzbergbahn AG (*©* **08652/25-61**).

BY BUS Regional bus service to Alpine villages and towns around Berchtesgaden is
offered by **RVO Regionalverkehr Oberbayern** (*©* **08652/94480**).

BY CAR Access by car is via Autobahn A8 from Munich in the north or Rte. 20 from
the south. The drive from Munich takes about 2 hours.

Visitor Information
For tourist information, contact the **Kurdirektion des Berchtesgadener Landes,**
Königsseer Strasse 2 (*©* **08652/96-70**), open Monday to Friday 8:30am to 5pm and
Saturday from 9am to noon.

SEEING THE SIGHTS
The **Schlossplatz ★**, partially enclosed by the castle and Stiftskirche, is the most attractive plaza in town. On the opposite side of the square from the church is a 16th-century
arcade that leads to Marktplatz, with typical Alpine houses and a wooden fountain from
1677 (restored by Ludwig I in 1860). Some of Berchtesgaden's oldest inns and houses
border this square. Extending from Marktplatz is the Nonntal, a landmark street lined
with more old houses, some built into the rocks of the Lockstein Mountain that towers
above. **The Stiftskirche (Abbey Church),** dating from 1122, is adjacent to the Königliches Schloss Berchtesgaden (see below). The church is mainly Romanesque, with Gothic
additions. One of its ancient twin steeples was destroyed by lightning and rebuilt in
1866. The interior contains many fine works of art; the high altar has a painting by Zott
dating from 1669. In the vestry is a small silver altar donated by Empress Maria Theresa
of Austria.

A minor but interesting museum, the **Heimatmuseum,** Schloss Aldelsheim, Schrof-
fenbergallee 6 (*©* **08652/44-10**), is devoted to Alpine woodcarving. Woodcarving as a
craft here predates the more fabled woodcarving at Oberammergau, and some of the best

examples in Germany are on display in the museum. Entry is allowed only as part of a guided tour in English, offered Tuesday to Sunday at 10am to 4pm for a charge of 2.50€ ($4). Free for ages 18 and under; closed in November.

Königliches Schloss Berchtesgaden   Berchtesgaden grew up around a powerful Augustinian monastery whose monks introduced the art of woodcarving, for which the town is noted to this day. When the town became part of Bavaria in 1809, the abbey was secularized and eventually converted to a palace for the royal family of Wittelsbach. Now it is a museum, devoted mostly to the royal collection of sacred art, including wood sculptures by the famed artists Veit Stoss and Tilman Riemenschneider. You can also explore a gallery of 19th-century art. There's a collection of Italian Renaissance furniture from the 16th century, and three armoires displaying many pistols and guns of the 17th and 18th centuries, plus swords and armor. Precious porcelain and hunting trophies are also shown. Visitors are ushered through about 30 of the castle's showcase rooms as part of tours that depart at 20-minute intervals throughout the day. Tours last an hour each and are conducted mostly in German, with a smattering of English. English-language pamphlets with descriptions of the castle are passed out in advance. Note that the castle is closed for the last half of August every year, during which time the Duke of Bavaria, heir to the throne of Bavaria and owner of the castle, comes for his summer holiday.

Schlossplatz 2. (℃ **08652/947-980.** Admission 7€ ($11) adults, 3.50€ ($5.60) students and seniors, 3€ ($4.80) children 6–17, free for children 5 and under. Mid-May to mid-Oct Sun–Fri 10am–noon and 2–4pm; mid-Oct to mid-May Mon–Fri 11am–2pm. Closed last 2 weeks in Aug. Bus: 9539.

Salzbergwerk Berchtesgaden (Kids)   These salt mines at the eastern edge of town were once owned by the Augustinian monastery. Operations began here in 1517. The deposits are more than 300m (1,000 ft.) thick and are still processed from four galleries or "hills." Visitors are given protective miner's clothing. Older children will enjoy the guided tours that begin with a ride into the mine on a small, wagonlike train. After a nearly 1km (¹/₂-mile) journey, visitors leave the train and explore the rest of the mine, sliding down a miner's slide and riding on the underground salt lake in a ferry. The highlight of the tour is the "chapel," a grotto containing unusually shaped salt formations illuminated for an eerie effect. The 1¹/₂-hour tour can be taken any time of the year, in any weather.

Bergwerkstrasse 83. (℃ **08652/60020.** Admission 14€ ($22) adults, 9€ ($14) students and children 4–16. May–Oct daily 9am–5pm; Nov–Apr daily 11:30am–3pm. Bus: 840.

ORGANIZED TOURS

Guided tours in English are offered by the American-run **Berchtesgaden Mini Bus Tours,** Königsseerstrasse 2 (℃ **08652/6-49-71**). Tours, including Obersalzberg, the Eagle's Nest, and the Bunker System, as an afternoon history package, are conducted daily from mid-May to mid-October, starting across the street from the train station at the Berchtesgaden tourist office (see "Visitor Information," above), where there's a tour information and ticket booth. The service also takes visitors to sights such as the Salt Mines and the Königssee. A 4-hour tour costs 40€ ($64) adults, 34€ ($54) for children 11 and under, and is free for children age 1 and under. One of the most popular tours offered is the "Sound of Music" tour to nearby Salzburg.

OUTDOORS IN THE AREA

Berchtesgaden has a world-class **ice-skating** rink, the **Eisstadion,** An der Schiessstätte (℃ **08652/6-14-05**). A local variation of **curling (Eisstock)** that uses wooden, rather than stone, implements is also played there. It's open from September to March.

The tourist office can arrange **hang gliding** or **paragliding,** which can be thrilling, if dangerous, from the vertiginous slopes of Mount Jenner. Mountain bikes can also be rented.

WHERE TO STAY

Alpenhotel Denninglehen ★ (Finds) This solid, traditional-looking mountain chalet, built in 1980, is set in a high Alpine meadow 6km (3²/₃ miles) east of Berchtesgaden, at an altitude of 900m (2,950 ft.) above sea level (Berchtesgaden is 500m/1,640 ft. above sea level). Ringed with snow in winter and grassy meadows and flower beds in summer, and within a short schuss from the ski slopes, it's a refreshingly rustic (albeit manicured) getaway for urbanites, with comfortable lodgings, clean air, and views that stretch for miles. Bedrooms are outfitted in either rustic, wood-sheathed contemporary style or more folkloric Bavarian and old-fashioned decor.

Am Priesterstein 7, 83471 Berchtesgaden/Oberau. ⓒ **08652/97890.** Fax 08652/64710. www. denninglehen.de. 25 units. 38€–48€ ($61–$77) per person. Rates include continental buffet. MC, V. Free parking. Closed last week of Dec and Jan 15–29. From Berchtesgaden, drive along Rte. 305, following signs to Unterau; take Rte. 319, following the signs to Oberau. **Amenities:** Restaurant; bar; indoor heated pool; sauna; fitness room. *In room:* TV.

Hotel Fischer ★ A 5-minute uphill walk from the Berchtesgaden railway station, in a spot overlooking the town, this hotel was built in Bavarian style in the late 1970s. Fronted with dark-stained wooden balconies against a cream-colored facade, it rambles pleasantly along the hillside. Each bedroom is cozy and traditional, with a regional theme and a small bathroom with a shower unit.

Königsseer Strasse 51, 83471 Berchtesgaden. ⓒ **08652/9550.** Fax 08652/6-48-73. www.hotel-fischer.de. 40 units. 54€–73€ ($86–$117) per person double. Rates include buffet breakfast. V. Parking 4€ ($6.40). Closed Nov to mid-Dec and mid-Mar to Apr 10. **Amenities:** Restaurant; bar; indoor pool; sauna; room service; solarium. *In room:* TV, hair dryer.

Hotel Watzmann (Value) Built as part of a brewery 300 years ago, the Watzmann is your best budget bet in town, although it doesn't have the style or amenities of the other properties described here. Set opposite the church on the main square, it has a large outdoor terrace, a cozy Bavarian-inspired decor, and dozens of turn-of-the-20th-century artifacts. Everyone in town seems to stop by sometime during the day or night for a beer, coffee, or lunch. Inside are huge carved wooden pillars, oak ceilings, wrought-iron chandeliers, and hunting trophies. The doors of the simply furnished guest rooms are painted with floral murals. Rooms are small but well maintained.

Franziskanerplatz 1, 83471 Berchtesgaden. ⓒ **08652/20-55.** Fax 08652/51-74. www.hotel-watzmann. com. 26 units. 40€–105€ ($64–$168) per person double. AE, DC, MC, V. Free parking. Closed Nov 1–Dec 25. **Amenities:** Restaurant. *In room:* No phone.

Hotel Wittelsbach Quiet, serene, and sedate, with a loyal clientele that includes many seniors who return year after year, this is a well-maintained hotel with century-old, four-story premises. It resembles a private, Jugendstil (Art Nouveau) chalet with pink exterior walls, lavish balustrades (most rooms have a private balcony), and a location within a small but verdant garden on one of the major thoroughfares of the town center. Bedrooms are comfortable, quiet, high-ceilinged, generously sized, and decorated in pale blue tones. The only meal offered is breakfast, served in a rustic, *gemütlich* (cozy) room loaded with local artifacts and a sense of Teutonic charm.

Maximilianstrasse 16, 83471 Berchtesgaden. ⓒ **08652/9-63-80.** Fax 08652/6-63-04. www.hotel-wittelsbach.com. 29 units. 74€–84€ ($118–$134) double; 100€–130€ ($160–$208) suite. Rates include breakfast buffet. AE, DC, MC, V. Free parking. **Amenities:** Breakfast room; room service; coin-operated laundry. *In room:* TV, minibar.

WHERE TO DINE

Demming-Restaurant Le Gourmet BAVARIAN/INTERNATIONAL   The Demming Hotel—old-fashioned and regional—has one of the town's best restaurants. Formerly a wealthy private house, it looks over a panoramic view of mountains and forests. Many locals regard dining here as an event. Only fresh ingredients are used in the well-prepared dishes, including hearty mountain fare, such as roast beef with chive sauce and an array of veal and fish dishes. Sometimes we wish the chef could be less timid in his cookery, but what you get isn't bad unless you're seeking zesty flavors.

Built in 1965, the five-story hotel lies on a quiet residential street and charges 50€ to 65€ ($80–$104) per person for a double room, with breakfast included. All rooms have a shower, phone, and TV, with balconies opening onto an Alpine view. Other amenities include an indoor pool, a sauna, a solarium, and the availability of massage.

Sunklergässchen 2, 83471 Berchtesgaden. ✆ **08652/96-10.** Reservations required. Main courses 13€–32€ ($21–$51). DC, MC, V accepted for hotel guests only. Daily 6:30–10pm. Closed Oct 28–Dec 15.

Hubertusstube INTERNATIONAL   You'll get an undeniable sense of Bavarian *Gemütlichkeit* in this richly paneled restaurant, where a trio of old-fashioned dining rooms, each with a century-old history of hospitality, offers well-prepared food and a view of the Alps. Specialties include filets of baby lamb flavored with garlic and served with leaf spinach and gratin potatoes. A small sirloin steak is roasted with a mustard coating, and a good-tasting veal steak is stuffed with ham and cheese and served with a mixed salad. Service is traditional and very polite.

In the Hotel Vier Jahreszeiten, Maximilianstrasse 20. ✆ **08652/9520.** Reservations recommended. Main courses 13€–25€ ($21–$40). AE, DC, MC, V. Daily 11:30am–2pm and 6–11pm.

Panorama Restaurant GERMAN/INTERNATIONAL   The decor includes lots of blond birchwood paneling and touches of pale blue, but virtually no one notices it because the windows encompass a sweeping view of Obersalzberg and the nearby mountains. Recommended dishes include braised trout with almonds, pepper steak, goulash or *Leberknödelsuppe* (liver-dumpling soup), veal or pork schnitzels, and a savory version of that traditional rib-sticker, *Schweinshaxen* (pork shank).

In the Alpenhotel Kronprinz, Am Brandholz. ✆ **08652/6070.** Reservations recommended. Main courses 10€–27€ ($16–$43). AE, DC, MC, V. Daily noon–3pm and 6–9pm.

DAY TRIPS FROM BERCHTESGADEN

Königssee ★★

This "jewel in the necklace" of Berchtesgaden is one of Europe's most scenic bodies of water. Its waters appear to be dark green because of the steep mountains that jut upward from its shores. On the low-lying land at the northern edge of the lake are a few charming inns and bathing facilities and also a parking lot, but the rest of the lake is enclosed by mountains, making it impossible to walk along the shoreline. The only way to explore the waters (unless you're like one of the mountain goats you may glimpse on the mountains) is by boat.

Electric motorboats (no noisy power launches allowed) carry passengers on tours around the lake in summer, and occasionally even in winter. The favorite spot on Königssee is the tiny flat peninsula on the western bank. It was the site of a basilica as early as the 12th century. Today the Catholic Chapel of St. Bartholomew is still used for services (except in winter). The clergy must arrive by boat since there's no other way to approach the peninsula. The adjacent buildings include a fisher's house and a restaurant, once a favored hunting lodge of the Bavarian kings. Here you can sample trout and salmon caught in the crisp, clean waters. At the southern end of the lake, you come to the Salet (or Salet-Alm), a spot where the tour boat makes a short stop near a thundering waterfall. If you follow the footpath up the hillside, you'll reach the summer pastures used by the cattle of Berchtesgaden Land.

Just over the hill is the Obersee, part of Königssee until an avalanche separated them 8 centuries ago. If you prefer a shorter trip, you can take the boat as far as St. Batholomä and back. To reach the lake from Berchtesgaden by car, follow the signs south from the town only 5km (3 miles). It's also a pleasant hour's walk or a short ride by electric train or bus from the center of town.

For information about boat excursions, call **Schiffahrt Königssee** at (C) **08652/96360.** An entire tour of Königssee requires about 2 hours. There are boats in summer every 15 minutes, so getting off one boat and climbing aboard another is easy if you want to break up the tour. During the summer, the first boat departs every morning at 8am and the last boat leaves at 5:15pm. In winter, boats leave about every 45 minutes beginning at 9:45am. The important stops are at Salet and St. Bartholomä. A round-trip fare for a lake tour is 15€ ($24) for adults and half-price for children.

Obersalzberg

The drive from Berchtesgaden to Obersalzberg at 990m (3,248 ft.) is along one of Bavaria's scenic routes. Here Hitler settled down in a rented cottage while he completed *Mein Kampf.* After he came to power in 1933, he bought Haus Wachenfeld and had it remodeled into his residence, the Berghof. Obersalzberg became the center of holiday living for Nazis such as Martin Bormann and Hermann Göring.

At Obersalzberg, you can walk around the ruins of Hitler's **Berghof.** Here, the 1938 meeting between Hitler and British Prime Minister Neville Chamberlain resulted in the Munich Agreement. Chamberlain came away hailing "peace in our time," but the Nazi dictator felt he had merely given the prime minister his "autograph" and continued preparations for World War II. The Berghof was destroyed in 1952 by Bavarian government authorities at the request of the U.S. Army—the Americans did not want a monument to Hitler. One of the only remaining structures from the Nazi compound is a guesthouse, the General Walker Hotel, used by U.S. troops stationed in Europe. Wear good walking shoes and be prepared to run into some VERBOTEN! signs in use during Hitler's heyday.

Hitler built the **bunkers** and air-raid shelter in 1943. Three thousand laborers completed the work in 9 months, connecting all the major buildings of the Obersalzberg area to the underground rooms. Many readers have expressed their disappointment when reaching this site, apparently thinking they would tour Hitler's sumptuously decorated private apartments. Instead, all they can see today are spooky, macabre-looking bunkers stripped of all their former trappings, which are a barren reminder of a tawdry dream about what was supposed to have been "A Thousand-Year Reich." A bunker, part of Hitler's air-raid–shelter system, is open for a visit. Newly opened are prison cells used by the *Reichssicherheitsdienst* (State Security Police). They were to be a last refuge for Hitler and other high officials of the Third Reich. Entrance to the bunker and prison cells is 2.50€ ($4); access is free for students, children 15 and under, and military personnel. They're open November to March Tuesday to Sunday from 10am to 3pm, from April to October daily 9am to 5pm.

An eerily fascinating point of interest is the **Kehlstein (Eagle's Nest)** ★★, which was erected on a high-altitude site by Bormann, who intended it as a 50th-birthday gift for Hitler. Built on a rocky plateau, and never intended as a military installation, its access was made possible by the construction of a 7km (4^{1}/$_{3}$-mile) road that was blasted out of solid rock beginning in 1937—an outstanding act of engineering. Ironically, Hitler visited the site very rarely, at the very most a total of only three times. Unlike Hitler's larger lodgings at Obersalzberg, which were demolished by the Allies at the end of World War II, the original granite-built teahouse on the mountain summit at the Kehlstein is still standing. Today it's the site of a restaurant, the **Kehlsteinhaus,** that's open mid-May to mid-October daily from 9am to 5pm. In winter, the site is completely closed because of snow blockages on its access road.

Between April and October, if you want to reach Kehlstein, you can either sign up for an organized tour with Eagle's Nest Tours (see below), or set out by yourself from the railway station at Berchtesgaden. Modern buses operated by the **RVO Bus Company** (for information, call the Berchtesgaden Tourist Office at ✆ **08652/9670**) charge 6€ ($9.60) per person for a round-trip transit from the Berchtesgaden railway station up to the Alpine hamlet of **Berchtesgaden-Hintereck.** Here, you'll find some souvenir shops, a documentation center, and a minimuseum showcasing the region's role as a place of rest and relaxation for Hitler. Also at Hintereck, you'll have the option of visiting a bunker and a grim series of rooms used as a military prison by the Nazi regime. Access to the minimuseum, the documentation center, the bunker, and the prison cells at Hintereck costs 5€ ($8) for adults. Access is free for students, children 15 and under, and military personnel. From April to October, they're open daily from 9am to 5pm; from November to March, they're open Tuesday to Sunday 10am to 3pm (closed Jan 1, Nov 1, and Dec 24, 25, and 31).

To continue uphill from Hintereck to Kehlstein, you'll have to transfer to the **Kehlstein Bus** that hauls passengers uphill, past sweeping panoramas, along a tight and winding Alpine road, to the base of an elevator shaft that will carry you the remaining way to the Kehlstein. Total transit time from Berchtesgaden to Kehlstein, without stops, is about 50 minutes each way. The Kehlstein bus line operates at roughly 20-minute intervals daily from 9am to 5pm from mid-May to mid-October. Round-trip passage, including the fee for the elevator, costs 18€ ($29) per person (free for children 4 and under). If you're hardy, you can skip the elevator and take a 30-minute uphill climb along a well-marked hiking trail instead. The **restaurant** at the summit, within the Kehlsteinhaus, is open during hours that correspond to the bus access described above.

The Kehlstein road is closed to private traffic. The only option for drivers of private cars involves parking in the lot at Hintereck and then riding the Kehlstein bus to the base of the elevator described above.

If you prefer to visit Kehlstein by guided tour, you'll find worthwhile English-language options at the American-run **Eagle's Nest Tours,** Königsseerstrasse 2 (✆ **08652/64971;** www.eagles-nest-tours.com). Tours, including Obersalzberg, Eagle's Nest, and the bunker system as an afternoon history package, are conducted daily mid-May to mid-October, starting at the Berchtesgaden Visitor Center. The service also takes visitors to sights such as the Salt Mines and the Königssee. A 4-hour tour costs 45€ ($72) adults, 30€ ($48) children 7 to 12, and free for children 6 and under. One of the most popular tours offered is the Sound of Music tour to nearby Salzburg, 35€ ($56) adults, 25€ ($40) children 6 to 12, and free for children 5 and under.

Obersalzberg is becoming an important health resort; the ruins of Bormann's Gusthof Farm are now the location of Skytop Lodge, a popular golfing center in summer and a ski site in winter.

Where to Stay

Hotel zum Türken   The Hotel zum Türken, located in Obersalzberg, is legendary. It's designed in the Alpine style and has terraces with views. On its facade is a large painted sign of "The Turk"—legend has it that the first owner was a veteran of the Turkish war. In the 1930s, anti-Nazi remarks led to trouble for the proprietor, Herr Schuster, who was arrested. Afterward Bormann used the building as a Gestapo headquarters; it then fell victim to air raids and looting in April 1945. Herr Schuster's daughter, Therese Partner, was able to buy the ruin from the German government in 1949. There is an old air-raid shelter directly under the hotel that can be visited every day from 9am to 3pm. The small- to medium-size rooms are well-maintained with neatly kept bathrooms. Most rooms have balconies with views of the valley.

83471 Berchtesgaden-Obersalzberg. ℭ **08652/2428.** Fax 08652/4710. www.hotel-zum-tuerken.com. 15 units, 12 with shower or tub. 72€–95€ ($115–$152) double without bathroom; 102€–148€ ($163–$237) double with bathroom. Rates include continental breakfast. AE, DC, MC, V. Free parking. **Amenities:** Breakfast room; bar; lounge. *In room:* Hair dryer, no phone.

InterContinental Resort Berchtesgaden ★★★   Set against snow-capped mountains, Hermann Göring's former rural retreat has been turned into one of the best hotels in the Bavarian Alps. It is just over a rise from the Berghof, the house where Hitler plotted his dirty deeds. You can ski in the winter, or golf, hike, swim, and raft in the summer. The opening of this luxurious spa and retreat on land formerly inhabited by Nazis plotting massive death has generated unfavorable press comment. But until the Nazis made it their private preserve, the Obersalzberg area was a vacation retreat. So, in a sense, the resort is returning to its origins with the opening of this hotel. The spacious bedrooms are furnished with deluxe styling, comfort, charm, and grace.

Hintereck 1, 83471 Berchtesgaden. ℭ **08652/97550.** Fax 08652/97559999. www.ichotelsgroup.com. 138 units. 223€–285€ ($357–$456) double; from 433€ ($693) suite. AE, DC, MC, V. Parking 15€ ($24). **Amenities:** 3 restaurants; bar; 2 heated pools (1 indoor, 1 outdoor); sauna; health club; business services; salon; room service; babysitting; laundry service; dry cleaning; nonsmoking rooms. *In room:* A/C, TV, minibar, coffeemaker, hair dryer, iron, safe.

3 BAD REICHENHALL ★

135km (84 miles) SE of Munich, 19km (12 miles) SE of Salzburg

The best German spas can call themselves *Staatsbad,* and Bad Reichenhall bears that title with pride. This old salt town is the most important curative spa in the Bavarian Alps. Mountain chains surround it, protecting it from the winds. Its brine springs, with a salt content as high as 24%, are the most powerful saline springs in Europe, and the town has been a source of salt for more than 2,400 years. The combination of the waters and the pure air has made Bad Reichenhall an important spa for centuries.

In 1848, King Maximilian of Bavaria stayed here, popularizing Bad Reichenhall as a fashionable resort. Today, visitors come from all over the world to take the waters that are especially recommended for the treatment of respiratory disorders such as asthma, chronic bronchitis, and sinus infection, as well as skin diseases. It is known for its holistic approach: Types of spa treatments include inhalation, brine drinking cures, mud baths, and breathing exercises. Although Bad Reichenhall takes the medical side of the cure seriously, a number of beauty and fitness programs are also featured.

ESSENTIALS
Getting There
BY AIR   The nearest airport is Salzburg (see "Berchtesgaden," earlier in this chapter). From Salzburg, it's a 20-minute train ride into Bad Reichenhall, with trains leaving every hour throughout the day, with a change in Freilassing.

BY TRAIN   Bad Reichenhall is connected to the airport at Munich (see chapter 3) by frequent train service through Rosenheim. The trip takes about $2^1/_2$ hours. For information and schedules, call ✆ **01805/996633** or check out **www.bahn.de**. Frequent bus and rail connections to and from Berchtesgaden take about 45 minutes. Buses or trains leave every hour from Berchtesgaden heading for Bad Reichenhall.

BY BUS   Regional bus service to and from Bad Reichenhall is provided by **RVO Regionalverkehr Oberbayern** (✆ **08821/948274**). From the spa, you can take a bus to various stops in the Bavarian Alps, including Berchtesgaden.

BY CAR   Access is by the A8 Autobahn, from Munich in the north and Salzburg in the south. Exit on Federal Hwy. 21 into Bad Reichenhall.

Visitor Information
For tourist information, go to the **Kur- und Verkehrsverein im Kurgastzentrum,** Wittelsbacherstrasse 15 (✆ **08651/6060**). It's open Monday to Friday 8:30am to 5pm and Saturday 9am to noon.

SIGHTS & ACTIVITIES
The ideal climate permits a complete spectrum of outdoor events, from excursions into the mountains for skiing or hiking to tennis tournaments. Gardeners and botanists will enjoy the spa gardens: The sheltered location of the town amid the lofty Alps permits the growth of several varieties of tropical plants, giving the gardens a lush, exotic appearance. There's also a wide choice of indoor activities, from symphony concerts to folklore presentations to gambling in the casino.

The great fire of 1834 destroyed much of the town, but many of the impressive churches survived. An outstanding example is **St. Zeno,** a 12th-century Gothic church showing a later baroque influence. Its most remarkable feature is its painted interior, centering on the carved altarpiece, the *Coronation of the Virgin.*

Bad Reichenhaller Saltmuseum, Alte Saline Reichenhall (✆ **08651/7002146**), a short walk from the Kurgarten, is home of the industry responsible for the region's growth and prosperity from Celtic times to today. Parts of the old plant still stand, but most of it was reconstructed in the mid–19th century by Ludwig I of Bavaria. The large pumps and huge marble caverns are impressive. Tours run May to October daily 10 to 11:30am and 2 to 4pm, and November to April Tuesday and Friday 2 to 4pm. Admission is 5.90€ ($9.50) for adults and 3.90€ ($6.30) for children.

WHERE TO STAY
Very Expensive
Steigenberger Axelmannstein ★★★   This first-class hotel, set in its own 3-hectare ($7^1/_2$-acre) garden, is the best in town for traditional charm and spa conveniences, far

superior to its closest rival, the Parkhotel Luisenbad (see below). Public rooms are tradi- tionally furnished with antiques and reproductions. Many of the well-furnished and spacious bedrooms have views of the encircling Bavarian Alps. The Parkrestaurant, opening onto a garden, attracts many nonresidents, as does the cozy Axel-Stüberl, with regional dishes. The wood-paneled Axel-Bar has live entertainment.

Salzburger Strasse 2–6, 83435 Bad Reichenhall. ☎ **08651/77-70.** Fax 08651/59-32. www.bad-reichenhall.steigenberger.de. 151 units. 180€–354€ ($288–$566) double; from 280€ ($448) suite. Rates include buffet breakfast. AE, MC, V. Parking 11€ ($18). **Amenities:** 2 restaurants; bar; indoor pool; tennis court; fitness center; sauna; room service; massage; laundry service; dry cleaning; nonsmoking rooms; cosmetic studio; solarium. *In room:* TV, minibar, hair dryer, safe.

Expensive

Parkhotel Luisenbad ★★   A world unto itself, Parkhotel Luisenbad is an 1860s hotel with a guest-room wing in a garden setting. It's a good second choice to the Steigenberger, especially if you like traditional hotels. Its best feature is the indoor pool with a glass wall, bringing the outdoors inside. The more modern rooms are handsome, with bold colors and tasteful furnishings, but many guests prefer the older, more traditional rooms. Rooms range in size from medium to spacious. The lobby and the Restaurant die Holzstube (see "Where to Dine," below) have been renovated in a classic provincial style and decorated in warm colors.

Ludwigstrasse 33, 83435 Bad Reichenhall. ☎ **08651/60-40.** Fax 08651/6-29-28. www.parkhotel.de. 83 units. 105€–215€ ($168–$344) double. Rates include continental breakfast. DC, MC, V. Parking 5€ ($8). **Amenities:** 3 restaurants; bar; lounge; indoor pool; sauna; room service; massage; laundry service; dry cleaning; nonsmoking rooms; mud baths. *In room:* TV, minibar, hair dryer, safe.

Inexpensive

Hotel-Pension Erika ★ (Finds)   Charming, intimate, and personalized, this Italianate-style hotel was built in a grandiose Renaissance style in 1898 by an architect who based his inspiration on a small palace he had admired near Venice. Today, with an interior that has been much renovated and modernized, it welcomes guests into a verdant garden in a location in the heart of Bad Reichenhall. Bedrooms are each outfitted in a combination of contemporary and vaguely Jugendstil design, in monochromatic color schemes of red, blue, yellow, or green, with lots of exposed wood. Most guests opt for the half-board plan, enjoying evening meals personally prepared by the owner, who cooks German, French, Italian, and Austrian cuisine with style and flair. The dining room is open only to residents of the hotel.

Adolf-Schmid-Strasse 3, 83435 Bad Reichenhall. ☎ **08651/95360.** Fax 08651/953-6200. www.hotel-pension-erika.de. 33 units. 35€–51€ ($56–$82) per person double; 49€–65€ ($78–$104) per person suite. Rates include breakfast. AE, MC, V. Parking 4€ ($6.40). Closed Nov–Feb; in-house restaurant closed Sun year-round. **Amenities:** Restaurant; lounge. *In room:* TV, safe.

Salzburger Hof (Value)   This three-story hotel is one of the best buys in town. Its public rooms are filled with old-Bavarian charm. Best of all are the compact guest rooms, most of which contain streamlined sofas, window desks, beds with built-in headboards, armchairs around a breakfast table, and well-kept bathrooms with a shower; all open onto tiny balconies. The room prices depend on the view.

Mozartstrasse 7, 83435 Bad Reichenhall. ☎ **08651/9-76-90.** Fax 08651/97-69-99. www.hotel-salzburgerhof.de. 25 units. 76€–96€ ($122–$154) double. Rates include continental breakfast. No credit cards. Parking: 2.50€ ($4). **Amenities:** Restaurant. *In room:* TV.

WHERE TO DINE

Restaurant die Holzstube GERMAN/INTERNATIONAL/ITALIAN   The old-fashioned tradition and service here attract many regular patrons. This is a place where you can watch the flowers bloom in the garden and enjoy a first-rate cuisine (with many diet-conscious selections). You might try one of the kitchen's own original recipes: for example, marinated and roasted medallions of venison *Königin Luise,* served with bacon, chanterelles, and whortleberries.

In the Parkhotel Luisenbad, Ludwigstrasse 33. ℂ **08651/60-40.** Reservations recommended. Main courses 15€–23€ ($24–$37); fixed-price menu 27€ ($43). DC, MC, V. Daily noon–2pm and 6–9pm.

BAD REICHENHALL AFTER DARK

Most guests looking for a night out head for the **Bayerische Spielbank Casino,** Wittelsbacherstrasse 17 (ℂ **08651/95800**), which offers roulette, American roulette, blackjack, and 50 types of slot machines. You must show your passport if you plan to do any gaming. It's open daily 3pm to 2am; admission is 2.50€ ($4). Men must wear jackets and ties. The **theater,** also located here at the Kurgastzentrum, site of the casino, is a setting for operas, operettas, plays, ballets, musicals, symphonies, folkloric evenings, and chamber-music recitals. The tourism office (see "Visitor Information," above) keeps a complete list of events and ticket prices. When weather permits, performances are given in an open-air pavilion. Tickets are 15€ to 40€ ($24–$64).

If you want to hang out with the locals, go to the **Axel Bar,** a woodsy bar in the Steigenberger Axelmannstein Hotel, Salzburgerstrasse 2–6 (ℂ **08651/7770**). Here you can dance to rather sedate disco music interspersed with folk tunes. Good old-fashioned Bavarian beer is the order of the evening at everybody's favorite beer hall, **Burgerbräu,** Waaggasse (ℂ **08651/6080**).

---

4 CHIEMSEE ★

Prien am Chiemsee: 85km (53 miles) SE of Munich, 23km (14 miles) E of Rosenheim, 64km (40 miles) W of Salzburg

Known as the "Bavarian Sea," the Chiemsee is one of the most beautiful lakes in the Bavarian Alps, set in a serene landscape. In the south, the mountains reach almost to the water. Many resorts line the shores of the large lake, but the Chiemsee's main attractions are on its two islands, Frauenchiemsee, with its interesting local customs, and Herrenchiemsee, site of the palace built by Ludwig II with the intent of re-creating Versailles.

ESSENTIALS
Getting There
BY TRAIN   Prien Bahnhof is on the major Munich–Rosenheim–Freilassing–Salzburg rail line, with frequent connections in all directions. Ten trains arrive daily from Munich (trip time: 1 hr.). For information, call ℂ **01805/996633** or visit **www.bahn.de.**

BY BUS   Regional bus service is offered by **RVO Regionalverkehr Oberbayern** (ℂ **08821/948274**).

BY CAR   Access by car is via the A8 Autobahn from Munich.

Contact the **Kur- und Verkehrsamt,** Alte Rathaus-Strasse 11, in Prien am Chiemsee (© **08051/69050**). It's open Monday to Friday 8:30am to 6pm. From May to September it is also open on Saturday during the same hours.

Getting Around

BY STEAMER From the liveliest resort, Prien, on the lake's west shore, you can reach either Frauenchiemsee or Herrenchiemsee via lake steamers. The round-trip fare to Herrenchiemsee is 6.20€ ($9.90); to Fraueninchiemsee it's 7.30€ ($12). Children 13 and under travel free. The steamers, operated by **Chiemsee-Schiffahrt Ludwig Fessler** (© **08051/6090;** www.chiemsee-schifffahrt.de), run year-round. Connections can also be made from Gstadt, Seebruck, Chieming, Übersee/Feldwies, and Bernau/Felden. Boats leave Prien/Stock for Herrenchiemsee May to September daily, about every 20 minutes from 9am to 5pm. The last return is at 6:50pm.

BY BUS Bus service is from the harbor to the DB station in Prien (Chiemsee-Schiffahrt) and around the lake by RVO.

EXPLORING THE ISLANDS

Frauenchiemsee

Frauenchiemsee, also called Fraueninsel, is the smaller of the lake's two major islands. Along its sandy shore stands a fishing village whose boats fish the lake for pike and salmon. At the festival of Corpus Christi, these boats are covered with flowers and streamers, the fishers are outfitted in Bavarian garb, and the young women of the village dress as brides. As the boats circle the island, they stop at each corner for the singing of the Gospels.

The island is also the home of a Benedictine nunnery, founded in 782. The convent is known for a liqueur called *Kloster Likör.* Sold by nuns in black cowls with white-winged head garb, it's supposed to be an "agreeable stomach elixir."

You can walk around the island in about 30 minutes to enjoy panoramic views of the lake. **Torhalle** (© **08054/7256**), a summer-only art gallery, is installed in the ancient hall that used to be the gatehouse of the Frauenwörth convent. Admission is 2.50€ ($4) for adults, 1.50€ ($2.40) for students, and free for 11 and under. The hall is open only May to October daily 11am to 6pm.

Herrenchiemsee ★★

Herrenchiemsee, also called Herreninsel, has the most popular visitor attraction on the lake, one of King Ludwig's fantastic castles.

Neues Schloss Begun by Ludwig II in 1878, this castle was never completed. It was meant to be a replica of the grand palace of Versailles that Ludwig so admired. A German journalist once called it "a monument to uncreative megalomania." However, the creation of the castle gave impetus to a revival of Arts and Crafts. One of the architects of Herrenchiemsee was Julius Hofmann, whom the king had also employed for the construction of his famous Alpine castle, Neuschwanstein. When money ran out and work was halted in 1886, only the center of the enormous palace had been completed. The palace and its formal gardens, surrounded by woodlands of beech and fir, remain one of the most fascinating of Ludwig's adventures, in spite of their unfinished state.

The palace entrance is lit by a huge skylight above the sumptuously decorated state staircase. Frescoes depicting the four states of existence alternate with Greek and Roman

The Fairy-Tale King

Often called "Mad" King Ludwig (although Bavarians hate that label), Ludwig II, son of Maximilian II, was only 18 years old when he was crowned king of Bavaria. Handsome Ludwig initially took an interest in affairs of state, but he soon grew bored and turned to the pursuit of his romantic visions. He transformed his dreams into some of the region's most elaborate castles, nearly bankrupting Bavaria in the process.

Linderhof, the first and smallest of Ludwig's architectural fantasies, was his favorite castle, and the only one completed. His most elaborate effort was his attempt to construct his own Versailles on the island of Herrenchiemsee, but best known is the multiturreted Disneyland-like Neuschwanstein. From a distance, the castle appears more illusory than real. It's the most photographed castle in Germany and one of Germany's greatest tourist attractions.

The "dream king" was born in 1845 at Nymphenburg, the summer residence of the Bavarian rulers. A bisexual loner who never married, Ludwig's most intense relationship was his friendship with the composer Richard Wagner. Ludwig was an admirer of Wagner when that composer's music was considered crude, loud, and even demonic by almost everyone; it was Ludwig's enthusiastic and generous support that gave Wagner the opportunity to develop his art. It is probable that Ludwig, who was not musical, was captivated less by the music than by the opera's world of fantasy. The king sometimes had Wagner's operas mounted for his own pleasure and watched them in royal and solitary splendor. In the magical grotto at Linderhof, he re-created the Venus grotto from the Munich opera stage design for *Tannhäuser*. Although the money he

statues set in niches on the staircase and in the gallery above. The vestibule is adorned with a pair of enameled peacocks, Louis XIV's favorite bird.

The **Great Hall of Mirrors** ★★ is unquestionably the most splendid hall in the palace and the most authentic replica of Versailles. The 17 door panels contain enormous mirrors reflecting the 33 crystal chandeliers and the 44 gilded candelabras. The vaulted ceiling is covered with 25 paintings depicting the life of Louis XIV.

The dining room is a popular attraction for visitors because of the table nicknamed "the little table that lays itself." A mechanism in the floor permitted the table to go down to the room below to be cleared and relaid between courses. Over the table hangs an exquisite chandelier of Meissen porcelain, the largest in the world and the single most valuable item in the palace.

The **state bedroom** ★ is brilliant to the point of gaudiness, because practically every inch of the room has been gilded. On the dais, instead of a throne stands the richly decorated state bed, its purple-velvet draperies weighing more than 300 pounds. Separating the dais from the rest of the room is a carved wooden balustrade covered with gold leaf. On the ceiling, a huge fresco depicts the descent of Apollo, surrounded by the other gods of Olympus. The sun god's features bear a strong resemblance to Louis XIV.

Herrenchiemsee 3. © **08051/68-87-0.** Admission (in addition to the round-trip boat fare) 7€ ($11) adults, 6€ ($9.60) students, free for persons 17 and under. Apr–Sept tours daily 9am–6pm; off season daily 9:40am–4pm.

lavished on Wagner came from his own fortune, Ludwig's ministers became alarmed and Wagner was persuaded to leave Munich, although the friendship continued at a distance.

Ludwig had few close friends. He was devoted to his cousin Sisi—Elisabeth, the empress of Austria—but estranged from the rest of his family. He led a solitary life, slept most of the day, and spent his nights going for long, lonely rides through the countryside, often dressed in full kingly regalia. More and more, he withdrew into his dream world; he ran up huge debts and refused all advice to curb his extravagant building projects.

Finally, the cabinet decided he had to go—his excesses were too much. He was declared insane in 1886 when he was 41 years old, and his uncle Luitpold was made regent. Three days later, he was found drowned in Lake Starnberg on the outskirts of Munich—he may have committed suicide, or he may have been murdered. His death remains a mystery. On the shore of the lake is a memorial chapel dedicated to him. He is buried with other royals in the crypt beneath the choir of St. Michael's Church.

Today, Ludwig enjoys something of a cult status in Munich. Was he really insane? His theatricality, self-absorbed lifestyle, morbid shyness, and outbursts of temper certainly made him a very strange person, but there is not much evidence of real insanity. He seems mainly to have been an eccentric who had the means and power to turn his fantasies into reality.

WHERE TO STAY

Bayerischer Hof   The rustic decor creates the illusion that this relatively severe modern hotel is older than it is. Of note is the painted ceiling in the dining room. The rest of the hotel is more streamlined—modern, efficient, and appealing, though the Yachthotel has more style and flair. Nonetheless, rooms are comfortable and bathrooms well equipped, with showers or tubs.

Bernauerstrasse 3, 83209 Prien am Chiemsee. (☎) **08051/6030.** Fax 08051/62917. www.bayerischerhof-prien.de. 46 units. 90€–110€ ($144–$176) double. Rates include buffet breakfast. AE, MC, V. Parking 7€ ($11). Restaurant closed in Nov; restaurant and hotel closed the last 2 weeks of Jan. **Amenities:** Restaurant; bar; lounge; laundry service; nonsmoking rooms. In room: TV, minibar, safe.

Inselhotel zur Linde (Value)   Set on the highest hillock on the Fraueninsel, this is a solid, richly textured, and historic inn with a tradition of welcoming overnight guests that goes back to 1396. Its premises are scattered among a pair of steep-roofed, old-fashioned Teutonic-looking buildings surrounded with a lush flowering garden and flanked by the island's largest and busiest beer garden. Bedrooms, each renovated in the late 1990s, are high-ceilinged, old-fashioned, and conservatively outfitted with lace curtains, various tones of beige and champagne, and traditional, Mittel European style. Don't expect much in the way of amenities here. You're housed in comfort, but without a lot of gadgets other than a telephone.

Haus 1, 83256 Fraueninsel im Chiemsee. © **08054/90366.** Fax 08054/7299. www.inselhotel-zurlinde.de. 14 units. 114€–124€ ($182–$198) double. Rates include breakfast. MC, V. Closed Mid-Jan to mid-Mar. **Amenities:** Restaurant; laundry service.

Yachthotel Chiemsee ★ The boating crowd flocks to this hotel, on the western shore of the "Bavarian Sea." This modern hotel offers attractively furnished rooms, all with king-size beds, and balconies or terraces, some opening onto the water. Lakeside rooms have two double beds and a pullout sofa for groups of four or more. There's a choice of restaurants, complete with a lakeside terrace and a marina, although you can order from the same menu in all three. The most elegant room, patronized for its view if not its food, is the Seepavillon. The Seerestaurant is slightly more rustic, but with an elegant flair, and the Zirbelstüberl goes Alpine-Bavarian all the way.

Harrasser Strasse 49, 83209 Prien am Chiemsee. © **08051/69-60.** Fax 08051/51-71. www.yachthotel.de. 97 units. 156€–186€ ($250–$298) double; 220€–360€ ($352–$576) suite. Rates include buffet breakfast. AE, DC, MC, V. Free parking. **Amenities:** Restaurant; bar; indoor pool; whirlpool; sauna; room service; laundry service; dry cleaning; solarium; squash court. *In room:* TV, hair dryer, safe.

WHERE TO DINE

Restaurant Mühlberger ★★ CONTINENTAL Set within a 2-minute drive (or a 5-min. walk) from the center of Prien, this is a cozy, relatively modern building whose exposed pine and coziness makes you think it might be older. The thoughtful and hospitable staff present menu items that reflect the diversity of local culinary traditions, and although lots of imagination is shown in the kitchen, some recipes evoke strong memories of the childhoods in many patrons. Examples include *Saibling* (a local freshwater whitefish) served in herb sauce with new potatoes, filet of veal with exotic wild mushrooms and a sauce made from a local white wine, a tender form of veal-based Tafelspitz (the boiled-beef dish that's always associated with Vienna and its last emperor, Franz-Josef), many well-flavored versions of chicken, and such saltwater fish dishes as tuna steak with a curried tomato sauce or turbot with béarnaise sauce. You may begin a meal here with a terrine of guinea fowl with pearl onions and end it with a house-made strudel layered with wild cherries, vanilla ice cream, and chocolate sauce.

Bernauerstrasse 40, Prien. © **08051/966-888.** Reservations recommended. Main courses 24€–26€ ($38–$42); fixed-price lunch 35€ ($56), fixed-price dinner menus 59€–70€ ($94–$112). MC, V. Thurs–Mon 11:30am–2pm and 6–10pm. Closed 3 weeks in Feb and 2 weeks in Nov.

5 BAD WIESSEE ★

53km (33 miles) S of Munich, 18km (11 miles) SE of Bad Tölz

If you've always believed that the best medicine is the worst tasting, you should feel at home in Bad Wiessee—the mineral springs of this popular spa on the Tegernsee are saturated with iodine and sulfur. However, the other attractions of this small town more than make up for this healthful discomfort. The spa, with a huge lake at its feet and towering Alps rising behind it, is a year-round resort. In summer, swimming and boating are popular; in winter, you can ski on the slopes or skate on the lake.

The springs are used for the treatment of many diseases, including rheumatism and heart and respiratory conditions. In spite of its tiny size, Bad Wiessee is advanced in its medical facilities, as well as in its accommodations and restaurants.

The main season begins in May and ends in October. During these busy times, you should definitely make a reservation. Many hotels close in winter, so be warned if you're an off-season visitor. In recent years, the town has become increasingly popular with **207** vacationers from Munich.

From Bad Wiessee, possible tours include visits to Munich, Chiemsee, and the castles of Neuschwanstein (see "Neuschwanstein & Hohenschwangau," later in this chapter) and Herrenchiemsee (see above). You can also visit Salzburg and Innsbruck in Austria. The tourism office (see below) will supply details.

ESSENTIALS

Getting There

BY TRAIN Travelers arriving by train disembark at Gmund, 3km (1³/₄ miles) away. At the railway station there, a flotilla of buses (btw. 9 and 11 per day, depending on the day of the week) meet every major train, with easy connections on to Bad Wiessee. For rail information, call © **01805/99-66-33.**

BY BUS Between three and five buses depart every day for Bad Wiessee from Munich's Hauptbahnhof, with additional stops along the Zweibrückestrasse, adjacent to Munich's Deutsches Museum. Travel time is about 90 minutes. Round-trip transport costs 19€ ($30) per person. For bus information, call © **08022/19-412.**

BY CAR Access from either Munich or Salzburg (Austria) is via the Autobahn A8. Take the Holzkirchen exit heading toward Bad Wiessee and follow the signs.

Visitor Information

For information, go to the **Kurverwaltung**, Adrian Stoop-Strasse 20 (© **08022/86030**). May to October, hours are Monday to Friday 8am to 6pm, and Saturday 9am to noon. In the off season, hours are Monday to Friday 8am to 5pm.

SIGHTS & ACTIVITIES

Bad Wiessee offers plenty of activities, apart from its health treatments. In summer, visitors can sail or windsurf on the lake, or head to the mountains for mountain biking and hiking. A drive up the **Wallberg Road** winds through the Moorsalm pasture to an altitude of 990m (3,248 ft.). There's also plenty of golf and tennis. In winter, experienced Alpine skiers are drawn to the Wallberg, and there are many cross-country trails as well. Wintertime hiking is also possible, because about 97km (60 miles) of paths are cleared of snow. The less adventurous can enjoy horse-drawn sleigh rides. You can also take a **mountain cable car,** which travels up 1,530m (5,020 ft.).

The town of Bad Wiessee has old-world charm. It's best explored via the old-fashioned steam train or by carriage ride. During the annual lake festivals in summer, locals don traditional clothing and parade through the town. The nearby **Tegernsee Ducal Palace** contains the former monastery of St. Quinn, founded in A.D. 746.

WHERE TO STAY

Hotel Lederer am See ★ This spa and holiday hotel is clearly one of the most distinguished choices in town. From the balcony of your room, you'll look out onto the Tegernsee and the Lower Bavarian Alps. The atmosphere is pleasant, with good service and attractive, well-maintained rooms, ranging in size from medium to spacious. The hotel stands in a large park, and there are a dock and an indoor pool for swimming, as well as a meadow for sunbathing. The hotel restaurant turns out international cuisine of a good standard. Sometimes there's a barbecue on the terrace facing the lake, followed by entertainment or dancing in the nightclub.

THE BAVARIAN ALPS

12

BAD WIESSEE

Bodenschneidstrasse 9–11, 83707 Bad Wiessee. ✆ **08022/82-90.** Fax 08022/82-92-00. www.lederer. com. 98 units. 95€–160€ ($152–$256) double. Rates include breakfast. AE, DC, MC, V. Free parking. Closed Nov. **Amenities:** Restaurant; bar; lounge; nightclub; indoor pool; outdoor tennis court; sauna; room service; laundry service; dry cleaning; solarium. *In room:* TV, hair dryer.

Hotel Rex   A modern hotel with much charm and character, Hotel Rex is set against a backdrop of the Lower Bavarian Alps. It's an ideal choice for a vacation by the lake. The decorator tried to make the place as warm and inviting as possible. The well-maintained guest rooms are furnished in Bavarian style and contain neatly kept bathrooms with shower or tub. The hotel has good food and caters to special dieters, and its Bierstuberl is a lively gathering place.

Münchnerstrasse 25, 83707 Bad Wiessee. ✆ **08022/8-62-00.** Fax 08022/862-01-00. www.hotel-rex.de. 57 units. 45€–69€ ($72–$110) per person double. Rates include breakfast. MC, V. Parking: 5€ ($8). Closed Nov 1–Apr 14. **Amenities:** Restaurant; bar; lounge; room service; laundry service. *In room:* TV, hair dryer.

Kurhotel Edelweiss   This chalet/guesthouse, built in the 1950s, is ornamented with wooden balconies and painted detailing around its doors and windows. Rooms are functionally but comfortably furnished and all come with well-kept bathrooms with shower-tub combinations. Additional, but less desirable, rooms are available in the motel-like outbuildings beside the main structure. The modern public rooms are suffused with a certain German kitsch. The Bavarian-style restaurant is open for hotel guests only. The staff is a bit gloomy—but the price is right.

Münchnerstrasse 21 (.5km/⅓ mile north of Bad Wiessee's center), 83707 Bad Wiessee. ✆ **08022/8-60-90.** Fax 08022/8-38-83. www.hotel-edelweiss-bad-wiessee.de. 38 units. 70€–98€ ($112–$157) double. Rates include continental breakfast. No credit cards. Free parking. Closed Nov. **Amenities:** Restaurant; lounge. *In room:* TV, hair dryer.

Park Hotel Resi von der Post (Value)   This enduring favorite has been around much longer than many of its fast-rising competitors. It has been considerably modernized and now has well-furnished, traditional guest rooms. The atmosphere in the hotel's restaurant is often bustling, as diners who live nearby fill up the place; many show up in Bavarian dress. Ask for the special cheese of the Tegernsee district, *Miesbacher.* Make reservations early for this hotel; it's usually booked up for the year by summer.

Zilcherstrasse 14, 83707 Bad Wiessee. ✆ **08022/9-86-50.** Fax 08022/98-65-65. www.hotel-resi-von-der-post.de. 25 units. 82€–99€ ($131–$158) double; 95€–118€ ($152–$189) suite. Rates include buffet breakfast. AE, DC, MC, V. Parking 5€ ($8). **Amenities:** Restaurant; lounge; limited room service. *In room:* TV, minibar, Wi-Fi.

WHERE TO DINE

Most visitors dine at their hotels, as Bad Wiessee is known for its hotels, rather than its restaurants. However, we offer one (but only one) well-recommended restaurant.

Freihaus Brenner ★ CONTINENTAL   This restaurant's setting is a cozy, steep-roofed farmhouse whose intricate murals and weathered balconies evoke the old-fashioned Teutonic world. The original version of this place was built in the early 1800s. Burnt to the ground around 1900, it was rebuilt nearby a few years later about 18m (60 ft.) from the main location. Today, young and energetic proprietors keep the recipes fresh and international and the service zippy, for clients who enjoy the *gemütlich* setting and the woodsy location overlooking the lake, about a 5-minute drive west from the center of Bad Wiessee. Menu items include selections from every country that borders Germany. There are also some Thai dishes. As far as local fare goes, we recommend roasted

duckling with red cabbage and potato salad and the wursts, which come in several varieties and are sometimes served with braised celery and new potatoes.

Freihaus 4. (©) **08022/82004.** Reservations recommended. Main courses 12€–26€ ($19–$42). MC, V. Daily
9am–10pm (warm food daily noon 2pm and 6:30–10pm).

6 GARMISCH-PARTENKIRCHEN

89km (55 miles) SW of Munich, 118km (73 miles) SE of Augsburg, 60km (37 miles) NW of Innsbruck

In spite of its urban flair, Garmisch-Partenkirchen, Germany's top Alpine resort, has kept
some of the charm of an ancient village. It's actually made up of two towns, the older
Partenkirchen and the more modern Garmisch. Even today, you occasionally see country
folk in traditional costumes, and you may be held up in traffic while the cattle are led
from their mountain-grazing grounds down through the streets of town.

Increasingly, this ski center is also promoting itself as a climatic health resort. Although
it is hardly the equal of such fabled German spas as Baden-Baden, it offers a number of
holiday packages for those seeking an array of programs that include walks in the hills,
massages, river rafting, mountain bike tours, water treatments (Kneipp), beauty treatments, water gymnastics, bubble baths scented with essential oils, steam baths, and so
much more. Information about these activities is available from the Garmisch-Partenkirchen Tourist Board (see "Visitor Information," below)

ESSENTIALS
Getting There
BY TRAIN The Garmisch-Partenkirchen Bahnhof is on the Munich–Weilheim–
Garmisch–Mittenwald–Innsbruck rail line with frequent connections in all directions.
Twenty trains per day arrive from Munich (trip time: 1 hr., 22 min.). For rail information
and schedules, call (©) **01805/99 66-33.** Mountain rail service to several mountain
plateaus and the Zugspitze is offered by the **Bayerische Zugspitzenbahn** at Garmisch
((©) **08821/79-70**).

BY BUS Both long-distance and regional buses through the Bavarian Alps are provided
by **RVO Regionalverkehr Oberbayern,** Finkenstrasse 3, in Garmisch-Partenkirchen
((©) **08821/94-82-74**).

BY CAR Access is via the Autobahn A95 from Munich; exit at Eschenlohe.

Visitor Information
For tourist information, contact the **Verkehrsamt,** Richard-Strauss-Platz 2 ((©) **08821/18-
07-00**), open Monday to Saturday 8am to 6pm and Sunday and holidays from 10am to
noon.

Getting Around
An unnumbered municipal bus services the town, depositing passengers at Marienplatz
or the Bahnhof, from which it is possible to walk to all centrally located hotels. This free
bus runs every 15 minutes.

EXPLORING THE AREA
The symbol of the city's growth and modernity is the **Olympic Ice Stadium,** built for
the 1936 Winter Olympics and capable of holding nearly 12,000 people. On the slopes

at the edge of town is the much larger **Ski Stadium,** with two ski jumps and a slalom course. In 1936, more than 100,000 people watched the events in this stadium. Today, it's still an integral part of winter life in Garmisch—the World Cup Ski Jump is held here every New Year.

Garmisch-Partenkirchen is a center for winter sports, summer hiking, and mountain climbing. In addition, the town environs offer panoramic views and colorful buildings. The pilgrimage **Chapel of St. Anton,** on a pinewood path at the edge of Partenkirchen, is all pink and silver, inside and out. Its graceful lines are characteristic of 18th-century style. The **Philosopher's Walk,** in the park surrounding the chapel, is a delightful spot to wander, just to enjoy the views of the mountains around the low-lying town. Along Frülingstrasse in Garmisch are some beautiful examples of **Bavarian houses,** and the villa of composer Richard Strauss is at the end of Zöppritzstrasse. The **church of St. Martin,** off the Marienplatz, is worth a look for its stuccowork.

This area of Germany has always attracted the German romantics, including the "dream king," Ludwig II. Perhaps with Wagner's music sounding in his ears, the king ordered the construction of a hunting lodge in the style of a Swiss chalet, but commanded that the interior look like something out of *The Arabian Nights.* The **Jagschloss Schachen** can be reached only by an arduous climb. The tourist office will supply details. Tours are offered at 11am and 2pm daily and often leave from the Olympic Ski Stadium heading for the lodge—but check this first.

WHERE TO STAY
Expensive
Alpina Hotel ★ In this Bavarian hostelry 3 minutes from the Hausberg ski lifts, guests have all sorts of luxury facilities, including a garden with wide lawns and trees and an open patio. Alpina nonetheless has many winning features. Its facade is graced with a wide overhanging roof and Tirolean-style entranceway and windows. Each guest room sports a personalized decor. Yours may have a snow-white sofa, chairs, walls, lamps, and carpet, with original paintings as accents, or it might feature sloped pine ceilings, a Spanish bedspread, and matching armchairs. The open tavern dining room has two levels, and an extensive brick wine cellar has a wide choice of vintages. Bavarian and international dishes are served in a beamed rustic dining room and on the sun terrace.

Alpspitzstrasse 12, 82467 Garmisch-Partenkirchen. ✆ 08821/78-30. Fax 08821/7-13-74. www.alpina-gap.de. 65 units. 162€–175€ ($259–$280) double. Rates include buffet breakfast. AE, MC, V. Parking 10€ ($16). **Amenities:** 2 restaurants; bar; indoor pool; fitness center; sauna; room service; laundry service; dry cleaning; all nonsmoking rooms; solarium. *In room:* TV, minibar, hair dryer, Wi-Fi (in some).

Grand Hotel Sonnenbichl ★★ The finest hotel in the area, but not the most atmospheric, is on the hillside overlooking Garmisch-Partenkirchen, 1.5km (1 mile) from the city center and 3km (1¾ miles) from the Bahnhof, with views of the Wetterstein mountain range and the Zugspitze from its front rooms (those in the rear open onto a rock wall). The hotel was built in 1898 by the family of Georg Bader. After World War II, it was used as a military hospital. Bedrooms are well kept and range from midsize to spacious. The decor is more or less Art Nouveau. The hotel serves excellent food. You can have light, modern cuisine in the elegant gourmet restaurant, the Blauer Salon, or Bavarian specialties in the Zirbelstube. Afternoon coffee and fresh homemade cake are served in the lobby or on the sunny terrace.

Burgstrasse 97, 82467 Garmisch-Partenkirchen. ✆ 08821/70-20. Fax 08821/70-21-31. www. sonnenbichl.de. 93 units. 168€–198€ ($269–$317) double; 245€–470€ ($392–$752) suite. Rates include

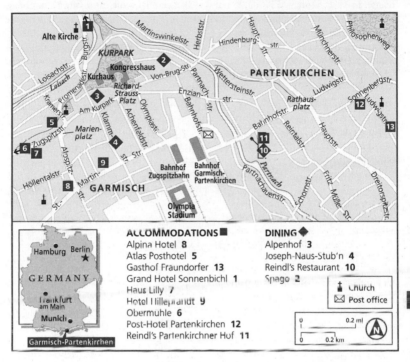

ACCOMMODATIONS ■
Alpina Hotel **8**
Atlas Posthotel **5**
Gasthof Fraundorfer **13**
Grand Hotel Sonnenbichl **1**
Haus Lilly **7**
Hotel Hilleprandt **9**
Obermühle **6**
Post-Hotel Partenkirchen **12**
Reindl's Partenkirchner Hof **11**

DINING ◆
Alpenhof **3**
Joseph-Naus-Stub'n **4**
Reindl's Restaurant **10**
Spago **2**

♦ Church
⊠ Post office

0   0.2 mi
0   0.2 km

THE BAVARIAN ALPS

12

GARMISCH-PARTENKIRCHEN

buffet breakfast. AE, DC, MC, V. Free parking. Take Rte. 23 toward Oberammergau. **Amenities:** 2 restaurants; bar; indoor heated pool; whirlpool; fitness center; sauna; room service; massage; laundry service; dry cleaning; solarium. *In room:* TV, hair dryer, safe.

Obermühle ★   This hotel is a 5- to 10-minute walk from Garmisch's center, in a quiet, isolated spot much favored by repeat guests. The Wolf family, the owners, have operated a hotel on this spot since 1634, although the present building was constructed in 1969. They still maintain the traditional hospitality that has characterized their family for so long. Although it's a bit sterile, the mountain panoramas from its beer garden and terrace are compensating factors. Most rooms have balconies with views of the Alps. Nearby are miles of woodland trails crisscrossing the nearby foothills. The rooms often have style and comfort, some with traditional Bavarian character. Bavarian and international dishes are featured in the excellent restaurant. The restaurant is cozy and the garden a pleasant place to wander.

Mühlstrasse 22, 82467 Garmisch-Partenkirchen. ℂ **800/780-7234** in the U.S., or 08821/7040. Fax 08821/704112. www.hotel-obermuehle.de. 90 units. 129€–170€ ($206–$272) double; from 210€ ($336) suite. Rates include buffet breakfast. AE, DC, MC, V. Parking garage 15€ ($24). Take Rte. 24 (Zugspitzstrasse) toward Griesen. **Amenities:** Restaurant; bar; lounge; indoor pool; sauna; room service; babysitting; laundry service; dry cleaning; nonsmoking rooms; solarium. *In room:* TV, beverage maker, minibar, hair dryer, Wi-Fi.

Post-Hotel Partenkirchen ★   The Post-Hotel Partenkirchen, which was founded in 1492, is one of the town's most prestigious hotels. In recent years, it has even surpassed its major rival, the Reindl's Partenkirchner Hof (see below). You'll experience old-world living in stylish, U-shaped rooms containing Bavarian baroque carved furnishings and antiques. The sunny balconies overlook a garden and offer a view of the Alps. Rooms are generally medium-size, though some are quite spacious.

Ludwigstrasse 49, 82482 Garmisch-Partenkirchen. (C) **08821/93630.** Fax 08821/93632222. www.post-hotel.de. 59 units. 100€–150€ ($160–$240) double; 170€–230€ ($272–$368) suite. Rates include buffet breakfast. MC, V. Parking 7€ ($11). **Amenities:** Breakfast room; bar; skiing; mountain climbing; room service; laundry service. *In room:* TV, minibar, hair dryer, safe.

Waxenstein ★ Finds   One of the most delightful places to recharge your batteries is not in Garmisch itself, but in Grainau, lying in a sunny spot, 2km (1.2m) from the center. The hotel opens onto panoramic views of the Zugspitze. The bedrooms and suites are spacious and elegantly furnished. Even if you're not an overnight guest, but touring the area, consider a visit to their Toedt's Restaurant, which serves market-fresh ingredients with excellent regional cooking.

Höhenrainweg 3, 82491 Grainau. (C) **08821/9840.** Fax 08821/8401. www.waxenstein.de. 41 units. 120€–155€ ($192–$248) double; 175€–195€ ($280–$312) suite. Rates include breakfast. AE, DC, MC, V. Free parking. **Amenities:** Restaurant; bar; outdoor pool; sauna; fitness center; room service; laundry service. *In room:* TV, hair dryer, minibar, safe, Wi-Fi.

Moderate

Atlas Posthotel ★   The history and identity of Garmisch are bound up in events that took place at this hotel in the heart of town. It began as a tavern in 1512. During the Thirty Years' War, it sheltered refugees from besieged Munich. In 1891, it was bought by the Berlin beer baron who invented Berliner Weissen, which quickly became one of the most popular brands in Garmisch. Rooms range from spacious to rather small and cozy, mingling Bavarian antique charm with modern comforts.

Marienplatz 12, 82467 Garmisch-Partenkirchen. (C) **08821/7090.** Fax 08821/709205. www.clausings posthotel.de. 44 units. 89€ ($142) double. Rates include buffet breakfast. AE, MC, V. Parking 3€ ($4.80). **Amenities:** 2 restaurants; bar; room service. *In room:* TV, minibar, hair dryer, Wi-Fi.

Gasthof Fraundorfer Finds   The family-owned Gasthof Fraundorfer is on Parten-kirchen's main street, just a 5-minute walk from the old church. Its original style has not been changed, so it retains the character of bygone days. There are three floors under a sloping roof, with a facade brightly decorated with murals depicting a family feast. You'll be in the midst of village-centered activities, near shops and restaurants. Rooms are furnished in a traditional Alpine manner. Two rooms have four-poster beds; all have firm mattresses. Some larger units are virtual apartments, suitable for up to five guests. Bathrooms are compact with shower stalls. The Gästehaus Barbara is in back, with 20 more beds, including a *Himmelbett* (heaven bed), which is loaded with soft, feather-stuffed pillows and comforters.

Ludwigstrasse 24, 82467 Garmisch-Partenkirchen. (C) **08821/9270.** Fax 08821/92799. www.gasthof-fraundorfer.de. 32 units. 78€–100€ ($125–$160) double; 115€–188€ ($184–$301) family room for 2–5 people. Rates include buffet breakfast. MC, V. Free parking. **Amenities:** Restaurant; room service (break-fast only); laundry service; dry cleaning; solarium. *In room:* TV, kitchenettes (in apts), hair dryer, safe.

Reindl's Partenkirchner Hof ★   Reindl's opened in 1911 and has continuously attracted a devoted following. Owners Bruni and Karl Reindl maintain a high level of luxury and hospitality in this Bavarian retreat. The annexes, the Wetterstein and the House Alpspitz, have balconies, and the main four-story building has wraparound veran-das, giving each room an unobstructed view of the mountains and town. Rooms are among the most attractive in town. The best are suites with panoramic views of mountains or the garden. Fine carpeting and rustic pine furniture add to the allure.

Bahnhofstrasse 15, 82467 Garmisch-Partenkirchen. ℭ **08821/943870.** Fax 08821/94387250. www. reindls.de. 63 units. 55€–75€ ($88–$120) per person double; 77€–135€ ($123–$216) suite. Rates include breakfast. DC, MC, V. Parking 10€ ($16). Closed Nov 10–Dec 15. **Amenities:** 2 restaurants; bar; lounge; indoor heated pool; health club; sauna; room service; laundry service; dry cleaning. *In room:* TV, minibar, hair dryer, Wi-Fi.

Inexpensive

Haus Lilly This spotlessly clean guesthouse wins points for its large breakfasts and the personality of its smiling owner, Maria Lechner, whose English is limited but whose hospitality transcends language. Each small room comes with a comfortable bed and free access to a kitchen. Bathrooms are small and have shower stalls.

Zugspitzstrasse 20–22 (a 15-min. walk from the Bahnhof), 82467 Garmisch-Partenkirchen. ℭ **08821/ 52600.** 8 units. 70€ ($112) double, triple, or quad. Rates include buffet breakfast. No credit cards. Free parking. **Amenities:** Breakfast room; lounge; room service. *In room:* TV, hair dryer.

Hotel Hilleprandt ⓥalue This cozy, tranquil chalet is a great budget choice, lying 450m (1,500 ft.) from the train station. Its wooden balconies, attractive garden, and backdrop of forest-covered mountains evoke an old-time Alpine building. However, a complete renovation has brought streamlined modern comfort. Rooms are small but comfortable, each with a private balcony and tiled tub-and-shower bathroom.

Riffelstrasse 17 (near Zugspitze Bahnhof and Olympic Ice Stadium), 82467 Garmisch-Partenkirchen. ℭ **08821/943040.** Fax 08821/74548. www.hotel-hilleprandt.de. 13 units. 42€–53€ ($67–$85) double; from 60€ ($77) suite. Rates include buffet breakfast. MC, V. Free parking. **Amenities:** Restaurant; breakfast room; lounge; fitness center; Jacuzzi; sauna; sun bed; room service; massage; laundry service; dry cleaning. *In room:* TV, hair dryer, safe.

ON THE OUTSKIRTS

Das Kranzbach ★★★ Ⓕinds You reach this unique property, a faux English manor house, by taking an old private toll road once constructed by King Ludwig II to reach his hunting lodge deep in a pine forest. This restored property, in a setting of forests, mountains, and meadows, boasts one of the finest spas in the area, with some two dozen treatment rooms. We prefer the rooms in the original building, the Mary Portman House. They are airier yet more simply decorated than the grander comfort of the annex, called "Scenic View," an oasis of wood and glass. The decor is a combination of traditional and extreme modern, including apple-green painted chairs and papier-mâché chandeliers. Spectacular views and cozy lounges with wood-burning fireplaces are just part of the allure of this swanky retreat.

82493 Kranzbach bei Garmisch-Partenkircken. ℭ **08823/92-800-0.** Fax 08823/92-800-900. www. daskranzbach.de. 90 units. 119€–199€ ($190 $318) per person double; 157€–227€ ($251–$363) per person suite. DISC, MC, V. Free parking. Lies 9 miles (15km) east of Garmisch-partenkirchen train station. **Amenities:** Restaurant; bar; laundry service; dry cleaning; room service; 2 pools (indoor and outdoor); spa; public Wi-Fi. *In room:* A/C, TV, minibar, hair dryer, safe.

WHERE TO DINE

Expensive

Post-Hotel Partenkirchen ★★ BAVARIAN/INTERNATIONAL Post-Hotel Partenkirchen is renowned for its distinguished Continental cuisine—in fact, its reputation is known throughout Bavaria. The interior dining rooms are rustic, with lots of mellow, old-fashioned atmosphere. Everything seems comfortably subdued, including the guests. Perhaps the best way to dine here is to order one of the fixed-price menus, which change daily depending on the availability of seasonal produce. They are almost invariably of excellent quality, plentiful, and a lot less expensive than ordering a la carte. The a la carte menu is extensive, featuring game in autumn. You can order fresh cauliflower soup followed by main dishes such as schnitzel cordon bleu or mixed grill St. James. The Wiener schnitzel is the best we've had in the resort.

Ludwigstrasse 49. 𝒞 **08821/9-36-30.** Reservations required. Main courses 13€–32€ ($21–$51). MC, V. Daily noon–2pm and 6–9:30pm.

Reindl's Restaurant ★★ INTERCONTINENTAL Reindl's is a first-class restaurant in every way. The seasonal menu offers modern cuisine as well as regional Bavarian dishes. Two notable appetizers are the scampi salad *Walterspiel* with fresh peaches, lemon, and tarragon, and the homemade gooseliver pâté with Riesling jelly. For a main dish, try *coq au Riesling* (chicken in wine) with noodles or veal roasted with *Steinpilzen,* a special mushroom from the Bavarian mountains. For dessert, try the Grand Marnier sabayon with strawberry and vanilla ice cream, or a *Salzburger Nockerl* (a dessert soufflé made with egg white, sugar, butter, and flour) for two.

In the Partenkirchner Hof, Bahnhofstrasse 15. 𝒞 **08821/943870.** Reservations required. Main courses 12€–22€ ($19–$35). DC, MC, V. Daily noon–2:30pm and 6:30–11pm. Closed Nov 5–Dec 15.

Moderate

Alpenhof ★ Value INTERNATIONAL Alpenhof is widely regarded as one of the finest restaurants in Garmisch, as are the hotel dining rooms at the Posthotel Partenkirchen and Reindl's Partenkirchner Hof. The cuisine is grounded in tradition, including a variety of Bavarian specialties, as well as trout meunière or pikeperch with a savory peppercorn sauce. Locals love the roast duck with red cabbage and potato dumplings. For dessert, try a soufflé with exotic fruits. In summer, the outside tables are lovely; in winter the cozy interior is flooded with sunlight from a greenhouse.

Am Kurpark 10. 𝒞 **08821/59055.** Reservations recommended. Main courses 9€–20€ ($14–$32). MC, V. Daily 11am–2pm and 6–10pm.

Café Riessersee BAVARIAN/INTERNATIONAL This cafe/restaurant on the shores of a small emerald-green lake is the ideal place to stop after you explore the Zugspitze. It's a great place for a leisurely lunch or afternoon coffee with cakes, ice cream, and chocolates, but it's worth visiting for the Bavarian dinner dishes as well. Dinner main courses center on fresh fish served from a big aquarium-style holding tank. Seasonal dishes are based on, for example, wild game, fresh fruits and wild berries, and forest mushrooms. During *Spargel* (asparagus) season, a menu is devoted entirely to asparagus.

Riess 6 (3km/2 miles from the center of town). 𝒞 **08821/95440.** Main courses 8€–20€ ($13–$32). AE, MC, V. Daily 11am–9pm.

Joseph-Naus-Stub'n ★ GERMAN/CONTINENTAL One of the most charming dining spots in town lies on the lobby level of a prominent and very visible hotel, the Zugspitze, which, with its traditional Alpine design, evokes a very large mountain chalet on steroids. Within a country-baroque decor that manages to be elegant and woodsy, but with a definite sense of almost ladylike grace, you can enjoy some of the most upscale and sophisticated cuisine in town. Menus change with the season, but the best examples include selections from an oft-changing array of oysters, crabs, North Sea sole and floun- der, trout, and zander, each prepared in a different way every night or according to your specifications. During the autumn and winter, the focus is on game dishes which includes filets of venison.

In the Zugspitze Hotel, Klammstrasse 19. (C) **08821/9010.** Reservations recommended Fri–Sat nights. Main courses 11€–20€ ($18–$32); fixed-price menus 26€ ($42) for 3 courses, 55€ ($88) for 6 courses. AE, DC, MC, V. Daily 5:30–10pm; Sun noon–2pm.

Spago MEDITERRANEAN/INTERNATIONAL   Its decor successfully mixes elements from Spain, Italy, and southern France into a hybrid, ochre-toned mélange of the three, and the clientele tends to include a higher percentage of American expatriates from the nearby army base than any other restaurant in town. A 5-minute walk from the railway station, this place is well accustomed to varying tastes and preferences, and it's relatively easy to strike up a conversation at the bar. Its menu includes pastas; burgers; steaks; a flavorful version of chicken breast in a crust of crushed cornflakes, served with wok-fried vegetables and Basmati rice; spinach-flavored lasagna; and even a mixed grill inspired by the wide-open spaces of the (mythical) American West, served with baked beans, baked potatoes, and sour cream.

Partnachstrasse 50. (C) **08821/966-555.** Reservations not necessary. Main courses 9€–26€ ($14–$42). AE, DC, MC, V. Daily 10am–11pm.

SHOPPING

Your best bets are in the traffic-reduced Ludwigstrasse in Partenkirchen and in the almost traffic-free zone from Richard-Strauss Platz to Marienplatz in Garmisch. A vast array of stores sells boots, boutique items, clothing, jewelry, art, antiques, and more. If you like traditional Bavarian dress but don't want to spend a lot of money, head for **Loisachtaler,** Burgstrasse 20 ((C) **08821/52390**). Here, Petra Ostler has assembled the area's finest collection of secondhand clothing. Take your pick: a Jägermeister loden coat, an Alpine hat with pheasant feathers, or a cast-off dirndl. They all look like new.

GARMISCH-PARTENKIRCHEN AFTER DARK

You can test your luck at the town's casino, **Spielbank Garmisch-Partenkirchen,** Am Kurpark 10 ((C) **08821/95990**). Admission costs 2.50€ ($4) per person, and you must be 18 or over (you must present a passport). The casino is open daily 3pm to 2am. Beginning at 8pm, blackjack tables are open. Friday and Saturday, games of seven-card stud poker are arranged (book in advance). Men must wear a jacket and tie.

If you'd like to meet the locals at night, head for one of the taverns for a beer. All major hotels have bars, but for a change of pace, go to the **Irish Pub,** Rathausplatz 8 ((C) **08821/3938**), and order a Guinness. This pub, in the center of town, attracts one of the most convivial crowds in the area.

Many hotels have dance floors that keep the music pumping into the wee hours, but for dancing of a different sort, check out the summer program of **Bavarian folk music and dancing,** held every Saturday night mid-May to September in the Bayernhalle, Brauhausstrasse 19. During the same season Saturday to Thursday, **classical concerts** are held at the Garmisch park bandstand. On Friday, these live shows move to the Partenkirchen bandstand. Check with the local tourist office (see "Visitor Information," earlier in this section) for details about these programs as well as a 5-day **Johann Strauss Festival** held in June.

TO THE TOP OF THE ZUGSPITZE ★★★

From Garmisch-Partenkirchen, you can see the tallest mountain in Germany, the **Zug-spitze,** 2,960m (9,700 ft.) above sea level. Ski slopes begin at a height of 2,650m (8,690 ft.). For a panoramic view of both the Bavarian and the Tyrolean (Austrian) Alps, go all the way to the summit. There are two ways to reach the Zugspitze from the center of Garmisch. The first begins with a trip on the cog railway, the Zugspitzbahn, which departs from the back of Garmisch's main railway station daily every hour from 8:15am to 2:15pm. The train travels uphill, past lichen-covered boulders and coursing streams, to a high-altitude plateau, the Zugspitzplatt, where views sweep out over all Bavaria. At the Zugspitzplatt, you'll transfer onto a cable car, the Gletscher Seilbahn, for a 4-minute ride uphill to the top of the Zugspitze. There, far-reaching panoramas, a cafe and restaurant, a gift shop, and many Alpine trails await. Total travel time for this itinerary is about 55 minutes, but you may want to linger at the first stop, the Zugspitzplatt, before continuing up.

The other way to get to the summit is to take the Zugspitzbahn for a briefer trip, disembarking 14km (9 miles) southwest of Garmisch at the lower station of the Eibsee Seilbahn (Eibsee Cable Car), next to a clear Alpine lake. The cable car will carry you from there directly to the summit of the Zugspitze, for a total transit time of about 38 minutes. The Eibsee Seilbahn makes its run at least every half-hour 8:30am to 4:30pm (July–Aug to 5:30pm).

Round-trip tickets allow you to ascend one way and descend the other, in order to enjoy the widest range of spectacular views. May to October, round-trip fares are 47€ ($75) for adults, 33€ ($53) for ages 16 and 17, and 28€ ($45) for children 6 to 15. November to April, round-trip fares are reduced to 37€ ($59) for adults, 27€ ($43) for ages 16 and 17, and 23€ ($37) for ages 5 to 15. Year-round, family fare for two adults and a child costs 104€ ($166). For more information, contact the **Bayerische Zugspitzbahn,** Olympiastrasse 27, Garmisch-Partenkirchen (© **08821/7970;** www. zugspitze.de).

From Garmisch-Partenkirchen, many other peaks of the Wetterstein range are accessible as well, via the 10 funiculars ascending from the borders of the town. From the top of the **Wank** (1,755m/5,758 ft.) to the east, you get the best view of the plateau on which the twin villages of Garmisch and Partenkirchen sit. This summit is also a favorite with patrons of Garmisch's spa facilities because the plentiful sunshine makes it ideal for the *Liegekur* (deck-chair cure).

HIKING IN THE BAVARIAN ALPS

Hiking is a national pastime in Bavaria. When winter snows melt, everybody seems to hit the trails, from preschoolers to seniors living on pensions. The tourist office in Garmisch-Partenkirchen will help you find trails of varying degrees of difficulty. After that, you just follow the signs. The Zugspitzbahn, the rail line between Garmisch-Partenkirchen and Eibsee, at the base of the Zugspitze, offers a brochure outlining seven trails most favored by hikers. You don't have to be an Olympic athlete to try them. Some hikes will take 4 to 5 hours, and a few are suitable for the entire family.

An easily accessible destination is the 1,240m (4,068-ft.) **Eckbauer** peak that lies on the southern fringe of Partenkirchen. The easy trails on its lower slopes are recommended

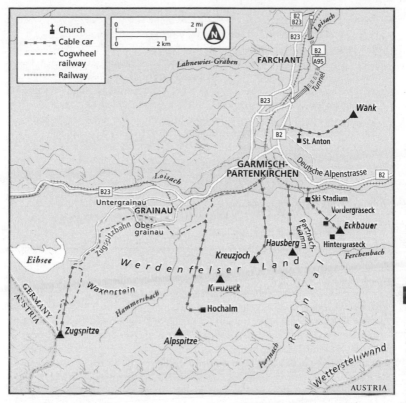

Church
Cable car
Cogwheel railway
Railway

0 — 2 mi
0 — 2 km
N

Lahnewies-Graben FARCHANT

B2
B23
Loisach
B23
B2
A95
Tunnel

B23

▲ **Wank**

B2

✝ St. Anton

GARMISCH-PARTENKIRCHEN

Deutsche Alpenstrasse B2

Loisach

B23

Untergrainau
GRAINAU
Ober-grainau

Zugspitzbahn

■ Ski Stadium

Vordergraseck
■ **Eckbauer**
■ Hintergraseck
Ferchenbach

Hausberg ▲

Kreuzjoch ▲

Werdenfelser *Land*

Partnach-Klamm

Eibsee

Waxenstein

Kreuzeck ▲

Hammersbach

■ Hochalm

▲ **Zugspitze**

GERMANY AUSTRIA

Alpspitze ▲

Reintal

Partnach

Wettersteilwand

AUSTRIA

for first-time Alpine hikers. You can even take a chairlift to the top, where in real Bavarian style, the Bergasthof will serve you a glass of buttermilk. In less than an hour, you can descend on relatively easy trails through a forest. The cable car stretching from Garmisch to the top of the Eckbauer departs year-round from a facility (the Eckbauerbahn) that sits adjacent to the ski stadium in Garmisch. The round-trip costs 11€ ($18) for adults, 6.50€ ($10) for children. For information on the Eckbauerbahn, call ☎ **08821/3469.**

More demanding are the slopes of the rugged **Alpspitz** ★ region, which begins about a mile southwest of Garmisch. The area is interlaced with wildflowers, unusual geology, Alpine meadows, and a network of cable cars and hiking trails spread over a terrain ranging in altitude between 1,200m (4,000 ft.) and 1,800m (6,000 ft.). The highest trails are around the summit of the Alpspitz at 2,600m (8,540 ft.).

One of the most appealing ways to gain a high-altitude panorama over this region is to take a trip up the Alpspitz. Begin your journey at the Kreuzeckbahn/Alpspitzbahn cable car terminus, a mile south of Garmisch. The cable car will carry you uphill along the Kreuzeckbahn for a 4-minute ride across a jagged landscape to the lowest station of the Hochalm cable car. Here the Hochalmbahn will carry you uphill for another 4 minutes to the top of the Osterfelderkopf, 1,980m (6,500 ft.) above sea level. Cable cars for

(Moments) A Dramatic Alpine Fantasy

Another scenic hike is through the **Partnachklamm Gorge,** a canyon with a roaring stream at the bottom and sheer cliff walls rising on either side of the hiking trail. Take the Graseck Seilbahn from its departure point at the bottom of the gorge, less than .8km (¹/₂ mile) south of Garmisch's ski stadium, and get off at the first station, which is adjacent to a cozy hotel, the **Forsthaus Graseck** ((✆ **08821/ 54006**). You might want to get a meal or drink at the Forsthaus first. Afterward, descend on foot along narrow paths by the sides of the stream as it cascades downhill. The path crosses the gorge and returns you to the point where you entered. Many readers have found this to be one of their most memorable adventures in Bavaria. The experience of walking along a rocky ledge just above a rushing river and behind small waterfalls while looking up at 360m (1,181 ft.) of rocky cliffs, is truly awesome (and sometimes wet).

From its departure point to the Forsthaus, the 3-minute cable car ride costs 3.50€ ($5.60) per person each way. For information about the Seilbahn, contact Forsthaus Graseck ((✆ **08821/54006**). The cable car operates at 20-minute intervals between 7am and 10pm (midnight on weekends).

both stages of this trip depart at 30-minute intervals daily 8:15am to 5:15pm. After your visit to the Osterfelderkopf summit, you can return to Garmisch via a different route, a direct downhill descent via the Alpspitzbahn, a 10-minute ride above jagged gorges, soaring cliffs, and grassy meadows.

Round-trip passage along this three-tiered Alpine itinerary costs 21€ ($34) for adults and 16€ ($26) for children 6 to 15; it's free for children 5 and under. These fares and times of departure can fluctuate. For the latest details, call either the information service for the above-mentioned cable cars ((✆ **08821/7970**) or check with the Garmisch **Verkehrsamt (tourist office)** on Richard-Strauss-Platz 2 ((✆ **08821/720688**).

8 OBERAMMERGAU ★

95km (59 miles) SW of Munich, 19km (12 miles) N of Garmisch-Partenkirchen

In this Alpine village, the world-famous Passion Play is generally performed every 10 years. It's the world's longest-running show (in more ways than one—it lasts about 8 hr.). It began in 1634 when the town's citizens took a vow to present the play in gratitude for being spared from the devastating plague of 1633. The actors in the play are still the townspeople of Oberammergau.

Oberammergau stands in a wide valley surrounded by forests and mountains, sunny slopes, and green meadows. It has long been known for the skill of its woodcarvers. Here in this village right under the Kofel peak, you'll find farms, as well as first-class hotels, cozy inns, and family boarding houses.

Numerous hiking trails lead through the mountains around Oberammergau to hikers' inns such as the Kolbenalm and the Romanshohe. You can, however, simply go up to the mountaintops on the Laber cable railway or the Kolben chairlift. Oberammergau also offers opportunities for tennis buffs, minigolf players, cyclists, swimmers, hang-gliding enthusiasts, and canoeists. The recreation center, **Wellenberg**, with its large Alpine swimming complex with open-air pools, hot water and fountains, sauna, solarium, and restaurant, is one of the most beautiful recreation centers in the Alps. The Ammer Valley, with Oberammergau in the (almost) center, is a treasure-trove to explorers, who use it as a base for visiting Linderhof Castle, the Benedictine monastery at Ettal, or the fairy-tale Neuschwanstein and Hohenschwangau castles (see "Neuschwanstein & Hohenschwangau," later in this chapter).

ESSENTIALS
Getting There
BY TRAIN The Oberammergau Bahnhof is on the Murnau–Bad Kohlgrum–Oberammergau rail line, with frequent connections in all directions. Through Murnau, all major German cities can be reached. Daily trains arrive from Munich (trip time: 2 hr.) and from Frankfurt (trip time: 7 hr.). For rail information and schedules, call ℂ **01805/99-66-33.**

BY BUS Regional bus service to nearby towns is offered by **RVO Regionalverkehr Oberbayern** in Garmisch-Partenkirchen (ℂ **08821/94-82-/4**). An unnumbered bus goes back and forth between Oberammergau and Garmisch-Partenkirchen.

BY CAR Oberammergau is 1¹⁄₂ hours from Munich and 5¹⁄₂ hours from Frankfurt. Take the Autobahn A95 Munich–Garmisch-Partenkirchen and exit at Eschenlohe.

Visitor Information
For tourist information, contact the **Oberammergau tourist information office,** Eugen-Papst Strasse 9A (ℂ **08822/9-23-10**), open Monday to Friday from 8:30am to 6pm and Saturday from 9am to noon and 1 to 5pm.

EXPLORING THE TOWN
Oberammergau has much to offer besides the play. Consider an excursion to either **Berg Laber (Mt. Laber)**, to the east of the town, or **Berg Kolben (Mt. Kolben)**, to the west. Berg Laber, which is slightly more dramatic, is accessible year-round via an enclosed cable-gondola (ℂ **08822/47-60**) that offers sweeping Alpine views. The 10-minute ascent costs 15€ ($24) per person. The top of Berg Kolben is accessible via a two-passenger open-sided chairlift (ℂ **08822/47-60**) whose exposure to high winds is a lot more primal. The cost is 12€ ($19) round-trip. Both operate mid-July to mid-October and mid-December to March daily 9am to noon and 1 to 4:30pm.

If you visit Oberammergau in an "off" year, you can still visit the **Passionspielhaus,** Passionwiese (ℂ **08822/3-22-78**), the modern theater at the edge of town where the Passion Play is performed. The roofed auditorium holds 4,700 spectators, and the open-air stage is a wonder of engineering, with a curtained center stage flanked by gates opening onto the so-called streets of Jerusalem. While today's theater and production methods are contemporary, the spirit of the play is still marked by medieval tradition. The play is divided into episodes, each introduced by an Old Testament tableau connecting predictions of the great prophets to incidents of Jesus's suffering. The entire community is involved—those without speaking parts are included in the crowd scenes. The auditorium is open daily 10am to 5pm; admission is 3.50€ ($5.60) for adults and 2€ ($3.20) for children ages 5 to 15 and students.

Aside from the actors, Oberammergau's most respected citizens include another unusual group, the woodcarvers, many of whom have been trained in the village woodcarver's school. In the **Pilatushaus,** Ludwig-Thoma-Strasse (© **08822/949511**), you can watch local artists at work, including woodcarvers, painters, sculptors, and potters. May to October, hours are Monday to Friday 1 to 5pm. You'll see many examples of these art forms throughout the town, on the painted cottages and inns and in the churchyard. When strolling through the village, watch for houses with frescoes by Franz Zwink (18th c.). The houses are named after fairy-tale characters, such as "Hansel and Gretel House" and the "Little Red Riding Hood House."

Heimatmuseum, Dorfstrasse 8 (© **08822/9-41-36**), has a notable collection of Christmas crèches, all hand-carved and hand-painted, from the 18th to the 20th century. It's open mid-April to mid-October Tuesday to Sunday from 2 to 6pm; off season, only on Saturday from 2 to 6pm. Admission is 6€ ($9.60) for adults and 1€ ($1.60) for students and ages 6 to 16. Free for ages 5 and under. The museum is closed October 29 to March 29.

SHOPPING FOR WOODCARVINGS

Oberammergau's woodcarvings are among the most sought after in the Germanic world, and many have graced the mantelpieces and shelves of homes around the globe. Most subjects are religious, deriving directly from 14th-century originals; however, to cater to the demands of modern visitors, there's been an increased emphasis lately on secular subjects, such as drinking or hunting scenes. Competition is fierce for sales of these woodcarvings, many of which are made in hamlets and farmhouses throughout the region. Know before you buy that even some of the most expensive "handmade" pieces might have been roughed in by machine prior to being finished off by hand.

Holzschittschule (Woodcarving School; © **08822/35-42**) has conditions of study that might remind you of the severity of the medieval guilds. Students who labor over a particular sculpture are required to turn it in to the school, where it's either placed on permanent exhibition or sold during the school's once-a-year sell-off, usually over a 2-day period in July.

Baur Anton, Dorfstrasse 27 (© **08822/8-21**), has the most sophisticated inventory of woodcarvings. The shop employs a small cadre of carvers who usually work from their homes to create works inspired by medieval originals. The outgoing and personable sales staff is quick to admit that the forms of many of the pieces are roughed in by machine, but most of the intricate work is completed by hand. Pieces are crafted from maple, pine, or linden (basswood). Prices start at 10€ ($16). Carvings are in their natural grain, stained, or polychromed (some of the most charming), and in some instances, partially gilded.

NEARBY ATTRACTIONS

Schloss Linderhof ★★

Until the late 19th century, a modest hunting lodge stood on a large piece of land, 13km (8 miles) west of the village, owned by the Bavarian royal family. In 1869, "Mad Ludwig" struck again, this time creating a French rococo palace in the Ammergau Mountains. Unlike Ludwig's palace at Chiemsee, Schloss Linderhof was not meant to copy any other structure. Unlike his castle at Neuschwanstein, its concentration of fanciful projects and designs was not limited to the palace interior. In fact, the gardens and smaller buildings at Linderhof are, if anything, more elaborate than the two-story main structure. It is his most successful venture, and the only one that was completed.

The most interesting palace rooms are on the second floor, where ceilings are much higher because of the unusual roof plan. Ascending the winged staircase of Carrara marble, you'll find yourself at the music room, known as the West Gobelin (tapestry) Room, with carved and gilded paneling and richly colored tapestries. This leads directly into the Hall of Mirrors. The mirrors are set in white and gold panels, decorated with gilded woodcarvings. The ceiling is festooned with frescoes depicting mythological scenes, including *The Birth of Venus* and *The Judgment of Paris*.

The king's bedchamber is the largest room in the palace and is placed in the back, overlooking the Fountain of Neptune and the cascades in the gardens. In the tradition of Louis XIV, who often received visitors in his bedchamber, the king's bed is closed off by a carved and gilded balustrade.

In the popular style of the previous century, Ludwig laid out the gardens in formal parterres with geometric shapes, baroque sculptures, and elegant fountains. The front of the palace opens onto a large pool with a piece of gilded statuary in its center, from which a jet of water sprays 32m (105 ft.) into the air.

The park also contains several other small but exotic buildings, including the Moorish Kiosk, where Ludwig often spent hours smoking a chibouk and dreaming of himself as an oriental prince. The magic grotto is unique, built of artificial rock, with stalagmites and stalactites dividing the cavelike room into three chambers. One wall of the grotto is painted with a scene of the Venus Mountain from *Tannhäuser*. The main chamber is occupied by an artificial lake illuminated from below; in Ludwig's time it had an artificial current produced by 24 dynamo engines. A shell-shaped boat, completely gilded, is tied to a platform called the Lorelei Rock.

Schloss Linderhof, Linderhof 12, 82488 Ettal (© **08822/92030**; www.linderhof. de), is open to the public throughout the year and makes an ideal day trip from Munich, as well as from Oberammergau. It's open April to September daily 9am to 6pm. From October to March, the grotto and Moorish Kiosk are closed, but the castle is open daily 10am to 4pm. Admission in the summer is 7€ ($11) for adults, 6€ ($9.60) for students, and free for children 14 and under. In winter, admission is 6€ ($9.60) for adults, 5€ ($8) for students, and free for children 14 and under.

Buses run between Oberammergau (from the railway station) and Schloss Linderhof seven times per day, beginning at 10:25am; the last bus leaves Linderhof at 6:58pm. Round-trip fare is 11€ ($18). For bus information, call **RVO Bus Company** (© **08821/948274**) at their regional office in Garmisch-Partenkirchen. Motorists from Oberammergau should follow signs to Ettal, about 5km (3 miles) away, and then go another 5km (3 miles) to Draswang; from there follow the signs to Schloss Linderhof.

Kloster Ettal ★

In a lovely valley sheltered by the steep hills of the Ammergau, Kloster Ettal, on Kaiser-Ludwig-Platz at Ettal (© **08822/7-40**; www.kloster-ettal.de), was founded by Ludwig the Bavarian in 1330. Monks, knights, and their ladies shared the honor of guarding the statue of the Virgin, attributed to Giovanni Pisano. In the 18th century, the golden age of the abbey, there were about 70,000 pilgrims every year. The Minister of Our Lady in Ettal is one of the finest examples of Bavarian rococo architecture in existence. Around the polygonal core of the church is a two-story gallery. An impressive baroque facade was built from a plan based on the designs of Enrico Zuccali. Inside, visitors stand under a vast dome to admire the fresco painted by John Jacob Zeiller in the summers of 1751 and 1752.

The abbey stands 3km (2 miles) south of Oberammergau, along the road to Garmisch-Partenkirchen. Admission is free, and it's open daily 8am to 7pm year-round.

Buses from Oberammergau leave from the Rathaus and the Bahnhof once per hour during the day, with round-trip fare 8€ ($13). Call the **RVO Bus Company** in Garmisch-Partenkirchen (© **08821/948274**) for information.

WHERE TO STAY & DINE
Moderate

Hotel Restaurant Böld ★ This inn has steadily improved in quality and is now among the town's premier choices. Only a stone's throw from the river, the well-designed chalet hotel offers comfortable public rooms in its central building and well-furnished guest rooms in its contemporary annex. All rooms have well-kept bathrooms with showers. Most units open onto balconies. The restaurant features both international and regional cuisine. In the bar, you'll find a tranquil atmosphere, plus attentive service. Raimund Hans and family are the hosts.

König-Ludwig-Strasse 10, 82487 Oberammergau. © **08822/91-20.** Fax 08822/7102. www.hotel-boeld. de. 57 units. 79€–125€ ($126–$200) double; from 135€ ($216) suite. Rates include continental breakfast. AE, MC, V. Free outdoor parking; 6€ ($9.60) in the garage. **Amenities:** Restaurant; bar; whirlpool; sauna; room service; nonsmoking rooms; rooms for those w/limited mobility. *In room:* TV, minibar, hair dryer.

Hotel Wolf ⓥalue An overgrown Bavarian chalet, the Wolf is at the heart of village life. Its facade is much like others in the area: an encircling balcony, heavy timbering, and window boxes spilling cascades of red and pink geraniums. Inside it retains some local flavor, although concessions have been made: an elevator, conservative room furnishings, a dining hall with zigzag paneled ceiling, and spoke chairs. The Hafner Stub'n is a rustic place for beer drinking light meals, which can be both economical and gracious. There's always a freshly made soup of the day, followed by a generous main course, such as Wiener schnitzel or roast pork with dumplings and cabbage.

Dorfstrasse 1, 82487 Oberammergau. © **08822/9-23-30.** Fax 08822/9-23-333. www.hotel-wolf.de. 32 units. 110€–135€ ($176–$216) double. Rates include buffet breakfast. DC, MC, V. Free parking. **Amenities:** Restaurant; bar; outdoor pool; sauna; room service; solarium. *In room:* TV, hair dryer, Wi-Fi.

Parkhotel Sonnenhof ★ Ⓚids Short on charm and Alpine rusticity, this modern hotel still has a lot going for it. First, it's far enough away from the crowds that descend in summer—often in tour buses. It offers peace and tranquillity but is within walking distance of the center. The hotel overlooks the Ammer River and a beautiful *Pfarrkirche* (parish church). Every room has a balcony with an Alpine vista, often of Oberammergau's mountain, the Kobel. Although devoid of old-fashioned charm, guest rooms are well maintained and filled with first-class comforts. The hotel has more luxuries than most in the area—for example, an indoor pool, sauna, and bowling alley. It's also a family favorite, with a children's playroom. Two of the restaurants serve international dishes, although the really good items here are the Bavarian specialties.

König-Ludwig-Strasse 12, 82487 Oberammergau. © **08822/9130.** Fax 08822/3047. www.parkhotel-sonnenhof.de. 61 units. 110€–145€ ($176–$232) double; 125€–160€ ($200–$256) suite. AE, DC, MC, V. Free parking. **Amenities:** 3 restaurants; bar; indoor pool; sauna; 2 children's centers; babysitting; laundry service; dry cleaning; nonsmoking rooms. *In room:* TV, minibar, hair dryer, safe.

Schlosshotel Linderhof ★ Ⓕinds This hotel originally was constructed about a century ago as one of the outbuildings of the famous palace. Designed with gables, shutters, and half-timbering in the style of a Bavarian chalet, it has been tastefully enlarged and renovated by members of the Maier family. Bedrooms are dignified and high-ceilinged, tasteful and comfortable, in a style that suggests 19th-century gentility. Much of its business derives from its cozy restaurant, which extends onto a stone terrace accented with parasols and potted flowers. An array of fixed-price menus focuses on such hearty regional food as pork schnitzels.

Linderhof 14 (near the palace), 82488 Ettal. © **08822/7-90.** Fax 08822/43-47. www.schlosshotel-linderhof.com. 29 units. 95€–120€ ($152–$192) double. Rates include breakfast. AE, DC, MC, V. Free parking. **Amenities:** Restaurant; lounge. *In room:* TV, fridge, hair dryer.

Turmwirt ★ (Finds) This cozy Bavarian-style 18th-century inn offers small, snug rooms, many with private balconies opening onto mountain views. Each comes with a small but well-maintained private bathroom with a tub-and-shower combo. The present building was constructed in 1889 and has since been altered and renovated many times, including a substantial enlargement in 1968. It's an intricately painted green-shuttered country house with a well-maintained homelike interior. The owners consist of three generations of the Glas family, who often present Bavarian folk evenings.

Ettalerstrasse 2 (5 min. from the town center), 82487 Oberammergau. © **08822/92600.** Fax 08822/1437. www.turmwirt.de. 22 units. 96€–110€ ($154–$176) double. Rates include buffet breakfast. AE, DC, MC, V. Free parking. **Amenities:** Restaurant; breakfast room; lounge; room service; laundry service; dry cleaning; nonsmoking rooms. *In room.* TV, minibar, hair dryer, safe.

Inexpensive

Alte Post Since 1612 this has been a provincial inn at the village center. Alte Post is built in chalet style—wide overhanging roof, green-shuttered windows painted with decorative trim, a large crucifix on the facade, and tables along a sidewalk under a long awning. It's the village social hub. The interior has storybook charm, with a ceiling-high green ceramic stove, Alpine chairs, and shelves of pewter plates. The rustic guest rooms have wood-beamed ceilings and wide beds with giant posts; most open onto views. The main dining room is equally rustic (with a collection of hunting memorabilia) and serves excellent Bavarian dishes.

Dorfstrasse 19, 82487 Oberammergau © **08822/91-00.** Fax 08822/91-01-00. www.ogau.de. 32 units. 65€–105€ ($104–$168) double. Rates include buffet breakfast. AE, DC, MC, V. Free parking. **Amenities:** Restaurant; nonsmoking rooms. *In room:* TV

Hotel Café-Restaurant Friedenshöhe (Value) The hotel name means "peaceful height." Built in 1906, the villa enjoys a beautiful location and is one of the better inns in town, although not in the same league as Böld or Parkhotel Sonnenhof. It was reconstructed into a pension and cafe in 1913. It hosted Thomas Mann, who stayed and wrote here. The guest rooms, furnished in tasteful modern style, are well maintained. The hotel offers an indoor terrace with a panoramic view, as well as an outdoor terrace. The Bavarian and international cuisine is known for the quality of its ingredients.

König-Ludwig-Strasse 31, 82487 Oberammergau. © **08822/94-484.** Fax 08822/43-45. www.friedenshoehe. de. 16 units. 60€–80€ ($96 $128) double. Rates include buffet breakfast. AE, DC, MC, V. Free parking. Closed Nov–Dec 14. **Amenities:** Restaurant; bar. *In room:* TV (on request).

Hotel der Schilcherhof (Value) This hotel is divided among three different old-fashioned and charming structures. This is old and rather courtly *Deutschland* with its surrounding gardens. Each unit is well kept and comes with a shower-only bathroom. In summer, the terrace overflows with beer and festivities. Five minutes away lies the Passion Play theater; also nearby is the Ammer River. In summer, you need to reserve well in advance to get a room. The house is built in the old style, with wooden front balconies and tiers of flower boxes, but has a fresh look.

Bahnhofstrasse 17, 82487 Oberammergau. © **08822/47-40.** Fax 08822/37-93. www.hotel-schilcherhof.
de. 26 units. 64€–84€ ($102–$134) double. Rates include full breakfast. AE, MC, V. Parking 5€ ($6). Closed
Nov 15–Christmas. **Amenities:** Breakfast room; lounge; bar; room service. *In room:* TV, hair dryer, no
phone.

---

9 MITTENWALD ★

106km (66 miles) S of Munich, 18km (11 miles) SE of Garmisch-Partenkirchen, 37km (23 miles) NW of
Innsbruck

This year-round resort has often been called the most beautiful town in the Bavarian
Alps. The village is noteworthy for its photogenic painted houses with their intricate
carved gables—even the baroque church tower is covered with frescoes. It's also noted as
a center for the highly specialized craft of violin making. On the square stands a monument to Matthias Klotz, who introduced violin making to Mittenwald in 1684.

In the countryside around Mittenwald, the Wetterstein and Karwendel ranges offer
constantly changing, scenic vistas. In winter, the town is a skiing center, and in summer,
an even more popular range of outdoor activities invites the visitor.

ESSENTIALS
Getting There
BY TRAIN   Mittenwald is reached by almost hourly train service, since it lies on the
express rail line between Munich and Innsbruck (Austria). From Munich, trip time is $1^1/_2$
to 2 hours, depending on the train. It is about 5 to 6 hours by train from Frankfurt. Call
© **01805/99-66-33** for information.

BY BUS   Regional bus service from Garmisch-Partenkirchen and nearby towns is frequently provided by **RVO Regionalverkehr Oberbayern at Garmisch.** Call © **08821/
94-82-74** for schedules and information.

BY CAR   Access by car is via the Autobahn A95 from Munich.

Visitor Information
Contact the **Tourist-Information Mittenwald,** Dammkarstrasse 3 (© **08823/33981;**
www.mittenwald.de). It's open Monday to Friday 8:30am to noon and 1 to 5pm, Saturday 9am to noon.

Horse and carriage trips or coach tours from Mittenwald to nearby villages are available; contact the tourist office for information.

SIGHTS & ACTIVITIES
Some 129km (80 miles) of hiking paths wind up and down the mountains around the
village. Chairlifts make the mountain hiking trails readily accessible. Of course, where
there are trails, there is mountain biking. A cycling map is available through Mittenwald's
administration office. Besides hiking or biking through the hills on your own, you can
take part in organized mountain-climbing expeditions.

Swimming in the brisk waters of the Lautersee and Ferchensee is a good way to cool
off on a hot summer's day. However, for those who find the waters too cold, Mittenwald
has a heated adventure pool.

Mittenwald has good spa facilities, with large gardens landscaped with tree-lined
streams and small pools. Concerts during the summer are held in the music pavilion.

The chief attraction of Mittenwald is the town itself, its most notable feature being its **painted houses** ★★ that line the main street. When Goethe came to call, he pronounced Mittenwald "a living picture-book." The village can be explored in about 1 1/2 hours since it consists of only about 3 sq. km (about 1 sq. mile). In winter, it's a picture postcard of snow-laden charm, and in summer, a mass of flowering facades with pots of geraniums clinging to the houses with richly decorated gables.

Between February 27 and March 4 every year, locals stage the ancient **Maschkere,** a festival in which they "cast out the demons of winter" by roaming noisily through the streets in costume and performing folk music.

The **Karwendelbahn Mittenwald** (*(C)* **08823/8480**) is a cable car operating in winter and summer, costing 21€ ($34) round-trip and running daily from 9am to 4:30pm. It takes skiers to a height of 2,244m (7,362 ft.). This elevation leads to numerous ski trails in winter that become hiking trails in summer. In winter, the 7km-long (4 1/3-mile) **Dammkar** skiing downhill slope is the big attraction for skiers. This run offers some of the best skiing and snowboarding in the Bavarian Alps.

Geigenbau-und Heimatmuseum This fascinating museum traces the history of violin making in Mittenwald and the development of the violin and other stringed instruments, from their invention through various stages of evolution. There is also a violin workshop.

Ballenhausgasse 3. *(C)* **08823/25-11.** Admission 4€ ($6.40) adults, 3€ ($4.80) students, 2€ ($3.20) for children 5–15. Tues–Fri 10am–noon and 1–5pm; Sat–Sun 10am–noon. Closed Nov 6–Dec 16.

St. Peter and St. Paul Church ★ Near the Heimatmuseum, this 18th-century church might be called "The Church of the Violin." The name of Matthias Klotz is carved on the back of the altar by the master violinmaker himself. Even some of the ceiling frescoes have angels playing the violin. As mentioned, Klotz is remembered by a bronze sculpture out front, the work of Ferdinand von Miller (1813–79). One of the great rococo churches of Bavaria, the church is filled with frescoes and elaborate stucco art. It was constructed by Josef Schmutzer and adorned by Matthäus Günther.

Ballenhausgen. No phone—check with visitor information. Free admission. Daily 8am–5pm (but hrs. can vary).

WHERE TO STAY
Moderate
Hotel Post ★★ The Post is the most seasoned and established chalet hotel in the village—it's been here since 1632, when it was a stop for stagecoaches carrying mail and passengers across the Alps. Although it doesn't offer the tranquillity or the scenic views of other Mittenwald hotels, it nevertheless is the city's finest address. Guest rooms are furnished in a comfortable though standard way. A delightful breakfast is served on the sun terrace, with a view of the Alps. On a cool day, take time out to enjoy a beer in the snug lounge/bar with an open fireplace. For a night of hearty Bavarian specialties, head for the wine tavern, which is full of Alpine charm with its deer antler collection, low beams, and wood paneling.

Obermarkt 9, 82481 Mittenwald. *(C)* **08823/938-2333.** Fax 08823/938-2999. www.posthotel-mittenwald. de. 82 units. 86€–140€ ($138–$224) double; 116€–170€ ($186–$272) suite. Rates include buffet breakfast. MC, V. Free parking. **Amenities:** Restaurant; bar; lounge; indoor heated pool; sauna; room service; massage; nonsmoking rooms. *In room:* TV, minibar, hair dryer, safe.

Inexpensive

Die Alpenrose ★   A particularly inviting place to stay is this inn in the village center at the foot of a rugged mountain. The facade is covered with decorative designs; window boxes hold flowering vines. The inn's basic structure is 14th century—it was once part of a monastery—although additions and improvements have been made over the years. The present inn is comfortable, with suitable plumbing facilities. The hotel's rooms are divided between the Alpenrose and its annex, the Bichlerhof; they're modernized but often with Bavarian traditional styling. The tavern room, overlooking the street, has many ingratiating features, including coved ceilings (one decoratively painted), hand-made chairs, flagstone floors, and a square tile stove in the center. In the Josefikeller, beer is served in giant steins, and musicians entertain guests in the evening. The dining room provides excellent meals, including Bavarian specialties.

Obermarkt 1, 82481 Mittenwald. ℂ **08823/9-27-00.** Fax 08823/3720. www.hotel-alpenrose-mittenwald. de. 19 units. 66€–85€ ($106–$136) double. Rates include buffet breakfast. AE, DC, MC, V. Free parking. **Amenities:** Restaurant; bar; room service. *In room:* TV, minibar, hair dryer.

Gästhaus Franziska   When Olaf Grothe built this guesthouse, he named it after the most important person in his life—his wife, Franziska. Both have labored to make it the most personalized guesthouse in town, with sympathetic attention given to their guests' needs. Rooms and suites are furnished tastefully in traditional Bavarian style. All have bathrooms with tub-and-shower combinations and balconies opening onto mountain views. Breakfast is the only meal served, but plenty of restaurants are nearby. Note that it's extremely difficult to obtain bookings between June 20 and October 2.

Innsbruckerstrasse 24, 82481 Mittenwald. ℂ **08823/9-20-30.** Fax 08823/92-03-49. www.franziska-tourismus.de. 18 units. 35€–41€ ($56–$66) per person double; 42€–47€ ($67–$75) per person suite. Rates include buffet breakfast. AE, MC, V. Free parking. Closed Nov 4–Dec 14. **Amenities:** Breakfast room; lounge; room service. *In room:* minibar, hair dryer, beverage maker.

WHERE TO DINE

Restaurant Arnspitze ★ BAVARIAN   Housed in a modern chalet hotel on the outskirts of town, this is the finest dining room in Mittenwald. Although you can also eat well at the inns previously recommended, over the years we've found the menus at this place more enticing. The restaurant is decorated in the old style; the cuisine is solid, satisfying, and wholesome. You might order sole with homemade noodles or veal steak in a creamy smooth sauce, then finish with one of the freshly made desserts.

Innsbruckerstrasse 68. ℂ **08823/24-25.** Main courses 17€–22€ ($26–$35). AE. Thurs–Mon noon–2:30pm and Wed–Mon 6–9pm. Closed 2 weeks in Apr.

10 NEUSCHWANSTEIN & HOHENSCHWANGAU

The 19th century saw a great classical revival in Germany, especially in Bavaria, mainly because of the enthusiasm of Bavarian kings for ancient art forms. Beginning with Ludwig I (1786–1868), who was responsible for many Greek revival buildings in Munich, the royal house ran the gamut of ancient architecture in just 3 short decades. Its culmination was the remarkable flights of fancy of Ludwig II (see "The Fairy-Tale King" box on p. 204). In spite of his rather lonely life and controversial alliances, both personal and political, he was a great patron of the arts.

In 1868, after a visit to the great castle of Wartburg, Ludwig wrote to his good friend, composer Richard Wagner: "I have the intention to rebuild the ancient castle ruins of Hohenschwangau in the true style of the ancient German knight's castle." The following year, construction began on the first of a series of fantastic edifices, work that stopped with Ludwig's untimely death in 1886 after he was deposed because of alleged insanity.

ESSENTIALS
Getting There
BY CAR From Munich, motorists can take the E533 toward Garmisch-Partenkirchen. At the end of the autobahn, the road becomes Rte. 95 for its final run into Garmisch. From Garmisch, continue west on Rte. 187 to the junction with Rte. 314, at which point you cut north to Füssen, where the castles are signposted.

Visitor Information
Information about the castles and the region in general is available at the **Kurverwaltung,** Rathaus, Münchnerstrasse 2 in Schwangau (© **08362/938523**). It's open Monday to Friday from 8am to 6pm, and Saturday 10am to 1pm.

VISITING THE ROYAL CASTLES
The name "Royal Castles" is limited to the castles of Hohenschwangau (built by Ludwig's father, Maximilian II) and Ludwig's Neuschwanstein. Ludwig's other extravagant castles, Neues Schloss (Herrenchiemsee) and Schloss Linderhof (near Oberammergau), are described in sections 4 and 8, earlier in this chapter.

There are often very long lines in summer to these popular attractions, especially in August. With 25,000 people a day visiting, the wait in peak summer months can range from 4 to 5 hours for a 20-minute tour. There is no way of beating the system other than arriving early in the morning to avoid the lines that have already begun to form by 8am.

Neuschwanstein ★★★
This is the fairy-tale castle of Ludwig II. Construction went on for 17 years until the king's death, when all work stopped, leaving a part of the interior incomplete. Ludwig lived in the rooms on and off for a total of only about 6 months from 1884 to 1886.

The doorway off the left side of the vestibule leads to the king's apartments. The study, like most of the rooms, is decorated with wall paintings showing scenes from the Nordic legends (which also inspired Wagner's operas). The theme of the study is the *Tannhäuser* saga, painted by J. Aigner. The only fabric in the room is hand-embroidered silk, used in curtains and chair coverings, all designed with the gold and silver Bavarian coat of arms.

From the vestibule, you enter the **throne room ★★** through the doorway at the opposite end. This hall, designed in Byzantine style by J. Hofmann, was never completed. The floor is a mosaic design depicting the animals of the world. The columns in the main hall are the deep copper red of porphyry. The circular apse where the king's throne was to have stood is reached by a stairway of white Carrera marble. The walls and ceiling are decorated with paintings of Christ in heaven looking down on the 12 apostles and 6 canonized kings of Europe.

The **king's bedroom ★** is the most richly carved in the entire castle—it took 4¹/₂ years to complete this room alone. Aside from the mural depicting the legend of Tristan and Isolde, the walls are decorated with panels carved to look like Gothic windows. In the center is a large wooden pillar completely encircled with gilded brass sconces. The ornate

THE BAVARIAN ALPS

12

NEUSCHWANSTEIN & HOHENSCHWANGAU

bed is on a raised platform with an elaborately carved canopy. Through the balcony window, you can see the 46m (150-ft.) waterfall in the Pollat Gorge, with the mountains in the distance.

The fourth floor of the castle is almost entirely given over to the Singer's Hall, the pride of Ludwig II and all of Bavaria. Modeled after the hall at Wartburg, where the legendary song contest of Tannhäuser supposedly took place, this hall is decorated with marble columns and elaborately painted designs interspersed with frescoes depicting the life of Parsifal.

The castle can be visited year-round, and in September, visitors have the additional treat of concerts in the Singer's Hall. For information and reservations, contact the tourist office, **Verkehrsamt,** Schwangau, at the Rathaus (© **08362/93-85-23**). The castle is open (guided tours only) April to September daily 9am to 6pm; October to March daily from 10am to 4pm. Admission is 9€ ($14) for adults, 8€ ($13) for students and seniors age 65 and over, and free for children age 16 and under. The castle is closed November 1; December 24, 25, and 31; and Shrove Tuesday.

Reaching Neuschwanstein involves a steep .8km (¹/₂-mile) climb from the parking lot for Hohenschwangau Castle (see below). This is about a 25-minute walk for the energetic, an eternity for anybody else. To cut down the climb, you can take a bus to Marienbrücke, a bridge that crosses over the Pollat Gorge at a height of 92m (302 ft.) From that vantage point, you can, like Ludwig, stop and meditate on the glories of the castle and its panoramic surroundings. If you want to photograph the castle, don't wait until you reach the top; you'll be too close to the edifice to photograph it properly. It costs 8€ ($13) for a round-trip. Marienbrücke is still not at the castle. From the bridge, it's another 10-minute walk. This footpath is very steep and not easy to negotiate for anyone who has trouble walking up or down precipitous hills.

The most traditional way to reach Neuschwanstein is by horse-drawn carriage, costing 6€ ($9.60) for the ascent, 2.50€ ($4) for the descent. Some readers have objected to the rides, complaining that too many people are crowded in.

Hohenschwangau ★

Not as glamorous nor as spectacular as Neuschwanstein, the neo-Gothic Hohenschwangau Castle nevertheless has a much richer history. The original structure dates back to the 12th-century Knights of Schwangau. When the knights faded away, the castle began to do so too, helped along by the Napoleonic Wars. When Ludwig II's father, Crown Prince Maximilian (later Maximilian II), saw the castle in 1832, he purchased it and in 4 years had it completely restored. Ludwig II spent the first 17 years of his life here and later received Richard Wagner in its chambers, although Wagner never visited Neuschwanstein on the hill above. (Many visitors wrongly assume that the king and Wagner had their meetings in the "Fantasy" castle of Neuschwanstein, when in fact they were here in Hohenschwangau.)

The rooms of Hohenschwangau are styled and furnished in a much heavier Gothic mode than those in the castle built by Ludwig. Many are typical of the halls of knights' castles of the Middle Ages in both England and Germany. There's no doubt that the castle's style greatly influenced young Ludwig and encouraged the fanciful boyhood dreams that formed his later tastes and character. Unlike Neuschwanstein, however, this castle has a comfortable look about it, as if it actually were a home at one time, not just a museum. The small chapel, once a reception hall, still hosts Sunday Mass. The suits of armor and the Gothic arches here set the stage for the rest of the rooms.

Among the most attractive chambers is the Hall of the Swan Knight, named for the wall paintings depicting the saga of Lohengrin—before Wagner and Ludwig II. Note the Gothic grillwork on the ceiling, the open spaces studded with stars.

Hohenschwangau, Alpseestrasse 24 (© **08362/930-830**), is open April to September daily 8:30am to 5:30pm; October to March daily 9:30am to 3:30pm. Admission is 9€ ($14) for adults and 8€ ($13) for children ages 12 to 15; children 11 and under enter free. There are several parking lots nearby where you can leave your car while visiting both castles.

WHERE TO STAY & DINE NEARBY

Hotel Lisl and Jägerhaus   This graciously styled villa, with an annex across the street, was seemingly made to provide views as well as comfort. Both houses sit in a narrow valley, surrounded by their own gardens. Most rooms have a view of at least one of the royal castles. In the main house, two well-styled dining rooms serve good-tasting meals. The restaurant features international as well as local cuisine.

Neuschwansteinstrasse 1–3, 87645 Hohenschwangau. © **08362/88-70.** Fax 08362/8-11-07. www. neuschwanstein-hotels.de. 47 units. 85€–170€ ($136–$272) double; 180€–220€ ($288–$352) suite. AE, DC, MC, V. Free parking. Closed Dec 21–26. **Amenities:** 2 dining rooms; bar; nonsmoking rooms. *In room:* TV, minibar, safe.

Hotel Müller Hohenschwangau   The location of this hospitable inn, near the foundations of Neuschwanstein Castle, makes it very alluring. The rooms are comfortable and have lots of rustic accessories. Bedrooms are inviting and have a bit of Bavarian charm. A well-maintained restaurant is lined with burnished pinewood, and a more formal evening restaurant has views over a verdantly planted sun terrace. Nature lovers especially enjoy hiking the short distance to nearby Hohenschwangau Castle.

Alpseestrasse 16, 87645 Hohenschwangau. © **08362/8-19-90.** Fax 08362/819913. www.hotel-mueller. de. 41 units. 140€–170€ ($224–$272) double; 187€–250€ ($299–$400) suite. Rates include buffet breakfast. AE, DC, MC, V. Free parking. Closed Jan–Feb. Füssen bus. **Amenities:** 4 restaurants; bar; outdoor pool; sauna; room service; all rooms nonsmoking. *In room:* TV, minibar (in some), hair dryer.

Appendix A: Fast Facts, Toll-Free Numbers & Websites

1 FAST FACTS: MUNICH

ATM NETWORKS See "Money & Costs," in chapter 3.

BUSINESS HOURS Most **banks** are open Monday to Friday 8:30am to 1pm and 2:30 to 4pm (many stay open to 5:30pm on Thurs). Most **businesses** and **stores** are open Monday to Friday 9am to 5pm (many stay open to 8 or 9pm on Thurs) and Saturday 9am to 2pm. On *langer Samstag* (the first Sat of the month) stores remain open until 6pm. Some (very few, actually) stores in Munich observe a late closing on Thursday, usually 8 or 9pm.

CASHPOINTS See "Money & Costs," in chapter 3.

CURRENCY See "Money & Costs," in chapter 3.

CURRENCY EXCHANGE You can almost always get a better rate at a bank than at your hotel. On Saturday and Sunday, or at night, you can exchange money at the Hauptbahnhof exchange, Bahnhofplatz, which is open daily from 6am to 11:30pm.

DENTISTS For an English-speaking dentist, go to **Klinik und Poliklinik für Kieferchirurgie der Universität München,** Lindwurmstrasse 2A (© **089/51-60-29-00**), the dental clinic for the university. It's always open for emergencies; for less urgent cases the doctors are available daily from 8am to noon and from 12:30 to 3pm.

DOCTORS The American, British, and Canadian consulates, as well as most hotels, keep a list of recommended English-speaking physicians. See "Embassies & Consulates," below.

DRINKING LAWS As in many European countries, the application of drinking laws is flexible. Laws are enforced only if a problem develops or if decorum is broken. Officially, someone must be 18 to consume any kind of alcoholic beverage in Germany, although at family gatherings, wine or schnapps might be offered to underage imbibers. For a bar or cafe to request proof of age of a prospective client is very rare. Drinking and driving, however, is treated as a very serious offense.

Beer, wine, and liquor are sold at most local supermarkets; many in Munich are open until 10pm. Munich doesn't have restrictive closing times for bars, many of which stay open until dawn, depending on the individual owners.

DRIVING RULES See "Getting There & Getting Around," in chapter 3.

DRUG LAWS Penalties for illegal drug possession in Germany are severe. You could go to jail or be deported immediately. *Warning:* Drug pushers often turn in their customers to the police.

DRUGSTORES For an international drugstore where English is spoken, go to **Bahnhof Apotheke,** Bahnhofplatz 12

(© 0831/522-66-11; www.bahnhof-apotheke.de; U-Bahn or S-Bahn: Hauptbahnhof), open Monday to Friday 8am to 8pm and Saturday 8:30am to 6pm. If you need a prescription filled during off-hours, call © 089/55-76-61 for open locations. The information is recorded and in German only, so you may need to get someone from your hotel staff to assist you.

ELECTRICITY In most places, the electricity is 220 volts AC, 50 cycles. Therefore, a transformer will be needed for U.S. appliances. Many leading hotels will supply one when asked. Otherwise, bring your own.

EMBASSIES & CONSULATES Offices representing various foreign governments are located in Munich. A **United States** Consulate is at Königstrasse 5, 80539 München (© 089/2-88-80). **Canada** maintains a consulate at Tal 29, 80331 (© 089/2-19-95 70). A Consulate General Office for the **United Kingdom** is located at Bürkleinstrasse 10, 80538 (© 089/21-10-90). The **Australian** government does not maintain an office in Munich, but if you should need assistance, contact the consulate in Berlin at Wallstrasse 76–79 10179 (© 030/8-80-08-80). **New Zealand's** embassy is also in Berlin, Friedrichstrasse 60 (© 030/20-62-10).

EMERGENCIES For emergency medical aid, phone © 112. Call the police at © 110, or the fire department at © 112. These are free calls.

HOLIDAYS The following public holidays are celebrated in Bavaria: January 1 (New Year's Day), January 6 (Epiphany), Easter (Good Friday and Easter Monday), May 1 (Labor Day), Ascension Day (10 days before Pentecost, the seventh Sun after Easter), Whitmonday (day after Whitsunday/Pentecost), Corpus Christi (10 days after Pentecost), August 15 (Feast of the Assumption), October 3 (Day of German Unity), November 1 (All Saints'

Day), November 17 (Day of Prayer and National Repentance), and December 25 and 26 (Christmas).

HOSPITALS Munich has a large number of hospitals with English-speaking staffs. Your hotel can put you in touch with the one nearest you. The German word for hospital is *Krankenhaus*. A good recommendation is **Städtisches Krankenhaus München,** Bogenhausen (© 089/92700; www.kh-bogenhausen.de).

INSURANCE Because Germany for most of us is far from home, and a number of things could go wrong—lost luggage, trip cancellation, or a medical emergency—consider some of the following options.

Medical Insurance For travel overseas, most U.S. health plans (including Medicare and Medicaid) do not provide coverage, and the ones that do often require you to pay for services up front and reimburse you only after you return home.

As a safety net, you may want to buy travel medical insurance, particularly if you're traveling to a remote or high-risk area where emergency evacuation might be necessary. If you require additional medical insurance, try **MEDEX Assistance** (© 410/453-6300; www.medexassist.com) or **Travel Assistance International** (© 800/821-2828; www.travelassistance.com; for general information on services, call the company's **Worldwide Assistance Services, Inc.** at © 800/777-8710).

Canadians should check with their provincial health plan offices or call **Health Canada** (© 866/225-0709; www.hc-sc.gc.ca) to find out the extent of their coverage and what documentation and receipts they must take home if they are treated overseas.

Travelers from the U.K. should carry their **European Health Insurance Card (EHIC),** which replaced the E111 form as proof of entitlement to free/reduced cost medical treatment abroad (© 0845/606-2030; www.ehic.org.uk). Note, however, that the EHIC only covers "necessary medical treatment," and for repatriation costs, lost money, baggage, or cancellation, travel insurance from a reputable company should always be sought (www.travel insuranceweb.com).

Travel Insurance The cost of travel insurance varies widely, depending on the destination, the cost and length of your trip, your age and health, and the type of trip you're taking, but expect to pay between 5% and 8% of the vacation itself. You can get estimates from various providers through **InsureMyTrip.com** (© 800/487-4722). Enter your trip cost and dates, your age, and other information, for prices from more than a dozen companies.

U.K. citizens and their families who make more than one trip abroad per year may find an annual travel insurance policy works out cheaper. Check **www.money supermarket.com** (© 0845/345-5708), which compares prices across a wide range of providers for single- and multi-trip policies.

Most big travel agents offer their own insurance and will probably try to sell you their package when you book a holiday. Think before you sign. **Britain's Consumers' Association** recommends that you insist on seeing the policy and reading the fine print before buying travel insurance. The **Association of British Insurers** (© 020/7600-3333; www.abi.org.uk) gives advice by phone and publishes Holiday Insurance, a free guide to policy provisions and prices. You might also shop around for better deals: Try **Columbus Direct** (© 0870/033-9988; www.columbusdirect.net).

Trip Cancellation Insurance Trip-cancellation insurance will help retrieve your money if you have to back out of a trip or depart early, or if your travel supplier goes bankrupt. Trip cancellation traditionally covers such events as sickness, natural disasters, and State Department advisories. The latest news in trip-cancellation insurance is the availability of **expanded hurricane coverage** and the **"any-reason"** cancellation coverage—which costs more but covers cancellations made for any reason. You won't get back 100% of your prepaid trip cost, but you'll be refunded a substantial portion. **TravelSafe** (© 888/885-7233; www.travelsafe.com) offers both types of coverage. Expedia also offers any-reason cancellation coverage for its air-hotel packages. For details, contact one of the following recommended insurers: **Access America** (© 866/807-3982; www.accessamerica.com); **Travel Guard International** (© 800/826-4919; www.travelguard.com); **Travel Insured International** (© 800/243-3174; www.travelinsured.com); and **Travelex Insurance Services** (© 888/457-4602; www.travelexinsurance.com).

INTERNET ACCESS Head for **Internet Cafe München,** Nymphenburger Strasse 145 (© 089/129-1120), which has 60 computer workstations, a bistro, and a bar, and is open daily 24 hours.

LANGUAGE Many Germans speak English, and English is usually spoken at major hotels and restaurants as well as in principal tourist areas. Nevertheless, a good phrase book to carry with you is *Berlitz German for Travellers,* available in most big bookstores.

LAUNDRY & DRY CLEANING Look in the Yellow Pages under either *Wascherei* or *Waschsalon* for a coin-operated laundromat near your hotel.

LEGAL AID Legal aid in Germany is administered by the Länder, a government agency. By federal law, anyone lawfully present in Germany can ask for legal aid. Forms to apply for legal advice and aid are available from any local courthouse or from a local lawyer. A national should also consult his or her local consulate.

LOST & FOUND Be sure to tell all your credit card companies the minute you discover your wallet has been lost or stolen, and file a report at the nearest police precinct. Your credit card company or insurer may require a police report number or record of the loss. Most credit card companies have an emergency toll-free number to call if your card is lost or stolen; the company may be able to wire you a cash advance immediately or deliver an emergency credit card in a day or two. Visa's emergency number outside the U.S. is ✆ **410/581-3836** or in Germany 0800-811-8440; call collect. American Express cardholders should call collect ✆ **336/393-1111.** MasterCard holders should call collect ✆ **314/542-7111.** If you need emergency cash over the weekend when all banks and American Express offices are closed, you can have money wired to you via **Western Union** (✆ **800/325-6000;** www.westernunion.com).

MAIL General delivery—mark it POSTE RESTANTE—can be used in any major town or city in Germany. You can pick up your mail upon presentation of a valid identity card or passport. Street mailboxes are painted yellow. It costs 1.70€ ($2.70) for the first 5 grams (about 1/5 oz.) to send an airmail letter to the United States or Canada, and 1€ ($1.60) for postcards. All letters to the U.K. cost .70€ ($1.10). To mail a package, go to one of the larger post offices in Munich. The **Postamt München** (main post office) is across from the Hauptbahnhof, at Bahnhofplatz 1 (✆ **089/599-0870**). If you want to have your mail sent to you, have it addressed Poste Restante, Postamt München, Bahnhofplatz 1, 80074 München, for general delivery. Take along your passport to reclaim any mail. The office is open Monday to Friday 7am to 8pm, Saturday 8am to 4pm, and Sunday 9am to 3pm. There are no longer fax, phone, or telex facilities available in the post office.

NEWSPAPERS & MAGAZINES The *International Herald Tribune* is the most widely distributed English-language newspaper in the city. You can also find copies of *USA Today* and the European editions of *Time* and *Newsweek.*

PASSPORTS Allow plenty of time before your trip to apply for a passport; processing normally takes 3 weeks but can take longer during busy periods (especially spring). And keep in mind that if you need a passport in a hurry, you'll pay a higher processing fee.

For Residents of Australia: You can pick up an application from your local post office or any branch of Passports Australia, but you must schedule an interview at the passport office to present your application materials. Call the **Australian Passport Information Service** at ✆ **131-232,** or visit the government website at www.passports.gov.au.

For Residents of Canada: Passport applications are available at travel agencies throughout Canada or from the central **Passport Office,** Dept. of Foreign Affairs and International Trade, Ottawa, ON K1A 0G3 (✆ **800/567 6868;** www.ppt.gc.ca).

For Residents of Ireland: You can apply for a 10-year passport at the **Passport Office,** Setanta Centre, Molesworth Street, Dublin 2 (✆ **01/671-1633;** www.dfa.ie). Those 17 and under or 65 and over must apply for a 3-year passport. You can also apply at 1A South Mall, Cork (✆ **021/494-4700**) or at most main post offices.

For Residents of New Zealand: You can pick up a passport application at any New Zealand Passports Office or download it from the website. Contact the **Passports Office** at ✆ **0800/225-050** in New Zealand or 04/474-8100, or log on to www.passports.govt.nz.

For Residents of the United Kingdom: To pick up an application for a standard 10-year passport (5-yr. passport for children 15 and under), visit your nearest passport office, major post office, or travel agency or contact the **United Kingdom Passport Service** at ✆ **0870/521-0410,** or search its website at www.ukpa.gov.uk.

For Residents of the United States: Whether you're applying in person or by mail, you can download passport applications from the U.S. Department of State website at **http://travel.state.gov**. To find your regional passport office, either check the U.S. Department of State website or call the **National Passport Information Center** toll-free number (✆ **877/487-2778**) for automated information.

POLICE Throughout the country, dial **110** for emergencies.

TAXES As a member of the European Union, Germany imposes a tax on most goods and services known as a **value-added tax (VAT)** or, in German, *Mehrwertsteuer*. Nearly everything is taxed at 16%, including vital necessities such as gas and luxury items such as jewelry. Food and books are taxed at 7%. VAT is included in the prices of restaurants and hotels. Goods for sale, such as cameras, also have the 16% tax already factored into the price. Stores that display a tax-free sticker will issue you a **Tax-Free Shopping Check** at the time of purchase. When leaving the country, have your check stamped by the German Customs Service as your proof of legal export. You can then get a cash refund at one of the Tax-Free Shopping Service offices in the major airports and many train stations, even at some of the bigger ferry terminals. Otherwise, you must send the checks to Tax-Free Shopping Service, Mengstrasse 19, 23552 Lübeck, Germany. If you want the payment to be credited to your bank card or your bank account, mention this. There is no airport departure tax.

TELEPHONES The phone numbers listed in this book are to be used within

Germany; when calling from abroad, omit the initial 0 in the city code.

If you're within Germany but not in Munich, use **089.** If you're calling within Munich, simply leave off the code and dial only the regular phone number. Local and long-distance calls may be placed from coin-operated public telephone booths. More than half the phones in Germany require an advance-payment telephone card from Telekom, the German telephone company. Phone cards are sold at post offices and newsstands. Rates are measured in units rather than minutes. The farther the distance, the more units are consumed. For example, a 4-minute call to the United States costs 41 units. All towns and cities in Germany may be dialed directly by using the prefix listed in the telephone directory above each local heading. Telephone calls made through hotel switchboards can double, triple, or even quadruple the charge, so try to make your calls outside your hotel. As an alternative, in some instances, post offices can send faxes for you, and many hotels offer Internet access—for free or for a small charge—to their guests.

Alternatively, you can dial the various telecommunication companies in the States for cheaper rates. From Germany, the access for **AT&T** is ✆ **0800/888-00-10. USA Direct** can be used with all telephone cards and for collect calls. The number from Germany is ✆ **01-30-00-10. Canada Direct** can be used with Bell Telephone Cards and for collect calls. This number from Germany is ✆ **01-30-00-14.**

To make international calls from Germany, first dial 00 and then the country code (U.S. or Canada 1, U.K. 44, Ireland 353, Australia 61, New Zealand 64). Next you dial the area code and number. For example, if you wanted to call the British Embassy in Washington, D.C., you would dial 00-1-202-588-7800.

For directory assistance: Dial ✆ **11837** if you're looking for a number inside

Germany, and dial ✆ **11834** for numbers to all other countries.

For operator assistance: If you need operator assistance in making a call, dial ✆ **0180/200-1033.**

Toll-free numbers: Numbers beginning with 0800 or 00800 within Germany are toll-free. *Be careful:* Numbers that begin with 08 followed by 36 carry a .35€ (55¢) surcharge per minute.

TIME Germany operates on Central European Time (CET), which means that the country is 6 hours ahead of Eastern Standard Time (EST) in the United States and 1 hour ahead of Greenwich Mean Time (GMT). Summer daylight saving time begins in Germany in April and ends in September—there's a slight difference in the dates from year to year—so there may be a period in early spring and in the fall when there's a 7-hour difference between EST and CET.

TIPPING If a restaurant bill says *Bedienung,* that means a service charge has already been added, so just round up to the nearest euro. If not, add 10% to 15%. Bellhops get 1€ ($1.60) per bag, as does the doorman at your hotel, restaurant, or nightclub. Room-cleaning staff get small tips, but you should tip concierges who perform special favors. Tip hairdressers or barbers 5% to 10%.

TOILETS Use the word *Toilette* (pronounced twah-*leh*-tah). Women's toilets are usually marked with an "F" for *Frauen,* and men's toilets with an "H" for *Herren.* Germany, frankly, doesn't have enough public toilets, except in transportation centers. The locals have to rely on bars, cafes, or restaurants—and using them isn't always appreciated if you're not a paying customer.

USEFUL PHONE NUMBERS U.S. Dept. of State Travel Advisory (✆ **202/647-5225,** staffed 24 hr.); U.S. Passport Agency (✆ **202/647-0518**); U.S. Centers for Disease Control International Traveler's Hot Line (✆ **404/332-4559**).

2 TOLL-FREE NUMBERS & WEBSITES

MAJOR INTERNATIONAL AIRLINES

Air New Zealand
✆ 800/262-1234 (in U.S.)
✆ 800/663-5494 (in Canada)
✆ 0800/028-4149 (in U.K.)
www.airnewzealand.com

American Airlines
✆ 800/433-7300 (in U.S. and Canada)
✆ 020/7365-0777 (in U.K.)
www.aa.com

British Airways
✆ 800/247-9297 (in U.S. and Canada)
✆ 087/0850-9850 (in U.K.)
www.british-airways.com

Continental Airlines
✆ 800/523-3273 (in U.S. and Canada)
✆ 084/5607-6760 (in U.K.)
www.continental.com

Delta Air Lines
✆ 800/221-1212 (in U.S. and Canada)
✆ 084/5600-0950 (in U.K.)
www.delta.com

Lufthansa
✆ 800/399-5838 (in U.S.)
✆ 800/563-5954 (in Canada)
✆ 087/0837-7747 (in U.K.)
www.lufthansa.com

Qantas Airways
✆ 800/227-4500 (in U.S. and Canada)
✆ 084/5774-7767 (in U.K.)
✆ 13 13 13 (in Australia)
www.qantas.com

United Airlines
📞 800/864-8331 (in U.S. and Canada)
📞 084/5844-4777 (in U.K.)
www.united.com

US Airways
📞 800/428-4322 (in U.S. and Canada)
📞 084/5600-3300 (in U.K.)
www.usairways.com

CAR RENTAL AGENCIES

Auto Europe
📞 888/223-5555 (in U.S. and Canada)
📞 0800/2235-5555 (in U.K.)
www.autoeurope.com

Avis
📞 800/331-1212 (in U.S. and Canada)
📞 084/4581-8181 (in U.K.)
www.avis.com

Budget
📞 800/527-0700 (in U.S.)
📞 087/0156-5656 (in U.K.)
📞 800/268-8900 (in Canada)
www.budget.com

Hertz
📞 800/654-3001 (in U.S. and Canada)
📞 087/0844-8844 (in U.K.)
www.hertz.com

Kemwel
📞 877/820-0668
www.kemwel.com

National
📞 800/CAR-RENT (800/227-7368)
www.nationalcar.com

MAJOR HOTEL & MOTEL CHAINS

Best Western International
📞 800/780-7234 (in U.S. and Canada)
📞 0800/393-130 (in U.K.)
www.bestwestern.com

Four Seasons
📞 800/819-5053 (in U.S. and Canada)
📞 0800/6488-6488 (in U.K.)
www.fourseasons.com

Hilton Hotels
📞 800/HILTONS (800/445-8667;
   in U.S. and Canada)
📞 087/0590-9090 (in U.K.)
www.hilton.com

Holiday Inn
📞 877/660-8550 (in U.S. and Canada)
📞 0800/405-060 (in U.K.)
www.holidayinn.com

Hyatt
📞 888/591-1234 (in U.S. and Canada)
📞 084/5888-1234 (in U.K.)
www.hyatt.com

InterContinental Hotels & Resorts
📞 877/660-8550 (in U.S. and Canada)
📞 0800/1800-1800 (in U.K.)
www.ichotelsgroup.com

Marriott
📞 877/236-2427 (in U.S. and Canada)
📞 0800/221-222 (in U.K.)
www.marriott.com

Radisson Hotels & Resorts
📞 888/201-1718 (in U.S. and Canada)
📞 0800/374-411 (in U.K.)
www.radisson.com

Ramada Worldwide
📞 888/2-RAMADA (888/272-6232;
   in U.S. and Canada)
📞 080/8100-0783 (in U.K.)
www.ramada.com

Sheraton Hotels & Resorts
📞 800/325-3535 (in U.S.)
📞 800/543-4300 (in Canada)
📞 0800/3253-5353 (in U.K.)
www.starwoodhotels.com

Appendix B:
Useful Terms & Phrases

1 GLOSSARY

GENERAL TERMS

Allee Avenue

Altes Rathaus Old town hall (a historical monument; no longer used as the headquarters of the city's officials)

Altstadt Old part of a city or town

Anlage Park area

Apotheke Pharmacy

Auf Wiedersehen Goodbye

Ausgang Exit

Bad Spa (also bath)

Bahn Railroad, train, course

Bahnhof Railroad station

Berg Mountain

Bitte Please

Brücke Bridge

Burg Fortified castle

Danke Thank you

Dom Cathedral

Domplatz Cathedral square

Drogerie Shop selling cosmetics, sundries

Eingang/Einfahrt Entrance

Eintritt Admission

Fahrrad Bicycle

Flughafen Airport

Gasse Lane

Gasthaus Inn, tavern, restaurant

Gasthof Inn

Gutbürgerliche Küche German home cooking

Hallo Hello

Hauptbahnhof Main railroad station

Hotelgarni Hotel that serves no meals or serves breakfast only

Insel Island

Kammer Room (in public building)

Kapelle Chapel

Kaufhaus Department store

Kino Cinema

Kirche Church

Kloster Monastery

Kneipe Bar for drinking; may serve snacks

Konditorei Cafe for coffee and pastries

Kunst Art

Land State

Marktplatz Market square

Neue Küche Cuisine moderne

Neues Rathaus New town hall (the seat of current city business)

Neustadt New part of city or town

Palatinate A region of Germany bordering France

Platz Square

Polizei Police

Postamt Post office

Rathaus Town or city hall

Ratskeller Restaurant in a Rathaus cellar serving traditional German food

Reisebüro Travel agency

Residenz Palace

Schauspielhaus Theater for plays

Schloss Palace, castle

See Lake *(der See)* or sea *(die See)*

Seilbahn Cable car

Speisekarte Menu

Spielbank Casino

Stadt Town, city

Stadtbahn (S-Bahn) Commuter railroad

Steg Footbridge

Strasse Street

Strassenbahn Streetcar, tram

Tagesmenu Menu of the day

Tankstelle Filling station

Teller Platter

Tor Gateway

Turm Tower

Ufer Shore, riverbank

Untergrundbahn (U-Bahn) Subway, underground transportation system

Verkehrsamt Tourist office

Weg Road

Weinstube Wine bar or tavern serving meals

Zimmer Room

---

2 MENU TERMS

MEATS & POULTRY (WURST, FLEISCH & GEFLÜGEL)

Aufschnitt Cold cuts

Beefsteak Hamburger steak

Brathuhn Roasted chicken

Bratwurst Grilled sausage

Eisbein Pigs' knuckles

Ente Duck

Frankfurter Hot dog

Gans Goose

Hammel Mutton

Kalb Veal

Kassler Rippchen Pork chops

Lamm Lamb

Leber Liver

Ragout Stew

Rinderbraten Roast beef

Rindfleisch Beef

Sauerbraten Marinated beef

Schinken Ham

Schnitzel Cutlet

Schweinebraten Roast pork

Tafelspitz Boiled beef usually served with applesauce and horseradish—a famous staple of Austria

Truthahn Turkey

Wiener schnitzel Breaded veal cutlet

Wurst Sausage

FISH (FISCH)

Aal Eel

Forelle Trout

Hecht Pike

Karpfen Carp

Lachs Salmon

Makrele Mackerel

Muschel Mussel

Rheinsalm Rhine salmon

Schellfisch Haddock

Seezunge Sole

EGGS (EIER)

Eier in der Schale Boiled eggs
Mit Speck With bacon
Rühreier Scrambled eggs

Spiegeleier Fried eggs
Verlorene Eier Poached eggs

VEGETABLES (GEMÜSE)

Artischocken Artichokes
Blumenkohl Cauliflower
Bohnen Beans
Bratkartoffeln Fried potatoes
Champignon Mushroom
Erbsen Peas
Grüne Bohnen Green or string beans
Gurken Cucumbers
Karotten Carrots
Kartoffel Potato
Kartoffelbrei Mashed potatoes
Kartoffelsalat Potato salad
Knödel Dumplings

Kohl Cabbage
Reis Rice
Rettich Radish
Rote Rüben Beets
Rotkraut Red cabbage
Salat Lettuce
Salzkartoffeln Boiled potatoes
Sellerie Celery
Spargel Asparagus
Spinat Spinach
Steinpilze Boletus mushrooms
Tomaten Tomatoes
Weisse Rüben Turnips

DESSERTS (NACHTISCH)

Auflauf Soufflé
Bienenstich Honey almond cake
Blätterteiggebäck Puff pastry
Bratapfel Baked apple
Dolce di Castagne Chestnut roll
Eis Ice cream
Kaffeecreme Coffee mousse
Käse Cheese
Kirschenstrudel Cherry strudel
Kirschtorte Black Forest cake
Kompott Stewed fruit

Obstkuchen Fruit tart
Obstsalat Fruit salad
Pfannkuchen Sugared pancakes
Pflaumenkompott Stewed plums
Schlagsahne Whipped cream
Schokolademus Chocolate mousse
Tarte Tatin A tart filled with, most often, apples
Topfenpalatschinken Cottage cheese pancakes
Zwetschkenknodel Plum dumplings

FRUITS (OBST)

Ananas Pineapple
Apfel Apple
Apfelsine Orange
Banane Banana
Birne Pear
Erdbeeren Strawberries

Himberren Raspberries
Kirschen Cherries
Pfirsich Peach
Weintrauben Grapes
Zitrone Lemon

Bier Beer
Ein dunkles A dark beer
Ein helles A light beer
Eine Tasse Kaffee A cup of coffee
Eine Tasse Tee A cup of tea
Eistee Ice tea
Geist Brandy
Hiesse Schokolade Hot chocolate
Kaffee Coffee
Kaffee mit Rahm/Milch/Zucker
Coffee with cream/milk/sugar
Kaffee mit Suss-stoff Coffee with
artificial sweetener
Kaffee Schwarz Black coffee
Koffeinfrei Decaffeinated coffee
Kräutertee Herb tea
Leicht Light (wine)
Likör Liqueur
Limonade Lemonade
Milch Milk

Mineralwasser Mineral water
Mit Eis With ice
Mit Wasser With water
Ohne Eis Without ice
Ohne Wasser Without water
Pur Straight
Rotwein Red wine
Saft Juice
Schaumwein Sparkling wine
Schnaps Schnapps
Schokolade Chocolate
Soda Club soda
Soda mit gas Soda with gas (to make
sure your club soda is carbonated)
Süss Sweet (wine)
Tee mit Milch Tea with cream
Tee mit Zitrone Tea with lemon
Trocken Dry (wine)
Wasser Water
Weisswein White wine

CONDIMENTS & TABLE ITEMS
(WÜRZE & TAFELGESCHIRR)

Brot Bread
Brötchen Rolls
Butter Butter
Eis Ice
Essig Vinegar
Flasche Bottle
Gabel Fork
Glas Glass
Kalte pikante sosse Ketchup
Löffel Spoon
Messer Knife

Öl Oil
Pfeffer Pepper
Platte Plate
Sahne Cream
Salat Zubereitung Salad dressing
Salz Salt
Senf Mustard
Tasse Cup
Teller Platter
Tischzeug Napkin
Zucker Sugar

COOKING TERMS

Gebacken Baked
Gebraten Fried
Gedämpft Steamed
Gefüllt Stuffed
Gekocht Boiled
Geröstet Roasted
Gut durchgebraten Well done

Heiss Hot
Kaltes Cold
Mittep Medium
Nicht durchgebraten Rare
Paniert Breaded
Pochiert Poached

INDEX

See also Accommodations and Restaurant indexes, below.

ACCOMMODATIONS